WORLD
HISTORY
WITH ATLAS

GEDDES &
GROSSET

Published 2006 by Geddes & Grosset,
David Dale House, New Lanark, ML11 9DJ, Scotland

© 2006 Geddes & Grosset

Pages 5–64
Co-authors: Liz Wyse and Caroline Lucas
Design and illustration: Ralph Orme
All maps with the exception of the maps on pages 16 and 62:
Malcolm Porter assisted by Andrea Fairbrass
Maps on pages 16 and 62: András Bereznay

ISBN 10: 1 84205 329 9
ISBN 13: 978 1 84205 329 4
Printed and bound in Poland

POLSKABOOK

Contents

Timelines

EUROPE	AMERICAS	ASIA	AFRICA
BC	**BC**	**BC**	**BC**
c. 20,000 Paintings showing hunting scenes in caves in southern France and Spain			
		c. 8000 First farming in the Middle East	
c. 6500 Agriculture in Greece			*c.* 5000 Agricultural settlements in Egypt
		c. 4000 Beginning of Bronze Age in the Near East	
		c. 3100 First writing on clay tablets	*c.* 3200 King Menes unites Egypt
	c. 3000 First ceramics in Mexico	*c.* 3000 First cities in Sumer	*c.* 2658 Beginning of 'Old Kingdom' in Egypt
		c. 2750 Growth of civilizations in Indus valley	*c.* 2650 First pyramid built for King Zoser of Egypt
c. 2200 Beginnings of Bronze Age Minoan civilization in Crete	*c.* 2000 First metal-working in Peru		
		c. 1750 Collapse of Indus Valley civilization	
c. 1600 Mycenaean civilization in Greece		*c.* 1600 Rise of Shang Dynasty in China	*c.* 1552 Beginning of 'New Kingdom' in Egypt
c. 1000 Destruction of Minoan Crete			1361–52 Rule of Tutankhamun in Egypt
c. 1200 Collapse of Mycenaean Empire	1200 Rise of the Oltec civilization	*c.* 1100 Chou Dynasty supplants Shang in China	
c. 1100 Phoenicians develop first phonic alphabet			
c. 800 Rise of city states in Greece		*c.* 720 Height of Assyrian power	*c.* 800 Carthage founded by Phoenicians
753 Foundation of Rome		*c.* 650 First iron used in China	
		586 Babylonian captivity of Jews	
510 Foundation of Roman Republic		*c.* 486 Death of Siddhartha Gautama, founder of Buddhism	
431–404 Peloponnesian War between Athens and Sparta		476–221 'Warring States' period in China	
334–327 Alexander the Great of Macedonia conquers Persia		*c.* 320 Mauryan Empire in India	
290 Roman conquest of central Italy			
264–146 Three Punic Wars between Rome and Carthage		221 Ch'in Dynasty	
146 Greece becomes part of Roman Empire		202 China under control of Han Dynasty	
31 Roman victory at the Battle of Actium			

EUROPE		AMERICAS		ASIA		AFRICA	
AD		**AD**		**AD**		**AD**	
43	Roman invasion of Britain			c. 0	Buddhism spreads from India to South East Asia and China		
116	Roman Empire at greatest extent			25	Han Dynasty restored in China	30	Egypt becomes Roman province
238	First raids on Roman Empire by Goths			131–36	Jewish revolt against Rome		
285	Roman Empire divided into Eastern Empire and Western Empire	c. 300	Mayan civilization rises to prominence in Central America	220	End of Han Dynasty: China splits into three states		
370	Huns from Asia begin to invade Europe			214	Great Wall of China built		
410	Visigoths sack Rome	c. 400	Pre-Inca civilizations in western South America	330	Constantinople becomes capital of Roman Empire		
449	Angles, Saxons and Jutes invade Britain			350	Huns invade western Central Asia	429–535	Vandal kingdom in northern Africa
486	Frankish Empire founded by Clovis			407–553	Early Mongol Empire	533–552	Justinian restores Roman power in North Africa
497	Franks converted to Christianity			552	Buddhism introduced to Japan		
597	St Augustine's Christian mission to England	c. 600	Height of Mayan civilization	c. 570 –632	Muhammad: founder of Islamic religion	641	Conquest of Egypt by Arabs
711	Second Muslim conquest of Spain			618	China reunited under T'ang Dynasty	c. 700	Rise of Empire of Ghana
793	Viking raids begin			622	First year of Islamic calendar		
800	Charlemagne crowned Holy Roman Emperor			635–74	Muslim conquests of Syria and Persia		
843	Treaty of Verdun divides Carolingian or Frankish Empire into three parts			730	First printing in China		
874	First Viking settlers in Iceland			821	Conquest of Tibet by Chinese		
886	Danelaw established in England			907	Last T'ang Emperor deposed in China	920 –1050	Height of Ghana Empire
911	Vikings granted Duchy of Normandy by Frankish king			939	Civil wars in Japan	969	Fatamids conquer Egypt and found Cairo
c. 1000	Vikings discover North America			960 –1127	Northern Sung Dynasty	c. 1000	First Iron Age settlement at Zimbabwe
1016	King Cnut rules England, Denmark and Norway			1127 –1279	Southern Sung Dynasty		
1054	Great Schism finally divides Church into Western Church and Eastern Church						

EUROPE	AMERICAS	ASIA	AFRICA
1066 Defeat of Anglo-Saxons by William the Conqueror			
1071 Normans conquer Byzantine Italy		**1071** Asia Minor conquered by Seljuk Turks	
		c. **1100** Polynesian Islands colonized	*c.* **1150** Beginnings of Yoruba city states (Nigeria)
1095–99 First Crusade	**1100** Toltecs build capital city at Tula in Mexico	**1156–59** Civil wars in Japan	
1147–49 Second Crusade			**1174** Ottoman Turks under Saladin conquer Egypt
1189–92 Third Crusade		**1174–87** Ottoman Turks under Saladin conquer Syria and Levant	
1202–04 Fourth Crusade and capture of Constantinople	Cuzco founded by the Incas		
1217–21 Fifth Crusade		**1206** Mongol Empire founded under Genghis Khan	*c.* **1200** Rise of Empire of Mali in West Africa
1228–29 Sixth Crusade	*c.* **1250** End of Toltec Empire in Mexico		
1237 Mongols invade Russia		**1234** Mongols invade and destroy Northern China	Emergence of Hausa city states (Nigeria)
1241 Mongols invade Poland, Hungary, Bohemia then withdraw			**1240** Collapse of Empire of Ghana
1248–54 Seventh Crusade			
1250 Collapse of Imperial power in Germany and Italy on death of Holy Roman Emperor, Frederick II		**1261** Beginning of Greek Palaeologian dynasties: ruled the Byzantine Empire until 1453	
1270–71 Eighth Crusade			*c.* **1300** Emergence of Ife kingdom, city state of the Yoruba (West Africa)
1271–72 Ninth Crusade			
1305 Papacy moves from Rome to Avignon	**1325** Rise of Aztecs in Mexico	*c.* **1334** Black Death in China	
1337 –1453 Hundred Years' War between France and England	Founding of city of Tenochtitlán	**1336** Revolution in Japan	
		c. **1370** Tamerlane begins conquest of Asia	
1378 –1417 Second Great Schism: break between Rome and Avignon, rival Popes elected	**1370** Expansion of Chimu kingdom in South America	**1368** Ming Dynasty founded in China	
	c. **1375** Beginning of Aztec expansion	**1380** Tartars (the Golden Horde) defeated by the Grand Duke	
1381 Peasants' Revolt in England		of Moscow	
1385 Portugal's independence from Spain assured		**1398– 1402** Tamerlane conquers kingdom of Delhi and Ottoman Empire	**1415** Portuguese begin to establish colonies in Africa
1415 Henry V of England defeats French at battle of Agincourt	**1438** Inca Empire established in Peru		
	1440–69 Montezuma I rules Aztecs		**1450** Height of Songhai Empire in northwest Africa
1453 England loses all her French possessions except for Calais	**1450** Incas conquer Chimu kingdom	**1453** Ottoman Turks capture Constantinople	**1482** Portuguese settle Gold Coast (now Ghana)
	1493 First New World settlement by Spanish		
1455–85 Wars of the Roses in England		**1498** Explorer Vasco da Gama reaches India around Cape of Good Hope	**1492** Spain begins conquest of North African coast
1492 Last Muslims in Spain conquered by Christians			

EUROPE	AMERICAS	ASIA	AFRICA
	1502–20 Aztec conquests under Montezuma II		1505 Portuguese begin establishing trading posts in East Africa
1517 Martin Luther nails '95 theses' to church door at Wittenberg		1517 Ottoman Turks conquer Syria, Egypt and Arabia	
1520 Zwingli leads Protestant Reformation in Switzerland	c. 1510 First African slaves taken to America		
1522 First circumnavigation of world by Portuguese navigator, Magellan	1521 Cortes conquers Aztec capital, Tenochtitlán		
1529–36 Reformation Parliament begins in England		1526 Foundation of Mughal Empire (till 1857)	
1532–36 Calvin starts Protestant movement in France	1533 Pizarro conquers Peru: end of Inca Empire	1533 Ivan the Terrible succeeds to Russian throne	
1540 Potato introduced to Europe from New World	1535 Spaniards explore Chile		
1545 Council of Trent marks start of the Counter-Reformation (till 1563)			1546 Destruction of Mali Empire in northwest Africa by the Songhai
1558 England loses Calais to French			
1562–98 Wars of Religion in France			1570 Kanem-Bornu Empire in the Sudan flourishes
1568 –1648 Eighty Years' War or Dutch Revolt			1571 Portuguese establish colony in Angola (Southern Africa)
1571 Battle of Lepanto: end of Turkish sea power			
1588 Spanish Armada defeated by English	1607 First successful English settlement in America at Jamestown, in Virginia		1591 Moroccans destroy Songhai Empire
1600 Foundation of English East India Company	1608 French colonists found Quebec		
1618–48 Thirty Years' War in Europe	1620 Puritans (Pilgrim Fathers) land in New England		
1649 Execution of Charles I in London	1624 Dutch settle New Amsterdam	1630s Japan isolates itself from the rest of the world	
	1654 Portuguese take Brazil from Dutch	1644 Ch'ing Dynasty founded in China by Manchus	1652 Foundation of Cape Colony by Dutch
1688 England's 'Glorious Revolution'	1664 New Amsterdam seized by British: later renamed New York	1690 Foundation of Calcutta by British	1686 French annex Madagascar
	1693 Gold discovered in Brazil		

EUROPE		AMERICAS		ASIA		AFRICA	
1700–14	War of Spanish Succession			1707	Break-up of Mughal Empire	1700	Rise of Ashanti power in the Gold Coast)
1704	Battle of Blenheim			1724	Hyderabad in India gains freedom from Mughals		
1707	Union of England and Scotland			1757	British rule in India established by battle of Plassey		
1740–48	War of Austrian Succession	1759	British capture Quebec from French				
1756–63	Seven Years' War	1775–83	American War of Independence	1768	Captain James Cook begins exploration of the Pacific		
1765	Invention of James Watts' steam engine	1776	Declaration of American Independence	1773–75	Peasant revolts in Russia		
	Beginning of Industrial Revolution in Britain	1789	Washington becomes first US president	1784	India Act gives Britain control of India	1787	British acquire Sierra Leone
		1791	Slave revolt in Haiti	1788	British penal colony at Botany Bay, Australia	1798	Napoleon attacks Egypt
1789	French Revolution						
1804	Napoleon proclaimed Emperor	1803	Louisiana Purchase doubles size of USA	1799	Napoleon invades Syria	1811	Muhammad Ali massacres Mameluke leaders and takes control in Egypt
1812	Napoleon's Russian campaign	1808–26	Independence movements in South America	1804–15	Serbs revolt against Ottoman Turks		
1815	Napoleon defeated at Waterloo			1819	British establish a trading post at Singapore	1814	British acquire the Cape Colony in South Africa from the Dutch
1821–29	Greek War of Independence	1821	Spain grants Mexico independence			1818	Zulu Empire founded in southern Africa
1825	First commercial steam railway	1840	Union of Upper and Lower Canada			1822	Liberia founded on the west coast of Africa for freed American slaves
1830	Revolutions in France, Germany, Poland and Italy	1845	Texas annexed by US	1840	Britain establishes sovereignty over New Zealand	1830	French begin conquest of Algeria
		1846–48	War between US and Mexico	1840–42	First Opium War between Britain and China	1835–37	Great Trek of Boers in South Africa
1845–46	Irish potato famine	1848	Gold is found in California	1842	Hong Kong ceded to Britain by China		
1848	Year of Revolutions	1861–65	American Civil War	1854 and 1858	Trade treaties between Japan and the US	1860	French expansion in West Africa begins
1854–56	Crimean War	1865	Assassination of US president, Abraham Lincoln	1856–60	Second Opium War	1869	Opening of Suez Canal
1861	Kingdom of Italy proclaimed			1857	Indian troops mutiny against British Army	1879	Anglo-Zulu War
		1867	Dominion of Canada formed	1877	Queen Victoria proclaimed Empress of India	1880–81	First Anglo-Boer War
1870–71	Franco-Prussian War		Alaska is purchased by the US from Russia	1885	Indian National Congress formed	1882	British occupy Egypt
1871	German Empire created			1886	Upper and Lower Burma united under British India	1884	Germany acquires African colonies
						1885	Belgium acquires Congo
1882–1914	Triple Alliance between Germany, Austria and Italy	1898	Spanish-American War	1894–95	First Sino-Japanese War	1886	Germany and Britain divide East Africa
						1899–1902	Second Anglo-Boer War

EUROPE		AMERICAS		ASIA		AFRICA	
1904	Anglo-French Entente			1901	Unification of Australia		
1905	First Revolution in Russia			1904–05	Russo-Japanese War		
		1911	Revolution in Mexico	1906	Revolt in Persia		
1912–13	Balkan Wars			1910	Japan annexes Korea	1910	Union of South Africa formed
		1914	Panama Canal opens			1911	Italy takes Libya from the Ottoman Empire
1914–18	First World War	1917	US enters First World War	1911–49	Chinese revolution		
1917	Russian Revolution			1922	Republic proclaimed in Turkey	1914	Egypt a British Protectorate
1919	Treaty of Versailles			1928	Chiang Kai-shek unites China	1919	Nationalist revolt in Egypt against British occupation
		1929	Wall Street crash heralds the Depression	1931	Japanese occupy Manchuria		
1920	League of Nations established			1934–35	Mao Tse-tung's Long March	1922	Egypt achieves independence
1922	Irish Free State created by Anglo-Irish Treaty of 1921	1933	Roosevelt introduces New Deal in the US	1937–45	Second Sino-Japanese War		
				1940	Japan allies with Germany	1935	Mussolini invades Abyssinia (Ethiopia)
	Mussolini takes power in Italy			1941	Japanese attack US fleet at Pearl Harbor		
1926	General Strike in Britain	1941	US enters Second World War	1942	Japanese fleet defeated by US at battle of Midway		
1933	Hitler becomes German Chancellor			1945	Nuclear bombs dropped on Japan	1949	Apartheid is established in South Africa
1936–39	Civil war in Spain			1946–49	Civil war in China		
1939–45	Second World War			1947	India, Pakistan and Burma gain independence		
1945	United Nations established			1948	Jewish state of Israel founded		
1948	Communists seize power in Czechoslovakia			1948–49	First Arab-Israeli War		
				1950–53	Korean War		
				1954–75	Vietnam War		
1956	Hungarian revolt crushed by Russians	1959	Cuban revolution	1956	Second Arab-Israeli War	1956	Suez crisis
1958	European Economic Community (EEC) comes into being	1962	Cuban missile crisis	1957	Federation of Malaya independent	1957	Ghana becomes independent, followed by other African states
		1963	President Kennedy assassinated	1962	Sino-Indian War		
		1963–73	US involvement in Vietnam War	1967	Third Arab-Israeli War	1960	Civil war follows independence in the Congo
1961	Berlin Wall built: beginning of Cold War in Europe	1969	Neil Armstrong becomes first man on the moon	1971	East Pakistan becomes Bangladesh	1962	Algeria gains independence from France
1968	USSR invades Czechoslovakia	1973	Political unrest in Chile culminates in a military coup	1973	Fourth Arab-Israeli War	1967–70	Civil war in Nigeria
1973	Britain, Eire and Denmark join EC (9 member states)	1974	Resignation of US President Nixon: Gerald Ford becomes US president	1974	Portuguese African colonies independent		
				1978	Fifth Arab-Israeli War		
1975	Restoration of monarchy in Spain			1979	Soviet invasion of Afghanistan	1979	General Amin flees from Uganda
					Shah of Iran deposed: Islamic republic declared		

EUROPE		AMERICAS		ASIA		AFRICA	
1980	Polish Solidarity Trade Union, led by Lech Walesa, confronts the Polish Communist government			1980-88	Iran-Iraq War	1980	Rhodesia, last British colony in Africa, becomes independent as Zimbabwe
		1981	US hostages in Iran freed				
		1982	Falklands War between Argentina and Britain: Britain retains Falklands	1984	Indian prime minister, Indira Gandhi, is assassinated	1981	President Sadat of Egypt is assassinated
1981	Greece becomes tenth member of the EC						
		1983	US troops invade Grenada				
1985	Mikhail Gorbachev elected new Soviet leader			1986	Overthrow of Marcos regime in Philippines	1985	Renewed unrest in South Africa
1986	Prime Minister Palme of Sweden assassinated. Spain and Portugal join the EC (12 member states)	1986	US raid on Libya	1987	Ongoing civil war in Lebanon	1986	Ethiopia has worst famine in more than ten years
			Nuclear arms talks resume between USA and USSR				
		1987	Falling dollar and Wall Street crash				
1989	Berlin Wall dismantled			1990	Gulf War begins: Iran invades Kuwait		
1991	Break up of the Soviet Union. West and East Germany are united	1989	US troops invade Panama		US and Allies send troops to Gulf region	1990	Nelson Mandela, African National Congress (ANC) political prisoner, is freed in South Africa: process of dismantling apartheid begins
1992	Bloody civil war in Yugoslavia: European Commission recognizes independence of Croatia and Slovenia	1992	Bill Clinton is elected US president	1994	Israel and PLO sign pact ending Israeli occupation of Gaza Strip and Jericho		
1993	Czechoslovakia is split into Slovakia and the Czech Republic			1995	Israeli Prime Minister Yitzakh Rabin is assassinated	1994	In South Africa ANC wins first multiracial election in Africa
1994–96	First Russian-Chechen War	1994	US troops invade Haiti to oust military government	1997	Hong Kong returned to Chinese rule		Massacre of Tutsis by Hutus in Rwanda leaves estimated 500,000 dead and 1.5 million homeless
1995	Dayton Peace Accords signed to end civil war in Bosnia and Herzegovina			1999	King Hussein of Jordan dies: Prince Abdullah is king		
					Allied jets attack missile sites in Iraq	1997	End of civil war in Zaire and country is renamed as the Democratic Republic of Congo
	Austria, Finland and Sweden join the EC now the EU (15 member states)				Inhabitants of East Timor vote for independence from Indonesia: UN sends in an Australian peacekeeping force when Indonesian militia go on the rampage		
1997	Labour Party wins British general election: Tony Blair is prime minister	1999	Self-governing region of Nunavut in northwest Canada comes into being			1999	UN troops pull out of Angola
1998	Good Friday Agreement in Northern Ireland						President Nelson Mandela of South Africa stands down from politics: Thabo Mbeki is new president
1999	Entire European Commission resigns following a report on corruption		Lost Mayan city found at border of Mexico and Guatemala		Military coup ends civilian government in Pakistan		

11

EUROPE		AMERICAS		ASIA		AFRICA	
1999–2002	Major combat in Second Russian-Chechen War	2000	President Fuyimori of Peru decamps to Japan	2000	Fijian government overthrown by armed coup	2000	Devastating floods in Mozambique
2000	Spain and Britain agree on administrative arrangements for Gibraltar	2001	George W. Bush becomes US president		Israel withdraws from South Lebanon	2001	More devastating floods in Mozambique
2001	Former Yugoslav president, Slobodan Milosevic, extradited to the Hague to stand trial for war crimes		IMF lends $8 billion to Argentina to stave off the country's financial collapse	2001	Ongoing violence in Israeli-Palestinian conflict		Zimbabwe approves legislation for white-owned farms to be confiscated without compensation
2001–02	Outbreak of foot and mouth disease rocks British agricultral industry		US is target of coordinated terrorist attacks on World Trade Center and the Pentagon: US Senate enacts anti-terrorism legislation		United Islamic Front for the Salvation of Afghanistan, with US and British air support, defeats the Taliban government	2002	Mt Nyiragongo erupts in DR Congo
2002	The euro, a single currency shared by 12 members of the EU, successfully launched	2002	US slaps a heavy tariff on steel imports	2002	East Timor recognised internationally as an independent state		Robert Mugabe re-elected as President of Zimbabwe
2003	London's biggest ever political demonstration against impending war in Iraq but British troops are part of Coalition forces that invade Iraq	2003	NASA spacecraft breaks up on re-entry: 7 astronauts killed	2003	US-led Coalition forces invade Iraq: US-led transitional authority is set up to oversee transference of rule to a civilian government	2003	Nigerian peacekeeping force enters Liberia to stop civil war
	Heatwave in Europe causes around 10,000 deaths among the elderly in France		US lifts much-criticized tariff on steel imports		North Korea withdraws from Nuclear Non-Proliferation Treaty	2004	African National Congress wins South African general election with 70% of the vote
2004	10 more countries join the EU (25 member states)		Invasion of Iraq by US-led Coalition Forces	2004	Insurgency in Iraq reaches new heights of violence in a sustained suicide bombing campaign		In Sudan, the government and the People's Liberation Army agree to end the civil war: ongoing violence in the Darfur region
	Swedish foreign minister, Anna Lindh, is stabbed to death in Stockholm	2004	Haitian President Aristide resigns and goes into exile		Asian Tsunami devastates shoreline communities in Indonesia, Sri Lanka and India		A UN report states that life expectancy in 7 African countries has fallen below 40
2005	Suicide bombers in London underground trains and a bus kill 52 people and wound over 700: British born al-Qaeda activists are identified as responsible		NASA lands a mobile robot on Mars	2005	Parliamentary elections held in Iraq: Shiites largest party but do not have majority vote	2005	A forced 'slum clearance' by the government of Zimbabwe drives fringe town dwellers back into the countryside
			Venezuela votes to keep President Hugo Chavez in office by 52% to 48%		Israel withdraws settlers from Gaza Strip		Ellen Johnson is elected President of Liberia: first woman president in Africa
			George Bush re-elected as US president		North Korea admits possession of nuclear weapons		
		2005	US continues its presence in Iraq				
			Hurricane Katrina devastates US Gulf coast				

The First Humans

Our closest relations in the animal world are chimpanzees and gorillas. By about 4 million years ago, the earliest human ancestors had evolved in Africa. They were called *Australopithecus* (which means 'southern ape'), but unlike apes they had the ability to walk upright. The first *Homo* (man) fossils which have been found date to 2 million years ago, but it was not until about 100,000 years ago that the first fully modern humans evolved in Africa. Over these millions of years of human evolution, the most noticeable development was in the size of the skull and the brain. As our ancestors' brains became larger, they developed other skills: the ability to make tools, to use language, to work together as a group, to create the first art.

During the cold phases of the last Ice Age, which lasted from about 2 million to 10,000 years ago, temperatures were, on average, 10–15°C lower than the present day. Humans were therefore forced to adapt to a hostile world. In cold climates, they learned to use fire, find or build shelters and make warm clothes. They became skilled at making tools and weapons, and were lethal hunters. By about 10,000 years ago modern humans had spread from Africa to the most remote corners of the globe. During cold periods, a great deal of water was locked up in the large ice sheets (glaciers) that covered much of the northern hemisphere. This caused sea levels to fall, revealing land 'bridges' that linked the continents, enabling our ancestors to cross from Asia into North America and from South East Asia into Australia.

When the ice finally retreated, large game, such as woolly mammoths, was increasingly scarce. Humans had to find new sources of food and began to experiment with the domestication of certain plants and animals – the agricultural revolution had begun.

Homo Habilis
Homo habilis ('handy man') was so called because of his ability to make tools. Feet and hand fossils show some similarities to modern humans' feet and hands. They indicate that he would have had a strong grip and would have been able to manipulate tools effectively. He was probably a meat-eater – tools were needed to separate the flesh from the carcass.

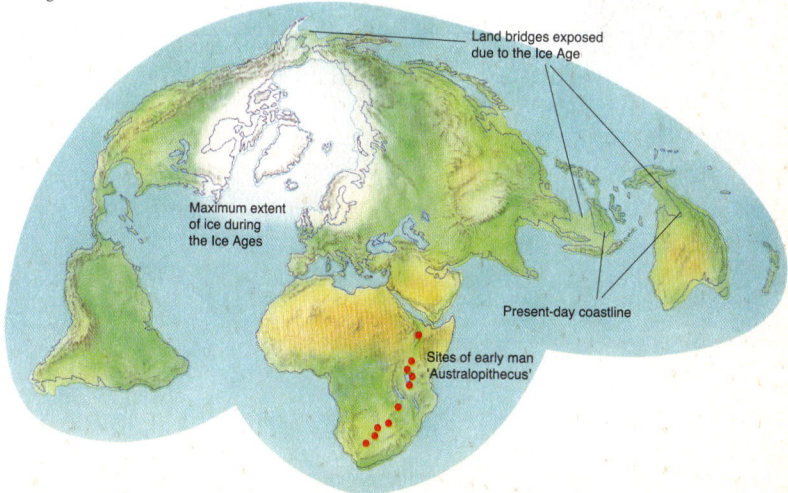

Land bridges exposed due to the Ice Age

Maximum extent of ice during the Ice Ages

Present-day coastline

Sites of early man 'Australopithecus'

The First Civilizations 3500–1000 BC

The cultivation of plants, such as wheat and barley, and the domestication of animals, such as sheep, goats and cattle, began in the Near East in about 8500 BC. As people turned to farming, they began to live in fixed settlements, which became small towns. In about 5000 BC, farmers moved down into the fertile river valleys of Mesopotamia, and built dykes and ditches to irrigate the arid land. Their labours bore fruit; surplus food freed some of the population from farming. These people became merchants, craftsmen and priests. As the settlements grew into cities, they became more organized; laws were made, writing evolved, and religious and public buildings were built.

Between 3500 and 1800 years ago, three great civilizations evolved in Mesopotamia, Egypt and the Indus valley of northern India. All three civilizations were located in the fertile valleys of great rivers. Each civilization was based on substantial cities, inhabited by several thousand people and containing imposing public buildings, such as temples and palaces. Each civilization had evolved a form of writing. All three civilizations show evidence of a strong, centralized administration or all-powerful rulers – in Mesopotamia, for example, rulers were buried with their sacrificed servants as well as a vast array of their worldly possessions.

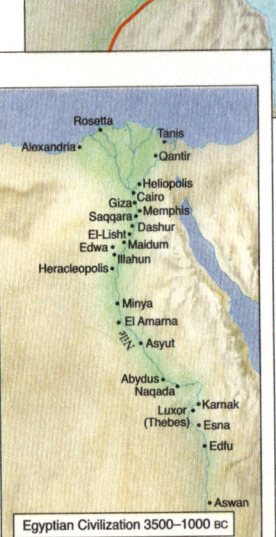

Egypt

The cities, tombs and temples of Ancient Egypt lined the banks of the River Nile. Every year the river flooded, depositing fertile mud along its banks – when the waters receded, these lands could be cultivated. During the Nile flood (August to October), the vast majority of the Egyptian population, who lived by farming, could work for the pharaoh, building temples, tombs and pyramids. During the Old Kingdom (c. 2685–2185 BC), when all of Egypt was under the rule of one pharaoh, the important centres were in the north, around Giza and Memphis. In the New Kingdom (c. 1552–1071), the main royal city was Thebes, in Middle Egypt.

Egyptian Civilization 3500–1000 BC

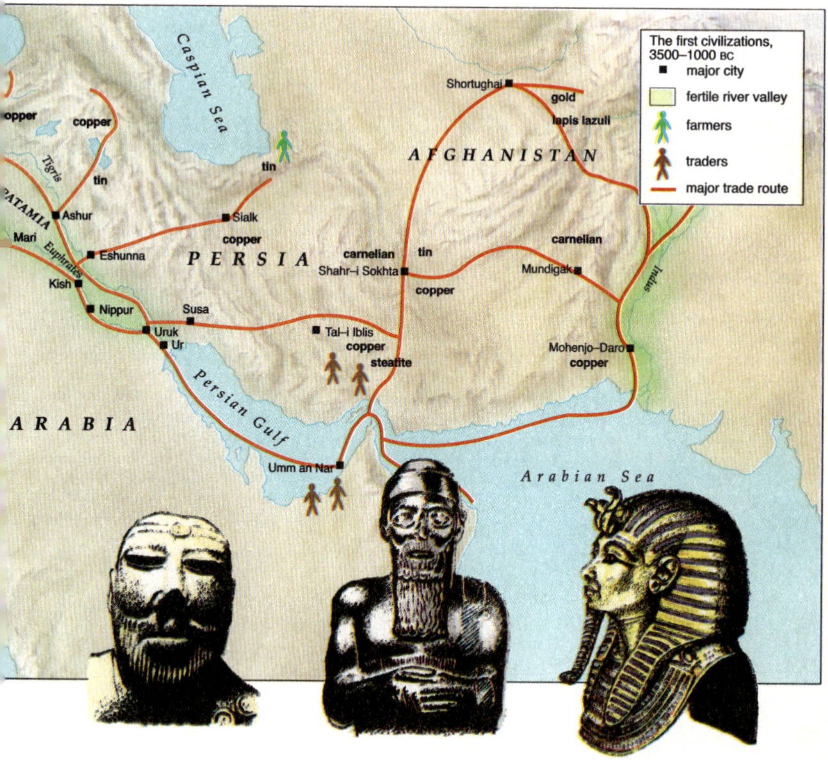

The map legend:

The first civilizations, 3500–1000 BC
- ■ major city
- fertile river valley
- 🧍 farmers
- 🧍 traders
- — major trade route

Map labels:
copper · copper · Caspian Sea · Shortughai · gold · lapis lazuli · AFGHANISTAN · tin · Tigris · tin · ...TAMIA · Ashur · Sialk · copper · Mari · Euphrates · Eshunna · PERSIA · carnelian · tin · carnelian · Kish · Shahr-i Sokhta · Mundigak · Nippur · Susa · copper · Uruk · Tal-i Iblis · Ur · copper · steatite · Mohenjo-Daro · copper · Persian Gulf · Indus · ARABIA · Umm an Nar · Arabian Sea

This head from the Indus valley city of Mohenjo-Daro, c. 2100 BC, may represent a priest-king.

Ishtup-Ilum, c. 2100 BC, was the ruler of Mari, a city-state in northern Mesopotamia.

The solid gold funeral mask of the Egyptian pharaoh, Tutankhamun, c. 1340 BC.

The Temple of Ur

The temple at the Mesopotamian city of Ur was a ziggurat, comprising an ascending series of terraces, made from mud-bricks, and decorated with mosaics. Each terrace would have been planted with a 'hanging garden' of trees. The temple was dedicated to the worship of the city's patron deity, the moon-god, Nanna. Surrounding the temple stood the houses of the lower town, which contained 20,000 people at its peak.

The Bronze Age 2000–1000 BC

Metal-working first occurred in Turkey and Iran in about 6000 BC, when people began to smelt copper and lead. By 3000 BC, it was a flourishing craft in the city-states of Mesopotamia and it became increasingly specialized as craftsmen began to experiment with mixing together different metals to produce alloys. By adding a small quantity of tin to copper they produced bronze, a harder metal that could be used for making stronger weapons, with sharper cutting edges. By about 2500 BC, copper was in use over a region that stretched from the Iberian peninsula to Scandinavia and, within a thousand years, bronze was being used by craftsmen in Europe. At this time, much of Europe was still thickly forested, and people lived in widely scattered agricultural villages. Tin, a vital component of bronze, was a rare resource, found mainly along the Atlantic coast of Europe. It was transported along long-distance trade routes and exchanged for other highly valued goods, such as Baltic amber and salt. Control of these precious resources led to the rise of a wealthy social elite, who turned to metalsmiths to produce bronze regalia, symbolic of their rank. Costly daggers, bronze sheaths and helmets, and metal breastplates were buried with chieftains in 'barrow burials' – graves that were crowned with large mounds of earth or stone. As the European population grew, there was increasing pressure on limited resources. Conflict began to break out between communities, and people began to build fortified villages or fortresses, which could be defended against groups of marauders. In Crete and the Greek mainland, two sophisticated Bronze Age societies began to emerge between 2000 BC and 1500 BC, centred on palaces which ruled over an agricultural hinterland. The Minoans of Crete built substantial palaces, whose magnificent wall paintings depict young acrobats leaping over a bull's horns. The Cretans

Trundholm Sun Chariot
Scandinavia flourished during the second millennium BC, growing rich on its trade in precious Baltic amber. Bronze-working was greatly valued. The sun was probably worshipped and sun symbolism was widespread. This bronze, wheeled model of a horse pulling a disc (the sun), was probably a revered religious object.

Mask of Agamemnon
When the royal tombs of Mycenae in mainland Greece were excavated in the nineteenth century, gold death-masks, tiaras, bowls, daggers and wine cups were found. One of the gold masks was associated with Agamemnon, the Mycenaean warlord celebrated by the poet Homer in his epic works, the Iliad and the Odyssey.

were skilled craftsmen and traders, and examples of Minoan jewellery and pottery have been found in Egypt, Greece and Italy. It is thought that a massive volcanic eruption on the island of Santorini in c. 1450 BC shattered Minoan civilization. On the Greek mainland, Mycenaean civilization was more warlike. Great Mycenaean cities, such as Mycenae and Pylos, were fortresses that ruled over the surrounding countryside, and Mycenaean traders dominated the eastern Mediterranean. But by 1000 BC internal conflict, or possibly foreign invasion, had brought about their downfall.

Meanwhile, in East Asia, the Shang state developed in c. 1800 BC from earlier agricultural communities that had evolved on the Yellow River. It was a feudal society, ruled by the Shang Dynasty of kings who lived in elaborate, luxurious palaces. The Shang were fierce soldiers, who used ancestor worship and human sacrifice to assert their power. Ancestors were consulted through oracle bones – animal bones heated to produce cracks which were then interpreted. Elaborate bronze vessels were used by the king and his aristocrats to offer wine and food to the spirits of their ancestors. But Shang rule was not to last, and in about 1100 BC the dynasty collapsed and the era of Chou China began.

Shang Bronze
Bronze halberds, with decorated hilts, were the main weapons of war in Shang China. Metalworking in China dates back to about 1800 BC, and bronze was widely used for everyday objects and weapons. More elaborate ritual vessels, cast from ceramic moulds, were decorated with vigorous animal motifs.

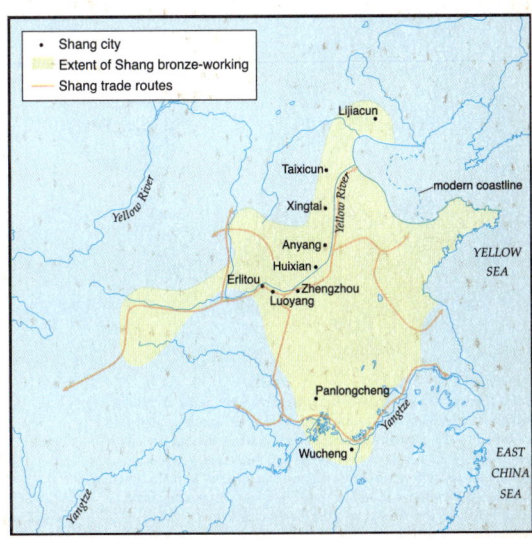

- • Shang city
- ▨ Extent of Shang bronze-working
- — Shang trade routes

Lijiacun

Taixicun

Xingtai

Yellow River

Yellow River

modern coastline

Anyang
Huixian
Erlitou
Zhengzhou
Luoyang

YELLOW SEA

Panlongcheng

Wucheng

Yangtze

Yangtze

EAST CHINA SEA

Greece 750–150 BC

Europe's earliest advanced civilization flourished on the island of Crete from 2200 to 1400 BC. Minoan civilization, centred on palace-cities, prospered by trading goods such as olive oil and pottery within the Mediterranean. Meanwhile, on the Peloponnese peninsula, another Bronze Age civilization was emerging, based on fortified palace-cities such as Mycenae. This more warlike civilization collapsed in about 1200 BC. A period known as the 'dark ages' followed but, in about 800 BC, populations began to expand, and small city-states, consisting of a city surrounded by towns, villages and agricultural land, began to evolve. By about 500 BC, Athens had become the richest and most important city-state in Classical Greece, as well as the cultural and intellectual centre of the Greek world. Democracy was born in Athens: Athenian citizens (free men) had the right to vote on all matters of government, and any citizen could serve for a year as a city magistrate, paid by the state. But, in 404 BC, Athens was crushed by Sparta, a rival city-state, where a small elite ruled over their subject peoples with the help of a well-trained army. In the fourth century BC the Greeks were united under the Macedonian leader, Alexander, who conquered the mighty empire of Persia. Wherever he went, he founded cities, spreading Greek culture and language throughout the Middle East.

·	main cities
▲	theatres
■	temples
→	route of Alexander
✗	battles

Adriatic Sea

ITALY

Tyrrhenian Sea

· Neapolis (Naples)
· Elea
■ Metap
· Sybaris
· Terina
· Cr
■ Hipponium
· Locri

■ Segesta
Selinus ■
Akragas · ■
Gela

Alexander the Great
Alexander the Great, son of King Philip of Macedonia, conquered a vast area, stretching from Greece to the borders of India from 334–323 BC. He died when he was just 33.

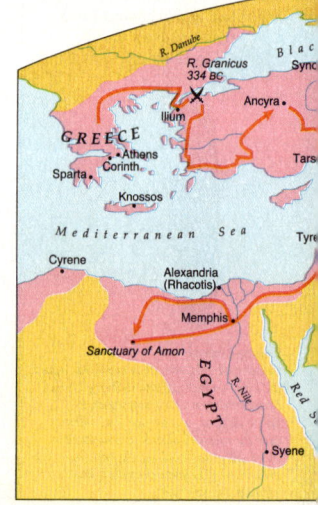

R. Danube
R. Granicus 334 BC
✗
Ilium
Ancyra ·
GREECE
· Athens
Sparta · Corinth ·
Knossos
Tars
B l a c
Sync
Tyr
Mediterranean Sea
Cyrene
Alexandria (Rhacotis) ·
Memphis ·
Sanctuary of Amon
EGYPT
R. Nile
Red S
· Syene

Athens
Most Greek cities clustered around a rocky outcrop, or acropolis, which could be defended in times of crisis. The Athenian acropolis is crowned by the famous Parthenon, dedicated to Athena, the city's patron deity. Below the acropolis, lay the market place, or agora, and the law courts and government offices. The Greeks were dedicated to the health of both mind and body, so large public gymnasia and amphitheatres were found in most Greek cities.

Greek Hoplites

Most of the Greek army was made up of infantrymen, or hoplites, who were armed with shields and long spears.

Black Sea
Apollonia

Byzantium
Chalcedon

Pella

MACEDONIA

ILLYRIA

Philippi
Maronea
Lampsacus
PHRYGIA
R. Granicus 334 BC

Neapolis
Thasus
Madytus
Abydus
MYSIA

Epidamnus
THESSALY
Acanthus
Sigeium
Assos
ANATOLIA

Methone
Lemnos
Mytilene
LYDIA
Sardis

Apollonia
Aegean Sea
Teos
IONIA

CORFU
Dodona
Chios
Ephesus
Magnesia
CARIA

Corcyra
LOCRIS
Priene
Halicarnassus

Ionian Sea
Oeniadae
Corcyra
ATTICA
Athens
Delphi
Corinth
Sunium
Delos

Elis
Nemea
Argos

Olympia
PELOPONNESE
Tegea
Kephalos

Megalopolis
Sparta
Melos

Messene
Gytheum

CRETE

Calidon

R. Jaxartes

Caspian Sea
R. Oxus
Alexandria Eschate

Maracanda

Gaugamela 331 BC
Meshed
Bactra
Drapsaca

Issus 333 BC
Nineveh
MEDIA
Ecbatana
Alexandria ad Caucasum

Thapsacus
Emesa
Alexandria (Herat)
Nicaea

R. Euphrates
R. Tigris
Alexandria Prophthasia
Bucephala 326 BC

Damascus
Babylon
Susa
R. Indus

Pasargadae
Sangela

Persepolis
PERSIA
Alexandria (Gulashkird)

ARABIA
Persian Gulf
Pura
Alexandria Sogdiana

Alexandria
Pattala
INDIA

Arabian Sea

Maximum extent of Alexander's empire

Alexander's route

Major battles

19

Rome 500 BC–AD 500

In 1000 BC Rome was no more than a collection of farming villages clustered around seven hills. Yet by 203 BC the Romans controlled the Italian peninsula, the whole of the Mediterranean Sea, Spain and Greece. The Romans had evolved a form of republican government: two rulers, or consuls, presided over the senate, drawn from the Roman aristocracy and rich landowners. But as the gulf between rich and poor within Rome grew wider, the ordinary people felt that they held none of the power. This discontent led to a series of bitter civil wars between powerful generals. In 27 BC, the Roman Republic became an empire under the rule of Augustus, the adopted son of the general and conqueror, Julius Caesar.

Under the rule of the Emperor Augustus more territories were conquered, the army was reorganized into an efficient and loyal fighting force, magnificent buildings and sculptures adorned all the empire's major cities. During this period a Roman citizen could travel from Mesopotamia or North Africa to the northern borders of England along straight, paved roads. Latin was spoken throughout the Roman Empire, the currency was universal. Even cities in distant provinces were built on the Roman model, with a forum (market place), basilica (assembly hall), temples, theatres, palaces, libraries and stadia, where huge crowds gathered to watch chariot racing and gladiatorial combat. As new provinces were conquered they brought wealth to the empire. But when the empire stopped growing, its vast size became a problem; the expenses of an army of over 300,000 men had to be met by increased taxes, which led to discontent, weakening the empire from within.

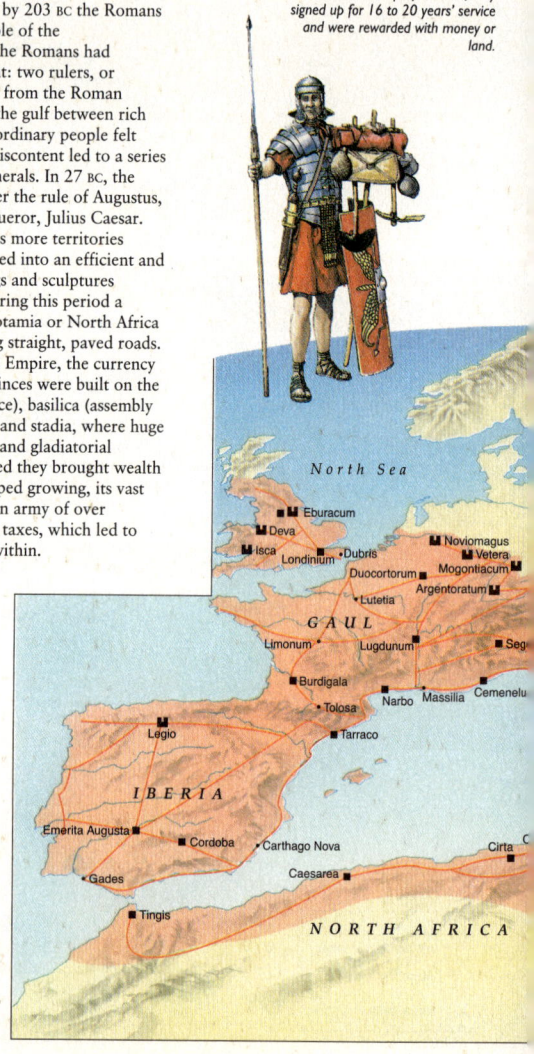

The Roman Army
The basic unit of the Roman army was the century, which consisted of 100 foot soldiers. Soldiers were professionals; they signed up for 16 to 20 years' service and were rewarded with money or land.

North Sea

- Eburacum
- Deva
- Isca
- Londinium
- Dubris
- Noviomagus
- Vetera
- Duocortorum
- Mogontiacum
- Argentoratum
- Lutetia

G A U L
- Limonum
- Lugdunum
- Segi
- Burdigala
- Tolosa
- Narbo Massilia Cemenelu
- Legio
- Tarraco

I B E R I A
- Emerita Augusta
- Cordoba
- Carthago Nova
- Cirta
- Gades
- Caesarea
- Tingis

N O R T H   A F R I C A

The Roman Empire
As new provinces were added to the Roman empire, the conquerors set about 'Romanizing' them. Towns and capital cities were built to follow the layout and design of Rome. Straight, paved roads and aqueducts linked these new settlements. In the countryside, land was cleared and irrigated so that it was ready for cultivation. A provincial governor was appointed to run the province and ensure that there were no revolts against Roman rule. Legions of the Roman army were sent to the provinces to help keep the peace and were often stationed in fortresses along the borders of the empire.

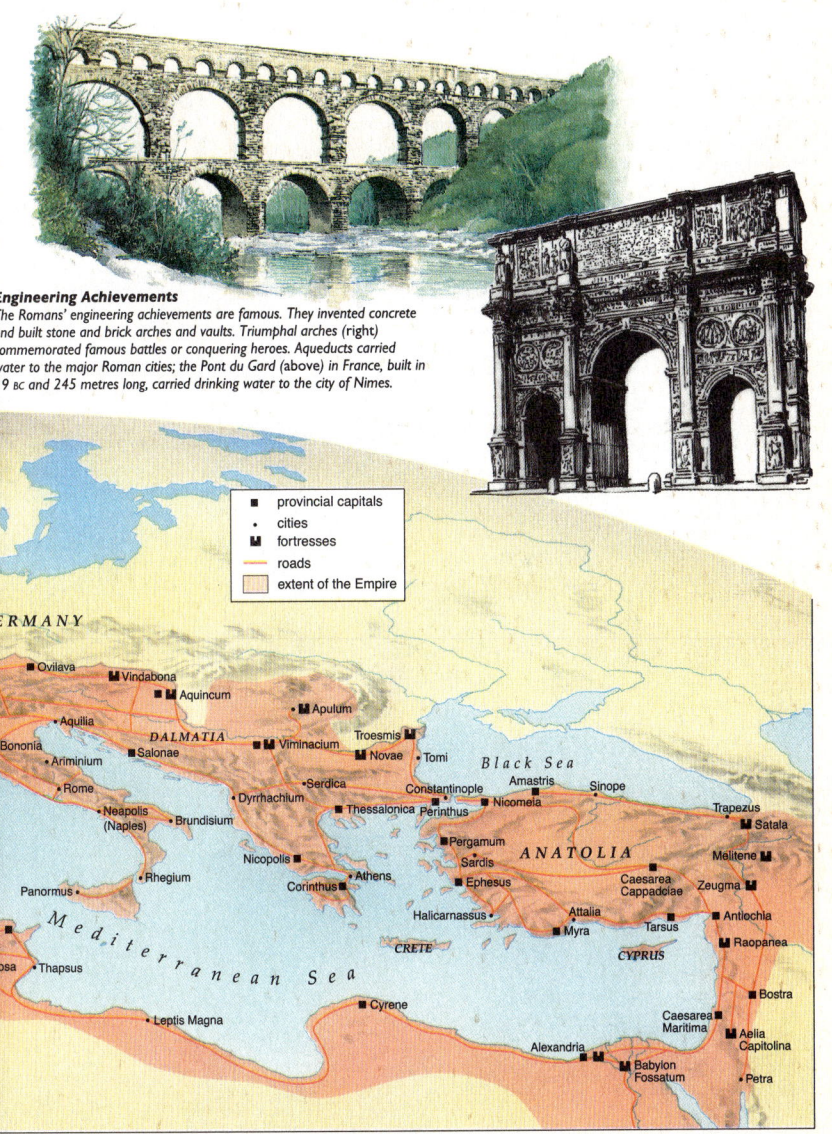

Engineering Achievements

The Romans' engineering achievements are famous. They invented concrete and built stone and brick arches and vaults. Triumphal arches (right) commemorated famous battles or conquering heroes. Aqueducts carried water to the major Roman cities; the Pont du Gard (above) in France, built in 19 BC and 245 metres long, carried drinking water to the city of Nimes.

Legend
- ■ provincial capitals
- · cities
- ⛊ fortresses
- — roads
- extent of the Empire

GERMANY

Ovilava
Vindabona
Aquincum
Aquilia
Apulum
Bononia
DALMATIA
Viminacium
Troesmis
Salonae
Novae
Tomi
Ariminium
Rome
Serdica
Constantinople
Amastris
Sinope
Black Sea
Neapolis (Naples)
Dyrrhachium
Thessalonica
Perinthus
Nicomela
Brundisium
Trapezus
Satala
Pergamum
ANATOLIA
Nicopolis
Sardis
Melitene
Rhegium
Athens
Ephesus
Caesarea Cappadciae
Zeugma
Panormus
Corinthus
Halicarnassus
Attalia
Antiochia
Myra
Tarsus
CRETE
CYPRUS
Raopanea
Mediterranean Sea
Thapsus
psa
Cyrene
Caesarea Maritima
Bostra
Leptis Magna
Alexandria
Aelia Capitolina
Babylon Fossatum
Petra

Europe Attacked AD 600–1100

The success of the Roman Empire led to its downfall, its sheer size making administration increasingly difficult. In the third century the empire split into the Byzantine Empire and the Western Empire. Throughout the 3rd century AD, nomadic tribes from central Asia, such as the Visigoths and Franks, had been pressing on Rome's northern frontiers. With the weakening of the empire, they broke through, sweeping south in search of new lands. These tribes were pastoralists; accompanied by their animal herds they travelled long distances, living in tented camps. With the collapse of the Western Roman Empire in the fifth century AD, one of the nomadic tribes, the Franks, became Europe's most powerful rulers. Under their great king, Charlemagne, the Frankish Carolingian Empire became known as the 'Holy Roman Empire' and extended from France to Italy.

Charlemagne
A gold bust of Charlemagne (742–814), King of the Franks.

- ○ Important Viking settlements
- • Other settlements

Viking routes

Areas under Viking control

Staraya Ladoga
Uppsala
Novgorod
Kaupang
Lindholm
Viborg
Århus
Grobina
Jelling
Loddekopinge
Odense
Limerick   Dublin
Cork   Wexford   Derby
Waterford   Nottingham
Norwich
London
Bremen
Hedeby
SAXONY
Aachen   Cologne
Rouen
Paris   Rheims   THURINGIA
FRANCIA
Nantes   SWABIA   BAVARIA
Arles
Rome
Kiev
Areas devastated by Magyars
Magyar invasion routes
MAGYARS
Constantinople
Extent of the Carolingian empire in AD 814

The Vikings

In the eighth century a seafaring people called the Vikings sailed in their longboats from Norway, Denmark and Sweden to find new lands to colonize. They raided coastal settlements, murdering and terrorizing the native populations and plundering their monasteries, returning to their homelands laden with treasure. In the mid-ninth century, instead of returning home, Viking raiders began to make permanent settlements. They were good farmers, adapting themselves to the culture of the peoples they conquered. Accomplished traders, they established trade routes throughout northwestern Europe. Some reached America. By crossing the Baltic Sea, Vikings entered the great river systems of European Russia, and in *c.* 862 formed the first Russian state in Novgorod. Using the south-flowing rivers, they penetrated the forests and frozen wastes of Russia, establishing trading stations as far as the Black Sea and the Mediterranean. Though fearless warriors, the Vikings were also good craftsmen, producing fine swords and beautiful woodcarvings.

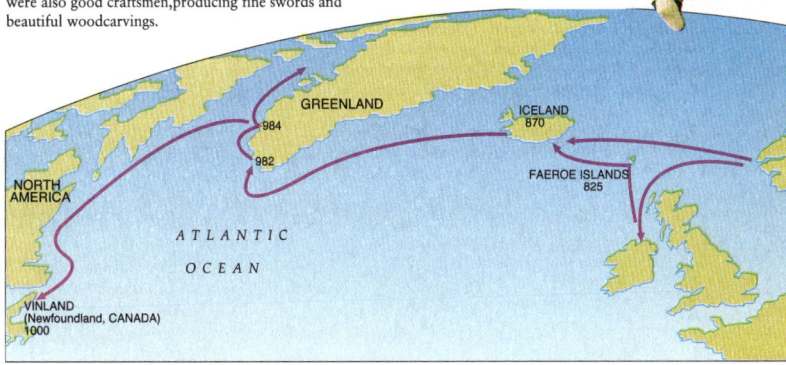

GREENLAND

984

982

ICELAND
870

FAEROE ISLANDS
825

NORTH
AMERICA

A T L A N T I C

O C E A N

VINLAND
(Newfoundland, CANADA)
1000

A Viking Settlement

The Vikings established a trading centre at Hedeby in Denmark where several major trade routes intersected. Over the years, Hedeby became a major trading centre. To protect the town from hostile German tribes, an earth embankment topped with a timber palisade was built around it. The houses were constructed of wood and earth. The entire family slept, ate, worked and played together in one small room. The house of a more prosperous Viking might have two or three rooms. Their food came from fishing, hunting and from local farms.

23

Asian Empires 100 BC–AD 1300

China was first united under the short-lived Ch'in Dynasty in 221 BC. The succeeding Han Dynasty (202 BC–AD 220) ruled a united China for over four centuries. During this period, China grew prosperous, with an efficient administration, extensive road and canal network, and a growing number of large towns. Paper was invented. Chang'an (or Xi'an), the Han capital, stood at the beginning of the Silk Road, the great trade route across central Asia. Merchants travelled the road, their camels laden with silk. After a long period of decline, the Han Empire collapsed and for 400 years China was fragmented. Its unification, begun during the Sui Dynasty, was consolidated by the T'ang (618–907), one of the greatest periods in Chinese history. Ch'ang-an became one of the world's largest cities. The T'ang were famed for their arts, literature and poetry. With the decline of the T'ang, a new dynasty, the Sung or Song (AD 960–1279), began. The Sung built a centrally controlled bureaucracy and army. Ocean-going junks laden with tea, silk and porcelain sailed for India and Africa. Urban centres grew and flourished. Printing was invented, developing later into movable type, 400 years before it reached the West. Among the Sung's finest products were its superb pottery and porcelain. The refinement of the Sung period lasted for 300 years until it was shattered by the Mongol invasion. In Japan, Imperial rule was established in about the fifth century AD. In the ninth century, Japan was dominated by military overlords, called shoguns.

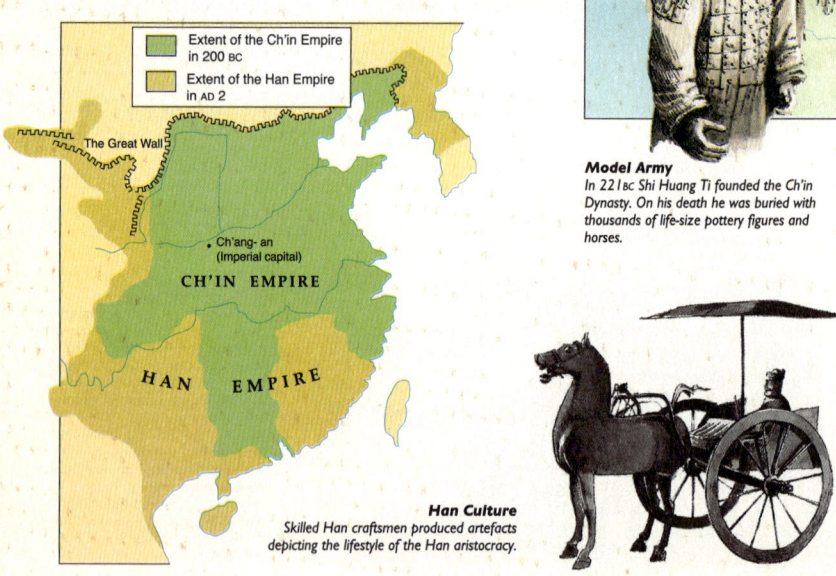

Samarkand

Area under Chinese military control

Extent of the Ch'in Empire in 200 BC

Extent of the Han Empire in AD 2

The Great Wall

Ch'ang-an (Imperial capital)

CH'IN EMPIRE

HAN EMPIRE

Model Army
In 221 BC Shi Huang Ti founded the Ch'in Dynasty. On his death he was buried with thousands of life-size pottery figures and horses.

Han Culture
Skilled Han craftsmen produced artefacts depicting the lifestyle of the Han aristocracy.

Area under
Tang control
in the 7th century

• Khotan

Great Wall

Lo-yang

Extent of
Sung China

T'ANG EMPIRE

Ch'ang-an

• Ningpo

• Ch'eng-tu

Canton

Feudal Japan
Buddhism spread from India in the sixth century. Temples like the Horyu-ji at Nara (left) were constructed. Samurai warriors (below right) protected the overlords.

Kyoto
Nara

Provincial borders
Provincial capitals
Fortresses

The Rise of Islam AD 632

In the seventh century the Prophet Muhammad founded the Islamic religion. Based on the simple message that there is no God but the one God, Allah, the religion united the warring nomadic tribes of the Arabian peninsula. Arab armies advanced east and west, engulfing the ancient world. By the time of the Prophet Muhammad's death in AD 632 the tide of conquest had spread from West Africa to the Far East. Today there are some 1.3 billion Muslims in the world.

While Western Europe struggled through the 'dark ages' (fifth–tenth century), the Arab world pushed forward the frontiers of learning in science, medicine, astronomy and mathematics. Arab merchants travelled the trade routes, carrying with them not only goods but a new and sophisticated culture. A prosperous Arab bathed in a 'Turkish' bath, strolled among the geometrically laid-out paths and water courses of his garden, or went shopping in the great covered markets – or souks – where everything was for sale under one roof. He could even send his son to university, whereas it was to be three hundred years before such centres of learning existed in Europe. Islamic architects designed exquisite buildings that contained intricate mosaics, brilliantly coloured glazed tiles and splashing fountains.

The Minaret
The tall slender minaret of the Ahmad ibn Tulun Mosque towers above the rooftops of Cairo, capital of Egypt.

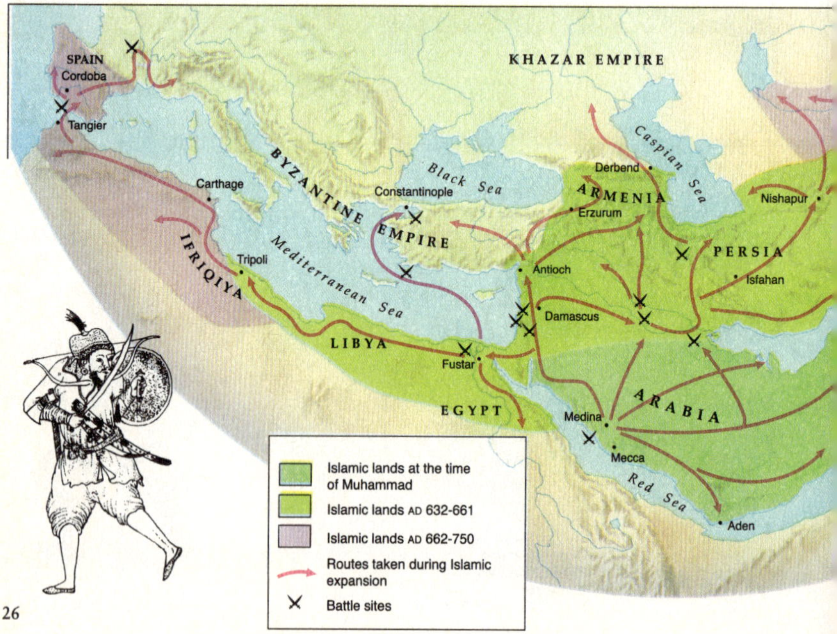

SPAIN
Cordoba
Tangier
KHAZAR EMPIRE
Carthage
BYZANTINE
Black Sea
Constantinople
Derbend
Caspian Sea
ARMENIA
Erzurum
Nishapur
IFRIQIYA
Tripoli
Mediterranean Sea
EMPIRE
Antioch
PERSIA
Isfahan
Damascus
LIBYA
Fustat
ARABIA
EGYPT
Medina
Mecca
Red Sea
Aden

- Islamic lands at the time of Muhammad
- Islamic lands AD 632-661
- Islamic lands AD 662-750
- → Routes taken during Islamic expansion
- ✕ Battle sites

Islamic Religion

The Islamic religion is based on a series of revelations that Muslims (followers of Islam) believe were received directly from God by the Prophet Muhammad (c. 570–632). These revelations are contained in the Koran, the Holy Book of Islam. Islam means submission to the will of God, known as Allah to Muslims. The Koran lays down strict rules for every aspect of a Muslim's life. A devout Muslim should pray to Allah five times a day, either in a mosque or wherever he happens to be so long as he kneels facing towards Mecca, the birthplace of Muhammad and the holiest city of Islam. The Koran also decrees that once in a lifetime every Muslim should make a pilgrimage to Mecca to worship at the Ka'aba, the holy shrine of Islam. It is also a Muslim's duty to fast during the daylight hours of the holy month of Ramadan.

Dome of the Rock
The magnificent Dome of the Rock in Jerusalem is one of the holiest places of Islam.

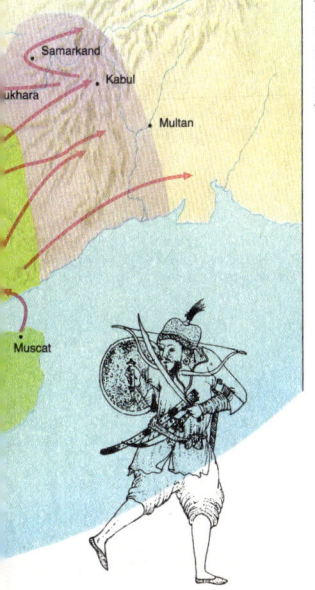

Samarkand

ukhara

Kabul

Multan

Muscat

Arab Trade

With the coming of Islam to North Africa in the eleventh century, Arab merchants opened up trade routes across the Sahara Desert. Their camel caravans carried salt, ivory, African slaves and gold from West Africa to the Mediterranean lands. Dates and grain were stored in pottery jars, like the one below from Syria. From the Arab markets, travelling merchants traded spices along the trade routes of Asia, returning with silk from China.

Europe in the Middle Ages 1100–1300

By the mid-tenth century, the invasions of the northern tribes, like the Vikings, had been halted. Western Europe was divided into kingdoms, ruled by kings or lords. Society was organized under a system called the feudal system whereby the king or lord gave land to nobles who in return swore an oath of loyalty and provided soldiers, or knights, for his protection. Throughout Europe these rulers built castles in strategic positions as defences against their potential enemies. Peasants were owned by the lord; they farmed his land for nothing but in return were given strips of land of their own and protected by his soldiers. Trade expanded during the Middle Ages, and towns developed into cities. As Christianity spread, the church played an increasingly important part in people's lives. Religious communities called monasteries were founded, where monks devoted their lives to prayer. As centres of pilgrimage, learning and medical care, they became an integral part of medieval life. The most powerful ruler in Western Europe was the pope, head of the Roman Catholic Church. The church owned vast amounts of land and grew rich on the payment of taxes.

Christianity

The Christian religion is based on the teachings of Jesus Christ whom Christians believe was the son of God. It began in Palestine, and after its adoption by the Romans in the fourth century, spread throughout Europe. Churches and cathedrals, like Santiago de Compostela in Spain, shown below, were built for worship and to glorify God.

Map

KINGDOM OF NORWAY
KINGDOM OF PICTS AND SCOTS
KINGDOM OF SWEDEN
IRELAND
KINGDOM OF DENMARK
PRINCIPALITY OF KIEV
ANGLO-SAXON KINGDOM
Aix-la-Chapelle
KINGDOM OF POLAND
Kiev
HOLY ROMAN EMPIRE
KINGDOM OF HUNGARY
NAVARRE
KINGDOM OF FRANCE
BURGUNDY
LEON
CASTILE
ARAGON
BARCELONA
CROATS
PAPAL STATES
Rome
SERBS
BULGARS
Constantinople
CALIPHATE OF CORDOBA
Cordoba
BYZANTINE EMPIRE

- ☐ Pagan religions
- ☐ Muslim religions
- ☐ Scandinavian-influenced religions

Craftsmen

Craftsmen, such as the carpenter below, tended to live in towns. They were independent of the feudal system and were paid for their work.

Daily Life

Most people lived as farmers, cultivating crops, such as wheat, barley and beans, and grazing livestock. The wool trade flourished in the Middle Ages, especially in England.

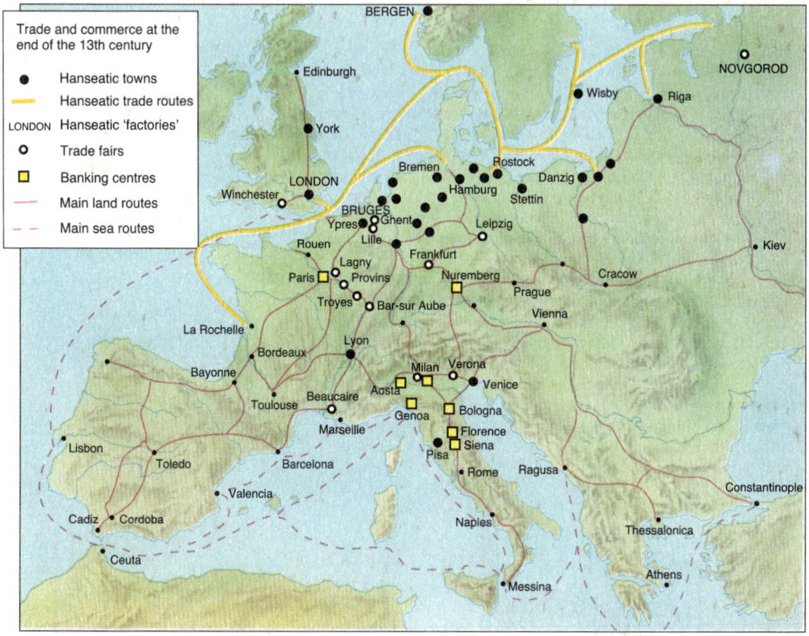

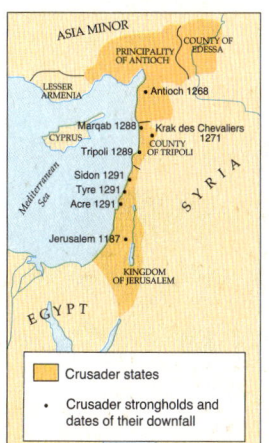

Map: Trade and commerce at the end of the 13th century

Legend:
- ● Hanseatic towns
- ━ Hanseatic trade routes (yellow)
- LONDON Hanseatic 'factories'
- ○ Trade fairs
- □ Banking centres
- — Main land routes
- - - Main sea routes

Map labels:

BERGEN

Edinburgh

NOVGOROD

Wisby · Riga

York

LONDON · Winchester

Rostock · Danzig

Bremen · Hamburg · Stettin

Ypres · Ghent · Lille · Leipzig · Kiev

BRUGES

Rouen · Lagny · Frankfurt

Paris · Provins · Nuremberg · Prague · Cracow

Troyes · Bar-sur Aube · Vienna

La Rochelle

Bordeaux · Lyon

Bayonne · Milan · Verona · Venice

Toulouse · Beaucaire · Aosta · Genoa · Bologna

Marseille · Florence · Siena

Lisbon · Pisa · Ragusa

Toledo · Barcelona · Rome · Constantinople

Cadiz · Cordoba · Valencia · Naples · Thessalonica

Ceuta · Messina · Athens

The Hansa
In northern Europe an association of trading towns, the Hansa, regulated commerce. Banking originated in the city states of medieval Italy. See above.

The Crusades
With the spread of Christianity, pilgrims journeyed to Palestine (or the Holy Land) to worship at the Christian holy places. When Seljuk Turks conquered Palestine in 1071, these pilgrimages were forbidden. This sparked off the Crusades, a series of military campaigns fought by Christians against Muslims for control of the holy places. The Crusaders built magnificent castles, like Krak des Chevaliers in Syria (below), to protect the pilgrim routes.

Map: Crusader states

ASIA MINOR

COUNTY OF EDESSA

PRINCIPALITY OF ANTIOCH

LESSER ARMENIA

CYPRUS

Antioch 1268

Marqab 1288

Krak des Chevaliers 1271

Tripoli 1289

COUNTY OF TRIPOLI

Sidon 1291

Tyre 1291

Acre 1291

Jerusalem 1187

SYRIA

Mediterranean Sea

KINGDOM OF JERUSALEM

EGYPT

Legend:
- ▨ Crusader states
- · Crusader strongholds and dates of their downfall

The Mongol Empire 1200–1405

Covering a vast area of northern Asia are the steppes – windswept grasslands inhabited by tribes of pastoral nomads grazing their sheep and horses. In the early thirteenth century the Mongol tribes were united under Genghis Khan (*c.* 1162–1227) who welded them into a formidable fighting force. The Mongol's first target was China. Despite the Great Wall, built by the Chinese in the third century BC to repel northern barbarians, the Mongol hordes invaded China, occupying it until driven out by the Ming Dynasty in 1368. In 1219 Genghis Khan's armies swept westwards, overrunning central Asia, Russia, entering Hungary and Poland and continuing their conquests until they reached the Black Sea. The Mongols then withdrew into central Asia, but within a few years a fresh onslaught began. Total domination of Europe and Muslim Asia was probably prevented only by the defeat of a Mongol army near Baghdad and by disputes between Genghis Khan's successors. Attempts to invade Java and Japan were also unsuccessful. In the late fourteenth century one of Genghis Khan's greatest successors, Tamerlane, led campaigns south of the Caspian Sea and as far as northern India. At its height, the Mongol Empire was the largest the world had ever seen. Though the hordes left a trail of death and destruction in their wake, once the empire was established it was followed by a period of peace and consolidation.

Yurt
The Mongols lived in tents, or yurts, which were perfectly adapted to their nomadic way of life. Greased animal skins or textiles were stretched over a wooden frame, then covered with handwoven rugs which helped to keep out the bitter winter cold. Inside the floor was covered with felt, skin or rugs. The yurt could be quickly dismantled and loaded onto a pony.

EUROPE

Liegnitz

Cracow

Gran

Ragusa

1242

Constantinople

AFRICA

Ain Jalut

Mongol Horsemen
Superb horsemen, the Mongols rode ponies that could travel immense distances without tiring. The Mongols could fire their arrows from the saddle at full gallop. Their manoeuvrability was aided by stirrups, such as those above, which were reputedly made for Genghis Khan himself. It was their speed, mobility and firepower that gave the Mongols their military superiority.

Trade

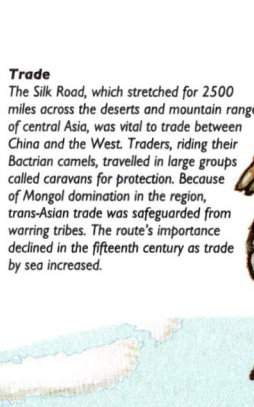

The Silk Road, which stretched for 2500 miles across the deserts and mountain ranges of central Asia, was vital to trade between China and the West. Traders, riding their Bactrian camels, travelled in large groups called caravans for protection. Because of Mongol domination in the region, trans-Asian trade was safeguarded from warring tribes. The route's importance declined in the fifteenth century as trade by sea increased.

Novgorod

KHANATE OF THE GOLDEN HORDE

MONGOLIA

Karakoram

JAPAN

New Sarai

1236

1219 Beshbalik

1211

Peking

1273

1223

CHAGATAI EMPIRE

Hsiliang

1216

1281

Tiflis

Kashgar

EMPIRE

Tabriz

• Bukhara

OF THE

1221

IL - KHAN

GREAT KHAN

CHINA

Baghdad *1258*

EMPIRE

Peshawar

Canton

1277 *1257*

Lahore

1285

1297

ARABIA

1296

Area under
loose Mongol
control

Pagan

to Java
1292

INDIA

| → | Campaigns of Genghis Khan and dates |
| → | Campaigns of his successors and dates |

31

Europe in Crisis 1300–1400

In the early fourteenth century Europe suffered from a number of disasters. A change in the climate caused harvests to fail, resulting in widespread famine. This was followed by a pandemic plague (called 'the Black Death'), and the beginning of the Hundred Years' War between England and France. This war was not one continuous conflict but a series of attempts by English kings to dominate France, which began with Edward III's claim to the French throne. The English armies won battles at Sluys, Crécy, Calais and Poitiers, but these were countered by later French victories, and by 1377 France had recovered most of its lost territories. War was renewed by Henry V of England who won a crushing victory over the French at Agincourt in 1415 and then went on to conquer much of Normandy. France's recovery was begun by Joan of Arc who led an army against the English at Orleans in 1429. By the mid-fifteenth century Calais was the only English possession left in France. The misery caused by war, famine, plague and high taxes led to popular uprisings, like the Peasants' Revolt in England in 1381.

Knights
Medieval knights went into battle wearing plate armour over a layer of chain mail.

Map legend:
- English domains in 1339
- English domains after Peace of Bretigny (1360)
- English bases in 1380

Sluys, Calais, Brussels, Cherbourg, Crécy, Agincourt, Paris, Brest, BRITTANY, Orléans, FRANCE, Poitiers, Lyon, Bordeaux, Bayonne, Carcassonne

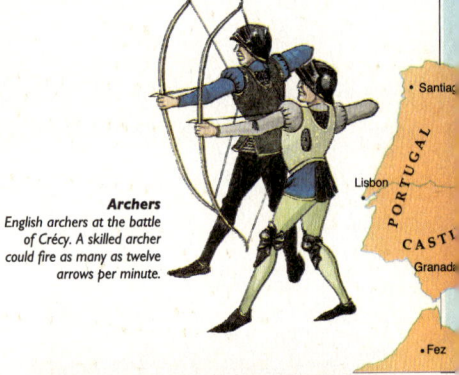

Archers
English archers at the battle of Crécy. A skilled archer could fire as many as twelve arrows per minute.

Santiago, PORTUGAL, Lisbon, CASTI, Granada, Fez

Changes in Warfare
The various conflicts during the Hundred Years' War were dominated by sieges of fortified castles and towns. An assault began with the mining of the outer walls and bombardment by cannon, as seen here in the siege of Rouen by the English in 1419.

SWEDEN

NORWAY Oslo • Stockholm

SCOTLAND

• Edinburgh

DENMARK
Copenhagen •

IRELAND

York •

Wexford •

• Lübeck

LITHUANIA

WALES

ENGLAND Amsterdam

SAXONY

Warsaw •

London •

HOLLAND
Bruges •

Brunswick •

SILESIA

POLAND

Kiev •

FLANDERS
Ghent •

HOLY

Rouen •

Mainz •

Cracow
•

Paris •

BOHEMIA

UKRAINE

BRITTANY

LORRAINE

ROMAN

Orléans •

BAVARIA

BURGUNDY

Munich •

Vienna •

Buda • • Pest

FRANCE

Basle •

EMPIRE AUSTRIA

HUNGARY

Lyon •

SAVOY

Milan •

Venice •

Bucharest
•

First cases
of plague
in 1346

BOSNIA

WALLACHIA

Marseilles •

SERBIA

BULGARIA

Constantinople

ARAGON

• Barcelona

PAPAL
STATES

Rome •

Adrianople •

Salonica
•

Toledo •

Naples •

OTTOMAN

Almeria •

EMPIRE

Palermo •

Athens •

| Areas with no or a low number of deaths caused by plague | The darker areas indicate where plague occured in 1347 and its gradual spread over the rest of Europe in just 4 years |

Messina •

Black Death

In the fourteenth century Western Europe was
ravaged by a terrible scourge called the Black
Death. Carried by infected fleas on rats, it made its
first appearance in the Crimea in 1346, probably
brought by ships from Asia. Victims were covered
by black swellings that oozed blood and were
incredibly painful. Few people who contracted the
plague survived. Its effect on the populations of
Europe was devastating: some towns and villages
were left virtually uninhabited. The dead had to be
buried in mass graves. It is estimated that some 20
million Europeans died.

The Ottoman Empire 1300–1500

Until the late thirteenth century the Ottoman Turks were nomadic tribesmen who patrolled the eastern borders of the Byzantine Empire. United by a strong leader – Othman or Osman I – in the early fourteenth century, they began their conquest of Eastern Europe, extending as far west as Hungary and the Balkans. In 1453, after a prolonged siege, the Ottomans captured Constantinople (now Istanbul), thus bringing to an end the Christian Byzantine Empire which had lasted some six hundred years.

Constantinople became the empire's cultural and administrative centre, and the residence of the sultan. In the Topkapi Palace overlooking the city, the sultan ruled his empire, surrounded by his family and protected by his personal bodyguard, the janissaries – Christians who had been captured by the Turks, converted to Islam and given a rigorous military training. No sultan could rise to power or maintain it without their support.

Under Suleiman I further expansion into Europe began, but with the failure of the siege of Vienna in 1529, westward expansion by land halted. In their shipyards in Constantinople the Ottomans built a magnificent fleet of galleys with which they ravaged the coasts of Spain, Italy and Greece. But in 1571 they were defeated in a great sea battle at Lepanto, off the coast of Greece. This defeat meant further expansion was only possible to the east. Expansion continued until 1680 when the empire's slow decline began.

Turkish Janissaries
Turkish janissaries served the sultan, both as soldiers and administrators, with unquestioning obedience.

Hagia Sophia
Influenced by both Muslim and Byzantine architecture, the Ottomans developed a style of their own. Magnificent mosques, surmounted by several domes and often with as many as six minarets, pierced the city skylines. St Sophia in Constantinople began life as a Christian church but was converted into an Islamic mosque when the city fell to the Turks in 1453.

Algiers

Tunis

Tripoli

SPAIN

Mediterranean

AFRICA

Maximum extent of the Ottoman Empire in 1680

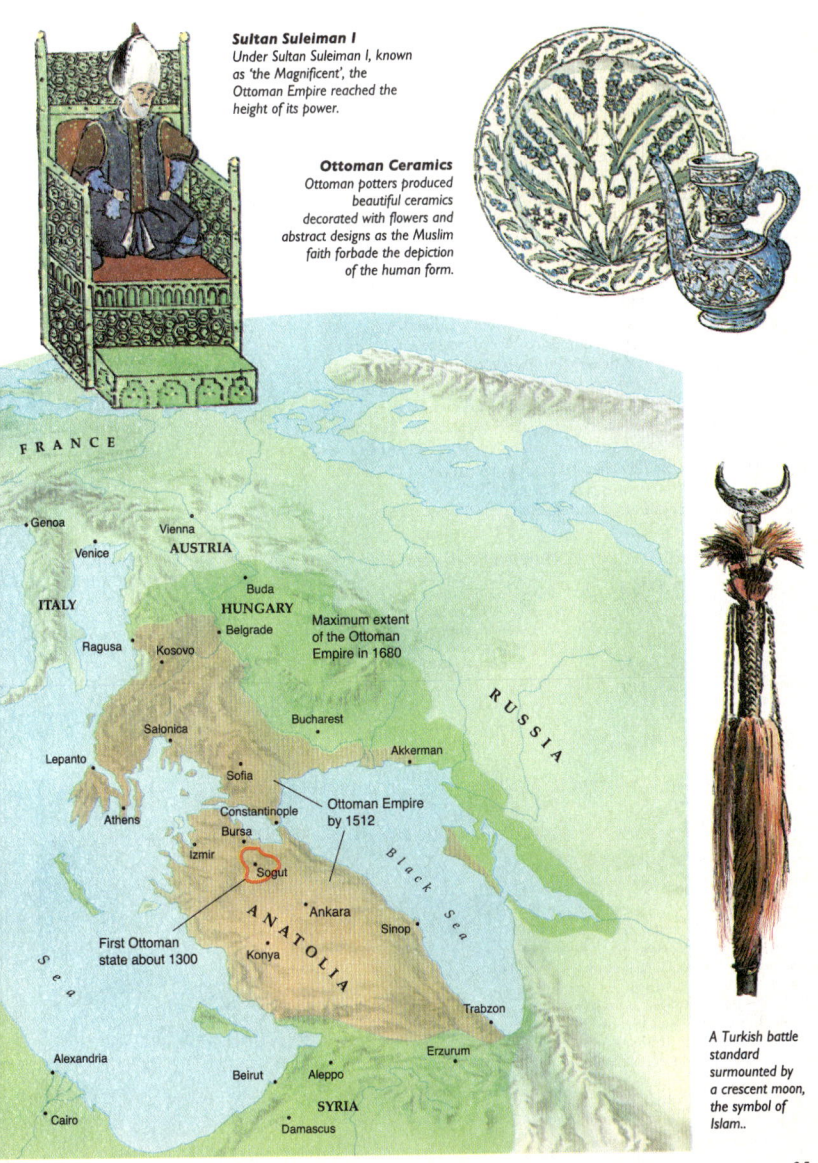

Sultan Suleiman I
Under Sultan Suleiman I, known as 'the Magnificent', the Ottoman Empire reached the height of its power.

Ottoman Ceramics
Ottoman potters produced beautiful ceramics decorated with flowers and abstract designs as the Muslim faith forbade the depiction of the human form.

FRANCE

Genoa

Vienna

Venice

AUSTRIA

ITALY

Buda

HUNGARY

Belgrade

Maximum extent of the Ottoman Empire in 1680

Ragusa

Kosovo

RUSSIA

Salonica

Bucharest

Lepanto

Akkerman

Sofia

Athens

Constantinople

Ottoman Empire by 1512

Bursa

Izmir

Sogut

Black Sea

ANATOLIA

Ankara

Sinop

First Ottoman state about 1300

Konya

Sea

Trabzon

Alexandria

Erzurum

Beirut

Aleppo

Cairo

SYRIA

Damascus

A Turkish battle standard surmounted by a crescent moon, the symbol of Islam..

35

The Americas from the Eve of Conquest to 1519

Sometime between 40,000 and 25,000 years ago hunters from Asia migrated to North America by crossing the Bering Strait. Living as hunter-gatherers, they gradually spread throughout the continent. Their descendants moved southwards, reaching Mexico in *c.* 20,000 BC. There they settled and became farmers, cultivating crops of maize and beans. Two warrior societies rose to power, first the Olmecs and then the Toltecs. The Olmecs are known for their huge helmeted stone heads and small jade axes, while the Toltecs erected temples and monumental stone warriors in their city at Tula. In the thirteenth century the Toltecs were succeeded by the warlike Aztecs, who established a powerful empire centred on their capital, Tenochtitlán, built on an island in Lake Texcoco – the site of Mexico City today. Believing that their gods required to be fed on human blood, the Aztecs waged continuous war on their neighbours, sacrificing their prisoners to the gods.

Further south, in the tropical rain forests of Guatemala and Belize, a sophisticated civilization called the Maya had been in existence since AD 300. Great builders, their huge temple complexes and spectacular pyramids can still be seen in the jungles of Yucatán. In Peru another great civilization, the Inca, had established its empire in the Cuzco valley in the twelfth century. The Inca and the Aztec were conquered by the Spanish conquistadors in the early sixteenth century.

Murder of Atahualpa
At its height, the Inca Empire stretched for 2000 miles along the Andes. In 1532 Spaniards, led by the conquistador Pizarro, invaded Peru, murdered the Inca leader, Atahualpa, (see left) and brought the empire to an end.

Totem Pole
Tribes who settled along the Pacific coast of North America erected painted wooden totem poles on which were carved symbolic animals and spirits.

Machu Picchu
In 1911, some four centuries after it was built, archaeologists discovered a remarkable Inca town high in the Andes. Extensive buildings and great terraces clung to the bare hillsides, evidence of a thriving community. Although only 70 kilometres from the Inca capital at Cuzco, Machu Picchu was never discovered by the Spanish conquistadors.

NORTHERN HUNTERS

L'Anse aux Meadows

FISHERMEN

HUNTER-GATHERERS

Huff Village

PLAINS HUNTERS

Hopewell

WOODLAND FARMERS

Mesa Verde

PUEBLO INDIANS

Moundville

FISHERMEN, DESERT-GATHERERS

DESERT-GATHERERS

MESOAMERICAN CIVILIZATION

Teotihuacan

Chichen Itza

MAYA

Tikal

AZTEC EMPIRE

FARMERS

MAIZE AND MANIOC FARMERS

SAVANNAH FARMERS

• Archaeological site

FARMING TRIBES

Moche

Huari

Machu Picchu

SAVANNAH FARMERS

INCA EMPIRE

SAVANNAH HUNTERS

GRASSLAND HUNTERS

FISHERMEN

An Indian Longhouse

Hunter-gathering tribes such as the Iroquois and Huron settled in the area of the Great Lakes of Canada. They lived in longhouses, built from saplings plaited with tree bark. The houses were large enough to accommodate several families.

Aztec Codices

The Aztec were so powerful that they demanded that towns from the Gulf of Mexico to the Pacific pay them a tribute. Adopting a very basic writing system involving pictures that had been used a thousand years before in Mexico, they recorded these tributes in a manuscript called a codex (pl. codices).

Maya Altar Carvings

The Maya were responsible for great technological advances: they invented the first system of writing known in the Americas, a calendar and a numerical system. Their great temple complexes were ornamented with sculptures and carved friezes. The relief above depicts ancient Maya rulers.

Migration

It is thought that when the great ice sheet retreated in the northern hemisphere, a temporary land bridge between Siberia and Alaska enabled migrants from Asia to cross into North America. Spreading south, they reached the Great Plains. Some migrants turned east, while others continued south towards Mexico where the first settlements began around 20,000 BC.

Europe: the Expansion of Knowledge 1400–1600

In the fifteenth century the great age of discovery began. Europeans sailed the seven seas in search of knowledge, goods to trade and new lands to conquer. Vasco da Gama's ships buffeted their way around the Cape of Good Hope, continuing east until they reached India. Christopher Columbus stumbled upon the Americas. Amerigo Vespucci gave his name to the American continent after his journeys along the coasts of what are now Brazil and Guiana. Ferdinand Magellan achieved the first circumnavigation of the world; the Spanish invaded Mexico and Peru; and the Portuguese explored Africa's west coast. The world began to take shape and maps began to look as they do today. These great voyagers returned with knowledge of other cultures and with their ships loaded with cargoes of gold, silver and tobacco from the Americas, ivory and slaves from Africa and spices from Indonesia. Trade routes formed a network across the oceans. The Dutch, Spanish, English, French and Portuguese founded colonies in foreign lands that grew into vast territorial possessions. In Italy a great flowering of the arts – known as the Renaissance, or rebirth – began. New forms of architecture, painting, music and literature evolved. Powerful families and wealthy members of the Church became patrons of the arts, commissioning work from artists like Raphael and Michelangelo and financing the construction of great cathedrals and palaces. The opening up of the world stimulated an interest in geography and cartography. Advances were made in navigation, astronomy and medicine, while the development of printing accelerated the spread of knowledge and new ideas throughout Europe and beyond.

European Christianity

From its early beginnings, European Christianity had been dominated by the Roman Catholic Church – so-called because it was ruled by the Pope in Rome. In the sixteenth century a German priest called Martin Luther led a movement of protest – later called the Reformation – against the corruption of the Catholic Church, which resulted in the establishment of the Protestant Church.

The Printing Press
Until the mid-fifteenth century, information was communicated by word of mouth or written by hand. In the 1450s communication was revolutionized by the printing press, invented by Johannes Gutenberg. The first book to be printed was the Bible. Individual letters were made which could be moved and reused – movable type. The interior of a printing shop on the left shows two men choosing the letters required to compose the manuscript page in front of them; paper is fed into the printing press and as each printed sheet comes off the press, a boy arranges it in order.

NORTH
AMERICA

PACIFIC
OCEAN

Magellan

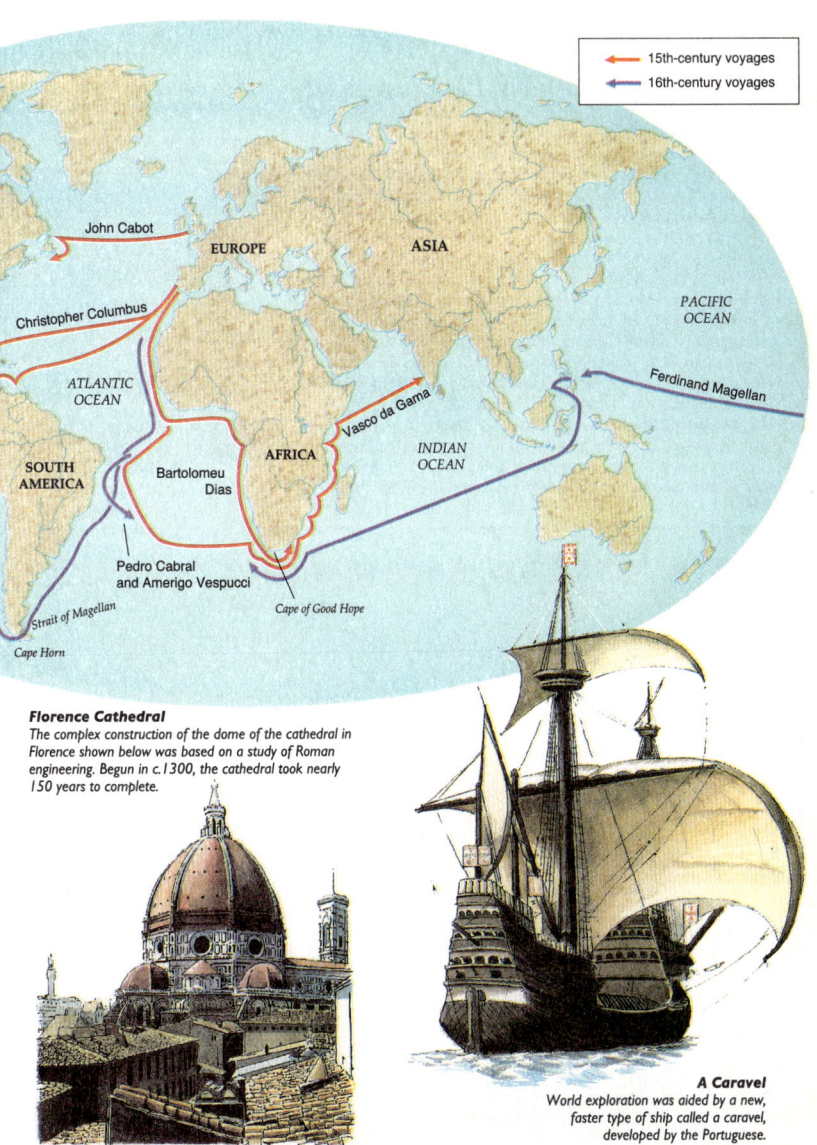

15th-century voyages
16th-century voyages

John Cabot

EUROPE

ASIA

PACIFIC OCEAN

Christopher Columbus

ATLANTIC OCEAN

Vasco da Gama

Ferdinand Magellan

INDIAN OCEAN

SOUTH AMERICA

Bartolomeu Dias

AFRICA

Pedro Cabral and Amerigo Vespucci

Cape of Good Hope

Strait of Magellan

Cape Horn

Florence Cathedral
The complex construction of the dome of the cathedral in Florence shown below was based on a study of Roman engineering. Begun in c.1300, the cathedral took nearly 150 years to complete.

A Caravel
World exploration was aided by a new, faster type of ship called a caravel, developed by the Portuguese.

39

Colonial Expansion 1500–1700

The great voyages of discovery had defined the areas of interest for the seafaring and trading nations of Western Europe. In the sixteenth and seventeenth centuries they began to expand their settlements into colonies and their colonies into empires. In the Americas the Spanish consolidated their empire in Mexico, extending it throughout Central America, to the Caribbean and southwards from Peru to Chile and beyond. The Portuguese settled Brazil. The success of these overseas empires was dependent on forced labour by the native populations – as in Mexico – or by Africans who were shipped from Africa to be sold as slaves. In North America French fur traders penetrated along the St Lawrence River deep into Canada; the Dutch settled along the Hudson Valley; in 1607 the English established a colony at Jamestown, Virginia. Trade was not the only motive for conquest and colonization; religion too played its part, some colonizers fleeing from religious persecution. In 1620 a group, later known as the 'Pilgrim Fathers', left England for America and founded a settlement at Plymouth. On the other side of the globe, the Portuguese founded a colony at Goa and set up slave-trading stations along the East African coast, while the Dutch established control of the spice trade in Indonesia. By the end of the seventeenth century, only Oceania remained undiscovered by the Europeans.

The Slave Trade
Between the mid-fifteenth century and the end of the seventeenth century, some 10 million Africans were crammed into the holds of slave ships and transported across the Atlantic to work the sugar, cotton and tobacco plantations of the European colonies. In the picture below sugar cane is crushed in a Spanish sugar mill.

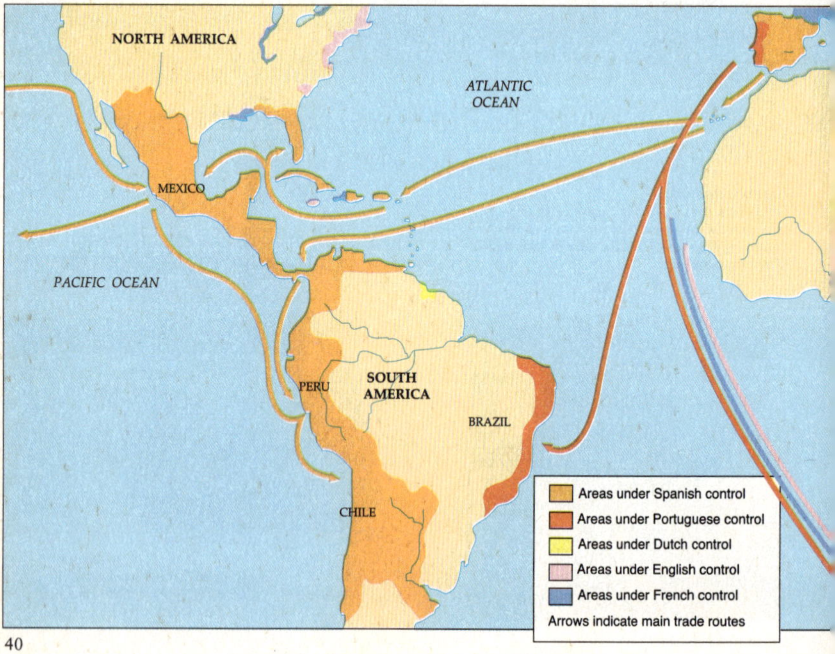

NORTH AMERICA

ATLANTIC OCEAN

MEXICO

PACIFIC OCEAN

PERU

SOUTH AMERICA

BRAZIL

CHILE

	Areas under Spanish control
	Areas under Portuguese control
	Areas under Dutch control
	Areas under English control
	Areas under French control

Arrows indicate main trade routes

New York

New York began as a Dutch trading post on Manhattan Island at the mouth of the Hudson River. Its fine natural harbour attracted a flourishing trade, especially in furs. Here ships enter the Great Dock. In 1664 New York was captured by the English.

A Benin brass statue of a Portuguese soldier.

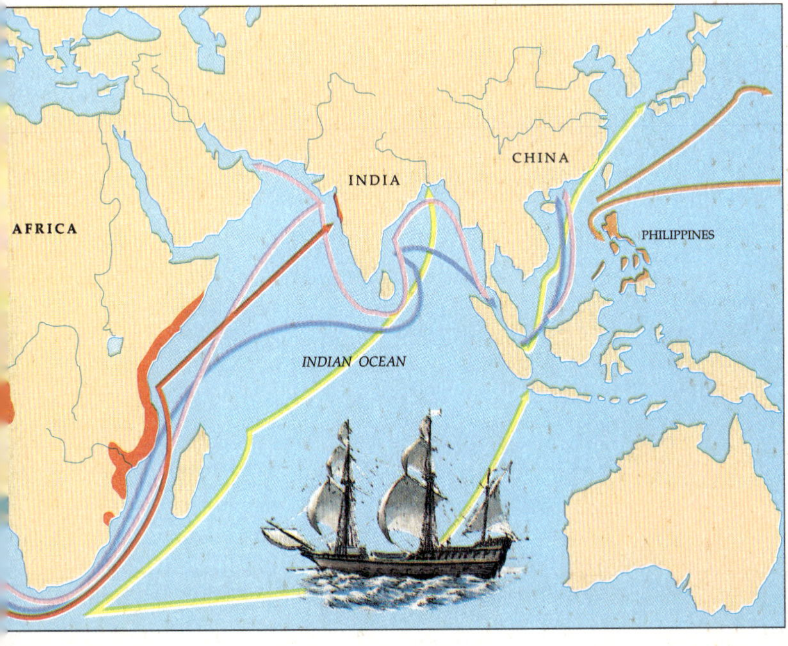

AFRICA

INDIA

CHINA

PHILIPPINES

INDIAN OCEAN

Asian Empires 1300–1700

Although Europeans had established trading ports in South East Asia, the continent remained largely unaffected by the European quest for colonization. Only the Indian subcontinent, invaded in the early sixteenth century by the Mughals, was radically altered by an alien culture. Of mixed Mongol and Turkish descent, the Mughals brought the Islamic religion to India. A series of remarkable rulers extended the empire and introduced the distinctive Islamic style of architecture which changed the face of Indian cities for ever.

China was ruled by an equally successful dynasty, the Ming, which brought peace and stability to a population twice the size of all Europe. The arts flourished, especially the production of silk and pottery. But threatened from without by Japan and a tribe from Manchuria called the Manchus, the Ming dynasty was ended in 1644 when the Manchus seized power and founded a new Imperial dynasty – the Ch'ing. During Ch'ing rule, the Chinese Empire reached its greatest extent, developed a successful economy and improved cultivation, especially of rice, the staple diet. Trade with Western nations, except Russia, was not permitted.

Throughout the 1400s and 1500s Japan had been torn by civil strife, but in the late sixteenth century a series of powerful warriors broke the power of the feudal overlords and restored peace and prosperity. In 1639 all foreigners were expelled from Japan and for the next 200 years it existed in virtual isolation from the rest of the world.

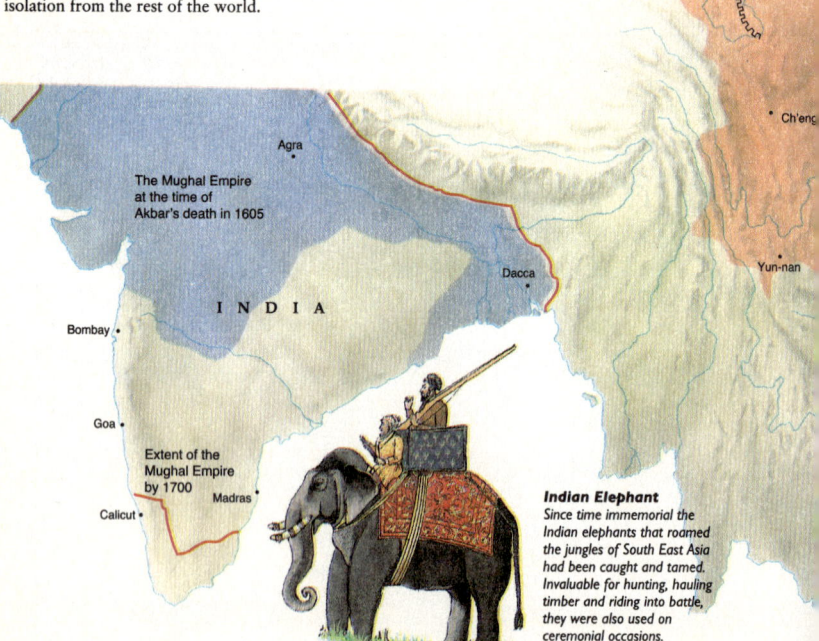

Great W

Ch'eng

Yun-nan

Agra

The Mughal Empire
at the time of
Akbar's death in 1605

Dacca

I N D I A

Bombay

Goa

Extent of the
Mughal Empire
by 1700
Madras

Calicut

Indian Elephant
Since time immemorial the Indian elephants that roamed the jungles of South East Asia had been caught and tamed. Invaluable for hunting, hauling timber and riding into battle, they were also used on ceremonial occasions.

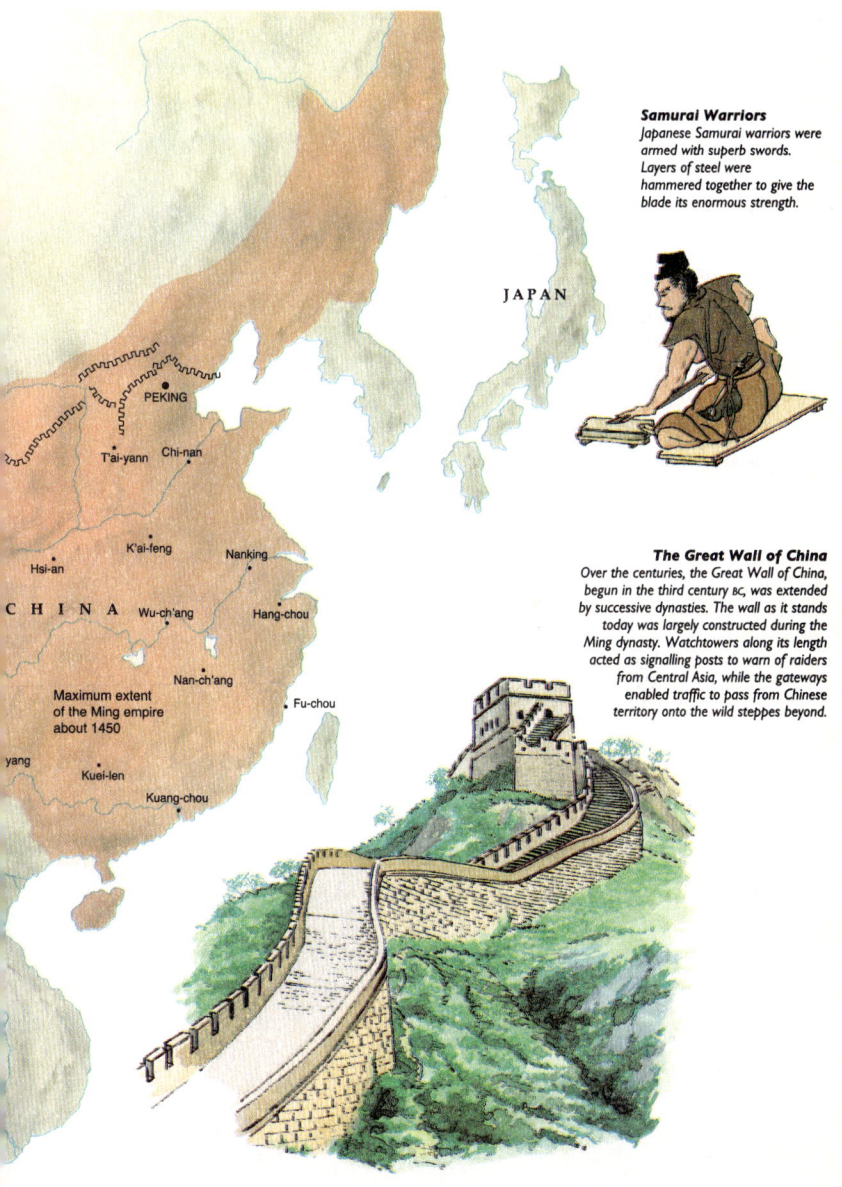

JAPAN

CHINA

PEKING

T'ai-yann Chi-nan

K'ai-feng Nanking

Hsi-an

Wu-ch'ang Hang-chou

Nan-ch'ang

Maximum extent
of the Ming empire
about 1450

Fu-chou

yang

Kuei-len

Kuang-chou

Samurai Warriors
*Japanese Samurai warriors were
armed with superb swords.
Layers of steel were
hammered together to give the
blade its enormous strength.*

The Great Wall of China
*Over the centuries, the Great Wall of China,
begun in the third century BC, was extended
by successive dynasties. The wall as it stands
today was largely constructed during the
Ming dynasty. Watchtowers along its length
acted as signalling posts to warn of raiders
from Central Asia, while the gateways
enabled traffic to pass from Chinese
territory onto the wild steppes beyond.*

Europe: Nations and Conflict 1600–1715

In the fifteenth and sixteenth centuries Europe was divided into a number of small states, but in the seventeenth century these states were absorbed into strong nations, larger and fewer in number, and ruled by powerful kings and emperors. The nations began to compete with one another for political supremacy in Europe. A nation's strength depended on its wealth, administration, military and naval forces and on its agriculture – 90 per cent of Europe's population still derived its living from the land. Conflicts which had previously been largely religious now became territorial. To maintain a balance of power in Europe, nations formed alliances with each other.

An illustrated drill manual of 1607 shows how soldiers in the Dutch army used their muskets.

The Thirty Years' War (1618–48)

This began as a religious war between the Catholic Habsburg emperors and their Protestant subjects in the Holy Roman Empire, but evolved into a major conflict involving the majority of the European states of the time. The war devastated central Europe, especially large areas of Germany, which was left with its economy in ruins and its population greatly reduced. The war was ended by the Peace of Westphalia in 1648.

A musketeer of the English Civil War period with his flintlock musket. Over his shoulder he carries his bandolier in which he kept his cartridge pouches.

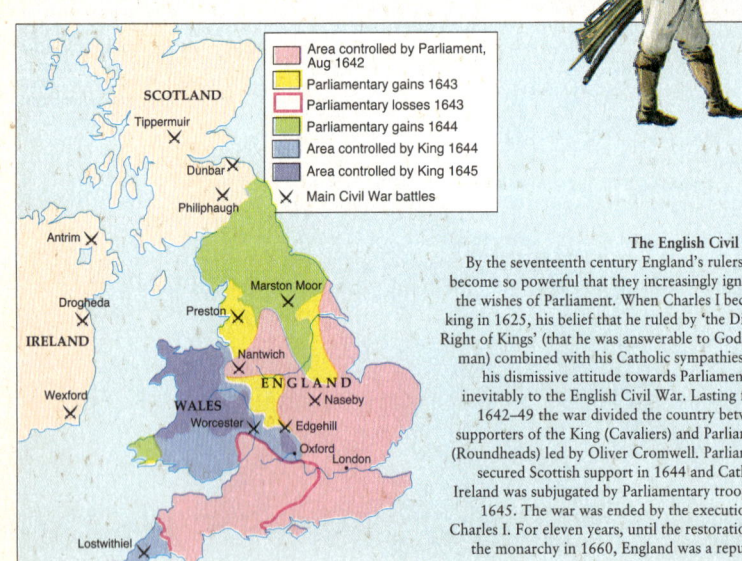

Legend:
- Area controlled by Parliament, Aug 1642
- Parliamentary gains 1643
- Parliamentary losses 1643
- Parliamentary gains 1644
- Area controlled by King 1644
- Area controlled by King 1645
- × Main Civil War battles

SCOTLAND
Tippermuir ×
Dunbar ×
× Philiphaugh
Antrim ×
Drogheda ×
Preston × Marston Moor ×
IRELAND
Nantwich
Wexford × ENGLAND
WALES × Naseby
Worcester × × Edgehill
Oxford
London
Lostwithiel ×

The English Civil War

By the seventeenth century England's rulers had become so powerful that they increasingly ignored the wishes of Parliament. When Charles I became king in 1625, his belief that he ruled by 'the Divine Right of Kings' (that he was answerable to God, not man) combined with his Catholic sympathies and his dismissive attitude towards Parliament led inevitably to the English Civil War. Lasting from 1642–49 the war divided the country between supporters of the King (Cavaliers) and Parliament (Roundheads) led by Oliver Cromwell. Parliament secured Scottish support in 1644 and Catholic Ireland was subjugated by Parliamentary troops in 1645. The war was ended by the execution of Charles I. For eleven years, until the restoration of the monarchy in 1660, England was a republic.

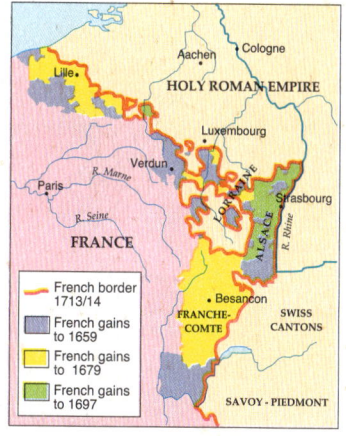

French border
1713/14

French gains
to 1659

French gains
to 1679

French gains
to 1697

Louis XIV's France
King of France from 1643 to 1715, Louis XIV was a prime
example of an absolute monarch. Aided by a few brilliant
ministers, he ruled France almost single-handedly, dispensing
with the French version of parliament, the Estates General.
During his reign France's frontiers were extended and French
culture became the envy of all Europe. But France's ascendancy
was bought at a price: the country was crippled by the taxes
required to finance the wars that Louis waged throughout his
reign.

Louis XIV
*Louis XIV's reign was the
golden age of French art and
literature. In his splendid
palace at Versailles the 'Sun
King' surrounded himself
with the aristocracy.*

The Rise of Russia
From the thirteenth to fourteenth centuries much of European Russia
was controlled by the Mongols. But in the fifteenth century the Princes
of Muscovy drove out the Mongols and created a centralized Russian
state. Ivan IV (known as Ivan the Terrible), the first tsar of Russia,
extended Russia's territories. During the reign of Peter the Great
(1682–1725) Russia became a vast empire stretching from the Baltic to
the Pacific. After travelling widely in Europe, Peter the Great began the
modernization of Russia by introducing Western ideas and
technology. He founded St Petersburg as the new Russian capital,
modelling its architecture on European examples.

*This wooden church on the
island of Kizhi on Lake Onega
bristles with the onion
domes and many roofs so
typical of Russian churches.*

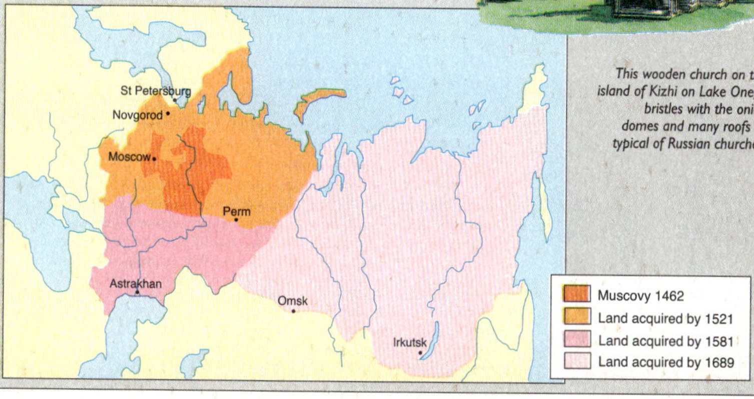

Muscovy 1462

Land acquired by 1521

Land acquired by 1581

Land acquired by 1689

The Age of Revolution 1770–1815

The eighteenth century was an age of prosperity, elegance and new ways of thinking. It witnessed the beginning of the Industrial Revolution, the rise of the press, the novel and the publication of the first encylopedias. The population of Europe doubled, and people moved increasingly from the country to the town. It was also the age of absolute monarchy. Western Europe was ruled by monarchs who presided over their subjects from magnificent palaces which became centres of art and fashion. In the latter part of the century minor upheavals erupted in many parts of the Western hemisphere, but these were overshadowed by major revolutions in France and America. The French Revolution sent shock waves throughout Europe, changing for ever the relationship between the rulers and the ruled, and precipitating over twenty years of conflict which devastated Europe.

George Washington
George Washington commanded the colonial forces which expelled the British from America.

The Stamp Act
A British tax collector is tarred and feathered by an angry mob of American colonists protesting against the Stamp Act imposed on them by the British parliament. The colonists argued that they could not be legally taxed since they were not represented in parliament.

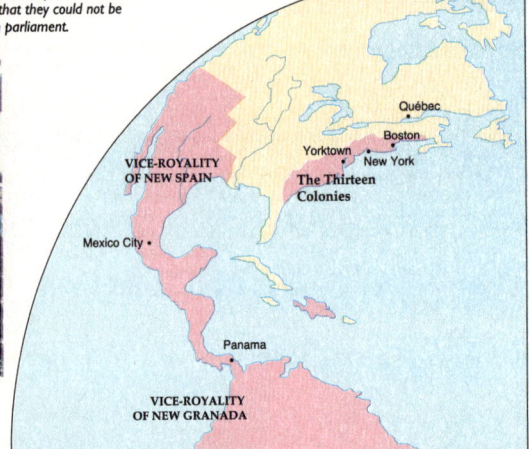

VICE-ROYALITY
OF NEW SPAIN

Québec
Boston
Yorktown · New York

The Thirteen
Colonies

Mexico City ·

Panama ·

VICE-ROYALITY
OF NEW GRANADA

The American War of Independence
Having defeated the French at Québec in 1759, Britain became the dominant power in North America. The original settlements – known as the Thirteen Colonies – now extended along the Atlantic coast. Increased resentment among the colonials against British rule led to war. In 1776 the Thirteen Colonies proclaimed the Declaration of Independence. With the defeat of British forces at Yorktown in 1781, America became independent.

Soldiers of the American War of Independence
The British 'redcoats' (left) were well-trained professional soldiers. The American volunteers (far left) were largely untrained and often ill-equipped.

Maximilien Robespierre
Robespierre was one of the most influential members of the French National Assembly, formed by the Third Estate to challenge the power of the aristocracy and the church.

Marie Antoinette
Louis XVI's Austrian queen, Marie Antoinette, went to her death on the scaffold nine months after her husband.

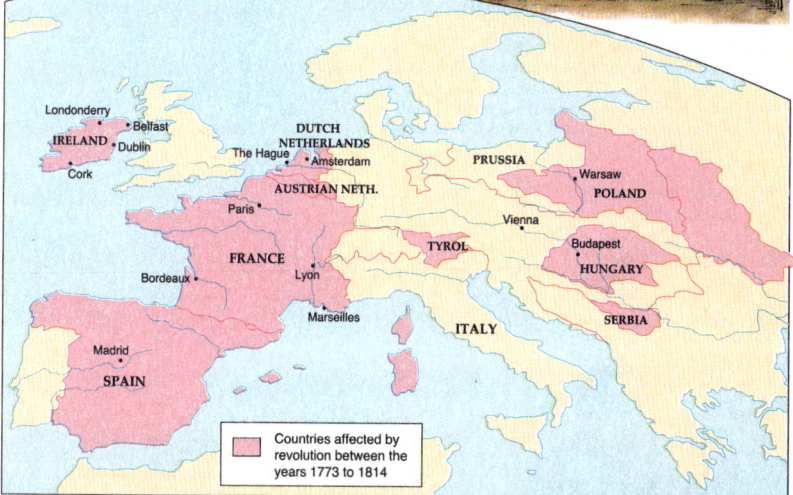

Londonderry
• Belfast
IRELAND • Dublin
Cork

DUTCH NETHERLANDS
The Hague • Amsterdam
AUSTRIAN NETH.
Paris •

PRUSSIA
Warsaw •
POLAND
Vienna •

FRANCE
Bordeaux • Lyon •

TYROL
Budapest •
HUNGARY

Marseilles •
ITALY
SERBIA

Madrid •
SPAIN

Countries affected by revolution between the years 1773 to 1814

The French Revolution

While the French aristocracy lived in luxury, the peasants, who made up over 90 per cent of the population, existed in a state of abject poverty. Opposition to the old order grew, erupting into full-scale revolution when a Paris mob stormed the Bastille prison. The monarchy was overthrown, the king executed and a republic established.

These cataclysmic events were followed by the Terror, in which some 40,000 people were guillotined. For the first time in history, the middle and lower classes had taken power into their own hands. In the picture on the right, French citizens of the Revolution march through Paris with a banner proclaiming 'Liberty or Death'.

The Napoleonic Years 1799–1815

Alarmed by the Revolution in France and the execution of Louis XVI, neighbouring states, including Britain, formed a coalition against France. The French then mobilized an army of some 750,000 men and went on the offensive. Led by Napoleon, the French forces defeated one European state after another but failed to drive the British out of Egypt. The first coalition broke up, leaving Britain as Napoleon's only opponent. A second coalition was formed, this time including Russia. In 1799, Napoleon seized control of the French government and appointed himself First Consul. After a brief period of peace, war was renewed in 1803. A year later Napoleon crowned himself Emperor of France. The French armies continued their inexorable progress, and by 1810 Napoleon was at the peak of his power. Only Britain continued to withstand his ambitions to dominate the whole of Europe. In 1805 the British navy confirmed its superiority at sea by defeating the French at Trafalgar, thus frustrating Napoleon's plans for invasion. When French forces invaded Spain, Britain sent an army commanded by Wellington to confront them. After six years of conflict, the Peninsular Wars ended in a French withdrawal. In 1812 Napoleon made the fatal decision to invade Russia. The French army's subsequent retreat from Moscow, and its crushing defeat by the allies at Leipzig, forced Napoleon's abdication and exile to Elba. But he escaped, gathered up an army and confronted the British and Prussians, commanded by his old enemy, Wellington, at Waterloo. The French were defeated. Napoleon again abdicated and was exiled to St Helena where he died in 1821. The French monarchy was restored, and Louis XVI's brother was crowned Louis XVIII. After nearly 23 years of war, the victorious powers met at the Congress of Vienna and began the task of reorganizing Europe.

Map labels:
GREAT BRITAIN
London
Brusse
Waterloo 1815
Paris 1814
Rheims
Montereau 1814
FRANCE
1806
Ma
Barcelon
Corunna 1809
Vitoria 1813
Salamanca 1812
Saragossa 1809
Madrid 1808
Valencia 1808
SPAIN
PORTUGAL
Lisbon 1809
Badajoz 1812
Bailen 1808
Trafalgar 1805
Gibraltar

Napoleon Bonaparte
Napoleon Bonaparte (1769-1821), a man of magnetic personality and vaunting ambition, was a military genius. A brilliant general and a skilful administrator, he introduced reforms that shaped modern France. The Code Napoléon reorganized the French legal system and is still used by a large part of the world today.

Napoleon's invasion of Russia, 1812

Napoleon's invasion of Russia in 1812 was the turning point in his fortunes. Prophesying a quick victorious campaign, he marched his armies over the frontier. After one of the bloodiest battles of the Napoleonic Wars, at Borodino, the Russians withdrew towards Moscow, luring the French deeper into Russian territory. When Napoleon reached Moscow, he found it almost deserted. A day later the Russian holy city was virtually destroyed by fire. Napoleon, with his goal in ruins, his supply lines threatened and the terrible Russian winter approaching, retreated.

The retreat became a disaster: short of food, transport and adequate clothing, and hounded by the Russians, the exhausted troops struggled through deep snow and icy winds towards the frontier. Of the 400,000 French soldiers who entered Russia, only 25,000 survived. For Napoleon, it was the beginning of the end of his empire.

Stockholm

SWEDEN

DENMARK
Hamburg   Copenhagen

WESTPHALIA   Berlin   PRUSSIA

Leipzig
ena 1806   1813   Bautzen 1813
Lutzen 1813
Hanau   OF THE   Ratisbon
1813   RHINE   1809
CONFEDERATION

Zurich 1799   Bassano 1796
Marengo
1800   Lonato 1796
Dego 1796   KINGDOM
Mondovi   OF ITALY
1796

GRAND DUCHY OF WARSAW
Friedland 1807   Berezina 1812
Austerlitz 1805
Aspern 1809
Vienna
AUSTRIA

St. Petersburg

1812

Smolensk 1812

Moscow 1812

Borodino 1812
Maloyaroslavets 1812

RUSSIA

Kiev

ILLYRIAN PROV.

Rome   KINGDOM
OF NAPLES

Constantinople

O T T O M A N   E M P I R E

SYRIA

Acre 1799

1798

Aboukir Bay 1798

Tabor 1799
El Arish

Alexandria

Battle of the Pyramids 1798
EGYPT

▦	Napoleonic Empire 1812
▦	other dependent states 1812
✕	Napoleon's victories
✕	Napoleon's defeats
→	Major campaigns and their dates

The Making of America 1800–1900

During the nineteenth century, the United States grew from the thirteen colonies strung out along the North Atlantic coast to become the world's most powerful and prosperous nation, stretching 'from sea to shining sea'. The push westwards began with the sale of Louisiana by the French to America. It cost the US government $15 million and immediately doubled the country in size. The opening up of the far west was a more gradual process: hunters in search of game and settlers seeking land to farm drifted ever deeper into the interior of the country. This relentless progression was disastrous for the American Indians, whose ancestral lands were overrun by settlers, miners and cattlemen, and whose game – particularly the buffalo – were slaughtered. Some Indian tribes fiercely resisted these incursions, but by 1890 they had been confined to reservations. The construction of the railway did much to open up the west, the gleaming rails penetrating the wilderness until by 1869 the east coast was joined to the west by 85,000 kilometres of track. The midwest was largely populated by immigrants from Europe in search of a new life and freedom from political or religious persecution; many also found work in the industrial cities of the north. Further west, from Texas to Montana, the plains became home to the cowboy and the cattle barons, who sent countless head of cattle by train to feed the growing populations of cities like Chicago. In the Deep South slaves worked the cotton and tobacco plantations. Despite the horrors of the American Civil War (1861–65), by the end of the nineteenth century the 48 separate states in North America had become the United States of today, with a population of 76 million.

American Civil War

The disparity between the rich industrial states in the north and the poverty of much of the population in the south was one of the main causes of the American Civil War. So too was the north's hatred of slavery, and its fear that it would be extended into the western states of America. When Abraham Lincoln became president in 1860, his declared opposition to slavery led to the withdrawal of eleven southern states (the Confederacy) from the Union. The war, which began in 1861, raged from Pennsylvania to Mississippi. It ended with the Confederacy's defeat in 1865; slavery was abolished. More Americans died in the American Civil War than in all the country's other wars combined.

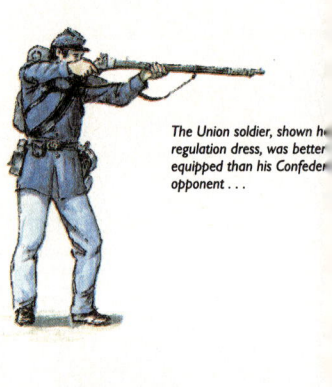

The Union soldier, shown he regulation dress, was better equipped than his Confeder opponent . . .

. . . but the Confederate so shown here in battle dress, better led.

Settlers

Pioneers returned from the far west with tales of limitless fertile land to be had for the taking. Families loaded their possessions into covered wagons and set off on the long hazardous journey. As the trails became established, forts (see map below) were built as staging posts and to provide refuge from hostile Indians.

Fort Benton
Fort Vancouver
Fort Union
Boston
Albany
Virginia City
New York
ROCKY MOUNTAINS
Fort Hall
Philadelphia
Fort Laramie
Missouri
Pittsburg
Washington
Fort Bridger
Chicago
Ogallala
Fort Leavenworth
Sutter's Fort
Salt Lake City
Abilene
Ohio
Bents Fort
Kansas City
Junction City
San Francisco
Fort Massiac
Colorado
Dodge City
Baxter Springs
Santa Fe
Fort Smith
Fort Yuma
Beans Store
El Paso
Fort Worth
Natchez
Mississippi

――	Settlers' routes
――	Cattle routes
○	Cattle towns
――	Fur traders' routes
⚒	Mining areas

Gold Rush

In 1848 a settler found a lump of gold in a stream in California. As news spread, gold-hungry adventurers from all over America and the world converged on California. In five years, half a billion dollars of gold were dug from the Californian mud. In 1850 the state became part of the Union.

51

Age of Empire 1800–1914

Until the early nineteenth century European imperialism had been motivated by trade. But the Industrial Revolution, which began in Britain in the mid- nineteenth century and spread throughout Europe, required cheap raw materials to feed its hungry machines. Countries like China and Japan, which had been closed to outsiders, now opened their doors to European trade.

Britain, which had retained trading posts at strategic points around the world, such as the Cape of Good Hope and Ceylon, now added others in the Far East, such as Hong Kong and Singapore, which became thriving British colonies. The opening of the French-built Suez Canal in 1869 gave Britain the justification for adding Egypt to its empire. Britain also laid claim to Australia and New Zealand. Since the establishment of the East India Company in the seventeenth century, British power in India had grown until it dominated the subcontinent.

Mexican Independence
The people of Mexico, resentful of Spanish rule and inspired by the ideals of the French Revolution, demanded their independence. Their struggle went on till 1821 when Spain granted Mexico its independence.

COLONIAL EMPIRES IN 1914

British	Portuguese
French	Italian
Dutch	Spanish
German	Ottoman
Belgian	Russian

—— Main sea routes

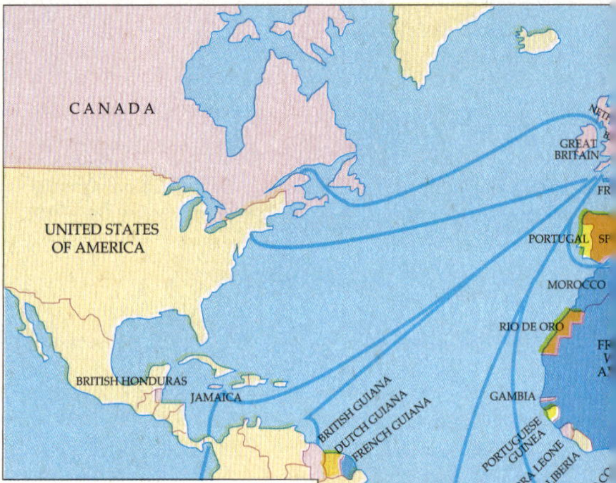

CANADA

UNITED STATES OF AMERICA

BRITISH HONDURAS

JAMAICA

BRITISH GUIANA
DUTCH GUIANA
FRENCH GUIANA

GREAT BRITAIN

PORTUGAL

MOROCCO

RIO DE ORO

GAMBIA

PORTUGUESE GUINEA

SIERRA LEONE

LIBERIA

GOLD CO

Trade Routes
By the end of the nineteenth century, a network of trade routes had been established around the globe. The opening of the Suez Canal saved ships from making the hazardous journey around the Cape. Mid-ocean islands, like Mauritius and the Seychelles, became important strategic footholds for the nations that possessed them.

Many of Britain's acquisitions were to protect its trade with India, its most prized possession, but in the late nineteenth century a fever for acquiring new territory gripped the European powers as each one tried to outdo the other in the size of its empire. It was Africa that bore the full brunt of this imperialism. Earlier in the nineteenth century, explorers and missionaries had penetrated deeper and deeper into the 'dark continent', establishing routes that could be used for trade. From the Cape to Cairo, the continent was carved up by the European nations, their culture and religion imposed upon the conquered peoples and borders established across tribal areas. Britain was foremost among the nations involved in the scramble for Africa and, with her other colonial conquests, by 1914 had built up the world's largest empire covering one quarter of the world's land surface.

Anglo-Boer War

In 1814 the British took control of South Africa from the original Dutch settlers – known as 'Boers' (farmers). Determined to maintain their independence from Britain, the Boers trekked into the interior and founded two republics, the Orange Free State and the Transvaal. When gold and diamonds were discovered in Boer territory, the massive influx of prospectors, and Britain's refusal to withdraw its troops from the Transvaal, led to war. Although British forces were superior in numbers, they were steadily out-fought by the brilliant guerilla tactics of the Boers. But the arrival of British reinforcements forced a Boer surrender in 1902.

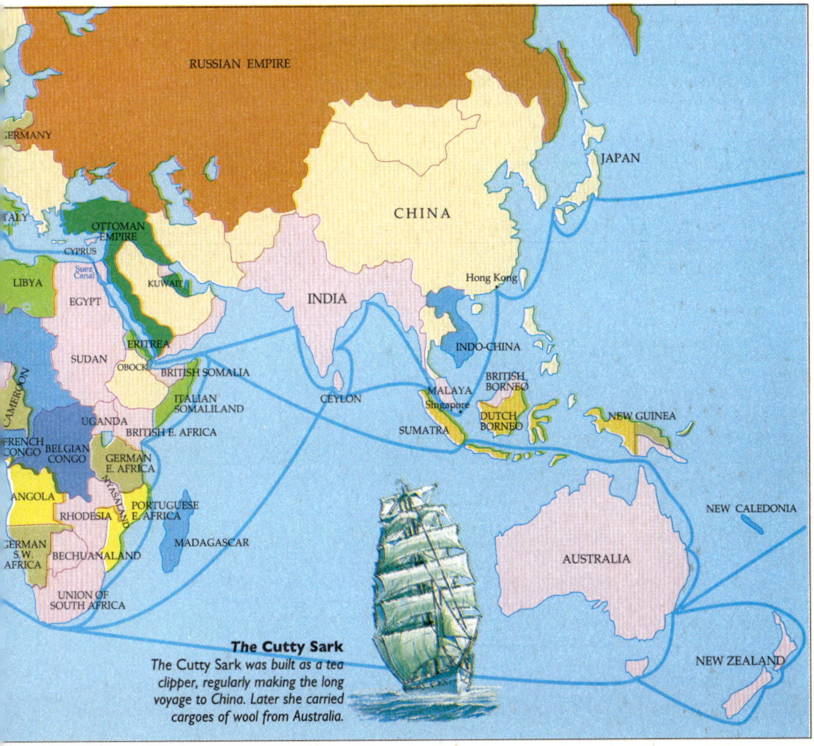

RUSSIAN EMPIRE

GERMANY

JAPAN

ITALY

OTTOMAN EMPIRE

CYPRUS

Suez Canal

LIBYA

KUWAIT

CHINA

Hong Kong

EGYPT

INDIA

SUDAN

ERITREA

OBOCK

BRITISH SOMALIA

INDO-CHINA

CAMEROON

UGANDA

ITALIAN SOMALILAND

CEYLON

MALAYA

BRITISH BORNEO

FRENCH CONGO

BELGIAN CONGO

BRITISH E. AFRICA

Singapore

DUTCH BORNEO

NEW GUINEA

GERMAN E. AFRICA

SUMATRA

ANGOLA

RHODESIA

PORTUGUESE E. AFRICA

GERMAN S.W. AFRICA

BECHUANALAND

MADAGASCAR

AUSTRALIA

NEW CALEDONIA

UNION OF SOUTH AFRICA

The Cutty Sark
The Cutty Sark was built as a tea clipper, regularly making the long voyage to China. Later she carried cargoes of wool from Australia.

NEW ZEALAND

The First World War 1914–1918

By 1900 Germany had become the most powerful industrial power in Europe. Fearing Germany's ambitions to increase its colonial empire, and alarmed by its formidable army and navy, France, Britain and Russia formed an alliance (Allied forces), while Germany allied itself with Austria (Central forces). In an atmosphere of mutual suspicion, an arms race developed. But it was increased tension in the Balkans – which had long been a centre of conflict – that precipitated matters. Serbia's emergence as the strongest state threatened the collapse of Austria's shaky empire in the region, which would isolate Germany in Europe. When the heir to the Austrian throne was assassinated in June 1914 at Sarajevo, Austria blamed Serbia and declared war. By August, all the European powers had mobilized and war was inevitable. Most of the fighting took place in Europe, but campaigns were fought as far afield as Mesopotamia (today's Iraq), the Middle East and in Germany's colonies in Africa and the Pacific.

During the course of the war, other countries, such as Greece and Italy, joined the war against Germany. At sea, the British navy was faced by German warships and submarines, which caused havoc to ships carrying supplies to the embattled French and British armies in France. In January 1917 American ships were sunk by German submarines. The United States entered the war, bringing massive reinforcements of men and arms to the aid of Britain and its allies. Germany surrendered in 1918: 10 million had died and over 20 million were wounded. For future generations the First World War became a symbol of the futility and senseless destruction of war.

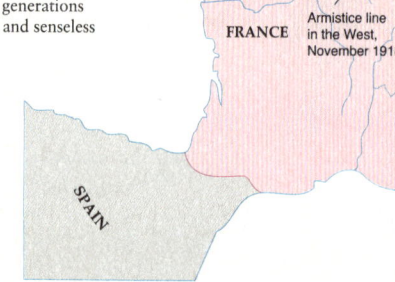

North Sea

GREAT BRITAIN

London

NETHERLA
Amsterdam

BELGIUM
· Brussel

Trench line in the West, 1914

Amiens ·

Farthest German advance in the West, 1914

Paris ·

L

Armistice line in the West, November 1918

FRANCE

S

SPAIN

Trench Warfare
In Western Europe the war took the form of two lines of opposing trenches stretching from the English Channel to the Swiss border. The British and French faced the Germans across an area of neutral territory, known as 'no-man's land'. Both sides fought in conditions of unbearable squalor. Living in the trenches, up to their knees in mud, their quarters infested by rats, they were shelled and gassed.

Key:

- Countries of the Central forces
- Countries of the Allied forces
- Territory held by Central Powers, December 1917
- Neutral countries

Main battles

NORWAY

SWEDEN

FINLAND

DENMARK
Copenhagen

Baltic Sea

R. Elbe

Berlin

R. Oder

GERMANY

Riga

Petrograd

Vilna

Minsk

RUSSIA

German penetration of Russia, March 1918

POLAND

Warsaw

Brest Litovsk

Farthest Russian advance in the East, 1914–15

Cracow

Kiev

R. Dnieper

Russian front, November 1915

Munich

Vienna

R. Danube

Budapest

AUSTRIA - HUNGARY

Trieste

Belgrade

ROMANIA

Bucharest

Odessa

Sebastopol

Black Sea

ITALY

Sarajevo

MONTENEGRO

SERBIA

ALBANIA

BULGARIA

Sofia

Constantinople

OTTOMAN EMPIRE

Mediterranean Sea

Salonica

GREECE

Inset map (Western Front):

Dunkirk

Antwerp

Passchendaele

Lille

BELGIUM

Charleroi

Liège

Namur

FRANCE

Rheims

Argonne

Chateau Thierry

Epernay

Verdun

Paris

Women at Work
As men went to war, women increasingly took their places in munitions factories, offices, hospitals and on the land.

Between the Wars 1919–1939

In 1919 a shattered Europe, crippled by the cost of the First World War, began the struggle toward recovery. The thirty victorious states met at Versailles (1919) to work out peace conditions. Germany was blamed for the war and made to pay huge reparations, which led to inflation, high unemployment and resentment against the European powers. In America a loss of confidence in the economy caused the collapse of the New York Stock Exchange in 1929: banks closed and thousands were thrown out of work. The American Depression sent shock waves round the world. Unemployment in America rose to 6 million by the end of 1930, while world unemployment doubled. The Great Depression had political repercussions: with promises of a 'New Deal' which would get people back to work, F. D. Roosevelt became US president. In Germany mounting unemployment and fear of social chaos created support for the National Socialist (or Nazi) Party, led by Adolf Hitler. The Nazis created jobs in the armed forces and munitions factories. Nationalism swept through Europe. In Italy the Fascist dictator, Mussolini, rose to power, pledging to increase Italy's prestige in Europe. In Spain a conflict erupted between Republicans and Nationalists – who were supported by Italy and Germany – which developed into three years of civil war. The failure of Britain and France to aid the Republicans in Spain encouraged Italian and German expansion in Europe. In the Far East, Japanese economic growth threatened the region's stability. The stage was set for the Second World War.

Wall Street Crash 1929
Thousands of panic-stricken investors thronged Wall Street after the collapse of the New York Stock Exchange in 1929. In the next three years 5000 American banks closed and thousands lost their savings.

Area occupied by Japan, 1933
Japanese-sponsored puppet state
Area under control of Nationalist government, 1928
Area subsequently under Nationalist control, 1929-37
Route of the long march

Mukden

Peking

KOREA

Yenan

C H I N A

Nanking

Tsunyi

Jui-chin

TAIWAN

The Chinese Revolution(1911–1949)
With the end of Imperial rule, provincial warlords controlled China. The misery they caused precipitated an upsurge of nationalism.

Chiang Kai-shek united much of China, ruling from Nanking with his Nationalist Party. But his Republic of China collapsed in the face of the Japanese invasion of Manchuria and civil war with Chinese Communists.

Led by Mao Tse-tung, the remnants of the Communist forces set off on 'the Long March', gathering widespread support as they journeyed north. After a brief truce, civil war resumed. The Nationalists were defeated and the People's Republic of China was proclaimed in 1949.

Adolf Hitler
To the German people, suffering the aftermath of the First World War, Hitler's promises of a return to prosperity ensured his rise to power. Hitler believed that the Germans were a 'master race' and that people who were not members of the master race, such as the Jews, must be eliminated.

The Russian Revolution (1917–21)
The First World War brought great hardship to the Russian people, and a loss of confidence in the government. In 1917 there was an uprising in St Petersburg and Tsar Nicholas II was forced to abdicate. A provisional government was formed, but the Bolsheviks (communists), led by Lenin, seized power, declared Russia a Soviet republic and made peace with Germany. The Revolution was followed by a conflict between anti-communist forces (the Whites), supported by certain Western powers, and the communists (the Reds). The conflict became widespread. The Whites were defeated. In 1921 the new Soviet Union was established.

SWEDEN

Boundary of Soviet territory, 1921

FINLAND

Leningrad ☆

Area controlled by Bolsheviks, 1919

Perm ☆

Baltic Sea

ESTONIA

Pskov ☆

Nizhniy-Novgorod ☆

Kazan ☆

Boundary of area controlled by Bolsheviks, 1918

Riga ☆

LATVIA

Moscow ☆

LITHUANIA

Smolensk ☆

GERMANY

Kaluga ☆

Penza ☆

Samara ☆

Orenburg ☆

Minsk ☆

POLAND

Tambov ☆

Saratov ☆

R. Ural

Zhitomir ☆

R. Dnieper

Kharkov ☆

Poltava ☆

R. Don

R. Volga

Yekaterinoslav ☆

Novocherkassk ☆

Boundary of Soviet territory, 1921

Odessa ☆

Rostov-on-Don ☆

ROMANIA

Simferopol ☆

Novorossiysk ☆

Caspian Sea

BULGARIA

Black Sea

Boundary of Soviet territory, 1921

TURKEY

☆ Principal Bolshevik towns

The Second World War 1939–1945

The Second World War was primarily fought between two large
alliances: the Axis Powers – a group of countries led by Germany and
Japan and including Italy – and the Allies – Britain, France, the Soviet
Union and the USA. Adolf Hitler's ambitions for a Greater Germany
had been demonstrated by his annexation of Austria in March 1938,
followed by the seizure of Czechoslovakia. British and French attempts
to curb German aggression by negotiation (the Munich agreement) had
failed. Fearful that Germany would overrun central Europe, Britain and
France guaranteed to protect Greece, Poland and Romania. When
Germany invaded Poland, Britain and France declared war. Surprised
but undeterred, Hitler invaded Denmark, Norway and the Low
Countries. The French, British and Belgian forces were forced to retreat
into northern France and to evacuate their armies from Dunkirk. The
Germans pressed inexorably into France. Italy joined Germany in the
war and France surrendered. By June 1940, with little cost in either
men or equipment, Germany dominated Western Europe. Only Britain
remained at war with Germany. Hitler's attempt to bomb Britain into a
surrender in August–September 1940 failed. The war now spread
farther east; Yugoslavia fell and Italy attacked Greece. In June 1941,
confident of victory, Hitler invaded Russia. Instead of yielding
to German aggression, the Russians resisted fiercely and
in December 1941 began a counter-offensive.

Tank Warfare
*The Germans were masters of tank warfare:
fast-moving tanks and mobile infantry,
supported by dive bombers, were used to
great effect in Poland, France and Greece.
But by 1942 the Allies were better equipped,
winning decisive tank battles in the deserts
of North Africa. In 1943, the Russians
successfully stemmed the tide of German
invasion in a massive tank battle at Kursk.*

Axis territory Sept. 1939
Axis satellites
Axis-occupied
Soviet occupied 1939–40
British Empire
Neutral countries
German advances

NORWAY
Bergen
FINLAND
SWEDEN
Leningrad
GREAT BRITAIN
North Sea
DENMARK
ESTONIA
LATVIA
Moscow
London
NETHERLANDS
LITHUANIA
Dunkirk
Berlin
E. PRUSSIA
BELGIUM
RUSSIA
Paris
GERMANY
Warsaw
FRANCE
Munich
CZECHOSLOVAKIA
POLAND
Kursk
SWITZ.
Vienna
PORTUGAL
Milan
HUNGARY
SPAIN
ITALY
YUGOSLAVIA
Belgrade
ROMANIA
Rome
Bucharest
Gibraltar
ALBANIA
BULGARIA
Black Sea
Spanish Morocco
MOROCCO
ALGERIA
TUNISIA
GREECE
TURKEY
CYPRUS
SYRIA
Mediterranean Sea
LEBANON
Tripoli
Tobruk
PALESTINE
TRANS-JORDAN
LIBYA
EGYPT

At the end of 1941 an event took place that altered the course of the war: Japan bombed the US naval base at Pearl Harbor in the Pacific. The US had been reluctant to become involved but Japan's unprovoked attack was a decisive factor and the US entered the war. A series of crucial battles in late 1942 and 1943 gave the initiative to the Allies on land and at sea. In June 1944 the Allies invaded France and liberated Western Europe, while Russia advanced on the eastern front. War in Europe ended on 8 May 1945.

Japanese controlled area, 1942
○ Allied bases

SOVIET UNION
KOREA JAPAN
CHINA
Hiroshima
Nagasaki
Midway I ○
BURMA
INDO-CHINA
THAILAND
Philippine Islands
PACIFIC OCEAN
Pearl Harbor ○
MALAY STATES
Borneo
Singapore
Netherland East Indies
New Guinea
Port Moresby
Darwin
AUSTRALIA

War in the Pacific
With the collapse of European empires in the Far East, Japan saw its chance for expansion. In 1941, it bombed Pearl Harbor and overran much of South East Asia. War in the Pacific now became inevitable. At Midway in 1942 Japanese naval power was shattered by the US fleet. Japanese land forces, however, fought on. In 1945, fearing Japanese resistance would continue indefinitely, the Allies dropped atomic bombs (above) on Hiroshima and Nagasaki, causing the death of 155,000 people in Hiroshima alone. Japan surrendered in August 1945.

Civilian Populations in the Second World War
In no previous conflict had civilian populations become so deeply involved. The bombing of Europe's cities took the war into people's homes. In the first four months of the German air raids on London – the Blitz – over 30,000 people were killed or injured. Hitler's persecution of the Jews and other civilians caused the death of more than 6 million people in German concentration camps.

The Postwar World 1946–1997

At the end of the Second World War much of Europe lay in ruins. Germany was divided into four zones, controlled by the victorious nations. Berlin, the pre-war German capital, was also divided into four zones. Under the dictator Stalin, the Soviet Union (USSR) took control of the eastern part of Germany and regained much of the territory it had lost at the end of the First World War. Repressive one-party (communist) regimes replaced the previous democracies. Fears that the Soviet Union would extend its control into the West accelerated the division of the continent into two armed camps, divided by the so-called 'Iron Curtain'. Mutual suspicion was aggravated by the formation in the West of the North Atlantic Treaty Organization (NATO) – which included the US – and the Warsaw Pact in the East. What became known as the Cold War developed between the two opposing blocs. The Western economies, stimulated by American aid, began to recover. In 1957 a number of them became founding members of the European Economic Community. But recovery in Eastern Europe was painfully slow. Harsh conditions led to widespread strikes and unrest. Uprisings in Hungary (1956) and Czechoslovakia (1968) were brutally suppressed by Soviet troops.

Nuclear Weapons
After the Second World War, the Soviet Union rapidly increased its hold on Eastern Europe and extended its control into the Baltic states. In the arms race between the US and the Soviet Union, each side stockpiled nuclear weapons like the Atlas missile above.

Map legend:
- Border of Germany 1937
- Allies control of Germany after 1945
- Annexed by Russia 194–45
- States which subsequently became communist
- 'Iron' curtain

ESTONIA
LATVIA
LITHUANIA
North Sea
Baltic Sea
E. PRUSSIA
NETHERLANDS
BRITISH
RUSSIAN
POLAND
BELGIUM
SOVIET UNION
LUX.
G E R M A N Y
AMERICAN
CZECHOSLOVAKIA
FRENCH
FRANCE
SWITZERLAND
AUSTRIA
HUNGARY
ITALY
ROMANIA
YUGOSLAVIA
Black Sea
BULGARIA
ALBANIA
TURKEY
Mediterranean Sea
GREECE

The West's fear of the spread of communism caused a series of confrontations around the world. In the civil war between communist North Vietnam and non-communist South Vietnam, America became involved on the side of the South, while China and the USSR supported the North. After enormous losses, America withdrew in 1975. When Gorbachev became leader of the USSR in 1985, a new era in East–West relations began. With the USSR on the verge of economic collapse, it could no longer afford to maintain its place in the arms race, and agreements were reached between the USSR and the US to reduce nuclear weapons. Discontented with communist rule, the republics within the USSR began to demand independence, and in 1991 the USSR officially ceased to exist. In the Far East, China had experienced two major upheavals: Mao Tse-tung's reforms, embodied in the Great Leap Forward (1958–59), met with opposition that Mao sought to suppress with the Cultural Revolution. A decade of chaos and political unrest followed, during which millions of Chinese died.

War in Vietnam
The retreat from empire caused conflict in both the Middle East and South East Asia. In Asia, the withdrawal of French colonists led to a communist takeover in North Vietnam. The US's involvement in the conflict, despite a huge injection of men and arms, ultimately led to their withdrawal and humiliation.

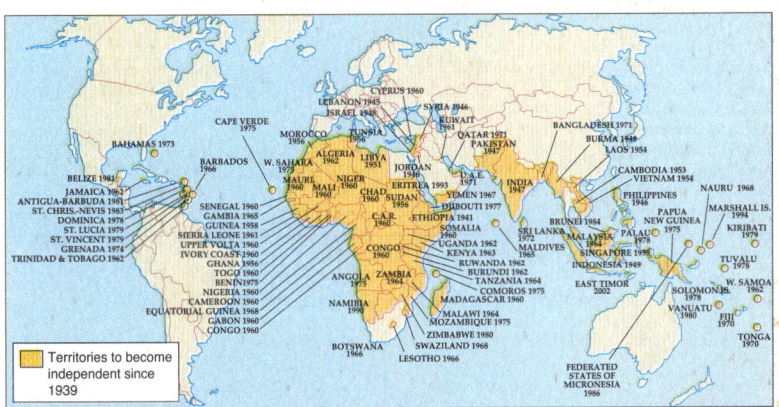

Territories to become
independent since
1939

Independence for Many
Within a few years of the end of the Second World War, virtually all of Europe's empires had collapsed. France lost Indo-China and Algeria; Indonesia regained the territories previously under Dutch control. India's long struggle for independence from Britain came to a successful conclusion in 1947. Independence for Burma, Sri Lanka (Ceylon) and Singapore followed. In Africa, all of the European colonies won independence mainly during the 1950s and 60s. In 1947, when Palestine was partitioned into a Jewish and an Arab state, the plan was disputed by the Palestinians and war broke out in 1948. Since then further wars have erupted between Israel and her Arab neighbours.

Civil War and Famine
For some African nations, independence brought new and terrible problems. Old tribal enmities, suppressed by colonial rule, resurfaced and boiled over into civil wars. In Ethiopia, civil war caused an appalling famine in 1984–1985 which shocked the world.

61

The World in Conflict 1985–2005

With the fall of the Berlin Wall in 1989, the Cold War era came to an end, and a new world order began to emerge. The USSR was broken into separate republics and former communist states in Europe gained their independence. In some regions, this fragmentation led to civil war, especially when it was fuelled by ethnic nationalism as in Yugoslavia. In the Middle East, disputes between Israel and her Arab neighbours remained unresolved, and Palestinians continued their violent struggle to eject Israeli settlers from the Autonomous Palestinian Territories. Islamic fundamentalism in Iran fuelled the tension, while Saddam Hussein, the dictator of Iraq, turned his attention to oil-rich Kuwait, igniting the Gulf War of 1991, when a US-led coalition of 29 states launched air and ground attacks against the Iraqis. In South Africa, political protest led to the breakdown of apartheid, with the first democratic elections held in 1994. The rest of the continent did not fare so well, however; ethnic warfare in east and central Africa led to the displacement of millions, and brutal genocide in Rwanda; in northeast Africa, Islamic fundamentalism continues to cause severe tension. On 11 September 2001, terrorists belonging to an Islamic group called al-Qaeda hijacked airliners filled with fuel and used them as bombs to attack the World Trade Center in New York City and the Pentagon in Washington, D.C. This attack unleashed a 'war against terror' by the US. In 2001, US troops invaded Afghanistan, ruled by the aggressively Islamic Taliban, and installed a democratic government. In 2003 they turned their attention to Iraq, and led a coalition of international forces into the country. They captured Saddam Hussein and eventually sponsored democratic elections, but Islamic insurgency against coalition forces continues to cause severe problems.

Terrorism
Terrorists are people who are prepared to risk their own lives to make a political point, whether it is to attack a hated target or an individual, or to destroy whole communities. Terrorist outrages are happening all over the world, and the US government has identified seven countries as state sponsors of terrorism.

US-led Intervention

Since September 2001, the US has been a leader in the war against terror. It has led international coalitions into Afghanistan and Iraq, using a wide variety of economic and other sanctions to pressure states into abandoning their support of terrorism. The price is high, however, and many coalition troops have lost their lives overseas.

Osama bin Laden

Considered the world's foremost terrorist, Osama bin Laden has been implicated in a string of deadly attacks against the United States and its allies. He is the chief suspect behind the World Trade Center attacks of 2001.

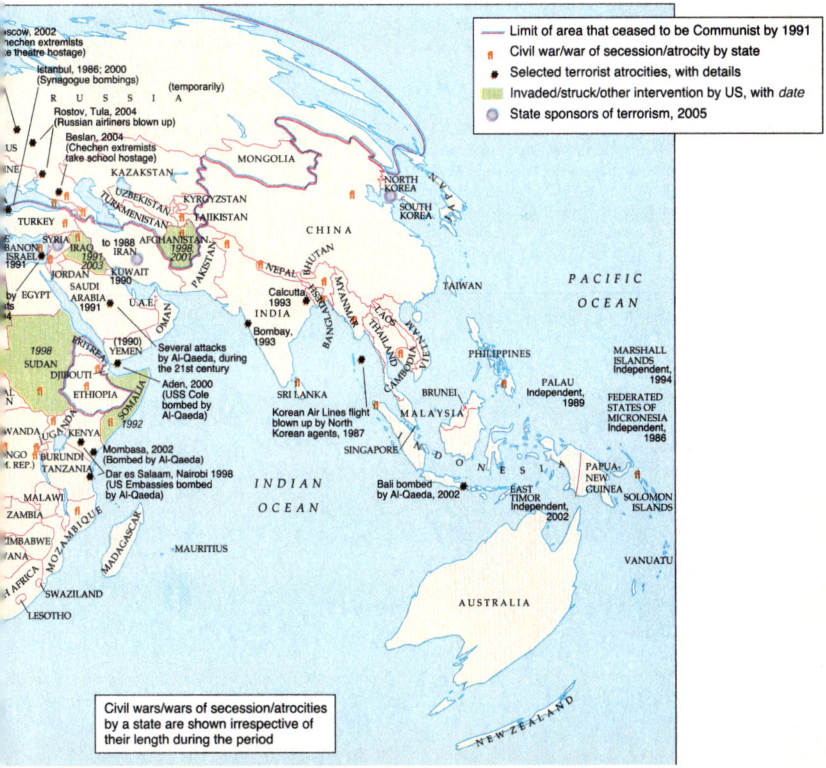

Limit of area that ceased to be Communist by 1991

🚩 Civil war/war of secession/atrocity by state

✴ Selected terrorist atrocities, with details

▨ Invaded/struck/other intervention by US, with *date*

◉ State sponsors of terrorism, 2005

---

scow, 2002
hechen extremists
e theatre hostage)

Istanbul, 1986; 2000
(Synagogue bombings)

(temporarily)

R U S S I A

Rostov, Tula, 2004
(Russian airliners blown up)

Beslan, 2004
(Chechen extremists
take school hostage)

US

NE

KAZAKSTAN

MONGOLIA

NORTH
KOREA

SOUTH
KOREA

UZBEKISTAN
KYRGYZSTAN

TURKMENISTAN
TAJIKISTAN

CHINA

TURKEY

SYRIA
ISRAEL
1991

IRAQ
1991
2003

IRAN

AFGHANISTAN
1998
2001

to 1988

NEPAL

BHUTAN

TAIWAN

PACIFIC
OCEAN

BANON
ISRAEL
1991

JORDAN

KUWAIT
1990

PAKISTAN

MYANMAR

LAOS

by EGYPT

SAUDI
ARABIA
1991

U.A.E.

OMAN

Calcutta,
1993

INDIA

BANGLADESH

THAILAND

CAMBODIA

VIETNAM

PHILIPPINES

MARSHALL
ISLANDS
Independent,
1994

ERITREA

(1990)
YEMEN

Several attacks
by Al-Qaeda, during
the 21st century

Bombay,
1993

PALAU
Independent,
1989

FEDERATED
STATES OF
MICRONESIA
Independent,
1986

1998

SUDAN

DJIBOUTI

ETHIOPIA

Aden, 2000
(USS Cole
bombed by
Al-Qaeda)

SRI LANKA

BRUNEI

MALAYSIA

Korean Air Lines flight
blown up by North
Korean agents, 1987

SOMALIA

1992

SINGAPORE

I N D O N E S I A

WANDA

UGANDA

KENYA

Mombasa, 2002
(Bombed by Al-Qaeda)

I N D I A N

O C E A N

Bali bombed
by Al-Qaeda, 2002

PAPUA
NEW
GUINEA

NGO
. REP.)

BURUNDI

TANZANIA

Dar es Salaam, Nairobi 1998
(US Embassies bombed
by Al-Qaeda)

EAST
TIMOR
Independent,
2002

SOLOMON
ISLANDS

MALAWI

ZAMBIA

IMBABWE
ANA

MOZAMBIQUE

MADAGASCAR

MAURITIUS

VANUATU

AFRICA

SWAZILAND

LESOTHO

AUSTRALIA

Civil wars/wars of secession/atrocities
by a state are shown irrespective of
their length during the period

NEW ZEALAND

The World Tomorrow?

Despite huge strides in technology in the twentieth century, with an estimated global population of more than 6 billion in the year 2005, many basic problems remain in the twenty-first century. Hunger and famine, war and disease stalk our world today just as they have done in the past. Will the citizens of tomorrow's world be any better off?

Urban populations have exploded in recent years: many Asian and African cities, such as Lagos and Bombay, are experiencing very rapid growth that is projected to continue at this pace. In 1950 there were just eight 'megacities' with populations of 5 million or more but by 2000 the number had grown to forty-one.

We are beginning to face the consequences of climate change and global warming: the United Nations Framework Convention on Climate Change has set an overall framework for intergovernmental efforts to tackle the challenge posed by climate change. For example, under the Convention governments now work together to gather and share information on greenhouse gas emissions, national policies and best practices.

There is a also a growing awareness – highlighted by the Earth Summits held in Stockholm (1972), Rio (1992), and Johannesburg (2002) – of the need to conserve the planet's natural resources, such as its wildlife and rainforests, and to develop alternative sources of energy – the present rate of oil consumption is now so great that oil supplies will have run out by 2050.

In 1997 pictures were received from a space probe on Mars and in 2004 another probe reached Saturn and sent back the closest photographs yet of the planet's rings. Manned space stations have circled the earth.

Will our exploration of space provide a pathway to future worlds? What will globalization bring? Can we save our world and its habitat? Can there be world peace and prosperity for all our peoples? The world tomorrow will certainly demand much from its citizens in the years to come.

World History: An Overview

1

Early Civilizations of Asia

Before History

Origins

Scientists estimate that the earth was formed some 4600 million years ago. Fossils of the simplest animals and plants have been found in rocks dating from 1000 million years later. The early development of life within those ancient seas was inconceivably slow. The first land plants and animals evolved in the Silurian Age, over 400 million years ago. The great dinosaurs ruled the earth for the 160 million years of the Mesozoic Era, which ended some 65 million years BC. The extinction of these giants provided the opportunity for the family of mammals to begin their colonization of the planet.

Some two million years ago, several groups of primates living around the forest edge in Africa began to show characteristics that might be called 'human'. These creatures began to plan their hunting expeditions and their use of weapons. Other animals use tools – no other animal makes tools for something it plans to do tomorrow!

Still, the development of man into the species *Homo sapiens* remained immensely slow. Some evolutionary pathways proved to be dead ends. But the spread of the family of man was relentless. For hundreds of thousands of years, small bands of these evolving people moved into new environments, hunting and gathering their food as they went. The animal, man, proved remarkably adaptable, surviving the cold of the Ice Ages and the heat of the tropics.

The First Agricultural Revolution

The last Ice Age rolled back some 12,000 years ago, leaving the world with much the same climate that it has retained until today. Comparatively shortly afterwards some people began to introduce major changes into the timeless pattern of life.

Wheat and barley live naturally in the area between eastern Turkey and the Caspian Sea. At some time people – probably the women – learnt that it was possible to plant the seeds and so reduce the work of gathering. Soon these new farmers began to select which seeds produced the best crop, and so improved the quality of the crops.

The introduction of cereal farming had radical effects on human life. Tribal groups lost their mobility as they had to settle in one place to tend the crops. When, in time, one group began to produce a surplus, it had to defend its goods against attack. Settlements then needed to be fortified and a military class grew up within the community. Once a community was producing a surplus of food, some people could undertake specialized roles within the community.

The domestication of animals was, no doubt, a long process. There was no sharp dividing line between the time when the people followed herds of wild animals as hunters, and the time when they drove the animals as herders. During the same years after the last Ice Age, people of southern Asia and Europe domesticated sheep, cattle and pigs. In the millennia that followed, tribesmen from the mountains of northern Iran and the steppes of Central Asia tamed the horse and camel.

Scholars differ about the pattern of development of settled agriculture. The traditional view was that all innovation happened in the Fertile Crescent of the Middle East, and skills spread outward, like ripples on a pond. Others hold that settled agriculture was discovered in many different places as conditions favoured it. Certainly the new methods appeared across Europe, as well as in India and Africa in the millennia that followed. Developments in the Far East and the Americas, at least, were independent of those in the Fertile Crescent. Millet and rice were cultivated in China and South East Asia from about 6000 BC. Here chicken, water buffalo and, again, pigs were domesticated. Change came later in the Americas, where maize, potatoes and other important crops were added to the world's store.

The Growth of Cities

As the agricultural age continued, so people began to gather into yet larger communities. The earliest discovered is Jericho, which grew up before 8000 BC. Two thousand years later, Catal Hüyük, in Anatolia, covered 32 acres. These cities provided protection and allowed for greater specialization of role for the inhabitants.

New skills were, indeed, needed. Copper was smelted in Anatolia in about 7000 BC, introducing the age of metals. The earliest known pottery and evidence of the first woollen textiles have both been found in Catal Hüyük.

City life also provided a centre for religious worship. A temple lay at the heart of the community, and religion and government were always closely allied to each other. The change in lifestyle brought with it a change in religious practice. Cave paintings, such as those of southern France give a glimpse of the cults of the hunter gatherers, which focused on animals and sacred places. These had much in common with the practices of people, such as some North American Indians, who lived similar lives within historical times.

Settled agriculture brought with it a new emphasis on birth and fertility, symbolized by the mother goddess figures found from widely dispersed areas of this early civilized world.

Sumerian Civilization

Irrigation

As would be expected, the earliest developments in city life happened in regions that had adequate natural rainfall. Some time after 5000 BC, however, groups from the north began to settle in the dry land of Mesopotamia. Here they drained the marshes and used the water from the Rivers Tigris and Euphrates to irrigate the fertile land.

The Rise of the Sumerian Cities

It appears as though two of the most vital inventions in the history of humans – the wheel and the plough – were made in Mesopotamia in around 3500 BC. These enabled farmers to cultivate the irrigated land in a more concentrated manner, so increasing the surplus production, leading to a spectacular flourishing of cities.

The most famous city, Ur of the Chaldees, was only one; also prominent were Eridu, Uruk (Erech), Opis, Nippur and Kish. Each city had its own special deity, and it served as the centre for a surrounding region of villages and farm land.

The Invention of Writing

In about 3100 BC the people of these Sumerian cities learnt how to represent their spoken language by the use of writing. The earliest characters were pictographic, and remain largely undeciphered. The Sumerians later developed the more flexible cuneiform script. The invention of writing marks the beginning of history, but the earliest documents were unremarkable. Written on the tablets of clay are lists showing the ownership of jars of oil and bundles of reeds. They do show, however, that some of the inhabitants were gathering serious wealth, which could be measured in hundreds and thousands of units.

Life in Sumeria

The cities were walled, but it appears that, in the early centuries, this was not a world of warring cities. Disputes were controlled by the exchange of embassies and by dynastic marriages, rather than by conflict. The laws that governed behaviour were not particularly strict.

The area was short of both wood and stone, and the Sumerian people depended heavily on clay for building and many other functions. The skills of the artisans became ever more refined. Gold, silver, bronze and polished stones were made into fine objects for the decoration of people, homes and temples. Weavers, leather workers and potters followed their specialized crafts. The scribes of later centuries wrote down a fine oral tradition of myths, epics and hymns. The world in which small family groups of hunters lived in cooperation had now been left far behind. Everyday life was controlled by a highly developed bureaucracy, which – for good or ill – was to become a hallmark of civilization. Kings were now divine beings, who were buried, not only with treasure, but also with their whole retinue to see them safely into the next life.

Egypt

In about 3200 BC, King Menes united the whole of the land of the lower Nile. The deserts that stretched on both sides of the river largely protected the Egyptians against the invasions that plagued Mesopotamia. Egyptian rulers had to face the armies of Assyria and 'the People of the Sea' from the Mediterranean, but the remarkable endurance of Egyptian civilization owes much to its isolation. Despite this, the Egyptians owed much to the Sumerians. In particular, they borrowed the early Sumerian system of writing, and adapted this into their own pictorial script. *Hieroglyphics* means 'the writing of the priests' and the art remained a closely guarded secret within the priestly caste.

For more than 2000 years dynasties followed one another; the country experienced bad times as well as good, but a continuity was maintained, unparalleled in the history of the world. Even when the land later fell under foreign rulers, Egyptian culture retained its remarkable integrity.

The Nile Waters

Egypt depended on the Nile. This was a kindlier river than the Tigris and Euphrates because each year it flooded the land on either side, providing natural irrigation for the fertile soil. The whole of Egyptian life was attuned to the rise and fall of the great river. The ruler – or pharaoh, as he would later be called – was the owner of the land and the giver of its life, and the ceremonials of kingship centred on the fertility of the land. The Book of Exodus describes how the rulers of Egypt were able to organize the storage of surpluses from good years to guard against crop failures in bad years.

The Calendar

The Egyptians studied the movements of the sun and stars, and they were the first to work out the year, consisting of 364¼ days. For the Egyptian farmer, this year was divided into three parts, each of four months – one of flooding, one of planting and one of harvesting.

The Capital Cities

Menes set up his capital in Memphis. Later pharaohs moved it to Thebes, but neither were true cities, like those of Sumeria. Their role was more as a centre of religion than a focus for daily life.

The wide deserts provided more protection from enemies than any city walls. Because of this physical isolation, Egyptian life could remain focused on its villages, rather than on larger centres of population.

Monuments and Art

The massive monuments of ancient Egypt remain objects of wonder. Imhotep, builder of the Step Pyramid at Saqqara, has left his name as the first architect known to history. Many thousands were marshalled to build these tombs for the rulers, working without winches, pulleys, blocks or tackles.

A modern visitor will look with awe at the pyramids and other great stone monuments, but it is the more modest paintings that give insight into the daily lives of the people. They show scenes of busy rural life, where peasants gather crops and hunt wild fowl by the Nile. They are happily free from the scenes of carnage and inhumanity, which are all too common in much of the art of the period. It was a world in which women had a high status and beauty was admired.

No doubt the peasants had to work hard to keep not only themselves but the whole apparatus of royal and priestly rule, but the river was kind and the land was fertile, and there was usually enough for all.

Migration and Trade

Semites and Indo-Europeans

The Semites were herders of sheep who originated in the Arabian peninsula. They were a warrior people, reared in the stern disciplines of life at the desert edge. The most powerful group in those early years were a people called the Amorites. They founded cities to the north of Sumeria – Babylon, Nineveh and Damascus. The Indo-Europeans were mainly cattle herders, who made their way into Mesopotamia from the north. Their gods emerge in the Pantheon of Greece and in the Vedic deities of India.

The Indo-Europeans had learned how to tame horses from their Asian neighbours. Most importantly, they brought iron. Iron weapons and chariots gave them a technological advantage over the earlier inhabitants of Mesopotamia. Control of iron therefore became an essential precondition of political power. The slow spread of iron technology had other important effects. An iron plough could break up land that had hitherto been too hard for agriculture. This created a rise in production, and hence an increase in population.

The Growth of Trade

Newcomers from both north and south were drawn into Mesopotamia by the rich lifestyle of the cities. But it happened that the area had no significant iron deposits, and was generally poor in other metals. This urgent need for raw materials was to be the driving force for the development of trade in the ancient world.

Money

It is remarkable how much trade was carried on before the development of currency as a method of exchange. Merchants from the civilized Fertile Crescent were able to take a range of manufactured goods to exchange for metals and other raw materials. Goods were also moved around the world as tribute, taxes and offerings to temples. The first coins date from about 700 BC, but their use spread slowly. Egypt, for instance, did not introduce a currency until about 400 BC.

Land Transport

The wheel was of no value in a world without roads. Columns of pack animals began to spread out from the Near East into the highlands of Iran and, through the Balkans, into metal rich Europe, opening up trade routes that would be travelled for many centuries.

Sea Transport

Improvements in the design of ships followed. Oars and sails were developed and rigging improved; decks were made watertight. The Red Sea and Persian Gulf became navigable all the year round, and the Mediterranean at least in summer. The growth in sea transport would ultimately change the centre of gravity of early civilizations away from the inland rivers towards the coastal regions. Ideas and empires could now spread along sea as well as land routes.

Against this background, the empires of the ancient Near East rose and fell.

Babylon, Assyria and the Hittites

Babylon

In 1792 BC, a ruler called Hammurabi came to power in the Semite city of Babylon. He can be looked upon as the first great emperor in the history of the world. Hammurabi's armies carried Babylonian power across most of the Fertile Crescent, from the Persian Gulf and the old Sumerian cities in the east, to the edge of mountains of Asia Minor and the borders of Syria in the west. Conquest was undertaken to secure essential supplies by the control of trade routes, and the exaction of tribute. Carvings show endless lines of conquered people bearing products to swell the stores of the great emperor, and the riches of Babylon became famous throughout the region.

Hammurabi was an absolute ruler, but he was anxious that his subjects should know the laws under which they had to order their lives. He therefore set up pillars in the temples on which were engraved all the laws that governed his kingdom, so that his subjects would be able to come and refer to them. This Code of Hammurabi was the first statement of the principle of 'An eye for an eye'.

Astrology played a vital role in all decision-taking, and this led to Babylonians to study the stars closely. By 1000 BC their astrologers had plotted the paths of the sun and the planets with great accuracy, and they were able to predict eclipses. They instituted the system under which the circle is divided into 360 degrees and the hour into 60 minutes.

The first great period of Babylonian power ended when the city was destroyed by the Hittites in 1600 BC. After that, Babylon remained an important centre of trade and culture, but a thousand years would pass before the city would achieve a late flowering of political power, under the great king, Nebuchadnezzar.

The Hittites

The Hittites, who destroyed the first Babylon, were an Indo-European people who had come into the area from the north, probably through the Balkans. After defeating Babylon, they dominated an even larger empire than that of Hammurabi, across the sweep of the Fertile Crescent, from their homeland in Anatolia, Asia Minor, to the Persian Gulf and the borders of Egypt. The power of the Hittites was based on their skill with iron. It was they who carried iron technology across the region.

Hittite power collapsed in its turn under pressure from 'the People of the Sea', who were also harassing Egypt at the same time. These People of the Sea, however, did not follow up their successes by founding an empire. Rather, they left a vacuum that was to be filled by the most terrible of the empires of the Ancient Near East.

Assyria

The centre of power now moved to the city of Nineveh on the middle reaches of the Tigris. Monuments of the great kings of Assyria, such as Tiglath-Pileser I and Ashurbanipal, show an empire based on brute military force and the use of terror to control conquered people. Whole populations, like the lost ten tribes of Israel, were moved from their homeland and resettled in other parts of the empire. In this way they lost the identity on which national resistance could be built.

Assyrian armies dominated the region from the twelfth to the seventh century BC. They marched north into the highlands of modern Turkey and Iran, looking for metals and other necessary supplies. They conquered Syria and Palestine, and, under Ashurbanipal in the mid-seventh century, they even drove the pharaohs of Egypt out of the Nile delta.

The Hebrews

Among the Semite invaders into the Near East was a group known as the Hebrews. The Bible record tells how Abraham, the father of the people, left the city of Ur to return to a purer nomadic way of life. His descendants experienced a period of bondage in Egypt, from which they emerged in about 1300 BC.

The Hebrews made their home in Palestine, and they had set up a monarchy by about 1000 BC. Hebrew power reached its peak under King Solomon, who died in 935 BC. The kingdom then split; Israel, the northern kingdom, was destroyed by Assyria in 722 BC and Judah, the southern, by Babylon in 587 BC.

The Hebrews do not feature in world history by virtue of their political success but because of their religious faith. They proclaimed a single deity whom they called Yahweh. The sacred writings of the Hebrews have been one of the major influences on the subsequent history of the world. Some themes need, therefore, to be identified.

Monotheism

Initially Yahweh was seen as the god of the Hebrews, who was set over the gods of other peoples of the area. In time, however, Yahweh began to develop a uniqueness that challenged the existence of other gods. A writer from the period of the Babylonian exile pronounced Yahweh to be the god of the non-Hebrew, as well as the Hebrew people.

Divine Law

The rulers of Babylon and Assyria were absolute monarchs, whose word was law and whose actions therefore could not be judged by any superior authority. The Hebrew prophetic tradition, in contrast, made it clear that a king, no less than any other person, operated under a divine law. Here, a ruler, who has unjustly taken a common man's vineyard, can be challenged by a prophet with the words 'Thou art the man!'

Man and Nature

The Hebrew creation myth, which was handed down verbally for many centuries before being written into the Book of Genesis, clearly sets man apart from the rest of creation. He is made in the image of God and given dominion over the beasts. The Bible has been the vehicle that has transmitted this perspective into Western culture.

Male-centred Religion

The Old Testament narrative describes the fierce rejection of the female fertility gods of the Fertile Crescent, which the Hebrews described as 'the Abomination of Desolation'. For the Hebrews, divinity was uncompromisingly male and woman is depicted as a secondary creation, born out of man's side. This rejection of the female strand of religion would later be modified in Catholic Christianity in the cult of the Virgin, but it has been influential in defining Western attitudes on the relationship of the sexes.

Persia

In about the year 1000 BC, Aryan people moved south into the land that is now Iran (the land of the Aryans). There were two dominant tribes; the Medes occupied the north of the country, while the Persians occupied the south.

In the early centuries the Medish tribes were subject to the Assyrians, but they rebelled against their masters, and in 612 BC Nineveh was sacked and the Assyrian Empire was destroyed by the army of the Medes. The success of the Medes, as of the Persians after them, was based on their successful harnessing of the horse as an instrument of war.

The power centre shifted south when the Persian king, Cyrus, united Medes and Persians to form what was to become the greatest empire of the Near East. At its height, the Persian Empire extended from Greece and North Africa in the west to the Indus valley and the edge of the Central Asian steppe in the east. Darius the Great had problems at either edge of the empire – with Greeks in the west and Scythians in the east – but the bulk of the Persian Empire held together well until 330 BC.

The official Persian religion was Zoroastrianism. This emphasized the struggle of good and evil, and was to give the Semites the concept of angels and hell fire. It did not, however, seek converts, and the people of the empire were left in peace with their own gods. Cyrus was greeted by the Jews as the instrument of Yahweh, and he even rebuilt King Solomon's Temple.

Darius was not as successful a conqueror as Cyrus, but he was an administrator of genius. Once a region had been brought within the empire, the royal satrap (provincial governor) worked to win the trust and loyalty of the conquered people. Regional traditions were respected and local people were given responsibility in managing their own affairs. The country was bound together by roads, which could be used for trade and even postal services, as well as for armies.

At its peak, the Persian Empire reached as far as the Indus valley, which was the home of another, distinct Asian civilization.

India

The Harappa Culture

The remains of cities, dating from about 2550 BC, have been found in the Indus valley. The pictogram writing of these early Harappa people has not been deciphered, but archaeologists have discovered houses built of burnt brick, with bathrooms.

There are the remains of canals and docks, and Indian products from this period have been excavated in Mesopotamia. Rice was grown, which may indicate that the cities had contact with the Far East, and the first evidence of cultivated cotton was also found here.

The Harappan cities had houses, granaries and temples, but no palaces. This suggests that the civilization was centred around its priests, rather than around warrior kings. They were therefore probably ill equipped to meet the challenge of invaders.

The Aryans

In about 1750 BC, Indo-European Aryans began to penetrate into the land from the north. They herded cattle, which were to become sacred creatures. Their religion is enshrined in the oldest holy books of the world, known as the Vedas. From these it is possible to get an image of nomadic people, standing round their camp fire at night, chanting hymns to the sun and other forces of nature.

The Aryans overran the northern part of the continent, but they did not completely destroy the people who had been there before them. They slowly spread from the Indus, clearing the dense forest of the Ganges valley and founding cities, such as Benares.

Hindu Castes

The racial structure of Aryan and non-Aryan people became enshrined in the caste system of India. There were three 'twice born' castes which are assumed to originate from the Aryan invaders: the *Brahmins*, who were the priests; the *Ksahiyas*, who were warriors; and the *Varsyas*, who were farmers and merchants. Only members of these castes were permitted to take part in the Vedic rituals.

The *Sudras*, who came below the lowest member of the twice-born castes accommodated the conquered people. Below them were the unclean *outcasts*, who did not enjoy any caste status.

The Cults

As time passed, people looked for religious expressions that could engage the emotions more fully than the Vedic hymns. The cults surrounding the gods *Vishnu* and *Shiva*, with their consorts, fulfilled their needs. It appears that Shiva, at least, was drawn from older pre-Aryan India. The cult of Shiva, who represented the great cycle of birth and death, life and destruction, was to express the Hindu world view most completely.

Buddhism

In the early part of the sixth century BC a prince of the warrior caste, called Siddartha Gautama, who became known as the Buddha, left his home to seek enlightenment. He first followed the strict Hindu practice of fasting, but he did not achieve his objective. In the end he found that true enlightenment could only be discovered by 'letting go' of his own self, and accepting that, in life, all things are changing. The Buddha rejected the caste system and his teachings took his followers out of Hinduism.

Although Hinduism and Buddhism separated, any contest for supremacy lay in the mind, for there were no wars of religion, like those that were to mark the West. The two religions share the same root. Both see man as an integral part of the natural world, not as a creature set apart from, and above it, as in the Hebrew tradition.

Buddhism received a great impetus with the conversion of King Ashoka of the north Indian Mauryan Kingdom in 260 BC. He abandoned his career of conquest and administered his kingdom in the light of the teaching, providing the people with social works and good laws. In the end, Hinduism was to retain its hold on the subcontinent, apart from Ceylon (Sri Lanka) in the south and the mountains of Tibet in the north, while Buddhism made its impact further east.

Central Asia

Across the Himalayas from India lay the great land mass of central Asia. This can be divided into three bands. Furthest north was the great wall of the forests of Siberia. The centre consists of the Asian grasslands. In the south are the deserts and mountains. The last two are influential in world history from the earliest times until about 1500 AD.

In the grasslands of the steppe lived a selection of nomadic tribes. They survived in marginal land, much as, in later times, the Plains American Indians would survive on the American prairie. The nomadic life could take peoples right across the grasslands, and they often fought each other for the control of land. Because the plain could only support a small population, drought, war or other impulses could set whole peoples on the move. This would produce a knock-on effect. Ripples could grow to waves. These would then break onto the boundaries of the lands that bordered on the steppes.

These were illiterate people, so their names and history are confused, but they appear in history as the Hsiungnu or Huns, the Avars, the Scythians, the Turks and the Mongols. They were terrible foes, who won their battles by great mobility and superb mastery of the horse.

Further south, in the desert region, lay the trade routes. From very early times Bactrian camels and horses carried goods along these trade routes, creating a link between Europe and the Near East to the west and China to the east. Most of the goods moved from east to west. At an early date, the Chinese learnt to make fine fabric from the web of the silk worm. Pepper and other spices also made light and high value loads. It was an immense and dangerous journey, but the profits were incentive enough to keep the caravans moving.

China

Isolation and Contact

The people of China have long known their nation as *Chung-hua,* the Central Nation. Educated people knew well of the existence of other cultures, but they were looked on as subordinate, and, indeed, tributaries of the great nation. Although the Chinese did maintain contact with the outside world, they were little influenced by it. Chinese culture was therefore able to establish a structure in the early centuries, which remained little altered throughout history.

The immediate concern of Chinese rulers, again from very early times, was to defend their northern border against the steppe nomads. This border, which would be marked by the world's greatest building work, the Great Wall, lay along the line where the decline in rainfall made settled agriculture impracticable.

Culture and Language

The huge country centred on three rivers, the Hwang-Ho, the Yangtse and the Hsi. They were divided by great mountain ridges. A wide range of climates could be found within the nation. China has been politically divided for long periods, but she has maintained a unity of culture beyond that achieved by any other people. An important reason for this is that, while the people of the west came to use to a phonic script, China retained the use of pictograms. The difference is fundamental. A phonic script is easily learned, but it needs to reflect the sounds of a language. People of different languages are therefore unable to communicate with each other without learning each other's language. This is inevitably culturally divisive. A pictogram script, in contrast, is hard to learn, but it is not linked to the sound of language. It can therefore be used to bind people who speak differently. China therefore developed a power to absorb and civilize the conquerors who, from time to time, spilled over her frontiers.

Literacy was the property of a cultured elite, whose whole education had, of necessity, been centred on diligence rather than creativity. This gave Chinese culture the twin characteristics of breadth and stability.

The State

Around 1600 BC, the first historical dynasty, the Shang, gained control of the northern Hwang-Ho river valley. Even at this early stage, the court had archivists and scribes. Like their successors of later dynasties, the kings saw themselves as the bringers of civilization to barbarian peoples.

About 1100 BC, the Shang were overthrown by the Chou who carried royal power to the central Yangtse river valley. Then, around 700 BC, the Chou in their turn were overthrown by pastoralists from the north. Eventually, in 476 BC , this brought in the time graphically known as 'the Period of the Warring States'.

Confucianism

K'ung-fu-tsu, who became known to the world as Confucius, was born in this period. He looked back from that period of unrest to an earlier time when the world was at peace and believed that the problems of his times arose from the fact that people had forgotten their proper duty. In an ordered world, everyone had a place in society. Some – rulers, parents, husbands – were 'higher'; others – subjects, children, wives – were 'lower'. Everyone, high and low, was bound together in ties of mutual duty and respect. The high had no more right to oppress the low than the low had to be disrespectful of the high. When these bonds were broken, the times became out of joint.

Confucianism therefore placed emphasis on 'conservative' institutions – the state, the civil service, scholarship, and, above all, the family. It was not a religion, in the sense of teaching about a god, but it brought a religious dimension to the worship of ancestors.

Social Structure

K'ung-fu-tsu accepted the most fundamental division in Chinese society. The common peasants were not allowed to belong to a clan, and they therefore had no ancestors to worship. Their lives consisted of an endless round of toil.

For those who were, more fortunately, born into a clan, China would become a land of opportunity. Even boys from poor homes could study to pass the necessary examinations, which would open up coveted civil service jobs. For those with more modest aspirations, growing cities offered opportunities in trade and the crafts.

The fortunate lived in an assurance that Chinese customs and the Chinese way offered *the* model of excellence, and all other people had to be judged according to the way in which they measured up to this standard.

2

Mediterranean Civilization

Early Seagoing People

Conquering the Oceans

The earliest civilizations centred on major river valleys. The rivers provided water and arteries of communication. Then the technology of sails and shipbuilding improved to a level that enabled men to venture onto the oceans. From early times, the Red Sea and the Persian Gulf provided important communication routes, which were orientated towards the east. But the Mediterranean, particularly in winter, is subject to violent storms. Further advances in marine engineering, such as the construction of watertight holds and improvements in sails and rigging, were needed before sailors could master this environment.

By about 500 BC ships were able to move freely in the Mediterranean, at least in summer, thus providing easier communication than was possible on land. There was then no distinction between a fertile north and an arid north shore. The whole region was fertile. Traders and rulers therefore saw the Mediterranean basin as a single unit, bound together by its ocean highway.

Minoa and Mycenae

In about 1900 BC in Crete, the Middle Minoan Period was at its height. Its earliest writing has not been deciphered, but excavations reveal fine palaces and developed communities. Its cities stood beside the sea, and the builders were already confident enough in the control their ships had over the eastern Mediterranean to dispense with fortifications.

Objects found in Crete and Egypt show that there was a lively trade between the two cultures. The Minoan sailors probably traded in timber, wood, olive oil and grapes over the whole of the Mediterranean area.

Inhabitants of the Minoan cities were the first people to enjoy the benefits of piped drains and sewers, and wall paintings show them dancing and playing sports, including the Minoan speciality of bull-leaping.

The Minoans set up colonies on the mainland, of which the most important seems to have been at Mycenae. This is the name given to Minoan civilization as it is found on the mainland. The culture spread across the Aegean to the coast of Asia Minor and to the city of Troy at the mouth of the Bosphorus.

Early Minoan civilization was destroyed by Indo-European people who poured into the region from the north. Some of these invaders settled in the Ionian peninsula to become Greeks. A later resurgence of Minoan civilization is thought to have been under Greek influence.

The stories written down centuries later by the poet Homer tell of the struggles between the Mycenaens of Troy and the less advanced Indo-European invaders.

The Phoenicians

Semite people, in general, liked to keep their feet on dry land. The exception were the people who lived in the area known as Phoenicia, which is now Lebanon and southern

Syria. They developed remarkable skills as sailors and for centuries their ships dominated the trade routes. Phoenician sailors reached the Atlantic Ocean and traded with tin miners in distant Cornwall. The Greek historian, Heroditus, even reports that one expedition rounded the southern cape of Africa.

The Phoenicians planted colonies to protect their trade routes. Most important, in about 800 BC they founded the city of Carthage. The colony was strategically placed to protect the ships that brought metal from Western Europe.

Phoenicia was never a power on land and, when the Assyrian king 'washed his weapons in the Mediterranean' in 868 BC, Phoenicia lost its independence. But the rulers of the great empires needed these fine sailors, and the Phoenicians therefore exercised influence beyond their military power.

Phoenicia is best known for its sailors. It did, however, make another major contribution to Western culture, by creating a phonic alphabet. The words *alpha*, *beta* and *gamma* are derived from the Phoenician words for an ox, a house and a camel.

The Greeks

In Mycenaean times, an iron-working Aryan people were moving south into the Greek peninsula. Myths of early battles with Mycenaean Troy are preserved in the works of the storyteller – or tellers – given the name of Homer.

The early culture was oral but, in around 750 BC the Greeks adopted and modified the Phoenician alphabet and committed the ancient legends to writing. These were to provide the starting point for the world's first great literary culture.

The beginnings of Classical Greek society date from the first Olympian Games, held in 776 BC. This event, held once every four years, drew together people who shared the Greek language and culture. The participants did not, however, come under one unified government.

Government

The Greek political structure was dictated by the geography of the region in which they settled. This was a land of mountain ranges, with small coastal plains that faced outwards to the sea. Each of these plains was settled by a self-governing community, which initially contained only as many people as the land would support. This was the basis of the *polis*, or city state.

Homer's *Iliad* provides a picture of an early feudal society of kings, nobles and common fighting men. Each city then followed its own course in working out the structure of government. The first struggle lay between the kings (monarchy) and the nobles (aristocracy). Then pressure came from other influential citizens (oligarchy) and from the general mass of free male citizens (democracy). When a state plunged into chaos, a strong man, who was often benevolent and public spirited, would emerge to bring order to the polis (tyranny).

The Greek concept of democracy was specific to the confined structure of the city state. It did not operate through representative institutions, but through the direct participation of citizens in the decision-taking process. The meeting place, or *agora*, not the temple or the royal palace, was now the centre of city life. The citizens who met here provided the city with its law courts and its political assembly. Debate and persuasion became vital skills. People could on occasion be swept away by the power of a demagogue, but within this forum they learned to listen and to analyse argument.

The fractured nature of Greek society did not provide peace and stability. The city states might join together in games, but they were as often at war with each other. For both good and ill, the people remained fiercely independent, more ready than any other people before, and perhaps even since, to question the structure of the society within which they lived.

Colonization

Since geography prevented expansion inland, the Greeks had an impetus to expand outwards, along the sea routes. Greek communities were established along the west and south coasts of Asia Minor, on the islands of the Aegean and as far east as Cyprus and westwards to Sicily and southern Italy, and even further into North Africa, France and Spain. These colonies were self-governing, but they often had links with powerful city states, such as Corinth or Athens. They served both as an overspill for excess population and also as trading bases across the Mediterranean Sea.

The Persian Wars

The conflict between Greece and Persia has been depicted as a struggle between an oppressive empire and a freedom-loving people. Reality is more complex. Close links had long existed between the Greeks and the Persians and many Greeks served within the Persian army. The trouble started when Greek city states in Asia Minor rebelled against Persian rule and Darius the Great of Persia moved to put down the insurrection. The Asian Greeks were supported by the European Greeks, and this brought the Persian Empire into conflict with an alliance of Greek cities, led by Athens and Sparta. The army of Darius was defeated at Marathon in 490 BC and the navy, led by his successor, Xerxes, failed ten years later at Salamis. This war drew the boundary of the Persian Empire to the east of the area of Greek settlement.

Athens and Sparta

The alliance that had defeated Persia did not survive the victory. Athens was much the largest of the city states, with a larger population than its farm land could support. Prosperity was based on the control of silver mines, which were worked by thousands of slaves. The city's very survival therefore depended on a structure of trade and colonies. Whatever freedom may have been enjoyed by Athenian citizens within their city, their rule of others was often oppressive. The Athenians demanded heavy tribute from client states and put down rebellion as violently as any Persian army.

Other trading city states, such as Corinth, felt themselves continually threatened by Athenian power. They found allies in the conservative, agricultural state of Sparta. The Peloponnesian War lasted for 27 years, and ended with the defeat of Athens in 404 BC. This led to a reaction against an over-mighty Sparta, and the destructive sequence of wars continued into the fourth century. The Greeks may have provided the world with a vocabulary of politics and an ideal of democracy, but their outstanding achievement lies, not in politics, but in the broader fields of culture.

Religion

Greek myth is drawn from the common Indo-European roots that created the Vedas (the sacred writings of Hinduism) in India and it has provided a fertile source of inspiration for Western art and literature for more than 2000 years. But it is harder, looking back through the twin filters of Semitic religion and rationalism that have shaped modern attitudes, to understand what the world of gods meant to the Greeks themselves. On the one hand, there was the piety of the common man which condemned Socrates for blaspheming against the gods; on the other, there was a strain of free-thinking, as expressed by Miletus a philosopher of the seventh century, who declared

'If an ox could paint a picture, its god would look like an ox'. The Greek religious tradition was real, but it was not an all-demanding way of life, like that of the Hebrews.

Philosophy and Science

The Greeks invented organized abstract thought and took it to a level that would dominate the philosophy of the Near East and Europe until very recent times. In the Greek perspective, there was no distinction between the arts, the sciences, and, indeed, religion. All were a part of the search for truth. In the sixth century, Pythagoras did not distinguish mathematics from philosophy and religion. The two greatest Greek thinkers, Plato and Aristotle, defined the twin, often opposing, channels through which all philosophy, and later, all theology, would flow.

Plato, a pupil of Socrates, was 23 years old when his home city of Athens was defeated by Sparta. His attempt to achieve a mental order was therefore born of the political disorder of the post-war years. Plato is the apostle of the *ideal* – the abstract of perfection, whether it be for the state, the individual, or in a mathematical equation. In his philosophy, all life is a striving towards an ideal of the good, containing truth, justice and beauty, which was the only reality in an imperfect world. Plato's Academy can lay claim to being the world's first university.

Aristotle came to Plato's Academy at the age of 17 and remained his master's devoted disciple. His interests, however, took him in the opposite direction, as he came to emphasize enquiry and experiment as the source of knowledge. While Plato stressed the *ideal*, Aristotle stressed the *real*; while Plato was drawn into the abstractions of mathematics, Aristotle found himself fascinated by the complexities of biology and literary criticism. For him, truth lay not in a distant abstract, but in a 'happy medium'. Aristotle is therefore seen as the father of the scientific method.

The Arts

Fifth-century Athens provided the most fertile environment for Classical Greek culture. The architecture of the Parthenon, the sculptures of Praxiteles and Pheidias provide an illustration in stone of the Platonic ideal. They provided generations of architects and artists, particularly from Europe, with a standard of perfection. Literature also flourished. Aeschylus, Sophocles and Euripides used the ancient myths to explore the depths of human experience and create tragic drama, while the irreverent Aristophanes pioneered the tradition of comedy. The disasters of the Peloponnesian Wars also inspired Thucydides to become the world's first scientific and literary historian.

The contribution of Greece to the world's cultural store is a fundamental theme of history. By the middle of the fourth century, however, the advances were largely confined to the Greek-speaking world. The diffusion of Greek culture into a wider world would be the work of a young and brilliant student of Aristotle.

The Hellenistic World

Alexander the Great

The state of Macedon lay to the north of Greece. It crossed the boundary that divided the civilized world from the barbarians. Philip II of Macedon developed his army into an efficient fighting machine and conquered the Greek city states. Philip died in 336 BC and was succeeded by his son, Alexander, Aristotle's pupil.

Alexander inherited his father's army and the Greek power base. The problem he faced was how he could pay the soldiers who had served Macedon so well. This search for money took Alexander the Great on spectacular campaigns. There was ample booty to be won across the Aegean in the Persian Empire. In 334 BC the Macedonian army defeated the Persians under their king, Darius III, at Issus. The army then marched south into Egypt, where Alexander founded the city that was to carry his name, Alexandria. He returned north, defeated the Persians once more and sacked the capital of Persepolis. Not content, he took his army eastward into Afghanistan and the Punjab. He would have gone further, but by 327 BC his soldiers insisted that the time had come to turn back.

The young man was one of the great soldiers of all time. The importance of his conquests, however, was that they were the catalyst that brought together the old civilizations of the Near East and the newer Greek culture. Alexander was Greek, but he was drawn to Eastern ways. He himself married a Persian nobleman's daughter, and, in a great symbolic gesture, he married nine thousand of his soldiers to Eastern women.

The Division of the Empire

Alexander died in Babylon in 323 BC at the age of 32, leaving no heir to succeed to his enormous empire. The land was divided between his generals. The Ptolemies based their power in Egypt, the Seleucids in the region of Syria and the Attalids around Pergamum. Parthia later became independent of the Seleucids. These were centralized states under absolute monarchs. The age of debate and democracy was certainly past. Over most of the Hellenistic world, this was a time of economic growth, but the Greek cities themselves declined.

Hellenistic Culture

Greek was now the official and commercial language of the whole area. The learning of the scholars became widely known and great libraries were set up at Alexandria and Pergamum. Among the books preserved were many of the writings of Plato and Aristotle.

Scholars in the Greek tradition worked in different parts of the Hellenistic world. Science flourished, as it would not do again for over 1500 years. In Alexandria, Euclid laid the foundation of geometry. Aristarchus correctly deduced the structure of the solar system 1800 years before Copernicus and Eratosthenes measured the circumference of the earth. Archimedes of Syracuse had the widest ranging genius of all.

Philosophers, such as the Stoics, could no longer question the ways of government, so they turned their thoughts towards the inner life of man. They led a quest for virtue and true contentment. Classical Greek styles provided powerful models for painters and sculptors, but Hellenistic artists retreated from the Platonic search for an ideal and worked instead to project the humanity of their subjects.

Religion

Greek religion was too restricted a vehicle for this new, expansive world. Mystery cults that demanded a more active devotion from their followers began to spread. Two of these became increasingly dominant: from Egypt came the myth of Isis and Osiris that told of a dying and a rising god; from Zoroastrianism came the mystery of Mithras, with its powerful image of redemption through blood.

The End of the Hellenistic World

The Hellenistic world in its turn fell to a new power from further west in the Mediterranean. The Roman victory at Actium in 31 BC marked the end of a great era. No battle, however, could put an end to Greek culture. The Roman poet, Horace, summed it up by saying that, although Greece was defeated, it took its conquerors prisoner.

Republican Rome

The Etruscans

In the years before 509 BC, central Italy was dominated by a people called the Etruscans. They can be seen in lifelike tomb sculptures, but little is known about their culture. They appear to have been an Indo-European people, who achieved dominance over other people by bringing iron working to a high level of perfection. Etruscan kings, the Tarquins, ruled in Rome until they were expelled, according to tradition, in 509 BC. The expulsion of the kings remained a powerful myth within the Roman state. Men looked back to the days of the Tarquins as the time when the rights of the citizen were subjected to the will of a single individual.

The Structure of the State

The new Roman state was based on agriculture. Indeed, *pecunia*, the name for a flock or herd of animals, became the Latin word for money.

There were different groups within Roman society. The old families who took pride in their status as *patricians*, assumed power in place of the deposed kings. The remaining free people were known as the *plebeians* or *plebs*. At first they were poor farmers, with little say in affairs of state. As Rome grew, however, many plebeians became more wealthy and they began to look for a share in the running of affairs.

Romans, be they patricians or plebs, took immense pride in their status as citizens. Roman citizenship became the unique badge of belonging to a pure and strong society, free from the softness and corruption of the Hellenistic world around them. Every man was liable to military service, which could be for as long as 16 years in the infantry or 10 years in the cavalry. Warlike virtues were admired by society and inculcated in boys through the home and education. At best, this could breed self-sacrifice to the common good; at worst, it could bring a lust for battle and bloodshed.

The organization of the Roman Republic was not unlike that of a Greek polis. The Roman *forum* took the place of the Greek agora. The *senate*, which was an assembly of patricians, wielded the real power. Two consuls, elected from its ranks, commanded the army in war and were responsible for government in time of peace. The demand of the plebs to be represented was met by the appointment of two tribunes. It therefore became possible for an unusually talented man, from a low family, to rise in the state. This structure lasted for 450 years. It carried Rome from being a small city state to the dominant force in the Mediterranean basin.

Early Expansion

In the early centuries, Roman armies were occupied with winning control over the Italian peninsula. If there was a ruthless character to Roman expansion, there could also be generosity in the terms given on surrender. Conquered people were given Roman citizenship and allowed a large measure of self-government. Once within Roman rule, they too were expected to provide troops for the army.

The Punic Wars

As Rome expanded, she had only one serious rival. Carthage had expanded beyond North Africa. Her ships controlled the sea and Carthaginian colonies were established in Sicily, Southern Italy and Spain. The two powers were bound to clash for supremacy in the western Mediterranean. The Romans built up a navy, and in the First Punic War (264–241 BC) they defeated the Carthaginians at sea and won Sicily.

The Second Punic War (218–202 BC) marked the decisive struggle between the two powers. When Hannibal crossed the Alps and defeated Roman armies at Lake Trasimene and Cannae, it seemed as though Roman power would be broken. In 202 BC, however, Hannibal was in turn defeated at Zama and Carthaginian power was destroyed. In 149 BC Rome found an excuse to fight a third Punic War. This time Carthage was flattened and the ground on which the city had stood was ploughed over.

The Rise of the Generals

Victory over Carthage had been bought at a high cost, and that cost was paid by the poor. Many peasant farmers, who were citizens, sold their land to the rich and so lost their means of support. This led to a period of internal unrest.

Wars were now being fought far from home, in the Hellenistic east and to the north in the land they called Gaul. Roads were built across the Roman Empire that enabled the army legions to move swiftly from one trouble spot to another.

But these distant armies could no longer be commanded by consuls with a term of only two years in office, and there arose a new breed of professional generals. These men often became fabulously rich on the booty of war, and, with a loyal army at their back, they could pose a threat to the traditional institutions of the Roman Republic. Marius made his name in Africa and Gaul, and then Sulla in the eastern Mediterranean. Julius Caesar was the most successful in this line of ambitious generals. In 49 BC he took an irrevocable step when he crossed the River Rubicon, which marked the boundary of Italy, and marched on Rome at the head of his army. By this action, he started the chain of events that led to his murder and the founding of Imperial Rome.

Christianity

Origins

The early years of the Roman Empire were to see the beginnings of another of the great religions of the world. The Jewish people had maintained a stubborn refusal to dilute their religion to meet the demands of Hellenistic rulers. At the time of Jesus of Nazareth, sects like the Essenes and the Zealots maintained a resistance to Roman rule.

Jesus was a Jew, but he appears to have rejected the path of political resistance and taught instead a message about the relationship of the individual to God and other men, closer to the teaching of some later rabbis. The content of Jesus' teaching was indeed to be influential, but his significance lay not in what he said but in what his disciples declared him to be.

The share of responsibility for his execution cannot be determined from the documents preserved, so it is unclear whether he was executed as a danger to the Roman state or as a critic of Jewish practice. Whichever it was, his disciples declared that they had witnessed his resurrection, and proclaimed that he was the Son of God. They picked up the words of the writer from the Babylonian exile and announced him as the saviour of the world, and not just of a chosen people. The holy books of the new religion were written down in the Greek language of the Hellenistic world, rather than in the more restricted Aramaic language that Jesus himself spoke.

Christianity and the Mysteries

Paul of Tarsus carried the message in a series of missionary journeys through the Greek-speaking world. There he spoke the language of the popular mysteries – of redemption through blood and of a dying and rising god. With Christianity, however, it was different, he declared. While the mysteries were based in mere images, Christianity was rooted in historical fact.

Paul and other missionaries always sought to found a Christian cell, which they called an *ecclesia*, the word used for the meeting of the Greek polis. Hellenistic culture provided a language for the new religion; Rome provided a structure that enabled it to spread. Missionaries could make use of the Roman roads, and they were not likely to be molested by bandits on the way.

There was no doubting the enthusiasm of the converts, but, for a long time, an outsider would not have readily recognized a fundamental difference between this religion and the mysteries. Heresies, like Gnosticism and Manichaeism were pulling Christianity away from its Semitic roots into the maelstrom of Hellenistic religion. The Roman army generally favoured Mithras. A long path of persecution lay ahead before Christianity would emerge as the dominant religion of the region.

Imperial Rome

The Emperor

At the battle of Actium in 31 BC, Julius Caesar's great-nephew, Octavian, brought Egypt into the Roman Empire and ended the years of civil war. Four years later he was given the title of Augustus and made consul for life. He was careful to preserve the honoured republican institutions, but the senate lapsed into impotence and all power now lay with him.

No rule of inheritance was ever established for the position of emperor. In the centuries that were to follow, incompetents would be matched by administrators and generals of ability, imbeciles by philosophers. Most emperors died violently. Succession first passed through the house of Caesar. During one century of good government, it became the practice for an emperor to adopt his successor. For long periods, however, power fell to the general who could command the largest army. But the mass of people would never see the emperor in person. For them, success or failure had to be judged on whether he was strong enough to prevent the huge empire from breaking into civil strife.

The practice of emperor worship was imported from the old Persian tradition. The act of reverence due to the god-ruler was the symbol that bound together the hugely diverse people who now lay under Roman rule. Pious Jews refused to perform this ritual, but this was recognized to be a part of their ancient tradition and it was generally overlooked. However, the refusal of Christians, who came from all parts and races, was looked upon as a serious threat to the unity of the empire.

Buildings

The great monuments of Rome date from the Imperial Age. Augustus himself restored eighty-two temples and boasted, 'I found Rome of brick and left it of marble.' Aqueducts, arches and the huge colosseum still stand as monuments to Imperial glory. The Romans were content to copy Greek styles to which they added impressive engineering skills.

The more prosperous Roman citizens built homes, such as have been preserved at Pompeii and excavated across the empire. Here they built for comfort, and artists, working in paint and mosaic, expressed a less pretentious view of life with humour and grace.

Natural Frontiers

The Roman armies had now carried their empire across Europe, Asia and Africa, until it had ten thousand miles of land frontier. Beyond lay barbarians, ever willing to invade and plunder. The task of defence was made easier by natural boundaries – the African and Arabian deserts and the great Rivers Rhine and Danube. This line of defence had two weak points, lying on either side of the Black Sea. In Asia, the entrance to the steppes lay open across the land of the Parthians. In Europe, generals were tempted to go beyond the Danube, across what is now Romania to the Carpathian Mountains. Roman armies suffered heavy defeats in both of these sectors. Claudius also carried the empire across the natural frontier of the North Sea to Britain. The expedition was designed to bring the glory of conquest and to win control of the fabled metal mines of the wild island.

The City of Rome

By Imperial times, Rome had grown to be a huge city. Since most of the work was done by slaves, much of the population was unemployed, and the citizens had become accustomed to a lifestyle supported by tribute from conquered peoples. No emperor could contemplate unrest in Rome, so the citizens had to be fed and kept amused on the famous diet of bread and circuses. Entertainments were on a massive scale. The Circus Maximus alone seated 190,000 people. Claudius built the huge harbour at Ostia, where grain, wild beasts and slaves were constantly being unloaded to feed the stomachs and the jaded palates of the people. The city gave nothing back to its empire.

East and West

Gradually a distinction began to emerge between the eastern and the western parts of the empire. The west, centred on Rome itself, covered western Europe and the old Carthaginian lands of North Africa. The east included the old Hellenistic world of Greece, Asia Minor, the Near East and Egypt.

The eastern side of the empire had a better balance to life. It contained ancient cities, but none dominated the region. It was self-sufficient in grain, wood, oil, wine and other essentials, with a surplus to buy in metal from the West and luxuries from the East.

The western part of the empire was not an area of ancient civilization. Since Carthage had been flattened, it had no cities to balance the metropolis of Rome, which constantly sucked in products, so upsetting the economic balance of the region.

In 285, the Emperor Diocletian appointed a co-emperor to rule the western sector. There was now an Empire of the East and an Empire of the West. In 324, Constantine accepted the dominance of the Eastern Empire by taking his capital to his new city of Constantinople.

The Triumph of Christianity

By this time, Christianity had established itself as a growing force. Diocletian tried to stem the tide, but Emperor Constantine accepted the new faith. Emperor worship may now have ceased, but even a Christian emperor could not shed the concept that he was the fountain of religion. He declared himself to be the thirteenth apostle and sat as chairman of the Council of Nicea, which established Christian doctrine. This set a precedent for the control of the church by the state.

At about the same time a group of hermits came together in Egypt to form the first monastery in the Christian tradition. This was destined to grow into an influential movement, capable of confronting the ambitions of Christian rulers.

The Barbarian Invasions

The century after Constantine saw increasing pressure on the European frontier of the Western Empire. Far away in the east, the Huns were on the move, and this created pressure on western tribes. The Huns themselves erupted into the heart of Europe under Attila in 440, to be defeated at Troyes (Châlons) in 451, but ahead of them, as if a prow wave, came Goths, Ostrogoths, Visigoths, Franks and Vandals.

The Romans found it difficult to defend the long land frontier and they recruited barbarians to strengthen the army. In 376 about 40,000 armed Visigoths were allowed across the frontier. Then in 410 the Goths sacked Rome. Vandals, who left their name for mindless destruction, crossed through Spain into North Africa and then returned for an even more destructive assault on the great city.

In northern Europe, Angles, Saxons and Jutes crossed the North Sea in 449, first to ravage and then to settle in the British Isles. The Celtic inhabitants, no longer protected by Roman legions, were driven back to the highland area of the West, and into Ireland, where the Christian faith survived and flourished.

Byzantium

Her Frontiers

With the ancient capital of Rome in barbarian hands, the Roman Empire can be said to have fallen. Those who lived in the Eastern Empire, however, recognized no such catastrophe. In 483, Justinian succeeded in Constantinople, and he set about the task of winning back the lost western lands. His armies recovered North Africa, Italy and Southern Spain. It appeared for a time as though the Roman Empire was still a reality. His conquests, however, were ephemeral. From his time onwards, the Empire of the East was under continual pressure.

In the east, Persia was a power of consequence once again, and behind her the steppe nomads were ever menacing. In the south, the empire faced growing Arab power. In the north, Slav people were pressing into the Balkans. The Emperor Heraclius led the Imperial armies in more successful campaigns, but the pressure was ever inwards towards what was to be the Byzantine heartland of Asia Minor, Greece, the Balkans and southern Italy.

Cultural Life

The people of Byzantium saw themselves as being direct inheritors of the old empire. Citizens of Constantinople still visited the bath houses; they still followed the chariot races with the passion of a modern football supporter. Justinian completed the work of centuries of Roman jurists by compiling the authoritative digest of Roman law.

Byzantium, however, soon developed a distinctive character that set it apart from the old empire. This drew both from the Greco-Roman and from Eastern traditions. Constantinople remained a home of classical scholarship – Plato was particularly popular, but his thinking became overlaid by layers of mysticism. Classical features were used in buildings, but the great dome that rose over Justinian's Church of the Holy Wisdom demonstrated new skills and a new aesthetic. Secular artists still worked within Hellenistic traditions, but religious artists, in paintings and mosaics, were beginning to express a particularly eastern Christian piety.

Religion

Early in the development of the Eastern Church there emerged a distinction between secular (living in the world) and religious (living out of the world) clergy. Secular clergy worked at the parish level and were allowed to marry. The ideal was set by the many hermits and monks who expressed their piety in extreme self-sacrifice. Religious icons became the focus of devotion for ordinary people.

Succeeding emperors maintained Constantine's position at the head of the church. Patriarchs, bishops and priests lay under his power. Emperors decided doctrine and mercilessly persecuted many of their subjects who held 'heretical' beliefs.

In the centuries after Justinian, the Eastern and the Western Churches drew gradually further apart. In the west, the Bishop of Rome claimed primacy and began to build a centralized structure. The church finally divided into western and eastern parts in the Great Schism of 1054. This was partly about authority, partly about abstruse issues of theology, but it mainly stemmed from lack of understanding of each other's piety.

The Arabs

Mecca

The desert land of the Arabian peninsula was inhabited by fierce and independent-minded Semitic tribes people, who were known as Arabs. They led a nomadic life of great hardship. One trade route between the Mediterranean and the Indian Ocean went across this land, passing through Mecca. The city was also a centre for pilgrimage to the sacred stone or *kaba*. The citizens of Mecca jealously guarded the revenues of both the trade and the pilgrimage.

Early in the seventh century a merchant, called Muhammad, had a vision and started preaching the message 'There is no god but Allah'. He came into conflict with the citizens of Mecca, and in 622 he left the city to live in Medina. This is the date from which the Arab world numbers its calendar.

Islam

The prophet Muhammad had met Christians and Jews and read many of their books, and the religion that he founded lies within the Semitic tradition. He preached one god, which for him ruled out the Christian concept of the Trinity. The word 'Islam' means 'submission', for the duty of the Muslim is to submit to the will of the one god. He gave his followers the five duties – daily prayers, alms, fasting, the keeping of Friday as a holy day, and the pilgrimage – but the message was one of great simplicity. Very quickly, the feuding tribes of the peninsula were given the sense of community, which has ever since been the distinguishing feature of Islam.

Muhammad taught his followers that Christians and Jews were 'people of the book'. They and their religion had, therefore to be treated with respect. Once they accepted Muslim rule, they might be taxed, but they should not be persecuted or converted by force.

The Arab Conquests

Once the Arabs were united, they started raiding towards the north in search of booty, into the lands controlled by Byzantium and Persia. Their invasions had startling and unexpected success, partly because the two empires had weakened one another by endless warfare. More important, however, was that taxation and religious persecution had made their governments deeply unpopular with the people. To 'heretical' Christians, the tolerant Muslim invaders seemed greatly preferable to either emperor.

The Persian Empire collapsed and the Byzantium Empire was pressed ever further backwards. Jerusalem fell in 638. It seemed as though Constantinople itself would fall, but in 717 the Arab armies were driven back from the city walls. By this time the Arabs not only controlled the Near East, but also North Africa and the whole of Spain. Their armies were even crossing the Pyrenees into the plains of Europe. Here, however, they found themselves in an alien environment of cold weather and barbarous people, so they turned back towards the south. The Arab armies carried Islam over this wide empire. Many conquered people converted; indeed Christianity disappeared completely from its old stronghold in North Africa.

The ultimate authority within the Islamic world lay with the caliphs. In 750 the ruling Umayyad house was overthrown and the new Abbasid rulers moved the capital to Baghdad.

Arab Culture

The Arabs possessed a powerful poetic tradition before the time of Muhammad and Islamic culture was founded in literature. The Koran, with its religious message and its classical language, provided a powerful unifying bond for one of history's more stable empires. Since the depiction of the human form was forbidden, art developed as elaborate geometric pattern. As the centre of the Islamic Empire moved out of the Arabian peninsula to Baghdad, so eastern influences became increasingly powerful. The Arabic language remained, however, the cement of the Islamic world. Although local dialects might vary, scholars from all parts continued to use the pure language of the Koran.

The Muslims did not come as the destroyers of civilization. The men from the desert quickly absorbed the cultures that they conquered. Their scholars read the Greek philosophers, and united them with the astronomy, mathematics and medicine of the East, so serving as the main channel for ancient learning in a troubled world. Muslim civilization reached one of its peaks in Spain, where the university of Cordova was a major centre of learning.

The eastern Mediterranean remained the centre of thriving trade. War might bring temporary disruption, but trading links with the East were never long severed. From India came spices, pepper and sugar; from China came porcelain and silks. The wealthy of Byzantium had an insatiable taste for luxury goods and the Arabs soon came to share these sophisticated tastes. Byzantium controlled the overland routes to China, which ended at the Black Sea ports. The Arabs controlled the sea routes by the Persian Gulf and the Red Sea to India, with links beyond to China and the Spice Isles.

Threats to Arab Civilization

In time, Byzantium ceased to be a threat to the Islamic Empire; indeed it seemed only a matter of time before Constantinople must fall. From the eleventh century, for some 300 years, Arab civilization would be subjected to assaults by Christian crusaders from Europe (Chapter 3) and successive waves of nomadic invaders from the steppes of Asia (Chapter 4). The latter were by far the more threatening of the two, and it was they who finally brought the great days of Near Eastern civilization to an end.

3

The Formation of Europe

Church and State

The Papacy

In the year 590, a new bishop of Rome or pope was elected who would later be known as Gregory the Great. He was a Roman from a senatorial family, but, in the chaos of his day, he had made the choice to become a monk. For a devout Christian, the monastic life seemed to be the only safe course to heaven in a violent and turbulent world. But Gregory saw that it was pointless to live with regrets for the past glories of Rome or hopes for help from Byzantium. The church now had a mission to the restless and threatening barbarian world. Gregory selected monks as missionaries and sent them to bring Christianity to the barbarian tribes. The best known of these was Augustine of Canterbury. At the same time, missionaries from Ireland were moving south from Scotland into England and northern Europe. The missionaries from Rome, however, succeeded in linking the growing church back to Rome.

For Gregory's successors the first priority was to establish the primacy of the bishopric of Rome, or papacy. Popes claimed that, since they stood in a direct line from St Peter, they had inherited his 'power to bind and loose'. A pope could therefore control men's eternal destiny by the weapon of excommunication. In an extreme situation, he could even place an interdict, which forbade the performance of any sacraments, on a whole country. In an age of faith this was a formidable sanction.

The popes had first to bring the Christian clergy under their control. Ordinary parish priests were generally illiterate peasants; bishops were temporal lords who used the church as a means of expanding family lands. Most were married men, who expected to pass their lands and livings on to their children. Their prime allegiance was therefore to the king or chief, rather than to a distant pope.

Monasticism

Only the monks were free from these temporal ties. The Rule of St Benedict, which imposed poverty, chastity and obedience, was now widely accepted. The monks were also almost alone in being literate in an uncultured world. This meant that they could reach positions of influence in both church and state.

The popes used monks as their representatives, and, wherever possible, promoted them to high positions within the church. In time the popes worked to extend their control over the secular clergy by forbidding clerical marriage altogether.

A Time of Turbulence

In the early centuries after the fall of Rome, the pope and his monks were able to establish respect and authority because they provided the only apparent stability in a troubled society. Groups of barbarians roamed through Europe, bound to their leaders by simple tribal ties. When they settled down and adopted Christianity, much of the old way of life continued. Society still had no recognizable political structure, in the modern sense. Disputes were settled by traditional 'rough justice', such as the ordeal and trial by battle.

Change continued slow in the dark forests of Germany. In time, however, the Franks and other groups in the western part of the European mainland adopted a form of Latin as their language, and paid some respect to the Roman legal system. The tribes who were more cut off in the British Isles, continued to speak their own German language, and developed law, based on past rulings, as preserved in the minds of the elders. So developed the divisions between the romance and Anglo-Saxon languages, and between Roman and common law which were to become important in later Western civilization.

Political and social order was beginning to emerge by the end of the eighth century, but then Viking ships brought new danger to European coasts. It is never easy to say why a people go on the move, but it appears as though population growth and weather problems disturbed the balance of marginal Scandinavian farming. Certainly the feared Norsemen set off on 'land takings' and voyages of plunder. Their ships spread out across the North Atlantic to Iceland, Greenland and North America; they emerged into the Mediterranean; they sailed down the great rivers of central Asia, setting up the Russian state, and reaching Constantinople; they won control of northern Britain and Normandy. In 1066, a family of Norse descent won the crown of England.

The Norsemen were not the only raiders. Men from the steppes, this time the Magyars, were pillaging from the east and Muslim Saracen raiders came from the south. Hardly any part of Europe escaped. The unfortunate monks of Luxeil had their monastery burned by Norsemen, Hungarians and Saracens.

The Holy Roman Empire

For a brief period a new power arose in Europe. In 771 the ruthless and talented Charlemagne succeeded to the whole of the Frankish kingdom. For the next 40 years he led his armies to victories on all his borders, even mounting the first counterattack against Islam in Spain. Charlemagne was more than a conqueror. He was a devout Christian, and did much to spread the faith – by the sword if necessary – across Europe. He also respected learning, and he could read himself, although writing defeated him. He encouraged the clergy to respect books and learning, he founded schools and brought the best minds of the day to his court.

On Christmas Day, 800, he was crowned by Pope Leo III in the church of St Peter in Rome. The people cried, 'to Charles Augustus, crowned by God, great and peaceful Emperor of the Romans, Life and Victory.' A new Roman Empire had been proclaimed.

The empire was based on one man's will, and, like Alexander's, it fell apart on Charlemagne's death. It was divided into three parts. The central kingdom did not survive, but the two other halves would ultimately become France and Germany. Charlemagne's eastern successor retained the title of Holy Roman Emperor, but his lands remained a loose confederacy. In 940 the Comte de Paris, Hughes Capet, won the French crown and established a monarchy that was to survive until the French Revolution. His family was the first European dynasty to establish the concept of a hereditary monarchy.

Powers Temporal and Spiritual

After Pope Leo III had placed the crown on Charlemagne's head, he stretched himself on the ground as a sign of honour to the emperor. Later popes would regret this gesture. The first objective of the popes was to win control within the church. This involved taking the right to appoint bishops away from the temporal rulers.

In the eleventh century, Pope Gregory VII and Emperor Henry IV came into conflict in the Investiture Controversy. Gregory was victorious, forcing Henry to stand barefoot in the winter snow as a sign of submission. Gregory then formulated the extreme claim that all power came from the pope, and he therefore had the right to appoint and depose kings and emperors. The Investiture Controversy was the first of a series of disputes between church and state. They involved, not only the Holy Roman Emperor, but also kings of France and England.

King, Lord and Parliament

The Feudal System

In those troubled times, people were prepared to sacrifice liberty in the interest of security. Kings and emperors were remote figures, so free men bound themselves to their local lord, who could give assistance when danger was near. When a man took such an oath of loyalty, he gave his lands to the lord, and then received them back as the lord's vassal. He had an obligation to follow his lord to war but as a mounted knight to set him apart from the common serfs. The lord, in his turn, bound himself to a higher lord, and the king stood at the apex of the pyramid. Only the serfs were nobody's vassal, because they had nothing to give in exchange for protection. They were not allowed to leave their villages, to go to school or to get married without their lord's permission.

By the end of the ninth century, this feudal system had spread to all but the most remote areas of Europe. Kings, like other lords, were concerned to extend their lands wherever they could by war and dynastic marriage. The two way nature of the feudal compact served as a check on royal power. In France, the Capetian kings stood at the apex of the pyramid, but for long periods their actual power did not extend beyond their own lands around Paris. So, when the King of England married a French heiress, he did homage to the French king for his lands in Aquitaine, but he did not permit any interference within his territory.

The Hundred Years' War between France and England was fought sporadically from 1337 to 1453. The English king may have laid claim to the crown of France, but it remained in essence a struggle between a dynastic monarch, determined to establish direct control over feudal lands on the one side, and an over-mighty subject, on the other. It was one of the catalysts that defined the meaning of the modern nation state. Writing some two hundred years later, Shakespeare would put words of nationalistic fervour into the mouths of John of Gaunt and Henry V. Such sentiments would have been incomprehensible in the time of Charlemagne or William the Conqueror, but they were beginning to have some meaning to their supposed speakers.

King and Parliament

William the Conqueror gave English kings more direct authority within their own realms. The feudal system was constructed to ensure that no lord could become 'over mighty'. Vassals, for their part were concerned that the king should not achieve unlimited power. In 1215, the lords forced King John to sign Magna Carta, which laid down two basic rights – that no free man could be imprisoned without a trial, and the king could not raise taxes without the consent of a Great Council. In 1295, King Edward I called what became known as the Model Parliament, because it set the pattern for future parliaments. Representation was by estates – the Lords temporal, the Lords Spiritual and the Third Estate, with the first two sitting together in an upper house. It was also established that parliament had the responsibility to act as the highest court in the land, to give advice to the king, to make laws and to vote taxes.

The Rise of the Towns

The inclusion of the third estate in Edward's Model Parliament was testament to the growing importance of trade in the European economy. Wealth was no longer the preserve of landowners and the church, so, to achieve maximum income, it was now necessary to consult with the representatives of the growing towns.

As towns grew in importance, kings gave them charters, which assured them freedom from interference by local landowners. Their walls were the symbol of their independence, and magnificent churches the evidence of their wealth. Trade provided a means by which low-born men could rise to positions of power within their own community, and even within the state. Different occupations were organized into guilds, which controlled terms of entry, quality standards and gave members a social structure.

The cities were often natural allies to kings who wanted to centralize power. Overmighty nobles might flourish in conditions of civil war, but merchants needed the peace that only a strong government could provide. Kings, for their part, recognized that the growing wealth that was the basis for national strength as well as royal revenue was generated not on noble estates but inside the town walls.

The Cloth Trade

The Lord Chancellor of England still sits in the House of Lords on a woolsack. This was a reminder to parliament that the nation's wealth rested on the woollen trade. England, however, stood in the lowly position of a primary producer; the business in finished cloth centred round Flanders. Flemish weavers jealously guarded the trade secrets that made their cloth the most sought after in Europe. From the thirteenth century, the economy of northern Europe became increasingly sensitive to fluctuations in the fortunes of the cloth trade.

The Crusades

The First Crusade

In 1095, the Byzantine Emperor Alexius I appealed to the pope for assistance against the Seljuk Turks. The pope answered by preaching a holy war. The motives of those, both noble and common folk, who took the cross, were very mixed. Many of the Norman lords who took the lead saw the opportunity of new land-taking, like that of their Viking ancestors; but there was also a real devotion. When the Crusaders arrived first in Byzantium and then in the Arab lands, they appeared like barbarians, with nothing to recommend them but their brute courage. When Jerusalem fell to them, they waded through blood to give thanks for the victory.

Outremer

The Crusaders established states in the conquered land. The Muslims resented these Christian enclaves in their territory, and they were therefore under constant pressure. In 1187, Saladin reconquered Jerusalem, and the Crusaders were unable to win it back. In 1291, the last Christian outpost fell to the army of Islam. The crusades gave the West two centuries of contact with a higher culture. Knights returned home with a taste for oriental luxury goods. Some picked up an interest in learning and mathematics, and methods of castle construction and siege warfare were modernized on Arab models.

The Later Crusades

Nine campaigns between the eleventh and the thirteenth centuries are known as crusades, as well as the tragic Children's Crusade. The movement turned inwards against European heretics. The simple Crusaders were not always able to distinguish which enemy they should fight. The Venetians encouraged the Fourth Crusade to turn on Byzantium. In 1204, Constantinople was captured by the Crusaders and the city remained in Christian hands until 1261. Although the rump of its empire would survive into the fifteenth century, Byzantium never recovered from the disaster.

Spain

At the same time, Christian forces were counterattacking against the Muslim Moors in Spain. In 1212, the Moors were defeated and driven back to Grenada. The reconquest of the peninsula was completed in 1492. A great culture was replaced by a fanatical Christian state, in which the Inquisition was used as a tool of persecution against Moors, Jews and many Christians whose views did not please the authorities.

Learning, Art and Society

Scholarship and Authority

As long as there was no nation state, there were no sharply defined national boundaries. Latin provided a lingua franca and the church a broadly based structure within which the educated of their day could communicate.

Through the troubled times any learning remained behind monastic walls. The books of early Christian fathers were copied and became the intellectual authorities of the new world. Men had lost confidence in their own ability to reach conclusions, either through logic or through experiment, and all argument therefore referred back to authority. Even quite trivial issues of dispute would be decided by the weight of authority that could be mustered on the one side or the other.

The authors of antiquity were largely unknown until around the twelfth century. Then translations began to be made into Latin from copies preserved in Islamic Spain and Sicily. The ancient dichotomy between Plato and Aristotle began to be reflected in arguments between nominalist and realist theologians. Thomas Aquinas, in particular, baptised Aristotle. This did not, however, lead to an increase in experiment. Classical authors joined the Christian fathers as valid sources of authority. In southern Europe, men still lived amidst the ruins of classical civilization. The classical and the Christian came together until, as in Dante's *Inferno* and Michelangelo's Sistine Chapel, they became indistinguishable from each other.

By the twelfth century, learning was emerging from monastic walls into the more open atmosphere of universities. The first was at Salerno, where Islamic and Byzantine influence was strong. Then came Bologna, Paris, Oxford and many others. Crowds would follow teachers, like Peter Abelard, who spoke a new and more restless language. University students were in religious orders of some sort, but the educational impetus continued outwards into the wider population. By later medieval times, an increasing number of lay people, particularly in the towns, were acquiring literacy.

Architecture and Painting

In early medieval times most stone buildings were either castles or monasteries. Many were fine buildings, but they added little to the techniques of antiquity. By the twelfth century, architects were developing their own signature. The Romanesque style of southern Italy was based closely on a study of classical models. In northern France and England there rose magnificent cathedrals in the Gothic style. Here the pointed arch and the flying buttress enabled them to give their structures both height and light.

Most painting, likewise, remained dedicated to the church. Altarpieces showed the Virgin and child, with patrons and saints; frescoes and stained glass windows reminded illiterate worshippers of Bible stories; monks, copying psalters and books of hours, under no pressure of deadlines, painted exquisite decoration. In Italy, the school of Sienna worked under direct influence from Byzantium. But painters, like architects and stone masons, were craftsmen who were happy to work for any patron, and, as the centuries passed, an increasing number of commissions were available for secular work.

Literature

Medieval literature, like that of any other period, was made up of different strands – folk tales and myths, national histories, historical chronicles, love poems and works of devotion. Early vernacular literature, like Norse sagas and the Anglo-Saxon *Beowolf*, helped to create national language areas. In the early centuries, however, Latin was the language of both secular and religious writing.

By the fourteenth century a new vernacular literature was emerging. The supreme example of this in English is *The Canterbury Tales*, written by a soldier and customs officer, Geoffrey Chaucer, for an audience of other lay people.

Times of Change

The Black Death

A sickness new to the human race was first reported in the Yangtze Valley in *c.* 1334 and, according to one estimate, some thirteen million Chinese died in the following years. Relentlessly it spread from east to west, leaving devastation in India and across Asia. In 1347, the plague spread across northern Italy and in the following years it is estimated that between a quarter and a third of the population of Europe perished. This first outbreak was the worst, but the disease returned periodically until the second half of the seventeenth century. Although it was a worldwide phenomenon, its effects have been most closely studied in Europe.

Initially it brought economic collapse; prices of all goods fell sharply and much farm land returned to nature. As life recovered, employers were faced with an acute labour shortage. This created strains within the social structure of both town and country. Guild regulations were flouted and the feudal structure began to crumble. There were major peasant uprisings, in France in 1358, in Florence in 1378 and in England in 1381.

The Late Medieval Church

Pious Christians were unable to understand why God could have created such destruction. The plague accentuated a Christian piety that identified God as judge and destroyer and the saints, particularly the Virgin Mary, as protector.

The church, like all institutions, moves through cycles of corruption and reformation. In early medieval times, reformation came from within. The last of these reforming movements was the founding of the friars by Francis of Assisi in 1209. Now the impetus for reform had grown weak. In the fourteenth century, popes taxed the faithful heavily to maintain a lavish lifestyle. After the Black Death these taxes fell all the more heavily on a smaller population. One fundraising technique was the offer of indulgences, by which punishment in the next world was remitted in exchange for payment in this world. During the fourteenth century, the church lost its independence when it moved under the protection of the King of France in Avignon. The Great Schism, when rival popes competed from Rome and Avignon, further undermined spiritual authority. Some Franciscans denounced papal luxury and were burned as heretics but their message was heard by the people.

Before the end of the fourteenth century, John Wycliffe in England and Jan Hus in Bohemia were preaching that man did not need the apparatus of the church to make contact with God. Hus founded what was to be the first Protestant Church, and Wycliffe translated the Bible into English.

The Reformation

In the early sixteenth century, the then pope set out to raise money for the rebuilding of St Peter's by selling indulgences. In 1517, the university lecturer, Martin Luther, challenged the papal representative to a debate by nailing his '95 theses' to the door of Wittenberg Cathedral. The church authorities sought to have him condemned, like heretics of old, but he found protection from German princes. The Protestant movement soon won followers, particularly in the trading towns and in northern Europe.

Luther did not initially see himself as the leader of a movement that would split the Western Church, but, as he preached the supremacy of the Bible and faith over the sacraments and traditional authority, the division quickly became irreconcilable. He found himself leading a mass movement, based on individual piety. Luther was the catalyst for another round in the ancient struggle between lay and secular powers. He only survived to preach because he was adopted by German princes, who saw his movement as a useful weapon against the power of the church.

Eastern Europe

Russia

It appears as though the Norsemen who settled the rivers of Russia brought no women with them, so the process of assimilation was rapid. In 980, Vladimir established the kingdom of Kiev and he married a sister of the Byzantine emperor. It is said that Russian envoys visited both Constantinople and the West to decide which form of Christianity should be adopted. They were overwhelmed by the splendour of Constantinople, and the Eastern link was forged. Kiev was destroyed in 1169 and the centre of power was driven northwards to Moscow. Trading and cultural ties with Byzantium were largely lost, and Russia was increasingly isolated until it was overrun by the Mongols in the thirteenth century. Russian independence can then be dated to the victory over the Tartars in 1380. The Grand Princes of Moscow emerged as rulers and Ivan III (1462–1505) adopted the title of 'Tsar' (Caesar) and the double-headed eagle, to substantiate the claim that, with Constantinople in Ottoman hands, the Russian monarchy had now inherited the imperial tradition.

Poland

When Vladimir made his choice of the Eastern Church, the Poles on his western frontier had just turned in the other direction. The missionaries who brought Western Christianity to Poland also acted as forerunners for waves of land-hungry German invaders, led by the fearsome Teutonic Knights. In late medieval times, a Polish state lay across the central European plain, with its prosperity based on grain exports to the West through the port of Danzig. It was, however, already showing signs of the damage that would be caused by its geographical location as a buffer between Western Europe, the Scandinavian north, Russia and the East and the disturbed cauldron of Slavs and Magyars in the Balkan south.

In both Russia and Poland, the serfs lived in great poverty, under the control of a wealthy landed class. Rulers were faced with a perpetual challenge from over-mighty subjects without being able to look for the support of any considerable middle class.

4

The Wider World

Asia Before the Mongols

India

For centuries after Ashoka, the Indian subcontinent was divided into warring states. The south, behind its mountain barrier, remained the home of non-Aryan people. They maintained contact with the Mediterranean civilizations through the Red Sea and Persian Gulf trading routes. In the northwest, the frontier and Indus valley remained open to Asian invaders. Invading Hunas, probably Huns, devastated this region, as they did lands both to the east and west.

In about 320 AD, the Guptas united the whole of northern India. This marked the great age of Hindu culture. In the fifth century, the decimal system was invented, so opening new areas of mathematics. Sculpture and literature flourished, both achieving a broad unity of style, characterized by a warm sensuality. Buddhist culture declined as Hinduism spread across Asia and into the islands of the Pacific. The island of Bali remains today a marker of this great expansion.

The Hindu Empire was in time challenged by the rise of Islam. Muslim traders – always effective missionaries for the Prophet – would have visited the western ports in the seventh century. By the eighth century, Muslim invaders were crossing the open northwestern frontier. By the twelfth century, they controlled the Punjab, and a century later they dominated the Ganges valley. The fateful religious divide was now established.

China

China was united more effectively by language and culture than it was by its political structure. The two most powerful dynasties were Han (c. 202 BC–AD 220) and T'ang (618–907). Their empires were comparable to that of Rome at its most powerful. During the T'ang Dynasty trade flourished, and China became a major sea power, with trade reaching from the Persian Gulf in the west to Indonesia in the east. The great Chinese dynasties had a life expectancy of about 300 years. They were founded by a great individual who combined military and administrative skills. In later years, as the succession passed to lesser men, the state would come under pressure from nomads to the north and rebellion at home. Imperial authority was upheld by officials, who preserved the traditions of K'ung-fu-tsu. Their main tasks were to take the census and keep the land register up to date. Beyond that, they maintained only a broad supervision over local lords, who raised taxes and performed the day-to-day tasks of administration themselves.

Great civil works were undertaken. The country was now bound together by canals, of which the most important was the Great Canal, which linked Peking with Hang-chou. Huge irrigation projects were undertaken to provide food for the ever-growing population. The casting of iron, printing, the magnetic compass, the use of paper money and explosives were all pioneered in China, but the conservative structure of society militated against the fullest exploitation of her inventions.

In the periods between the great dynasties, the country relapsed into warring states. There were times of disaster, when armies ravaged large areas, but in general, conditions changed little for the mass of peasants, whose life was always more closely governed by local lords than by distant emperors. But, while Europe remained divided into her warring states, China could always be drawn together once again by a dynamic new dynasty.

The Sung Dynasty (960–1279) was never as powerful as its great predecessors and in 1127 it lost the northern part of the country to Ch'in invaders. In the following century and a half, the Southern Sung Dynasty lacked military power, but the period is viewed by many as the high point of Chinese culture. The Imperial capital of Hangchou was a centre of wealth, culture and leisured living, far beyond any other city in the world.

Sung art was influenced by the Zen school of Buddhism. Painters, such as Ma Yuan, worked with an economy of line and colour to make a visual statement about man's position within the world order. Potters made dishes that looked 'like ivory, but were as delicate as thin layers of ice'.

The Seljuk Turks

The name 'Turk' is given to widely dispersed people, originating on the Asian steppes, who spoke a common language. In the tenth century, a chief called Seljuk settled with his people near Samarkand and was converted to Islam. The tribe organized an army based on slaves, mainly recruited from southern Russia and the Caucasus, who were known as Mameluks. Backed by these fearless warriors, Seljuk's grandsons built an empire, from Azerbaijan and Armenia, into the ancient lands of the Middle East. They overran Persia, captured Baghdad, Jerusalem and Egypt and invaded Byzantine lands in Asia Minor.

Later Seljuk rulers found it difficult to hold this vast empire together. While their efforts were largely directed against European crusades, they faced trouble in other parts of the empire. In Egypt, for instance, Mameluke soldiers established a virtually independent government. The Seljuk Empire therefore became vulnerable to another and greater threat from the Asian steppes.

The Mongols

Genghis Khan and his Successors

In 1206, a chief called Temujin, better known to the world as Genghis Khan, united the Mongol tribes who lived in the area today called Mongolia. These were wild, nomadic peoples in the tradition of the horsemen who had come from the steppes throughout recorded history. Genghis Khan then established dominance over the more numerous Turkish peoples from the land to the north of the Himalayas. He came to believe that he was destined to rule the world, and he embarked on the greatest programme of conquest in history. His followers were magnificent horsemen. As a nomad people, they could survive on dried milk and the blood of their horses. Released from the constraints of supply, they were therefore uniquely mobile. They were also utterly ruthless. Cities that accepted them were often treated with leniency; those that resisted were liable to be levelled to the ground, and the population massacred. As the reputation of the Mongol horde was carried ahead, rulers capitulated to avoid their dreadful destruction.

By the time that Genghis died in 1227, the Ch'in Empire of northern China had fallen, and Mongol armies had swept across the open grasslands of Asia as far as Russia and the Caucasus. Still the advance continued. In 1237–38, the Russian state was overwhelmed by horsemen who rode down its frozen rivers, achieving the winter conquest that would later elude both Napoleon and Hitler. When a great khan died the armies returned to their homeland to debate the issue of succession. Europe might have been overrun had Genghis Khan's successor not died in 1241. The armies did not again threaten Europe; to the Mongols, it seemed a poor land, hardly worth conquering. They did, however, return to the Middle East, capturing Baghdad and destroying the Caliphate of Abbasid in 1258. The tide of conquest finally turned here too when, in 1260, theMamelukes of Egypt organized the armies of Islam to defeat a Mongol army at Ain Jalut, near the town of Nazareth.

Mongol China

The Mongol Empire was now divided into four, with the eastern section the portion of Genghis' grandson, Kublai. He led a Mongol assault on the southern Sung Empire, which fell in 1279. Further expeditions were launched into South East Asia and even, unsuccessfully, against Japan. While his grandfather, Genghis, had devastated the north, Kublai respected the civilization that he conquered. Although he spoke little Chinese, he was a patron of literature and, like conquerors before him, he adopted Chinese ways. Mongol rule had now united the whole territory between Europe and China under a single authority and the ancient overland routes were opened once again. In 1275, members of the Polo family from faraway Venice reached the court of Kublai Khan. When the young Marco Polo finally returned to Venice in 1299 he gave the West its first information about the civilization of the East. Readers in the more primitive Europe found it hard to believe that such a land of riches could exist far to the east, but some two centuries later a Genoan sailor called Christopher Columbus would own and make notes on a copy of the Venetian's narrative.

For the Chinese, however, the Mongols remained a dynasty of foreigners. Prosperity declined sharply and there was a wave of unrest, and the Mongols were overthrown in 1368 by a new Ming Dynasty. This survived its allotted three centuries until 1644 when it was in turn overthrown by new invaders from Manchuria, who established the Manchu Dynasty.

Later Mongol Conquests

In about 1370, Timur the Lame (Tamerlane), a chief from the region of Samarkand, proclaimed that he was the man to revive the Mongol Empire. In the next 30 years, he ravaged the Middle East, Asia Minor, southern Russia and northern India with a brutality matched only by his distant kinsman, Genghis Khan. The ancient lands of the Fertile Crescent, so long the focus of world civilization, never recovered from his invasion. The Mongol Khanate of the Golden Horde in Russia was fatally weakened. He died in 1405, when on his way to carry his conquests into China.

In time the Mongol people of Central Asia and the Middle East came to accept the religion of Islam. The weakness in Mongol power lay in the fact that there was no established law of succession. Tamerlane's successors, like other Mongols, were concerned with domestic issues as they contested succession. Fifth in line from Timur was the more attractive Babur, an accomplished soldier who was also interested in literature, music and architecture. The kingdoms of northern India were at that time in a state of permanent warfare. In 1526, Babur won a series of victories, and by the time of his death in 1530 he had established Mongol – or Mughal – rule in northern India.

Mughal India
Akbar

In 1556 Babur's grandson, called Akbar, inherited a weak and divided empire as a boy of fourteen. He also inherited the ancestral belief that no empire can survive unless it is continually expanding, and throughout his reign he kept his armies constantly on the offensive. He continued old Mongol tactics. If a city resisted, it would most likely be destroyed and its people massacred; but if people accepted his authority, they found him a generous ruler. By 1600, his Mughal Empire controlled the whole of the subcontinent, except for Ceylon (Sri Lanka) and Vijayanagar in the south. Akbar built a huge capital at Fathpur-Siki, which was to be the model for Mughal public buildings of incomparable grandeur, culminating in the Taj Mahal of his grandson, Shah Jahan.

The country was divided into provinces, but all authority sprang directly from the emperor himself. Although a ruthless conqueror, Akbar was anxious to bind his people together effectively, and he was concerned at the religious division that existed between his Hindu and Muslim subjects. He was suspicious of all dogmatism, and devout Muslims accused him of backsliding when he abolished the poll tax payable by Hindus and worked to find a compromise between the two religions.

The Decline of the Mughal Empire

Akbar was an outstanding ruler, but his empire suffered from weaknesses inherited from his Mongol tradition. In Europe, structures of government were coming into existence that transcended the personality of the ruler. In Mughal India, however, authority continued to be overdependent on the ability of one man. The instability of the empire can be illustrated by events at the end of the reign of Akbar's grandson, Shah Jahan. In 1657, he fell ill, triggering a ferocious civil war between his sons; the victorious Aurangzeb was a devout and intolerant Muslim, and under his rule Akbar's united empire began to fall apart.

The Ottoman Empire

The Foundation of Empire

Mongol successes in central Asia created more movement of nomad tribes out of the grasslands. In the late thirteenth century, one Ertughrul led a band of followers, who were equally devoted to Islam and to plundering, into the Seljuk lands of the Middle East. Ertughrul's son, Othman (Osman), overthrew the Seljuk sultans, and founded the great empire that was to bear his name.

Othman's successors defeated the Byzantine army. They captured Asia Minor, and, in 1361, crossed into Europe to establish Ottoman power in the Balkans. Constantinople was now an isolated fortress in Ottoman lands, and in 1453 it fell to Sultan Mehmet II.

The Spread of Empire

Ottoman power reached its peak in the century after the fall of Constantinople. In the early sixteenth century, Selim I marched southwards, defeating the Mamelukes of Egypt and capturing Mecca, where he was proclaimed Caliph of the Islamic world. His successor Suleiman I, the Magnificent, turned north. In 1526, he defeated the Hungarian army at the great battle of Mohács. Three years later his armies laid siege to Vienna.

Africa

Trans-Saharan Trade

Historians of early sub-Saharan Africa are restricted by the lack of written records and the destructive capacity of termites, working on wood and mud brick. The continent, however, was far from isolated. A thriving trade existed across the Sahara trade routes between North Africa and the grassland region that lies across the continent from near the Atlantic to the Nile.

The staple product being carried southward was salt – an essential commodity for people living in a hot climate. The Muslim traders who crossed the desert carried various luxury goods, and also brought their religion and literacy in Arabic script. On the return journey they carried gold, slaves and leather goods. Before the time of Columbus, Europe was heavily dependent on African gold, and 'Morocco' leather has always originated south of the Sahara. A key focal point of this trade was Timbuktu, on the Niger, which became famous as the meeting point of the camel and the canoe. The town was already well enough known to be marked on a Spanish map in the late fourteenth century.

The gold and probably most of the slaves came from the forest region still further south, so trade reached out in both directions. Among the most active traders were the Hausa people, who were based in city states, such as Kano and Zaria. They would be late recruits to Islam and they never organized into larger political units.

African Empires

Broadly based political structures did, however, come into existence in southern Sudan to control the two-way trade. The Empire of Ghana (eighth to the eleventh centuries) was succeeded by Mali (twelfth to fourteenth centuries) and Songhai (fourteenth to sixteenth centuries). Kings like Musa Mensa, who ruled Mali in the early fourteenth century, were well known across the Islamic world and even beyond for their wealth and learning. The trade in gold appears also to have stimulated the growth of forest kingdoms, such as Benin and Oyo. These would grow in importance with the arrival of European ships on the coast in the fifteenth century. Far to the east, the kingdom of Ethiopia maintained its isolated Christian tradition, again with power based on trade with the north by way of the Nile.

There was also traffic in gold and slaves down the coast of East Africa. The unique stone ruins of Zimbabwe provide evidence to support the reports of inland states in this region.

America

America was the last continent to be settled by man and it remained the most isolated. Traditional hunter/gatherer lifestyles were successfully followed by people of widely differing culture across wide areas of North America and within the many forest regions of South America until they suffered under the impact of European invaders. The cultivation of maize and then of other crops, however, made possible the development of more complex civilizations.

Central America

The earliest civilization was that of the Olmecs, which flourished on the coast of the Gulf of Mexico in the seventh century BC. Many of the characteristics of later civilizations of the region can already be recognized in these people. In their capital of Teotihuacan, they built huge pyramids, apparently dedicated to the same gods that would be worshipped by people of the region in later generations.

The most accomplished civilization of the region was the Maya, centred on the Yucatan peninsula, which reached its peak in the ninth century BC. The Mayans used a pictogram form of writing. Like the Babylonians, they laid emphasis on the calendar and the heavenly bodies and they developed great skill in mathematics and astronomy, working out the duration of the year and learning how to predict eclipses. They were the first people in the world's history to achieve a sense of the vast span of time. Mayan sites, like those of ancient Egypt, are not cities, but vast complexes of temples and other ceremonial buildings.

The Maya were succeeded by the Toltecs, and they were overthrown in their turn by the Aztecs, who dominated the region from the thirteenth century. The Aztecs appear to have been the first to introduce mass human sacrifice. This practice came to dominate the whole of their strategy for the region. As victims were best found in warfare, they had no motivation to create conditions of peace, but rather encouraged a general unrest among subject people.

The Aztecs had a tradition that the white-skinned and bearded god, Quetzalcoatl, would one day return from the east. When the invading Spaniards appeared to fulfil this prophesy, there were many subject people who were prepared to take their side against their feared Aztec masters.

The Andes

The long spine of the Andes is perhaps the most improbable setting for any of the world's civilizations. Between 600 and 1000 AD, a people called the Huari brought some political unity to this area. In the twelfth century, the Incas, based on Cuzco in modern Peru, were only one of many smaller groupings. They then conquered an empire that by the fifteenth century stretched 2000 miles from Quito in modern Ecuador to the deserts of Chile.

The Incas were a non-literate people. Instructions were carried to distant parts of the empire by messengers. Again, lacking the wheel, these messengers travelled on foot over a road network, built with great engineering skill. Inca power was centred on heavily fortified cities, where invading Spaniards were to find a wealth of beautiful objects made of gold and stone.

The Incas were not as oppressive to their subject people as the Aztecs, but there were still many who were prepared to support the small force of Spaniards, under Francisco Pizarro, who arrived in 1531 to conquer and loot the Inca Empire.

5

The Triumph of Europe

The Background to Conquest

New Perspectives

The Mappa Mundi, in Hereford Cathedral, illustrates the medieval perspective of the world. Jerusalem lies in the centre of the world, with the three known continents – Asia, Africa and Europe – arranged around the Mediterranean Sea. Phoenician and Viking ships may have sailed the wider oceans, but these lay at the edge of the known universe.

By the fifteenth century, changes were taking place. The reports of Marco Polo's travels in the East were becoming widely known. No profit-orientated merchant could ignore his descriptions of markets loaded with silks, velvets and damasks. He had travelled beyond China to the islands of the Pacific and described how cheaply spices could be obtained. It was still impossible to keep meat animals alive through the European winter, so all except the breeding stock were slaughtered and salted down at Michaelmas. By spring such meat was barely edible without pepper, cinnamon and nutmeg to disguise the taste.

In 1400, a copy of the Hellenistic Ptolemy's *Geography* was brought from Constantinople and published in the West. It contained many errors, but did show that the world was round and not a flat dish. During the century, this became the accepted view of scholars.

The Ottoman conquests helped stimulate interest in alternative routes to East Asia. Through medieval times the majority of luxury goods had been brought by the Asian overland routes. These were now threatened by a hostile power. The Genoese, traditional allies of Byzantium, were particularly threatened by the new developments. Ottomans and Venetians alike combined to shut them out from the profitable business.

Logic demanded that traders should turn their attention to the oceans that lay beyond the enclosed Mediterranean world. Luxury goods were high value and low bulk cargo. Projected returns on investment on one cargo reaching Europe were astronomical.

Technical Advance

During the fifteenth century major technical advances were also made in Europe, which brought such a project within the bounds of the possible. Before that time European ships had been square rigged on a single main mast. Such a ship could be manned by a small crew, but could not sail efficiently into the wind. Arab ships used a lateen sail. This could sail into the wind but such a large crew was needed that it could never go far from land where food could be obtained. Shipbuilders now constructed multi-masted vessels, with both square and lateen sails, which could both be handled by a small crew and sail into the wind.

If ships were to sail far out from land, then navigational techniques needed to improve. By 1500, European sailors were skilled in the use of the magnetic compass, either re-invented or brought from China, and in measuring latitude. Almost 200 more years would pass before similar advances were made in calculating longitude. Great advances were also made in cartographical techniques, with the Dutch leading the way.

European craftsmen also developed gunnery to new levels. King John II of Portugal took particular interest in the problems of mounting modern guns on board ship. Success in these experiments meant that European ships could command the seas. In previous centuries, ships came together with grappling hooks to allow soldiers to fight a conventional battle. Now the European ship could sink an enemy ship without allowing it to come close enough to bring the soldiers into action.

Population and Prices

The intellectual climate was favourable, commercial incentives were strong, and the required technology was available. As with Norsemen and Mongols, however, a further 'push factor' was needed to trigger off a major movement of European people. Demographers have shown that western Europe had recovered from the Black Death and a cyclical population increase was in progress. Pauperism was on the increase, and also, in populations organized on the basis of primogeniture, the landless younger sons of gentry families were looking for any way of making a fortune.

Historians now link the population rise with an inflationary trend that persisted through the sixteenth century. On average, prices quadrupled between 1500 and 1600. Since wages and savings did not always keep up with the rising prices, this created conditions of hardship that could have made emigration seem attractive.

Religion

Christians of the period generally held that unbelievers possessed no rights. The pope declared that Christian kings had a right to conquer heathen lands. Some Catholic friars and, later, Jesuits did identify with the cause of the native people, but even their mission stations were instruments of colonial control. The Protestant record was, if anything, worse; 300 years would pass before Protestant Christians made any serious attempt to protect the rights of and to share their faith with non-European people.

Asia

The Portuguese

By 1400, Portugal was free from Muslim rule and had established itself as a separate country from Spain. Its geographical position made it a natural Atlantic pioneer. In the first half of the fifteenth century, the king of Portugal's brother, Henry 'the Navigator', established a school for sailors at Sagres, by Cape St Vincent, and sent out expeditions to explore ever further south into the Atlantic. Slowly they pushed the boundaries of exploration beyond the Azores and to Senegal.

In 1488, twenty-eight years after Henry's death, Bartholomew Diaz rounded the Cape of Good Hope and established that the way to India lay clear. In 1498, Vasco da Gama took his ship to Calicut in south India. Indian merchants were happy to sell to the newcomers as they offered higher prices than the Arabs. He returned with a cargo of pepper, cinnamon, ginger, cloves and tin. It was reported that the king of Portugal and Vasco da Gama's other backers made a 6000 per cent return on their investment. A century of human and financial investment had finally paid a dividend. In 1503, the Portuguese established a permanent base in India, at Cochin, followed in 1510 by Goa, and later by Seurat.

In 1509, the Arabs sent a fleet, manned by 15,000 men, to drive the Portuguese from their seas, but the European superiority in ships and gunnery proved decisive in a battle off Diu. From that time, European fleets exercised control over the world's oceans. Arab and oriental sailors could no longer confront them in battle, but only operate as pirates.

In 1517 the first Portuguese ship arrived off the coast of China and, according to European custom, fired their guns in salute. The Chinese found these barbaric Europeans 'crafty and cruel', but had to respect their guns, which 'shook the earth'. In 1521, Portuguese ships had reached the Spice Islands. In 1557, they established their trading base at Macao, off the Chinese mainland.

The Dutch

The Portuguese successfully protected their Africa route against encroachment by other European nations until the last years of the sixteenth century. Then, in 1594, a group of Dutch businessmen fitted out four ships to sail to the Far East. They carried the products of Europe – woollen and linen fabrics, glassware, ornaments and different kinds of ironware, including armour. The ships reached East Asia and found that the people welcomed their quality goods. In 1602, the Dutch parliament, the Estates, set up the Dutch East India Company to follow up this initiative. The Malacca Strait, in modern Indonesia, became the focus of their empire, with headquarters on the island of Java. The Dutch then set about driving the Portuguese out of their Asian empire. Only a few Portuguese outposts, such a Goa and Macao, survived the assault.

Once in control, the Dutch traders ruthlessly set about eliminating all competition. In 1623, ten English merchants were tortured and killed at Amboyna. But the Dutch were not content to exclude other European competition from their market. Chinese junks were shut out of their traditional markets as even local trade was channelled into Dutch ships. By now Europe was becoming glutted with spices, so the Dutch governor, Jan Coen, set about controlling production to keep prices high. On one occasion he destroyed all the nutmeg trees on the Banda Islands and either killed or sold into slavery the entire population of 15,000 people. He burnt villages along the coast of China in an attempt to control the whole region, but complained that China, like India, was 'too extensive for discipline'.

The English

The English East India Company was founded two years earlier than the Dutch, but it lost the race to control the Spice Islands. After Amboyna, the Dutch and the English were bitter commercial rivals. The English had to accept that the prize of the Pacific trade was closed to them and had to make do as a second best with establishing themselves in India. The trade in coffee, tea and cotton goods was of lower value than that from further east but, as the English trading stations at Madras, Bombay and Calcutta grew in importance, tea gained status as a fashionable drink. When Dutch power waned in the later years of the seventeenth century, English ships were able to use their Indian bases for trading with China and the Pacific Islands.

The French

The French East India Company had now replaced the Dutch as the main competition. French merchants, however, operated under difficulties. They came from a nation whose power was centred on its land army. While naval and commercial interests were influential in London, they carried little weight in Paris. In times of war, French ships were exposed to the powerful English navy and French overseas outposts were at all times starved of resources.

It long seemed impossible for any European nation to establish political control in the subcontinent. Then the death of Aurangzeb in 1707 marked the end of the Mughal Empire as an effective force, and the subcontinent split into warring states. From that time, the trading companies became increasingly involved in politics.

America

The Spanish

On 2 January 1492, the troops of the 'Catholic Monarchs', Isabella of Castile and her husband, Ferdinand of Aragon, finally drove the Moors out of Grenada. In the cheering crowd was a Genoese sailor, Christopher Columbus. Like another Genoese, John Cabot, he had decided that the Indies could best be reached by sailing westwards. Both turned to western European monarchs with a natural interest in Atlantic trade. Columbus won the support of Isabella, and in August his three ships sailed from Palos, to reach San Salvador on 12 October.

Columbus was bitterly disappointed that he did not find the eastern markets described by Marco Polo. In later voyages, he explored the Caribbean Islands and reached the mainland. He died in 1506, still convinced that he had reached the Indies. Before then, however, another Italian, Amerigo Vespucci, this time in Portuguese pay, had established that this was indeed the continent that subsequently carried his name. In the year that Columbus sailed, the Spanish pope, Alexander VI, issued a bull, awarding to Spain and Portugal all lands already discovered or to be discovered in the west, towards the Indies or the ocean seas, with the dividing line between the two on the line of longitude 45 degrees west. This ruling gave Brazil to Portugal and the rest of the continent to Spain. The Spanish, however, never established effective control to the north of a line from modern Georgia in the east to California in the west.

In 1519, Magellan led an expedition to explore this new world. When the remains of his expedition returned in 1522, having circumnavigated the globe, the basic facts of world geography were finally established.

Meanwhile the Spaniards were establishing their power in the 'New World'. In 1513, Balboa crossed the Isthmus of Panama and reached the Pacific Ocean. In the east, Portuguese guns could win naval battles, but they could never bring down great empires. In the west, however, the Spaniards found that civilizations crumbled before them. There was too large a gap between the technology of the New World on one side and the firearms, horses and armour of the Old World on the other. Perhaps most importantly, the American 'Indian' people were psychologically ill equipped to confront the brutal European soldiers. Many were killed by the newcomers; many lost the will to live when forced to work in unfamiliar ways; even more died of the plague and other diseases for which they lacked immunity. According to one estimate, twenty-five million people lived in what was to become New Spain when Columbus landed, but only a million and a half survived a century later.

The Spaniards may not have found silks and spices, but they found gold. What to the native Americans was a decorative metal was, to the Spaniards, the basic unit of exchange and measurement of wealth. For gold, Cortes and Pizarro destroyed the Aztec and Inca civilizations. Unsuccessful searches for gold established Spanish rule in what is now the south of the United States, from Florida to the Great Plains, and the Californian coast. All kinds of gold objects were melted down and shipped back to Spain, where the new riches funded the emergence of Spain as a major power.

The gold was soon plundered, and no significant mines were discovered. A sustainable flow of wealth was, however, established by the opening of silver mines in Peru. Spain now controlled both sides of the Isthmus of Panama and a merchant fleet was built on the westward, Pacific side. A trading base was established at Manila in the Philippines, and galleons carried trading goods across the wide Pacific. These luxury goods from the Orient, along with silver from Peru, were then carried across the Isthmus of Panama and loaded onto the Atlantic treasure fleet for Spain.

In the early years of colonization, few women left Spain for the New World, and settlers took Indian wives. The culture, and even the religion of New Spain therefore developed a syncretism between Spanish and Indian traditions. In time, the importation of black slaves from Africa further complicated the ethnic mix. It has, however, remained generally true, even into modern times, that the social position and wealth of any individual could be gauged by skin colour.

The English

John Cabot was convinced that Columbus had got his sums wrong. He believed correctly that China was far out of range of any ship following a southerly route. By his calculation, the journey could be made at a more northerly latitude. Sailors from Bristol, England, were already fishing the Newfoundland Banks and knew the North Atlantic well. Cabot therefore won support from King Henry VII of England and in 1496 reached the coast of North America. It was not obvious that the north of the continent was embedded in the Arctic ice and Cabot's son, Sebastian, led a long line of English sailors in search of the North-West Passage. The English sea dogs, Drake and Hawkins preferred the warm waters of New Spain to the cold northern seas. They first operated as traders, and then, after being attacked by Spaniards, as privateers.

The gold of New Spain and the luxury trade of the Orient offered instant riches. Returns on investment in North America were likely to be less spectacular. By the 1580s, however, Sir Walter Raleigh and others were advocating colonization of the land of Virginia, which was now claimed by England. Attempts were made to establish colonies in 1585 and 1589, but both failed. The first successful colony was established at Jamestown in 1607. In 1620 a group of 'Pilgrim' refugees set up a colony at New Plymouth, Massachusetts, and later moved to the better site of Boston.

The English settlements were based on a farming economy. Disease, spreading from New Spain, had recently ravaged the native American Indian tribes, leaving much of the land vacant. The surviving people practised a mixed hunting and farming economy, based on shifting cultivation, so to newcomers much of the land appeared to be empty. As land-hungry settlers kept on arriving and pushing inland towards the Appalachian Mountains conflict with the Indian people was inevitable.

The Dutch

In 1614, the United New Netherlands Company established a colony at the mouth of the Hudson River. The Dutch recognized the potential of the trade in beaver fur and used the Hudson to make contact with the Indian people of the interior. This settlement divided the English colonies of Virginia and New England, and hostility between the two Protestant countries, aroused in the far Spice Islands, spilled over into the New World. In 1664, the English drove the Dutch from North America.

At the height of their powers, the Dutch carried their assault on the Portuguese Empire into the New World by annexing Brazil in 1637. The Portuguese settlers rebelled against them and they were driven out in 1654, leaving Brazil as the western outpost of a once great Portuguese Empire.

The French

In 1603 the French explorer, de Champlain, first sailed into the St Lawrence River. He too was still searching for the elusive route to the East. He established settlements that were to become Montreal and Quebec and pressed on to explore the inland waterways of the interior. The French settlers were comparatively few in number and they received little support from their home government. Champlain and those who came after him exploited Indian rivalries to establish a flourishing trading empire, based on the fashion trade in beaver fur. As the animals were hunted to near extinction in the east, the 'beaver frontier' moved west, taking the hardy French after them.

French explorers followed the Great Lakes waterway into the interior and then the Mississippi to the Gulf of Mexico. Here they established the French outpost of New Orleans. Their North American empire, named Louisiana, after Louis XIV, now followed the waterways in a huge, but lightly populated arc. At first the French and English colonists only came into contact with each other in the Hudson Valley. The risk of conflict grew, however, when the French tightened the noose around the English colonies by taking control of the River Ohio. At the time, however, colonial wars, which decided the fate of India and North America, were seen as little more than a sideshow beside the main European conflicts.

The Old Colonial System

The Dutch can be credited with the development of mercantilism, which became known as the old colonial system. This was not developed specifically for North America, but, when applied by the English in their American possessions, it became a root cause of later conflict between the colonists and the mother country. It was assumed that overseas colonies existed to promote the interests of the mother country, by extending its economic base. Colonists were expected to produce cash crops. Some, like rice from the Carolinas or tobacco from Virginia, could not be produced in northern Europe. Softwood timber from New England was also of vital strategic importance for shipbuilding at a time when European forests were finally disappearing. Buying these goods from a national source saved the mother country the foreign exchange, which would be required to purchase them from abroad. By selling these crops, the colonists earned money that would be spent on manufactured goods. This in turn assisted the manufacturing industries and strengthened the merchant marine of the mother country. Any business between the colony and a third country had to be transacted through the mother country. This had the further benefit of boosting customs revenue.

The trade-off was that the mother country was responsible for providing the colonists with protection, be it from local populations or from hostile Europeans. This involved the Westminster government in the expense of funding wars against the French and their Indian allies. The system came under pressure when the colonies began to move away from their original role as providers of raw materials to develop their own manufacturing industries.

Africa

The Atlantic Slave Trade

The Portuguese were the first to discover that West Africa had human resources, which were to be exploited in a slave trade that continued for some 350 years. A base was established on the coast as early as 1448, from which comparatively small numbers of slaves were shipped back to Portugal.

Then, an acute labour problem began to develop in the new American plantations. The obvious solution was to recruit American Indians. Heavy field work, however, proved alien to them. Many died, often by suicide, when forced to work on European plantations. European labour was also brought in, both by the forcible transportation of convicts, and by indentured labour schemes, under which immigrants were bound to their masters for a given number of years. Again, however, expectation of life was short, and the labour problem remained unresolved.

Portuguese ships then began to take slaves directly to their colony of Brazil. In 1562, John Hawkins began the English slave trade between West Africa and the Caribbean. Dutch, French, Danes and later sailors from both North and South America joined in the business. European nations established forts on the West African coast to protect the interests of their slave traders.

It is estimated that some eight to ten million slaves were carried across the Middle Passage to America. The economies of European cities, such as Nantes, Bristol and later Liverpool, were based on slaving, and the business was accepted as a part of the national commercial interest.

The individual suffering of slaves would ultimately receive wide publicity; the impact the trade had on African society is harder to quantify. European sailors rarely penetrated inland to find their own captives. Domestic slavery already existed on the continent, and Africans initially sold their own slaves to purchase European goods. In time, however, demand outstripped this source of supply. Military confederacies, such as Dahomey and Ashanti, grew up to fulfil the double function of protecting their own members, and feeding slaves to the European forts. When Europeans later penetrated the continent, they discovered that these states often acted with a savagery untypical of African society further inland. The demand for slaves created an endemic state of war that penetrated inland, far beyond any direct European contact. The resulting depopulation appears, however, to have been balanced to some degree by improvements in the African diet as a result of the importation of American crops, such as the yam and cassava.

Colonization

The first African colonies had the prime function of protecting and providing staging posts for national ships on trade routes to the East. The Portuguese had previously established outposts in Mozambique and Angola that would achieve the distinction of being the longest lasting European overseas colonies. In 1652, Jan van Riebeck set up a Dutch colony at the Cape of Good Hope, to serve the eastern convoys as a 'tavern of the seas'. In the eighteenth century, the French established an interest in the Indian Ocean islands of Madagascar, Mauritius and Reunion. The slave coast of West Africa remained unattractive for colonization. European slavers and soldiers themselves suffered a high mortality rate from tropical diseases, particularly yellow fever and malaria.

East Africa

At this time, East Africa lay off the main trading routes, and the region offered little to attract European merchants. Arab dhows still sailed undisturbed to Zanzibar and their caravans penetrated deep inland. Here again, slaves featured prominently as a trading commodity alongside gold and ivory. The area remained an Arab area of influence until European missionaries and traders penetrated the area in the nineteenth century.

6

The Nations of Europe

Italy and the European Powers

The City States and the Papacy

In the fifteenth century, the northern half of Italy was the most advanced part of Europe. The great trading cities of Genoa and Venice brought in wealth and broad contact was maintained, both through trade and cultural exchange, with Arab and Byzantine civilizations. The country probably benefited from the fact that it was never brought under unitary political control.

The broken terrain of Tuscany and Umbria suited the development of independent city states, not unlike those of ancient Greece. Florence and Sienna, like Athens and Sparta of old, built up confederacies to counterbalance the power of the other. In the late fourteenth century, the banking family of Medici took power in Florence. Times were not always easy, but they led the city to its unique flowering of culture.

In the north, another ring of states, with Milan as the most powerful, controlled the trading routes across the Alps. In the centre, the pope ruled the Papal States as any other temporal monarch, and involved himself in the politics of the peninsula, attempting always to extend the patrimony of St Peter. During this period the lifestyle of the popes was little different from that of any other monarch. They led troops into battle, promoted family interests, including those of their children, and built themselves enormous monuments. Julius II's decision to build himself a tomb set off the chain of events that triggered the Reformation in distant Germany – the tomb would be too large for St Peter's, so the church had to be rebuilt and this involved raising money by the granting of indulgences.

The Theory of Kingship

Within this turbulent world of Italian politics, only the fittest survived. Niccolo Machiavelli worked for the Florentine state, travelling widely as a diplomat. He wrote a book, *The Prince*, which was based on these experiences. It contained advice for the Medici family on the theory and practice of government. Political decisions, he argued, could only be taken on a cool, indeed callous, assessment of the security needs of the state and of its ruler. Medieval concepts of the mutual duties of ruler and subjects were cut away in this first exposition of what would later come to be called 'real politik'.

Medieval monarchy was based on a feudal alliance between a king and his tenants in chief. In the sixteenth century, power was being drawn to the centre at the expense of both the magnates and of representational institutions. For Machiavelli's prince, power was its own justification. The theory of centralization was later taken further with the formulation of the concept of the divine right of kings. Rulers, it was said, held power directly from God; rebellion was a sin and criticism of the royal will was tantamount to treason.

Foreign Invasion

In 1494, Charles VIII of France crossed the Alps at the head of an army of 30,000 men. He laid claim to the kingdom of Naples and on his way south, through Rome itself, his army left a trail of destruction. Other foreign armies followed. Artists continued to work, producing some of the greatest works known to man, but the days of the city state were over and Italy would henceforth be a pawn in the real politik of the great powers. In 1527, the ragged, unpaid and hungry army of the great Holy Roman Emperor Charles V ran wild in the streets of Rome, and the city was sacked for the first time since the barbarian invasions.

The Empire of Charles V

Throughout medieval times, kingship was fundamentally a matter of family inheritance. Charles was the ultimate beneficiary of this dynastic system. From his mother, the mad Joanna, he inherited his grandparents' crowns of Castile and Aragon. On the paternal side, he inherited from his grandfather the title of Holy Roman Emperor, and from his grandmother the lands of the Duchy of Burgundy. As the King of Castile he controlled Spanish land in the New World; as Emperor he ruled Austria, Hungary, Bohemia and much of Germany; as Duke of Burgundy he possessed the Netherlands, which was the richest part of all Europe. His empire was larger than that of Charlemagne.

France was now shut in on all sides, and its king was determined not to let Italy fall to Charles' empire. The crusading spirit was finally laid to rest as the pope and the king of France allied with the Ottoman Turks against Charles.

This great empire, like that of Charlemagne, carried the seeds of its own destruction. Charles was unable to function adequately as ruler of such dispersed lands, and resentment grew, particularly in the Netherlands, at the taxes raised to support Italian wars. Charles was also depressed at his inability to control the spread of Protestantism within his own lands. He abdicated in 1556 and the empire was divided. The title of Holy Roman Emperor passed to his brother, Ferdinand I, while the more valuable western share of his empire, consisting of Spain and the old Burgundian lands, went to his son, Philip II. There were now two Habsburg dynasties in Europe.

Protestantism and the Counter Reformation

The Spread of Protestantism

Martin Luther's new beliefs found most followers in northern Europe, particularly in Germany itself and in Scandinavia. The impetus behind the further spread of Protestantism came, not from Germany but from Geneva. John Calvin was French, but he achieved prominence in the Swiss canton. He preached a harsh form of Protestantism; since God was all-powerful, he had predestined a minority of people – the elect – to salvation and the rest to damnation. The elect had to show their status by a strict adherence to a way of life. Within Geneva, moral sins, such as adultery, were severely punished. Calvinism proved to be a more militant faith than Lutheranism. It appealed in the Netherlands, in England and on the west coast of France, in Scotland and later in the Lutheran heartland of Germany.

All Protestantism stressed the direct communion of the individual with God, and it is not therefore surprising that it quickly showed a capacity to fragment. In 1532, an extreme group, the Anabaptists, took control of the German city of Münster, preaching not only rejection of infant baptism, but polygamy and a radical social gospel. In the extreme Protestant sects, authority lay not in any higher political or ecclesiastical power, but in the local 'gathered church'. These separatist churches were persecuted in Protestant and Catholic countries alike, but it was this tradition that would ultimately implant itself in the New England colonies of North America, and profoundly influence the development of American society.

Tolerance was not a cherished ideal in sixteenth century Europe, but by 1530 it had become clear that Protestantism was too powerful a movement to be readily suppressed. In that year the Peace of Augsburg laid down the principle of 'cuius regio, eius religio' – the country would follow the religion of the ruler. This left rulers free to persecute within their own dominions.

Sweden and England Break with Rome

Two European monarchs took their nations out of communion with the Roman Church. Both were motivated by national and financial, rather than by religious reasons. In 1523, the young Swedish nobleman, Gustavus Vasa, succeeded in his struggle to make Sweden independent from Denmark, and was proclaimed king. Lutheranism had already made progress among his people. In 1527, he broke with Rome as a symbol of his country's new national independence, and he enriched his hard pressed government with church lands.

Henry VIII of England had shown no personal inclination towards the reformed religion; indeed he had written a pamphlet attacking Luther and persecuted Protestants. In 1530, however, he became involved in a dispute with the pope over his divorce to Catherine of Aragon. Using selective intimidation, he won the support of parliament for a breach with Rome, and then for the plundering of the monastic lands. The Church of England, reformed in doctrine, but conservative in practice, was the creation of Henry's Archbishop of Canterbury, Thomas Cranmer. After a short return to Catholicism under Mary I, Henry's daughter, Elizabeth, declared that the English Church should be a home for all men of goodwill. Separatist Protestants and politically active Catholics were still persecuted, but England did escape the worst violence of these years.

The Counter Reformation

The Roman Church had been on the defensive against an aggressive Protestantism for 25 years when Pope Paul III called his bishops together for the Council of Trent. Paul represented a new generation of popes, anxious to clear away the scandals of the past, and re-establish the Western Church on a firm footing. The discussions were dominated by bishops from Spain and Italy, where Protestantism had found no foothold. The Council brought in reforms – indulgences, for instance, were abolished – but it made no concessions to Protestant faith. By the time that the Council had finished its debates in 1563, the lines of division were clearly drawn.

Catholicism was now on the counteroffensive. As in the past, monasticism provided the papacy with its frontline troops. In 1540, Ignatius Loyola, who had been a fellow student in Paris with John Calvin, established the Society of Jesus, or Jesuits. Members were bound to total loyalty to the pope, and this provided the reforming papacy with a means of circumventing special interests within the church. Jesuits became particularly prominent in education and in missionary work.

Spain and the Netherlands

The Expulsions

Even without Charles' eastern lands, Philip II's Spain remained the dominant power in Europe. He controlled southern Italy and Sicily and succeeded in conquering Portugal. Spain's European power was now underpinned by the revenues of a two huge overseas empires.

The nation's weakness was not clearly evident at the time. When the Moors were finally defeated, Muslims and Jews had been promised security within the Christian state. The presence of infidels, however, proved too much for its Catholic rulers, still driven by the intolerance of the Inquisition. Moors, Jews, and converted Moors, the Moriscos, were all driven out of the country. These, however, were the very trades-people and skilled craftsmen on whom the economy of the nation rested. As a result, Spain became heavily dependent on imported goods, particularly from the prosperous northern Netherlands. On occasions, the Panama fleet had to be diverted and sail direct to unload its treasure in the Netherlands.

The Spanish Netherlands

The old Burgundian lands covered both of the modern states of Belgium and Holland. The greatest centres of prosperity, with Antwerp outstanding, lay in the south. The northern part, mostly consisting of land drained from the Rhine delta, contained the finest farmland in Europe, but, even with intensive agriculture, it could not feed the growing towns. Calvinist Protestantism had won adherents both in the north and in the south.

Charles V was born in the Netherlands, and during his reign the two religions coexisted with reasonable tolerance. The accession of the Spanish-born Philip II, however, brought change. As king, he was determined to bring the old Burgundian noble families under his control, and, as a faithful son of the Roman Church, he meant to stamp out heresy in his land. The Spanish Duke of Alva was sent with an army to bring the area under control.

Dutch Independence

In 1572, William, Prince of Orange, led the people of the Netherlands in revolt. As Spanish armies established control of the south, many Protestants moved north behind the protection of the dykes, and the religious division between the Catholic south and the Protestant north was established. In 1581, the followers of William of Orange declared their independence from Spain. No matter how bitter the fighting, the trade between Spain and her rebellious provinces never ceased. Philip was in no position to cut off this channel of supplies for his people and the Dutch were happy to drain the enemy of wealth. William was murdered on Philip's orders in 1584, but the struggle continued until Spain made a truce in 1609. Almost 40 years would pass before Spain finally recognized the independence of the Dutch people, but in practice Holland had established its independence from its traditional ruling house.

The Dutch Republic

The new nation was unique in that power was based on trade, rather than on inherited land. A successful Dutchman did not plan for the day when he would put aside the cares of trade and live as a gentleman – his objective was to hand a thriving business to his heirs. The people lived by a strict work ethic, and made the most of the limited resources of their small land.

National wealth was founded on north–south trade, carrying products, such as grain, timber and iron, from the Baltic to the overpopulated Mediterranean lands. Dutch flyboats, little more than floating holds, plied the oceans: 'Norway was their forest, the banks of the Rhine and the Dordogne their vineyard; Spain and Ireland grazed their sheep; India and Arabia were their gardens and the sea their highway.' Scholars also provided vital information for the sailors and, in doing so, laid the foundation of modern geography.

The Decline of Spain

The loss of the Netherlands was the clearest marker of Spain's fall from its position of being Europe's dominant power. In 1588, a Spanish naval armada was also defeated by the English fleet. In 1640, Portugal re-established her independence under the house of Breganza. Spain could have overcome military reverse; the basic problem was that Philip II and his successors concentrated on military and colonial affairs at the expense of the economy, which had been shattered by the mass expulsions.

The French Wars of Religion

The French Monarchy

In the middle of the sixteenth century, French royal power stood at a low ebb. Financial stringency led to offices being sold to the highest bidder, and, partly as a result, the size and independence of the aristocracy was ever increasing. Calvinism was strong in Brittany and Normandy, and growing in power further south on the Atlantic coast and in Languedoc. Its strength was based on craftsmen and some poorer nobles, followed by a growing number of peasants. By 1562, there were over fifteen hundred 'Huguenot' congregations, many led by Geneva-trained pastors. The Catholics were themselves divided into two parties – the moderates, led by the regent, Catherine de' Medici, who at first planned to keep the peace by giving a measure of toleration to the Protestants, and an extreme Catholic party, who wanted to see heresy stamped out.

The Wars

Fighting broke out after extremist Catholics massacred a Huguenot congregation at Vassy in 1562. The ensuing wars were fought with great ferocity on both sides. In 1572, three thousand Huguenots were massacred in Paris on St Bartholomew's Day, and in 1588 the king, Henry III, was ejected from his own capital by extreme Catholics. In 1584, the Huguenot Henry of Navarre had become heir to the throne. He succeeded in bringing the war to an end by turning Catholic and reaching an agreement with his former Protestant followers in the Edict of Nantes (1598). This left the Huguenots with freedom of worship in large areas of the country, as well as certain fortified cities. These now effectively lay outside royal control.

Germany

The Empire after Charles V

Emperor Charles V's brother, Ferdinand, saw himself as a faithful Catholic and soldier of the Counter Reformation. His own lands and the south of Germany remained Catholic. The Protestant forces set against him were divided. In the north were the Lutheran powers of Denmark, Saxony and Brandenburg. The Calvinist stronghold lay to the west around the Rhine. Ferdinand dreamed of winning back the whole of Germany to Catholicism, while at the same time bringing it once again under Imperial rule.

Ferdinand was unable to achieve his ambition because his empire was exposed on its eastern flank. In the south-east, the Ottoman Empire reached the peak of its power under Suleiman I, and even threatened Vienna itself. In the northeast, Sweden was establishing control of the Baltic Sea while Poland and Russia both pressed on German land.

The Thirty Years' War

In the early seventeenth century, the religious divisions became more sharply fixed. In 1608–09, the Catholic League and the Calvinist Union were set up as rival military blocks. The first of a series of wars broke out in 1618, when the Calvinist Elector Palatine was elected king of Bohemia. The Catholic armies, led by virtually independent war lords, won early successes, but this rallied the Lutheran armies to the Protestant cause. The Protestant champion turned out to be Gustavus Adolphus, King of Sweden, who won a series of battles before he was killed at Lützen in 1632.

By this time the religious battle lines were becoming blurred. Catholic France, under Cardinal Richelieu, was prepared to fund Protestant armies and even to intervene directly to prolong the war and so prevent a re-emergence of Imperial power in Germany. This brought in Catholic and Habsburg Spain on the Imperial side.

The war was a disaster for the people of Germany. Roaming armies stripped the countryside of food; the devastation caused by the Imperial sack of Magdeburg in 1629 rivalled that of a Mongol army. When the war limped to a close in 1648, the countryside was impoverished and depopulated. Ferdinand's ideal of a Catholic Germany, united under the empire, was destroyed. Protestantism was unassailable in the north, and the effective power of the emperor in the German-speaking lands was henceforth limited to his Austrian heartland. In the Treaties of Westphalia, Ferdinand had to accept the independence of Switzerland – a reality since the end of the fifteenth century – and the King of Spain that of the Netherlands. France and Spain both made territorial gains in German lands. Most significant for the future, the new power of Brandenburg had emerged in the north.

Brandenburg-Prussia

In 1640, 'the Great Elector', Frederick William of the House of Hohenzollern, inherited Brandenburg and the eastern territory of Prussia. A man of great energy, he set about creating a well-run, modern state. His twin tools were an efficient civil service and a highly disciplined army, which served as a model for later German armies. The Great Elector's work was consolidated a century later by Frederick II ('Frederick the Great'). He had no vision of a united Germany, but he ruthlessly expanded his family lands at the expense of the Holy Roman Empire.

The Hegemony of France

Richelieu

Henry IV of France was assassinated in 1610 by a Catholic fanatic, leaving a country at peace, but with many problems. The Huguenots were a state within a state; the nobles were over powerful and contributed little to the national life; the peasants were desperately poor and over-taxed.

In 1624, Henry's son and successor, Louis XIII, appointed Cardinal Richelieu as head of the royal council. For eighteen years, Richelieu worked single-mindedly to establish royal power within the nation. He had no wish to persecute the Protestants, but he destroyed the independent Huguenot fortresses, including La Rochelle and Montauban. He made examples at a high level to bring the nobles under his control. Regional government was delegated to directly appointed intendants, who exercised the complete range of royal power.

Richelieu's foreign policy was directed at limiting the power of Spain and improving national security by achieving 'natural frontiers' at the Rhine and the Alps. For this, he was prepared to ally with Protestants and to prolong the misery of the Thirty Years' War.

Richelieu represented the apotheosis of the Machiavellian ideal; his policy was driven by a cold analysis of *raison d'être*. He did not, however, recognize that some improvement in the lot of the poor was essential if the state was to be securely based. Shortly after Richelieu and his royal master died, during 1642–43 there was a series of popular uprisings across the country, which were known as the Frondes.

Louis XIV

The young king who succeeded, Louis XIV, was to rule the country until 1715. His domestic and foreign policy was a continuation of that laid down by Richelieu. All real power lay in the hands of non-noble ministers and the intendants, while the nobles were emasculated by being drawn into the glittering court of Versailles.

Unlike Richelieu, however, Louis determined that he would not rule over heretics. He revoked the Edict of Nantes, facing Protestants with the choice of conversion or expulsion. Like Isabella of Castile, he was thereby driving a productive group out of the nation. Economic conditions did improve, but the poor continued to suffer harshly enforced penal taxation.

Much tax revenue was spent on foreign wars. As France had organized leagues and associations to limit the power of Spain, so now others united to contain France. The driving force in the anti-French Grand Alliance was William of Orange, Stadholder of the Netherlands. His power strengthened when, in 1688 he also became king of England as William III. The War of the Grand Alliance (1689–97) was followed by the War of the Spanish Succession (1701–14), which sought to prevent Louis from unifying the crowns of France and Spain by dynastic succession.

Eighteenth-century France

In 1715, France was clearly the leading power in Europe. Major losses of overseas territory to England in India and North America during the Seven Years' War (1756–63) did not appear as significant at the time as they were later to become. Financial weakness, however, underlay the pageantry of the French monarchy. The huge noble class – estimated at up to a quarter of a million strong – had lost political power but not financial and legal privilege. The state sank ever more deeply into debt, but had no means of tapping the huge reserves of noble wealth. Here lay the seeds of revolution.

England

Sea Power

When Roman soldiers were posted to Britain, they considered that they were being consigned to the edge of the civilized world. Through medieval times, the British Isles remained on the periphery of the known world. The discovery of America moved the centre of gravity away from the Mediterranean towards the Atlantic Ocean. Geography therefore now favoured England.

As an island nation, the English were perforce a seafaring people. By 1500, however, this seafaring tradition had not been converted into naval power. The defeat of the Spanish armada in 1588 proved to be a turning point. The battle was won by strategy rather than by fighting force, but the Elizabethan sea dogs created a national myth that would survive into modern times. Governments, reluctant to involve troops in European land battles, laid the greatest stress on building up naval power and securing naval supplies. The navy provided protection for the island, maintained links with overseas colonies, and secured trade routes against competition.

Monarchy and Parliament

The Tudor monarchs, Henry VIII and his daughter, Elizabeth, dominated sixteenth-century English politics. The English nobility were few in number, and were generally content to concentrate their efforts on field sports and the efficient management of their estates. While parliamentary government was withering on the continent, in England the old institutions remained robust. Henry found it convenient to use the

House of Commons as his ally against the church, and Elizabeth was able to manage parliament, even if sometimes with difficulty, both as a source of revenue and as a channel of government.

When Elizabeth died in 1603, the succession passed to the Scots House of Stuart, which, through family and cultural ties, was more influenced by the French model. Very early, James VI of Scotland and I of England became involved in disputes with both the legal and parliamentary establishment. James proclaimed the divine right of kings, which, he claimed, gave the king the power to appoint and dismiss judges and to raise taxes. Jurists recovered documents such as Magna Carta from obscurity to defend ancient privileges against the new royal pretensions. Implicit in their arguments lay the notion that royal power was derived from the consent of the people – however the people might be defined. The conflict was made more acute by the fact that personality did not match pretension. The Tudors had maintained authority through the force of their personalities, rather than through modern concepts of kingship. James was intelligent but personally unimpressive; his son Charles I was an inadequate recluse.

The Civil War

Charles I soon found himself in direct confrontation with parliament. In 1628, parliament presented a Petition of Right against the use of arbitrary royal power; in 1629, Charles dissolved parliament and began eleven years of direct rule. Many aspects of royal government were unpopular to influential subjects. An attempt was made to impose 'high church' worship, not only on England but also on Calvinist Scotland. An increasing number of cases were heard in royal prerogative courts, rather than in the courts of common law. Direct taxes, such as ship money, were levied without parliamentary approval. It seemed to many as though Charles would soon follow Richelieu's example and centralize all government.

The outbreak of war in Scotland brought financial disaster and Charles was forced to recall parliament in 1640. A struggle for power led to the outbreak of the English Civil War in 1642. Historians have long argued the economic, religious and social issues that lay behind the conflict; certainly it was very different in nature from the violent upheavals that would later shake France and Russia. Parliamentary power was based in the rich south-east, while the king's was centred in the poorer north and west. The Parliamentary victory was due both to this difference in resources, and to the leadership of Oliver Cromwell, who emerged as the outstanding general in the conflict. He kept his New Model Army under such firm control that it could march across countryside and leave fields and property as they had been before the army passed.

The Commonwealth

The Parliamentarians broke into factions after the defeat of the king in Scotland. In 1648, one faction seized power with army support and staged the trial of Charles I. The king's execution in 1649 provoked a shocked response across Europe. No action could have expressed the rejection of divine kingship more vividly. In 1653, Cromwell staged a military coup and assumed power as Lord Protector. Cromwell died in 1658 and a brief attempt was made to continue the Protectorate under his son. But this failed and in 1660 the army again was responsible for bringing Charles II back to London.

The Glorious Revolution

The saga of the conflict between the Stuarts and their parliaments was not, however, over. Charles II was mistrusted, both for his French sympathies and for his leaning towards Catholicism, but he still depended on parliament for revenue. In 1685, he was succeeded by his Catholic brother, James II. Three years later James was forced to leave the country, to be replaced by his Protestant daughter, Mary and her husband, the Dutch William of Orange, who exercised the practical power during their rule. William was more interested in securing an English alliance against France, than he was in pursuing power struggles with the English parliament. He therefore accepted laws that established that the king would henceforth require parliamentary consent to raise money and keep a standing army in peace time. It was also agreed that he could not alter or suspend any act of parliament.

In 1714, the English throne passed to the German House of Hanover. Since the new king could not speak English, day-to-day government passed to a prime minister and a cabinet, drawn from the majority party in the House of Commons. Political power had now finally passed from the monarchy to the property-owning classes, who were represented in parliament. In the century that followed, parliament largely used its power to improve the position of the landowning class, often at the expense of the poor. English politics had, however, run against the European tide, which favoured greater centralization in the hands of the monarch.

The Act of Union

Throughout history, there had been strife between England and her smaller, poorer northern neighbour, Scotland. The Union of the Crowns in 1603 did not put an end to this. In 1707, however, the two countries became formally united in the Act of Union. Two clan uprisings followed in 1715 and 1745, in favour of the exiled Stuarts, but these were suppressed. Scottish engineers, doctors and scholars were shortly after to make a major contribution to the great surge in the national prosperity of the united Great Britain.

Russia

Boyars and Serfs

Across the continent, the Russian state was following a very different pattern of development. The noble boyars held their land from the tsar in return for defined services. Since Russia had no law of primogeniture, this class was getting ever larger, and most of its members poorer, as estates were split one generation after another. The mass of the people remained in the medieval condition of serfdom. Families were owned by their masters, had no right to move of their own free will and had no redress except in their masters' court.

The relationship of tsar and boyars was often marked by bloody conflict. Ivan IV ('the Terrible') allied himself with the merchant class and the common people in an attempt to break noble power. He achieved many real reforms before mental disorder led him, in the latter years of his reign, to behaviour that anticipated that of Joseph Stalin in the twentieth century.

National Objectives

Russian development was hindered by the lack of a warm weather outlet to the ocean. The port of Archangel was icebound in winter, and all year the journey round northern Scandinavia was long and dangerous. The port of Rostov in the south was of little use as long as the Ottoman Turks controlled the mouth of the Sea of Azov and the Dardanelles. National policy therefore became directed at winning a port on the Baltic Sea. This brought Russia into conflict with the advanced military state of Sweden, which regarded the Baltic as a Swedish lake.

The Russian tsar could mobilize huge armies by raising levies, but there was no adequate support structure. Forces were sent to war with the vague hope that they would be able to live off the land. Often countless thousands of soldiers starved, and those who did manage to survive were in no condition to fight the world's most efficient army.

Peter the Great

Peter succeeded to the Russian throne in 1682 at the age of ten, and suffered huge indignities from guards and boyars while still a child. Once a man, he announced his intention to bring his nation up to date and orientate it towards the West. A man of little education but enormous energy, he immersed himself in every detail of Western science and technology. In a famous visit to the West, he was equally at home working in disguise as a dock worker in Holland and meeting with scientists in England. His methods of enforcement were effective, if sometimes eccentric.

The vindication of Peter's work came in 1709 when his army won a decisive victory at Poltava over the Swedish army under Charles XII. Russia had won its outlet to the Baltic Sea, and here Peter decided to build his capital of St Petersburg.

Peter's great failure was that, like Louis XIV in France, he failed to do anything to improve the lot of the Russian poor. Someone had to pay for wars against Turkey and Sweden, for the modern weapons, for new ships and for the fine capital city. The poor were taxed and taxed again until they were left with the barest minimum necessary to keep themselves and their families alive. It is a measure of the depth of the misery and the capacity of the Russian people to absorb suffering that revolution did not erupt in violence for another 200 years.

7

The Western Mind

The Renaissance

Italy

The word *Renaissance* was coined in the nineteenth century to describe the rebirth in Italy of the classical ideal in art, architecture and letters. The Middle Ages were looked upon as a dark period before the great transformation of the fifteenth and early sixteenth centuries. Recent study has shown that the picture was more complicated; classicism remained strong throughout the Middle Ages, and there was more cross fertilization between Europe north and south of the Alps than had been assumed.

Any gallery visitor can, however, see the astonishing change that happened in visual perception within a comparatively few years. Across northern Italy artists experimented with new forms. In the words of the art historian, Giorgio Vasari, Giotto 'restored the art of design'; in Umbria, Piero della Francesca used mathematics to work out laws of perspective, well beyond any classical achievement; in Florence, Michelangelo combined an analytical eye with his huge talent to create a new vision of the human, or at least male, form. Even when painters and sculptors continued to work on church commissions, they now used live models to give a new sense of naturalism.

There was a keen awareness among the artistic community that they were living in an exciting new age. The Medicis and other patrons commissioned works with secular themes, often drawn from Greek mythology. Artists were no longer like the faceless craftsmen who had produced so many medieval treasures. Art had found a new self-consciousness.

The same secular-driven innovation was reflected in music and literature. There was a passionate interest in all aspects of antiquity. Some sculptors even buried their own work and dug it up again, claiming it as a classical discovery. Old manuscripts were found in monastic libraries or brought from the East and studied with a new intensity. Enthusiasm for antiquity did not preclude Christian belief; rather the classical tradition was seen as one element in divine revelation, so producing a syncretism that alarmed conservative churchmen.

By the mid-sixteenth century the Italian Renaissance was losing its impetus. The first unique burst of innovation could not be maintained. The Counter Reformation Church now demanded a more orthodox treatment of subject matter, both in literature and in painting. Much great work continued to be done, particularly in the Veneto region. Palladio used Roman models in creating the architectural style that would bear his name, while Titian and his contemporaries were laying the foundations of what would become the baroque style. Generations of artists and patrons continued to travel to Italy to absorb the culture both of its classical past and of the present.

The Northern Renaissance

Some of the great painters of the Flemish school crossed the Alps and were much admired by Renaissance artists. Perhaps because they were not surrounded by antiquities in their home environment, however, they never made a sharp break with the gothic. Italian styles took many years to become established north of the Alps.

Northern Europe's unique contribution came in the field of scholarship and literature. Here writers were free from the restrictions of the Counter Reformation and fear of the Inquisition. Protestants wanted to make the Bible available to all. The translations of the scriptures by Martin Luther and William Tyndale were immensely influential in formalizing the written forms of German and English respectively. Traditional interpretations of the Bible were challenged when Erasmus of Rotterdam produced a version of the New Testament in the original Greek. Latin slowly ceased to be the universal language of scholarship. While a return to the vernacular liberated learning from the cloisters of the church, it also fractured the international culture, which had reached its peak in the twelfth century.

A strong secular tradition now flourished in England. Chaucer had already written for the newly educated merchant class. In 1510, John Colet, Dean of St Paul's Cathedral and close friend of Erasmus, made a gesture to the secularization of learning when he closed his cathedral school and refounded it under the control of a trading guild. The combination of Tyndale's language and Renaissance scholarship had created a uniquely favourable environment when in 1585 an actor called William Shakespeare left his native Stratford to chance his fortune in London.

The great flowering of French literature came in the seventeenth century. Corneille and Racine were still in essence Renaissance writers, handling classical themes with a Palladian sense of form and style.

Printing

Most importantly, the re-invention of printing by movable type provided the means of dissemination of both religious and secular literature. Whether the innovation be credited to Johannes Guttenberg of Mainz or Lourens Coster of Haarlem, the technique provided the means of dissemination of the works of any author. Books became cheaper as print runs grew longer. In the following centuries, print was used to promote colonies, to circulate scurrilous pamphlets, to produce works on magic, as well as to disseminate works of scholarship, religion and literature. In 1702, *The Courant*, the world's first daily newspaper, was published in London. Soon afterwards works of popular fiction began to come off the presses. Print had become an integral part of Western life.

The Advancement of Science

The Copernican Revolution

In Hellenistic times, the idea had been posited that the earth rotated round the sun, but this had not won general acceptance and in the sixteenth century it was still generally accepted that the heavenly bodies rotated around a stationary Earth. In 1543, however, the Polish scholar, Copernicus, published a book arguing the theory of heliocentric astronomy.

Copernicus' theory received little attention. During this time, however, Dutch craftsmen were experimenting with glass lenses. They made spectacles and also telescopes for use at sea. One of these telescopes fell into the hands of the Italian teacher, Galileo Galilei, and he turned the instrument towards the skies. By studying sun spots, the phases of Venus and the rings of Jupiter, he provided clear proof that Copernicus had been correct.

Galileo delayed publishing his findings because he recognized that they must arouse a storm of controversy. Authority, both of the Bible and of ancient authors, clearly supported a geocentric universe, and the church was still held to authority as the arbiter of truth. He published his findings in 1632, but, faced with the terror of the Inquisition, he recanted in 1633.

Descartes – the Turning Point

Tradition states that, after formally accepting that the Earth remained stationary, Galileo muttered 'it goes on moving'. Certainly the scientific impetus continued. In 1637, the French philosopher, Descartes, published *Discours de la Méthode*, which laid down what has become known as the Cartesian method. He argued that the experimental scientific process was the arbiter of truth. The pursuit of truth now involved breaking down knowledge into ever smaller areas of study. Medicine, for instance, became concerned with analysing the symptoms of disease in minute detail – arguably at the expense of a more integrated approach to the healing process.

In his dictum *Cogito ergo sum* – 'I think, therefore I am' – Descartes proclaimed the individualism that was to be the hallmark of modern European society. Western man had at last emerged from the shadow of past authorities, be they religious or classical. Personally a devout Catholic, Descartes rejected authority as an arbiter of faith and proclaimed that it had to be discovered through the human intellect. This was recognized as a fundamental challenge to the church, and Louis XIV personally ensured that Descartes was denied Christian burial.

Northern Europe

The condemnation of both Galileo and Descartes, and continued activities of the Inquisition placed scientists who lived in Catholic countries in an invidious position. In Protestant countries, scientists might meet hostility from those who defended religious authority, but they did not face persecution. The impetus for scientific innovation therefore passed to northern Europe.

The first Protestant scientist was the German, Kepler, who provided information on the movements of planets. Dutch scientists, continuing their work with lenses, developed the microscope. This opened up whole new areas of study in such fields as the biological sciences. In England, the cause of experimental science was argued by the Lord Chancellor, Francis Bacon, who had early visions of its potential. In 1628, William Harvey published his accurate theories on the circulation of the blood in his book *On the Motion of the Heart and the Blood in Animals*.

Advances in navigation, first in Holland, and then in France and, above all, in England, drove forward skills in cartography and geographical study. Progress in astronomy and in the construction of clocks were spin-offs from this navigational programme. Landsmen could now own clocks and watches that told the time with great accuracy. People began to organize their lives around them, and to treat the hours and minutes of the day with a new respect.

The revolution started by Copernicus was completed by Isaac Newton, who published his *Principia Mathematica* in 1687. While Galileo argued the structure of the universe, Newton demonstrated the gravitational mechanism by which it worked. In the words of the poet, Alexander Pope:

Nature and nature's laws lay hid in night:
God said, 'Let Newton be!' and all was light.

Until Newton's time, humans were the uncomprehending playthings of fate or divine providence. Now they began to understand that the everyday events of life were driven by a structure of causation. Later generations of scientists have maintained the process. Mendel worked out the structure of genetic inheritance, Darwin illustrated the mechanism evolution, Pasteur demonstrated the causes of disease, Crick and Watson unravelled the DNA code. These and many other insights make up the intellectual baggage of Western man.

Enlightenment to Romanticism

The Philosophes

The new enlightenment was to find its home in France, but the pattern of thinking owed much to seventeenth-century British writers, notably John Locke, who published his *Essay Concerning Human Understanding* in 1690. Locke said that many religious issues were beyond human knowledge, and he argued for tolerance and reliance on reason and reasonableness. His work reflected a wide change of mood, signalling the end of two centuries of religious strife; never again would the battle lines of Europe's terrible wars be drawn along religious lines.

The scientific advances of the seventeenth century encouraged philosophers of the following century to see the world as an ordered machine, much like one of the new clocks. There was an optimistic view that the universe was driven by a well-oiled logic, and, if people could only behave in a reasonable manner, the world's problems could be readily overcome. Past religious passions now appeared irrelevant. Many thinkers no longer saw God as an imminent cause of good or evil, but as a great watchmaker, an ultimate mover, who no longer had immediate relevance to life. The poet, Alexander Pope, himself a Catholic, again provided the aphorism of the age with the couplet;

> *Know then thyself; presume not God to scan;*
> *The proper study of mankind is man.*

The dominant personality among the *philosophes* was the Frenchman, Voltaire. He was a satirist, rather than an original thinker, and he turned his barbed pen on anything that he saw as repressive or pretentious. Voltaire had problems with the French authorities, but he and his circle sowed seeds of scepticism about the old order, which would have immense repercussions in the later years of the century.

Evangelicalism

The first reaction against the intellectual emphasis of the age came with a religious revival that developed in parallel in England and her North American colonies, both within and outside the Church of England. John Wesley set the emotional tone of the movement, sharply in contrast with the language of the *philosophes*, when he described how he 'felt his heart strangely warmed'. This new Protestantism appealed primarily not to authority, but to the conversion experience. Until then, the Protestant Churches had left missionary work almost entirely to the Catholic orders, but, by the end of the century, the worldwide tide of Protestant missions was beginning to flow, with incalculable, if often ambiguous, effects on non-European cultures.

Romanticism

If John Wesley represented the religious, Swiss-born philosopher, Jean Jacques Rousseau, led the secular reaction against Cartesian intellectualism. He proclaimed that man was pure when in the simple state, be that the uncorrupted form of a noble savage, or a newborn child. The quest for goodness therefore involved a return to nature. Rousseau, more than any other person, taught people to look on their environment as a place of beauty. Since the time of Hannibal, travellers had crossed the Alps, without pausing to recognize them as anything other than a barrier on the road to Italy. Now, as if overnight, Rousseau's Swiss mountains were discovered as majestic things of beauty.

As romanticism emphasized the emotions above the intellect, so it elevated the creative artist as the person most able to express those emotions. The great milestones of the movement, such as Wordsworth and Coleridge's *Lyrical Ballads*, Beethoven's *Eroica Symphony*, the late paintings of Turner, explored new forms and emotions. This could lead to excess, but it also opened the way to the achievements of those such as the French Impressionist painters and the great romantic composers.

Social Reform

At about the same time, first clearly surfacing in the 1770s, a transformation began to occur in attitudes to social issues. For centuries, Europeans had been shipping Africans to slavery with no apparent compunction. Now powerful antislavery movements made themselves heard in France, Denmark, England and other countries. Movements for the reform of vicious penal systems, the abolition of the 'hanging codes' and for the humane treatment of the insane can be dated to the same time. Educational reform also became a cause for the future.

Credit for this new mood of social reform has been given to the pen of Voltaire, the preaching of Wesley and the ideals of Rousseau. All played their part. In education, for instance, evangelical passion to bring truth to the poor led directly to the opening of so-called 'ragged schools' in England, while Rousseau was laying the foundations for the quite separate development of child-centred learning, which was carried forward by the Swiss educator, Pestalozzi. The cause of reform was uniquely in the air, and the traditional political structures were ill equipped to contain it. Europe was ready for the cataclysm of the French Revolution.

8

Revolution

The French Revolution

The Estates General

In 1776, the British government was faced with a major revolution in its American colonies (Chapter 11). King Louis XVI of France, recognizing this as an opportunity of regaining some of the ground lost in the Seven Years' War, involved France in the conflict. In military terms the intervention was successful; in financial terms it was a disaster. The French government, always in financial straits, was now unable to function. The shortfall could no longer be met by the time-honoured device of increasing taxes on the poor, but those able to pay could only be taxed with their own consent. Members of the aristocracy recognized an opportunity for winning concessions from the monarchy in return for money, and they insisted that Louis should recall the French parliament, the *Estates General*, which had not met for 150 years.

The body met in three separate houses – the House of Aristocracy, the House of Clergy and the Third Estate. This last house represented the property-owning middle classes and was largely made up of professional men. They had no vision of themselves as revolutionaries, but they were influenced by the ideas of the *philosophes* and of the American Declaration of Independence. Louis anticipated doing his business with the other two houses before disbanding the body, but the Third Estate had equal representation with the other two, and could count on considerable support in the House of Clergy. In the summer of 1789, the Third Estate declared that it constituted a National Assembly. Louis gave way before its demands and the body set about a huge programme of constitutional, administrative and social reform.

Popular Unrest

Since the time of the Frondes, French kings had been acutely aware of the dangers of uprisings among the poor, who remained unrepresented in the National Assembly. There was unrest in many parts of the countryside in 1789, but the most immediate danger came from the poor of Paris, who found themselves caught in a spiral of inflation, most crucially in the price of bread. By 14 July, it was estimated that only three days' supply remained in the storehouses of the capital.

The mob possessed armaments, but little ammunition. This lay under close guard in the royal castle of the Bastille. On 14 July, the mob stormed the Bastille, leaving Louis quite helpless. He could not use his army because the loyalty of rank and file soldiers was in doubt. Many of the aristocracy were now fleeing France and in June 1791 Louis and his family made their bid to escape. They were captured and brought back as prisoners to the capital. The National Assembly maintained the king as a figurehead until he signed the new constitution in September. The body then disbanded itself to make way for the new Legislative Assembly.

War and the Terror

Since the National Assembly had barred any of their number from seeking re-election, the new body was made up of inexperienced men. The dominant figures were Danton, who surrounded himself with members from the Gironde, in southern France, and the little lawyer, Robespierre, whose power was based on the Jacobin Club. Protagonists of the new order now felt under siege. The king could still serve as a focal point for a royalist counter-revolution, and both Austria and Prussia were issuing threats. Robespierre argued that peace should be preserved, but Danton believed that the nation could only be united by war. He urged his fellow countrymen to 'dare and dare and dare again', and Frenchmen responded to his cry that the *patrie* was in danger. In April 1792, France declared war on Austria, and Prussia came in on the side of Austria. Early news from the war was disastrous, and the capital was gripped in a fever. On 30 July, a contingent marched into the capital, singing the song that would become the national anthem. They demanded that Louis be dethroned and a republic proclaimed. The men of Marseilles were soon joined by a huge citizen army that, chanting the *Marseillaise*, threw itself on and routed mercenary enemy soldiers at Valmy on 20 September. Two days later, France was declared a republic. Louis was placed on trial in December and executed on 21 January 1793.

The citizens' army swept across the Netherlands and at last achieved the 'natural frontiers' that had been beyond the reach of the armies of Louis XIV. The victors proclaimed liberty and equality for the poor of all lands, but in practice all too often they laid new tax burdens on those same poor to pay for the cost of the war.

In February 1793, France faced a coalition of Britain, Austria, Prussia, Holland, Spain, Sardinia and Italian states. Action taken against the Catholic Church also provoked civil war in the conservative regions of the Vendée and Brittany. Effective power now passed from the Assembly to a Committee of Public Safety. In June, Danton's Gironde fell to Robespierre's Jacobins, and the period known as 'the Reign of Terror' began. Among the victims were successive waves of politicians, including both Danton and his Girondins, and Robespierre and the Jacobins. As a result, power passed to a new generation of second-rate men who did not command the respect of the nation.

Meanwhile, the French citizen army, now reinforced by the first use of conscription in modern times, was more than holding its own in the war. Britain, while formidable at sea, was poorly equipped for a land war and the old enemies, Prussia and Austria, failed to coordinate their effort. The French armies, now led by a new generation of generals, remained firmly entrenched on the Rhine.

The Empire

The rise of Napoleon

In May 1798, a French army led by the Corsican Napoleon Bonaparte was sent to invade Egypt in an attempt to cut British trade routes. Land victories were made worthless when the British fleet, commanded by Admiral Nelson, destroyed the French supply fleet, and so cut the army off from Europe. In August 1799, Napoleon abandoned his army and returned to France to challenge the discredited leaders of the nation. His gambler's throw succeeded and on 9 November he staged a coup d'état and assumed the title of First Consul. He set about centralizing power in his own hands; in 1802 he became consul for life, and in 1804, he followed the example of Charlemagne by crowning himself as Emperor Napoleon I. Any dismay at this negation of the ideals of the revolution was overwhelmed by the relief of ordinary Frenchmen at the return of ordered and firm government.

Imperial Government

Napoleon had a genius for administration. After an initial purge of remaining Jacobins, he set about healing old divisions and reuniting the country. He recognized that the continuing civil war in the Vendée could not be brought to an end unless the state came to terms with the Catholic Church, so the old religion was restored to its position as the national faith. He set about recruiting the ablest men into government, regardless of whether they held republican or royalist sympathies. Most enduringly, he personally supervised a detailed revision of the whole of the French legal system into the *Code Napoléon*. Had Napoleon been content to hold the Rhine frontier and bring sound administration to France, his rule could have been outstandingly successful. But he was by instinct a general and the symbolic identification with Charlemagne at his coronation illustrated his determination to build the greatest empire that the world had seen. 'I am destined to change the face of the world,' he declared. But Napoleon, like Louis XVI, discovered that wars could only be fought at a financial cost, which had to be passed on in taxes to the ordinary people of France and the conquered countries.

The Napoleonic Wars

The great struggles of previous centuries had achieved little more than change the line of a frontier here and there. In the three years from 1805, Napoleon completely redrew the map of Europe. He owed his success to the army that he had inherited from the Revolution. Opposing generals recognized that the citizens' armies of France were carried forward on a tide of national energy, which had been released by the Revolution. Napoleon added to this a military professionalism, identified with the magnificent Imperial Guard. The surge of victories carried the army across Europe as far as Bohemia, north into Scandinavia and south into Italy and Spain. Ancient rulers were replaced by members of the Bonaparte family or generals from the army. Even then, however, Britain, Spain and Russia remained as weak points in the French Continental System.

Giving priority to the invasion of Britain, Napoleon gathered barges at the Channel ports. Any hope of carrying out this operation, however, ended in 1805 when the French fleet was destroyed at the battle of Trafalgar. Britain therefore remained an implacable foe across the Channel.

The victorious French army in Spain found itself unable to overcome a fierce guerilla resistance that made full use of the broken terrain. The British despatched a force under the general who would later become the Duke of Wellington. In August 1812, after a relentless campaign, Wellington led his army into Madrid.

As Madrid fell, Napoleon was on the other side of Europe, leading 450,000 men on his disastrous campaign against Russia. He had already heavily defeated the Russian army and he believed that serfs would flock to join him once they heard that he had proclaimed their emancipation. He defeated the Russian army again at Borodino and marched on across the scorched countryside to occupy Moscow. But, when the Russians burned their own capital city around his army, and winter began to set in, he was forced to order the terrible retreat. In the end, only a tenth of his great army survived the ordeal. The Imperial Guard was reduced to some 400 men; 80,000 horses had died, leaving Napoleon with no effective cavalry to put in the field.

Defeats in Spain and Russia shattered the myth of invincibility and by 1814 Napoleon had lost everything. Paris fell on 30 March, and he abdicated his Imperial crown on 11 April. In France, however, loyalty to the deposed emperor remained strong, and, when he escaped from exile in 1815, men flocked to join his army. The 'Hundred Days' adventure ended when he was defeated by the combined British and Prussian armies at Waterloo on 18 June.

Napoleon passed the remainder of his life in well-guarded exile, but the Napoleonic legend lived on. As French power declined, people remembered that it was the Little Corporal who had led them to glory.

Reaction and Revolution

The Return of the Old Order

After the defeat of Napoleon, members of the old ruling houses moved back into their palaces. The statesmen met in Vienna to reorganize the continent. The Congress of Vienna took little account of nationalist aspirations. Poland was awarded to Russia; Venice and Lombardy to Austria; the Rhineland was taken from France and given to Prussia; the southern Netherlands were incorporated into Holland; Norway was made a part of Sweden.

The Austrian Prince Metternich was the main architect of this restoration of the old order. He fully recognized the huge changes in political consciousness brought about by the French Revolution, but he believed that these had to be suppressed, and that structures should return to return to their dynastic roots. He opposed all representative institutions, and established the Holy Alliance as a coalition of powers dedicated to suppress ideas of liberty and nationalism, wherever they might show themselves. Of the major powers, only Britain – itself, however imperfectly, a representative government – stood apart to uphold a more liberal tradition.

The policy of intervention was successfully invoked when the Spanish people rose in rebellion in 1820. Austria also put down rebellion in her Italian possessions. Metternich was wise enough to see himself as the defender of a dying way of life. In 1821, the people of Greece rose against their Turkish masters. True to his principles, Metternich gave Austrian support to the Ottoman Turks, but the rebels won backing from Russia and Britain and achieved their independence in 1830.

Also in 1830, the people of Paris rose again and replaced the conservative king with his more liberal cousin, Louis Philippe, and revolutions broke out in Poland and across Germany. In the same year, the Catholic Belgians rebelled against their Dutch masters. The conservative powers threatened to intervene, but Britain, in a gesture that would be called in 84 years later, guaranteed Belgian independence.

The Year of Revolutions

The unrest of 1830 was a prelude to the much greater upheavals of 1848. In January, rebellion broke out in Sicily. In February, the people of Paris drove Louis Philippe, now a figure of fun, into exile. In March, Venice, Parma, Milan and Sardinia all rose against Austria. As the year progressed, there was revolution in Poland and Hungary. Smaller German princes fell, most never to return. Uprisings in Berlin and Vienna even brought the powerful Prussian and Austrian states to the point of collapse, and the elderly Metternich had to follow Louis Philippe into exile.

The Hughes Capet French monarchy was finished for ever, and, after a period of civil war the French people turned again to the magic name of Napoleon, in the person of his nephew, Louis Napoleon. He followed family tradition by staging a coup d'état and assuming the title of Emperor Napoleon III. Across the rest of Europe, the ruling houses re-established control over their dominions.

New Nations

The Unification of Italy

A decade later, Camillo Cavour, a statesman in the Italian kingdom of Savoy, set about achieving by, political means, what had been beyond the powers of the revolutionaries. In 1858, he met with Napoleon III to discuss how Austrian rule might be ended and Italy unified under his king, Victor Emmanuel of Savoy. In 1859, French armies inflicted heavy defeats on the Austrians at Magenta and Solferino. In 1860, the popular soldier, Garibaldi, led 'the thousand' against the rulers of Sicily and Naples. He handed these territories over to Victor Emmanuel. For a time, Austria held on to Venice but the city fell in 1866. Finally the Papal States were brought into a united Italy in 1870. The political task was complete, but the new country faced formidable problems of poverty, and large numbers of people, particularly from the south, emigrated to find a better life.

The Unification of Germany

In 1862, Otto von Bismark, a nobleman of Junker descent, became the prime minister of Prussia. His first speech was ominous for the future of European peace. 'The great issues of our day cannot be solved by speeches and majority votes – but by blood and iron.' The German-speaking people were already showing a formidable potential, but to achieve it all they had to be united into a nation state. Only Austria or Prussia could be the focus of such a state. Bismark determined that it should be Prussia.

In 1864, the two powers collaborated to annex the German-speaking lands of Schleswig and Holstein from Denmark. Then, two years later, Prussia went to war with Austria. On 3 July 1866, the Habsburg army was devastatingly defeated at Sadowa. The Habsburg monarchy retained Austria, but Germany was now effectively united. In 1870, Germany went to war with France, and the Napoleonic legend was laid forever on the field of Sedan.

As Bismark's army occupied Paris, there could no longer be any doubt that Germany was the dominant power in continental Europe. The violent methods by which this had been achieved were no innovation in European politics. The new state was based on admirable organization. German cities were models of organization and sanitary efficiency. A state school place was provided for every child, and illiteracy rates became the lowest in the world. The poor, who until that time had emigrated in large numbers, now showed their confidence in the government of their country by staying at home, and by playing their part in constructing the impressive industrial base of the new nation.

9

A Changing World

The Infrastructure of Change

Population

The population of Europe had been growing relentlessly since the time of the Black Death. Demographers have argued why, for instance, the increase was particularly pronounced in the sixteenth century. It appears as though women started marrying younger, and therefore having a longer child bearing life. But this leaves unanswered the question why such a social change should have occurred. The eighteenth century again saw a steady population increase across western Europe, which predated the major medical advances of the following century. A modest alleviation of the harsh conditions of rural life, the improvement of the housing stock, and some advances in public health may all have contributed to a reduction in the death rate.

Rulers generally welcomed a rising population; it provided a larger manpower pool for the military, and increased the tax base of the nation. In 1798, however, an English clergyman, called Thomas Malthus, published his *Essay on Population*. The world, he argued, possesses limited resources. As population grows, so the most vulnerable – the poor – must inevitably experience disaster and hunger. Malthus' work was influential, but his warnings were not, in the short term, authenticated by events. The reason for this was that, at the same time that the population was increasing, Europe was experiencing a green revolution, which greatly increased the amount of food available to meet the growing demand.

The Second Agricultural Revolution

The first great change in farming practice came with the introduction of settled agriculture at the beginning of historical times (Chapter 1). Even in Babylonian cities, farming families had to produce a surplus to feed craftsmen, priests and warriors. By the beginning of the eighteenth century, little had changed. It is estimated that in England eight out of ten people still lived in the countryside and that, on average, one farming family had to keep one other family from the produce of its land. People still ate bread baked from their own wheat and drank beer brewed from their own barley. Animals, except for breeding stock were still slaughtered and salted down for the winter.

Once again, change originated in small, highly urbanized, seventeenth-century Holland. Dutch farms had to be more efficient than those of their larger neighbours, and major improvements were pioneered, particularly in the development of root vegetables, largely for animal winter feed, and in high-yield artificial grasses, such as alfalfa and lucerne.

In the eighteenth century, the English gentry, unlike their neighbours in France, lived on their estates and it became fashionable to take an interest in farming. George III set the tone by contributing articles to a farming journal. Some began to introduce the Dutch innovations on their estates. New crops and methods of rotation were introduced and selective breeding produced remarkable improvements in the quality of livestock.

These improvements could not be introduced without radical changes in the organization of the countryside. Improved agriculture could not be successfully introduced in the old communal fields, so enclosures, which had been taking place for two centuries, were given a new impetus. In the change from peasant holdings to larger farms, worked by landless labourers, many lost land and ancient rights. The production of food, however, became a much more efficient process. By the late eighteenth century, British farmers were in a position to support a huge increase in the nation's urban population.

Financial and Human Resources

Any major economic expansion needs to be built on a sound financial base. Britain's growing international trade brought prosperity, and her island position meant that wealth did not have to be dissipated on the maintenance of a large standing army. By the standards of the time, she also had a sophisticated and well-capitalized banking industry.

It is harder to establish a link between the skills required for technological advance and the social and educational structure of the day. Few of the innovators of the new age came from the conventional academic background, which had produced Isaac Newton; they were more typically self-taught, or the products of Scottish or dissenting education.

Economic Theory

In 1776, Adam Smith published *The Wealth of Nations*, which laid the basis of modern economics. He argued the benefits of competition in a free economy, against both state control and the abuses of monopoly powers. His arguments were influential both in government and business circles, initially in Britain and later in the United States and elsewhere.

The First Industrial Revolution

Iron and Coal

Since the time of the Hittites, iron working had been centred on the great forests. The charcoal used in the smelting process consumed large quantities of timber, which was also vital for building and naval supplies. Over the centuries, the forests receded to the more remote areas. By the end of the seventeenth century, Britain faced something of a crisis. In the fourteenth century, German craftsmen had learnt how to make cast iron, so that the metal could now be used to make a wider range of products, but there was an acute shortage of the wood needed to drive the blast furnaces.

Early in the eighteenth century, the Darby family of Shropshire finally solved the problem of how iron could be smelted from coal. As this technique became widely known, industry moved from the forests to the great coalfields that lie across Europe in a band from mid-Russia to Wales. Surface coal was soon exhausted and deep mines were sunk to exploit the seams. Iron goods could now be produced in bulk.

Steam Power

As early as Hellenistic times, it had been recognized in theory that steam could be used to drive an engine, but the technological basis was lacking. The need for pumps to drain the new deep mines made progress all the more essential. The Scottish engineer, James Watt, made the essential breakthrough when he separated the cylinder from the condenser. As a result, industry could now be liberated, not only from the forests, but also from the banks of fast flowing rivers.

Water Transport

Before the eighteenth century, land transport was rudimentary over most of Europe. Once again, the Dutch had pioneered the use of the canals, which drained their country for transporting loads. The French government also constructed the magnificent Canal du Midi, designed to prevent goods having to be carried around the coast of Spain. France also had a high quality road network, built by forced labour, but these, like those of the Romans, were built for military use.

In 1861 the Duke of Bridgwater opened a canal that linked his coal mine at Worsley with the growing town of Manchester. The potential for improved communications to lubricate economic growth was illustrated when the price of coal in Manchester fell immediately by a half. The great revolution occurred, however, when steam power was applied to locomotion. Here the initiative was taken in the United States, where inland waterways provided the essential communication links for the new nation. In 1807, Robert Fulton sailed the steamboat *Clermont* from New York to Albany in 32 hours – a journey that had previously taken four days. Two years later, steam power was applied to ocean navigation.

Railways

The world's first commercial railway was opened in Britain in 1825, between Stockton and Darlington. Huge sums of money were invested in railway building in many nations, but, despite massive construction programmes, especially in the United States and Germany, Britain retained her initial advantage. The age of cheap and rapid communication brought important social, as well as economic, change as the structure of society began to reflect the new mobility.

Cotton and the Factory System

There had long been a market for fine fabrics in western Europe. By the early eighteenth century a substantial silk industry had grown up in France, which reduced dependence on imports. At this time, cotton was still a luxury fabric and ready woven cloth was imported from India. Entrepreneurs then began to import raw cotton, which was put out for manufacture to domestic workers. Whole families worked immensely long hours at carding, spinning and weaving to earn a modest subsistence. The early machines were invented by enterprising craftsmen to help boost domestic output.

The first large spinning factory was built by Richard Arkwright at Cromford, near Derby, in 1771. By the early nineteenth century all the stages of cotton cloth production had been brought within the factory system. Britain, backed by her huge merchant marine, had established a dominant position in the world supply of textiles. One machine, tended by a woman or a girl, could now do the work of many domestic workers, and traditional producers, from Britain itself to India, lost their livelihood.

Despite being a closely guarded secret, the new technology was bound to become known. The United States was already showing itself a fertile ground for industrial development and a substantial industry grew up in New England.

Urban Growth

The population of Europe continued to grow rapidly throughout the nineteenth century, but the increase was now concentrated in the urban centres. In the nineteenth century, the population of London increased from about 900,000 to some 4.7 million, that of Paris from 600,000 to 3.6 million; small country towns turned into conurbations. This growth in Europe was matched by the comparable expansion of New York and the Midwestern cities of the United States.

The urban centres grew faster than their service infrastructure, and so the industrial revolution became identified with slum housing, malnutrition and cholera, on a scale that remains common in the burgeoning cities of modern developing countries. For most of the workers, however, the change from rural to urban poverty was not the disaster that has often been painted. The poor had always lived on the edge of subsistence; there were indeed reverses, as during the 'hungry forties', but the overall tendency was towards an improvement in living standards. Pasteur's discovery of the germ causation of disease stimulated major sewage and other sanitation projects in the second half of the century.

The Second Industrial Revolution

The Decline of Britain

Visitors to the Great Exhibition, which was held in London in 1851, would not have readily recognized that the age of British industrial supremacy was already nearing its end. Britain possessed half of the world's mileage of railway lines, and half of its merchant marine. Five years later, the British inventor, Henry Bessemer, would present his Convertor, which made possible the mass production of steel. The nation's lead still appeared unassailable.

In hindsight it is, however, possible to recognize the signs of decay. Too much investment lay in the industries of the first industrial revolution, which were vulnerable to competition from low cost countries; the educational system, both for the rich and poor, was ill equipped to provide training in the more technical skills needed to meet the ever-growing complexities of industry; British industry was already at times failing to capitalize on the skills of the inventors.

Germany and the United States

In the second half of the century, two powers demonstrated great economic potential. German military expenditure funded the expansion of the mighty firm of Alfred Krupp, which was soon competing with British companies for the supply of railway and shipyard equipment. The electric dynamo was invented simultaneously in Britain and Germany, but the German firm of Siemens reaped the benefits. In 1885, Carl Benz produced the first working automobile using the internal combustion engine, so initiating the greatest transport revolution in the world's history.

The United States was also showing both creativity and economic power. Inventive geniuses, like Bell and Edison, found that the young nation, with its growing market base, provided an ideal environment for the exploitation of new technology. The telegraph, the telephone, the domestic sewing machine, mechanized agricultural machines, the safety lift, air conditioning, the electric light, the phonograph, the cine camera and the aeroplane were all American contributions to the more sophisticated second phase of industrialization. Andrew Carnegie and Henry Ford also showed the American capacity to build great operations on the inventions of others.

Capital and Labour

Trades Unions

Throughout history, there had always been a sharp divide between the rich and the poor, but the working people within the new factory system became acutely aware of the polarization between those who owned the means of production and their employees. By gathering workers together in large units of production, the owners made it practicable for them to organize in defence of their living conditions.

Robert Owen, a working man turned successful cotton master, attempted to establish a model industrial society at New Lanark, Scotland; he introduced schools and all kinds of leisure activities for the working people, and still was able to show a profit for the mill. He became dissatisfied with this paternalistic approach and set up a cooperative venture in New Harmony in America. This proved less successful, and he returned to Britain, where he founded the ambitious Grand National Consolidated Trades Union. This was a bid to harness the power of the working people so that they could control the industries in which they worked. Owen's union failed, as did most of the early attempts to organize labour. Unskilled workers, faced by organized management, lacked credible bargaining power. Over much of Europe, they were further weakened by being divided between opposing Christian and socialist unions.

The battle between capital and labour could be seen in its rawest state in the United States. The owners mobilized city and state authorities and hired private armies to break strikes. Also there were as yet no antitrust laws to prevent employers from combining to achieve their objectives. The workers responded by organizing themselves into violent secret societies, like the Molly McGuires of the Pennsylvania coal mines. At Andrew Carnegie's Homestead works at Pittsburgh in 1892, the two sides confronted each other in a pitched battle.

At Homestead, as elsewhere, management emerged victorious because there was always unskilled 'blackleg' labour on hand to fill the jobs of those who went on strike. At the end of the century, however, there emerged a new generation of union leaders who recognized that progress could best be made by organizing the skilled labour that was now vital for the more sophisticated industries. In The United States, in 1886, Samuel Gompers organized these skilled trades into the more successful American Federation of Labour. In the years that followed, the rights of organized labour were increasingly recognized by the legal systems of the industrialized nations.

Socialism

During the time that Robert Owen was experimenting with new structures, continental thinkers were beginning to challenge the laissez-faire theories of Adam Smith. Most influential was the French nobleman, Claude de Saint-Simon, often looked on as the founder of socialism, who published his critique of the new industrial age in the 1820s. He argued for the replacement of the existing ruling elite by a 'meritocracy', which would manage the economy for the general good of the population, rather than for individual gain.

Saint-Simon's ideas gained ground in France. In 1848, Paris experienced two distinct revolutions. The first unseated the French king; the second was a bloody confrontation between workers, proclaiming the new socialists ideas, and the bourgeoisie, who defended traditional property rights.

Communism

Karl Marx watched the destruction of the Paris workers in 1848 with distress but without surprise. He had been associated with the revolutionary movement in his native Germany before being forced into exile. He believed that history showed two struggles. The first, as in all earlier revolutions, had been between the feudal authorities and the bourgeoisie. The second, in his own day, lay between the bourgeoisie and the proletariat.

Marx held that the value of goods lay in the labour that had been expended in their production, and the interests of the proletariat lay in winning a fair return for that labour. That was in conflict with the interests of the owners, or bourgeoisie, who were dedicated to achieving a profit on the product. Within a capitalist society the proletariat was therefore alienated from the production process, and both sides were inevitably locked in class war. The objective for the proletariat was to win control of the machinery of government by revolution, and then to use the new communist state to control the 'commanding heights of the economy' – land, transport, factories and banks.

Marx and his friends tried to gather the revolutionary movement into the unity without which he believed it could never be effective. In 1864, the First International meeting of the Communist party was held in London, with delegations from France, Germany, Italy, Switzerland and Poland, as well as Britain. The party, however, quickly showed its capacity for splitting into factions. When, by the beginning of the next century, none of the great industrial nations had fallen, many thought that the communist challenge had passed away. It was not anticipated that the revolution would come in Russia, which, under Marx's definition, still lay within the feudal stage of development.

Change and Society

Education

The movement for educational reform can be traced to the late eighteenth century, but another century had to pass before change affected the lives of working people. In Germany and the United States, and later in Japan, politicians recognized that, if a nation were to remain competitive in the new world, it needed an educated labour force. All across the industrial world there was a huge increase not only in basic education but also in the provision of higher education. Literacy and numeracy were at last seen as functional skills, rather than as the prerogative of a privileged élite.

The Women's Movement

Before the middle of the nineteenth century, individual voices had been raised to protest against the subjugation of women in Western society, but the origin of a formal movement can be placed in 1848, the year of revolutions. In that year, a group of women, with men supporters, met at Seneca Falls in New York State and laid out a programme that was to be the blueprint for the women's movement. The resolutions demanded voting rights, equality before the law, the right to hold property, justice in marriage, equal opportunity in education, free access to jobs and an end to the pervasive double standard in morality. The political struggle became identified with the names of Susan Anthony in the USA and later with the Pankhurst family in Britain. Many advances were made, particularly in educational provision, but the radical change came with the First World War. Women who undertook a wide range of men's work could no longer be denied basic rights.

Leisure

Towards the end of the century working hours began to be reduced and, perhaps for the first time in history, the less privileged found themselves with time for leisure activities. Virtually all the major sports that are popular across the world today were codified during these decades, and this happened mainly in Britain, where the industrial achievements brought the earliest benefits. By the beginning of the twentieth century, the bicycle and the railway excursion were giving urban dwellers a new sense of freedom. Many problems remained, but those who lived in the industrial societies experienced a genuine improvement in their quality of life. This improvement made the programmes of the revolutionaries less attractive than Karl Marx and his followers had anticipated.

10

America

The Birth of the United States

The Causes of Conflict

When the Seven Years' War ended in 1763 it appeared that Britain had achieved her aims in the New World. The French colonies in Canada had fallen under British rule and the stranglehold on the Thirteen Colonies by French forts on the River Ohio had been broken. Very shortly, however, it became clear that strains were building up in the relationships between the American colonists and the mother country.

Under the mercantilist system, it was taken for granted that the colonies existed for the benefit of the mother country. As American economies strengthened, however, they began to generate their own momentum. Slaving ships from New England, for instance, now competed directly with those from Bristol on the Guinea Coast.

The American colonists had already developed the westward momentum that remains a feature of the nation today. Pioneers were penetrating into the rich lands to the west of the Appalachians. Britain, as the colonizing power, was responsible for their security, and the London government therefore had to decide whether to expand its budgets to provide these pioneers with protection. To the annoyance of many colonists, a decision was taken that a limit should be drawn along the ridge of the Appalachians. The government further decided that the American colonies should be taxed to help pay security costs. When the traditional colonial assemblies refused to vote the funds, the British government decided to establish the principle of its right to impose direct taxation. The Stamp Act, the Sugar Act and the duty on tea were all stages in the deteriorating relationship. None were in themselves onerous, but they created genuine anxiety: sugar molasses, for instance, was turned into rum, which was the staple of the slave trade; and any tax could be used to make American ships uncompetitive with their British rivals.

War of Independence

Tension centred on the largest city and trading port of Boston, where fighting started in 1775. In the following year, representatives from the Thirteen Colonies, now to become states, met in Philadelphia to declare themselves independent. The famous and highly influential Declaration of Independence, drafted by Thomas Jefferson, justified the act of rebellion in terms that drew from Locke and the *philosophes*. It declared that government derives from the consent of the governed and the misgovernment, listed in detail, broke that tie of consent.

The colonists faced serious problems in organizing themselves to fight a major European power; there was little natural unity, and money to fund the conflict proved as hard to raise as it had been under British rule. American success was largely the result of the outstanding leadership qualities of George Washington and the ability of the colonists to adapt to a guerilla style of warfare, well suited to the heavily forested terrain. In 1781, the British army surrendered at Yorktown and two years later, Britain accepted defeat.

The Constitution

It was not immediately clear, however, whether one or thirteen new nations had emerged from the conflict. Many in Washington's army remained unpaid and no mechanism existed for a central government to raise money from the states. The Constitutional Convention of 1787 was faced with serious division between the interests of large and of small states, and between those who wanted to see a strong central government and those who preferred to see real power continue to lie with the individual states. The final document, which was ratified in 1788, steered a compromise course between the interests. The Executive, Legislature and Judiciary all had their own spheres of responsibility, and acted as a control on one another by a complex structure of checks and balances.

Canada

The successful rebellion by the American colonies left the British government reluctant to expend further effort and resources on colonization. Many loyalists from the south had moved north, and the division between the French and English population remained deep. The colonies covered much sparsely populated territory and communications remained poor. The people were united only in a common hostility to any threat of annexation by their more powerful neighbour to the south.

In the first half of the nineteenth century, progress was made towards the establishment of a confederacy. In 1867, the British North America Act brought together four provinces into a federal Dominion of Canada. To protect minority French interests, language and education remained provincial concerns and other provinces joined the federation in subsequent years. In 1885, the last rivet was driven into the Canadian Pacific Line, bringing together east and west and opening up the prairies for agricultural development.

Latin America

To the south, the countries of Latin America remained under the colonial control of Spain and Portugal. The successful rebellion of the British colonies was shortly followed by the collapse of the old monarchies in the face of Napoleon's army. Links with the old countries were cut during the European wars, and this generated an outburst of nationalist fervour.

Spain fought a series of devastating wars to recover control of her American empire. In 1810, the Mexican priest, Manuel Hidalgo y Costilla, led the poor in a rising, but independence was not finally won until 1821. Power then passed, not to the poor, but to the wealthy classes of Spanish descent. Rulers like Santa Anna treated the country as a personal *hacienda*, and the situation of the poor became, if anything, worse than it had been in colonial days.

In 1811, Venezuela declared its independence under the 'Great Liberator', Simon Bolivar. He had travelled in Europe and was particularly influenced by the writings of Voltaire, and he now saw himself as the George Washington who would bring unity to the Spanish-speaking countries of South America. He won a series of victories against Spain, and independence seemed assured, provided the conservative European powers did not follow Metternich's plan and intervene to uphold the old order. This was prevented by American President Monroe, who warned off any intervention by proclaiming his doctrine of 'hands off America'.

Bolivar seemed on the verge of creating a United Republic of Columbia, which could have become a power comparable to the USA. He was, however, unable to hold the new country together, and one part of the country after another broke off to form new nations. As in Mexico, the privileged classes preserved power for themselves. The European nations competed to invest, particularly in Argentina, and there was a steady stream of immigration from the Old World, but the old inequalities remained, and the economies of many of the new Latin American countries became dangerously dependent on single primary products.

The path to independence was smoother in Brazil. The Portuguese royal family decided not to defend its rights and in 1822 the country was declared an independent empire by consent. Here, too, old social inequalities remained and, as late as 1888, Brazil was the last American country to abolish the Atlantic slave trade.

Slavery and the American Civil War

King Cotton

Dr Samuel Johnson spoke for many when he poured scorn on the American ideals of liberty which were denied to the black slave population. The continuance of the institution of slavery was one of the issues discussed in the Constitutional Convention. There were three broad points of view: opponents of slavery wished to see the institution outlawed in the new nation; representatives of the southern states would not contemplate joining a union that deprived them of their property; moderates, like Washington himself, opposed slavery, but they believed that they could let history take its course. Slavery, they argued, was outdated and it would wither away of its own accord. Events proved them wrong.

The new English cotton mills created an insatiable demand for raw cotton. The native short staple cotton was an uneconomic crop until in 1793 Eli Whitney invented a gin that enabled it to be cleaned in large quantities. In the decades that followed huge areas of the south were given over to cotton cultivation. This created a demand for slaves. The Atlantic slave trade was declared illegal, but many were smuggled into the country; others were 'sold down the river' by plantation owners from the more northerly slave states.

This resurgence of slavery led to widespread unrest. Slave risings broke out and an increasing number of slaves used the freedom road to escape north. White and black activists combined in a highly organized antislavery movement. Anger rose when, in 1850, Congress passed the Fugitive Slave Law, which gave southern owners the right to pursue their property into the free northern states.

Slave and Free States

The House of Representatives, elected by population, was dominated by the free states. The Senate was more finely balanced. As new states were added to the Union, the balance was maintained. California and Oregon tilted the balance towards the free states. 'Bleeding' Kansas, a fierce bone of contention, fell to the slave party. When, in 1860, a republican from Illinois called Abraham Lincoln was elected president, the slave states felt that the political balance had swung irretrievably against them. In March 1861, eleven southern states declared their secession from the Union and the following month they attacked the federal Fort Sumter.

The Civil War

Over six hundred thousand men died in the four years of war that followed. The southern armies were highly motivated and generally well commanded, but they were bound to lose a long war of attrition. The industrial north had a larger population, more industrial production and more miles of railway. This was the first major war in history fought with armaments that were the products of the industrial revolution, and great battles, like Antietam and Gettysburg presaged the terrible loss of life at Verdun and on the Somme half a century later. When the war ended in April 1865, the south lay devastated. Lincoln was assassinated five days later.

Civil Rights

The war had been fought over the right of the south to secede from the Union. Slavery was abolished in the process. Lincoln's Emancipation Proclamation was given the force of law by the Thirteenth Amendment of 1865, and further amendments wrote civil rights into the American Constitution. In the years of reconstruction, black legislators took their seats, and it appeared as though political and social equality might be close. Gradually, however, by a process of manipulation and terrorization, the white supremacists regained control of the southern states. The liberal fervour of the antislavery years was now spent, and the Supreme Court proved unwilling to uphold even the most clearly defined constitutional rights. Disillusioned, many blacks migrated to the booming industrial cities of the north, where they encountered new forms of discrimination.

The situation only began to improve with the great Civil Rights Movement of the 1960s, when Dr Martin Luther King provided a rallying point for his people's aspirations and liberal white sympathizers were again mobilized, as they had been a century before in the antislavery campaign.

The Westward Movement

Thomas Jefferson

Of all the founding fathers, Jefferson had the clearest vision that the new nation could become a great power and that this had to be based on an exploitation of the great potential of the continent. He was the architect of the system whereby new states could be added to the Union. By 1803, Napoleon had decided that the Mississippi lands of Louisiana, which remained French, were of no value, and Jefferson, now president, negotiated to buy them for $15,000,000 – and in doing so doubled the land area of the United States. In 1804, he sent out an expedition led by Lewis and Clark to cross the continent and report back on its potential.

Jefferson's vision of the west as a land of opportunity gradually captured the American imagination. It was argued that the American people – by which was meant the white American people – had a 'manifest destiny' to possess the continent from the Atlantic Ocean to the Pacific Ocean.

The Dispossession of the American Indian People

During the early years of the nineteenth century, Americans of European origin were pushing into traditional Indian territory beyond the Appalachians. Every expedient was used, from purchase to forced expulsion, to drive the Indian people back into the western grasslands, which remained unattractive to white settlers.

The nomadic buffalo culture of the plains Indians was based on horses originally acquired from the southern Spanish settlements, and it was therefore a comparatively recent development. In the middle of the century, migrants were attracted, not to the featureless plains with their extremes of climate, but to the far west. For a brief period, wagon trains and nomadic Indians were able to coexist. By the 1870s, however, the white settlers began to move into these last hunting grounds. The buffalo were hunted to deprive the Indian people of their livelihood and to provide food for railway construction workers; then the railway link with the eastern markets made the grasslands attractive for cattle farming. Finally new agricultural machinery and irrigation techniques made large-scale wheat farming economic. With the buffalo herds destroyed, and their whole way of life undermined, the surviving Indian people were driven back into ever more arid and infertile reservations.

Oregon Country

Lewis and Clark reported on fertile land on the Pacific coast around the mouth of the River Columbia. Many Americans were prepared to go to war with Britain over British Columbia, but agreement was reached on the 49th parallel boundary. This left ample scope for colonization in the northwest. The wagon trains that followed the Oregon trail brought farming families into this attractive region.

The Southwest

The new Mexican state claimed the whole of the southwest of the country, from Texas to California and as far north as Utah and southern Wyoming. Spanish settlement had been based on missions, which were often widely dispersed, and the non-Indian population of the region remained low. Between 1846 and 1848 the United States and Mexico were in an intermittent state of war, which ended with the capture of Mexico City and defeat for Mexico. Under the Treaty of Guadalupe Hidalgo (1848), the United States won the whole of the southwest. The existing property rights of the Spanish-speaking people were, in theory, protected, but, in practice, they had no means of protecting them against the newly arrived 'Anglos', who controlled the courts.

Shortly before the treaty was signed, gold was discovered at Sutter's Mill in northern California. This set off the Gold Rush, which brought fortune hunters flocking to California from the east, and, indeed, from many parts of the world. The influx of population in turn created a farming boom and California was rapidly converted from a thinly populated region, largely consisting of mountains and desert, to the world's most rapidly expanding economy.

Immigration

From Europe

Any measurement of the population rise of Europe from the middle of the eighteenth to the end of the nineteenth centuries should properly include, not only statistics on those countries themselves, but also of the millions who emigrated to destinations in many parts of the world – as well as their descendants. Figures cannot be collated, but people of European stock took over great areas of the world, often at the expense of the indigenous population.

In order to overcome human reluctance to disrupt living patterns, there needs to be a 'push factor' propelling people from their homes, and a 'pull factor' drawing them to a new environment. As in the early years of colonization, the growing wealth of the United States drew economic, political and religious refugees from Europe. The British still came. Many of the Mormons who pulled their handcarts across the plains to Utah originated from among the cotton mills of Lancashire. The depopulation of the Scottish glens provided a new stream, although most preferred to go to Canada. The Catholic Irish, angered by English Protestant rule and by unjust land laws had long been ready recruits; the disastrous potato famine of 1845–46, which is estimated to have claimed the lives of a million people, turned the stream into a flood.

People now came from new countries of origin. Norwegian families, long accustomed to extremes of climate, left their marginal fiord farms to farm in the harsh environment of Wisconsin and the Dakotas. Germans fled from the political and social upheavals of their country. Peasants from southern Italy, condemned to live on the brink of subsistence under rapacious landlords, took the boat to America. Towards the end of the century, people were coming from further east. Russian Jews fled the pogroms; Poles fled Russian oppression. All funnelled through Ellis Island to emerge, often penniless, and speaking no English, onto the streets of New York. They worked as they could, in clothing sweatshops, on construction, in domestic service. Each new national group faced discrimination as those who were settled in jobs and homes tried to protect their position from the work-hungry newcomers.

The New Immigration

The capture of the southwest brought a significant Spanish-speaking population within the United States. Civil war in Mexico and an increasing divergency of the standards of living brought an increasing number of immigrants across the border. Most came as migrant workers, following the crops into California and far beyond. In good times, they were welcomed as cheap labour, but in times of depression they proved easy targets for discrimination. In the twentieth century, immigrants from Puerto Rico and other Caribbean islands increased the Hispanic population of the eastern side of the country.

Asian immigration began when Chinese labourers were recruited to work in the 1849 Gold Rush. Distinctive in those early days in their 'queues' and national clothing, they found themselves at the bottom of the immigrant 'heap', increasingly shut out from desirable employment and property ownership by Chinese Exclusion Acts. They, like subsequent Asian immigrants, preserved a respect for education, which enabled them to improve their status rapidly when the legal discrimination was brought to an end.

The United States Abroad

The Continent

The Monroe Doctrine was originally proclaimed to protect emerging Latin nations seeking to establish independence from European colonial powers. In the later years of the century it was used to promote the continent as a sphere of US interest.

One major thrust lay through the Caribbean towards South America. In 1903, effective control over the Isthmus of Panama was wrested from Columbia and the Panama Canal linking the two oceans was opened in 1914. War with Spain in 1898 ended with the acquisition of Puerto Rico and Cuba.

American interests also led expansion across the Pacific. Alaska was purchased from Russia in 1867, providing the westward bridge of the Aleutian Islands. Midway Island was won in the same year, followed by Samoa and the Hawaiian group. The war with Spain finally brought Guam and the Philippines within the American empire.

Although the United States was no longer a new country, the need to absorb waves of immigrants fostered an introversion and at times an aggressive nationalism. Many American statesmen, wishing to distance their country from what they saw as the destructive quarrels of the old world, proclaimed a policy of isolationism. The history of the twentieth century and the twenty-first century was to show that the world's greatest power could not successfully stand back from international events.

11

The Age of Imperialism

India

The East India Company

The battles in the eighteenth century between rival trading companies were fought, not to win territory, but to establish trading advantage. In 1757, however, the British East India Company's army in Bengal first captured the French trading station, and then defeated the Nawab's army, at Plassey. The Company then found itself, by default, the inheritor of Mughal power. Now irretrievably involved in politics, it gradually extended its control over large areas of the subcontinent.

Company officials never lost sight of the fact that their objective was to turn in a profit. As the Company extended its control over all internal as well as external trade, the standard of living of many Indians declined. Company officials took the opportunity of amassing private fortunes, often by corrupt means. In the days before steamships and the opening of the Suez Canal, India was far distant from home. Men travelled out as bachelors and many took local women and lived much as Indian princes.

The writings of Adam Smith had discredited the old mercantilist ideas that had been the justification for early colonization, and after the American revolution the British government was reluctant to become involved in further colonial expansion. To bring the East India Company under control it assumed dual control of its Indian possessions in 1784. In line with prevailing doctrines of free trade, the Company therefore lost its monopoly trading rights and was reduced to an administrative organization.

Modernization

The evangelical fervour of the age brought Protestant missionaries of many denominations to the subcontinent. Most had a simple desire to replace the traditional religions of Hinduism and Islam. They started schools that offered Western education and encouraged converts to adopt Western dress and habits. These missionaries looked to the Christian rulers of India for protection and active encouragement.

The new generation of administrators was less directly motivated by the profit motive and more by a desire to bring the benefits of modern life to the people of India. Many had a genuine, albeit paternalistic, respect for Indian culture, and they resisted the missionaries' attempt to overturn traditional ways. These administrators did, however, believe in reform. Laws, based on Western practice, were introduced to stamp out traditional practices, such as the burning alive of widows and the killing of infant girls. The products of the industrial revolution, such as the electric telegraph and railways, were also enthusiastically introduced.

The Mutiny

The modernization programme inevitably created tension. Railways, for instance, were looked upon as a threat to the caste system. There was also powerful resentment against British acquisition of new land, particularly in the northern Muslim province of Oudh. The introduction of a new form of greased cartridge, smeared with animal fat, was the immediate cause of the Indian Mutiny of 1857. This was as much a traditionalist reaction against modernization as it was a rebellion against the ever-expanding foreign rule. Many educated Indians, like the operators of the Delhi telegraph, died at the hands of the mutineers. The mutiny was put down with as much ferocity as it had been waged. The British parliament at last accepted direct responsibility for government. In 1877, Queen Victoria was proclaimed Empress of India and her rule over India became the symbol of British power and imperialism.

The Raj

The new rulers determined that the mistakes that had led to the mutiny should not be repeated. They therefore took care to respect the rights of the traditional ruling class. When early representative institutions were introduced, this ruling class was called upon to represent the Indian people. The aspirations of the rising intelligentsia were therefore overlooked. Indeed, the contempt for the educated 'Westernized native', which was to be characteristic of British imperialism, was first shown in India. The first meeting of the Indian National Congress was held in Bombay in 1885, but a further 20 years would pass before independence appeared on the Congress agenda.

Throughout history, India, like China, had shown a capacity to absorb its conquerors; the British alone resisted assimilation. The new rulers of the Indian Civil Service were drawn from the élite and many acquired a knowledge of Indian language and customs, but, in the wake of the Mutiny, a barrier existed between the two races that could not be crossed. Fast and comfortable steamships now linked Europe and India, and the journey time was much reduced when the Suez Canal opened in 1869. Administrators and traders increasingly kept their roots in Britain, while serving tours of duty overseas. Also men were now joined in India by their womenfolk. Few of these *memsahibs* had work that brought them into contact with Indian people, so their cultural values were never seriously challenged.

In the second half of the century new concepts of racial superiority were fashionable, particularly in northern Europe. Europeans had long treated other races as inferior, but they had not theorized about it. Now concepts of racial superiority were becoming fashionable, partly based on popular Darwinism. The European rulers of India, as of other colonized people, were therefore ill equipped to understand nationalist aspirations when they did come to the surface.

China

The Manchu Empire

In the middle of the seventeenth century, invaders from Manchuria overthrew the Ming emperor and established the foreign Manchu (Ch'ing) Dynasty. Following the ancient pattern, the early rulers were able men, who established a working relationship with the mandarin administrators, and for more than a century the land experienced one of its more prosperous periods.

By the end of the eighteenth century, however, problems were growing. It is estimated that the population trebled, from 100 to 300 million between 1650 and 1800, and it would reach 420 million by 1850. In China, Malthus' forecasts on the effects of population growth proved accurate. All available land was already under cultivation, so production could not match increased demand. The situation became disastrous in the terrible northern famine of 1887–89, when some ten million people starved to death. As social problems became worse, so the quality of Imperial government deteriorated into corruption and mismanagement. Resentment boiled and people remembered that the Manchu were a foreign race.

In 1786 rebellion broke out in Shantung, and this was followed in 1795 by the White Lotus Uprising on the borders of Szechwan and Shensi. These were the preludes of a century of peasant unrest on a scale far beyond anything experienced in human history before that time. It is estimated, for instance, that more people died in the T'ai-p'ing Rebellion of 1851–64 than in the whole of the First World War, while huge Islamic risings of the north and southwest left wide areas of the country devastated. The Manchu Dynasty, however, managed to cling to power through all these upheavals.

China and the West

Since the earliest times, China had always had a favourable balance of trade with Europe. There was a demand in the West for porcelain and silks, but, apart from a few clocks and toys, Europe had little to offer in return. Towards the end of the eighteenth century the balance took a turn for the worse. There was a fashion in Europe for Chinoiserie, reflected in some of the art of the period. More important, tea became the staple drink of many Europeans. This could only be bought by a steady drain of silver bullion.

Western merchants were convinced a huge Chinese market, was waiting to be opened up, but contact was strictly controlled through a few merchants in Canton. Attempts to open the market ended in frustration. In 1793, George III of Britain sent an emissary to the Manchu court with gifts. Emperor Qianlong thanked King George for his 'submissive loyalty in sending this tribute mission' from 'the lonely remoteness of your island, cut off from the world by intervening wastes of sea', but the mission achieved nothing of substance.

The Opium Wars

In the early years of the nineteenth century, British traders found that the drug, opium, could right the adverse balance of trade and reverse the flow of silver bullion into China. A great deal of Indian farmland was placed under the crop and the harvested drug shipped to China by British traders. Apart from the direct damage done by the opium, the opium trade was a breach of Chinese law and in 1839 a large quantity was destroyed. In the First Opium War that followed, the Chinese forces proved ill equipped to fight a modern war, and they were defeated. In 1842, the Treaty of Nanjing forced China to open up to foreign trade and missions, and Britain won control of the trading outpost of Hong Kong.

Thirteen years later, the British prime minister, Lord Palmerston, decided to assert British authority once again. His declared policy that half-civilized governments, such as China, 'all need a dressing down every eight or ten years to keep them in order' made him popular at home. He was prepared to defend British citizens against the valid operation of foreign law and in 1856 he defied parliament to take Britain, with French help, to war with China again. The Imperial army was weakened by the T'ai-p'ing Rebellion and in 1860 the allied army marched into Peking and burned the Imperial Palace.

European Influence and Reaction

Although China herself remained nominally independent, her influence in Asia was much reduced. Russia used the British and French invasion as a cover for occupying the northern Amur river, so winning the Pacific outlet of Vladivostok; Britain won Burma, against fierce local opposition; France defeated Chinese armies to win Indo-China; Korea won its independence, only to fall later to Japan; Japan conquered Taiwan; even the United States closed in by conquering the Philippines, again in the face of fierce nationalist resistance. Within China itself, the European powers jockeyed for privileges. Even more of a threat to China, the country was now open to Western missionaries who, along with the Christian gospel, brought cultural assumptions profoundly at odds with traditional Confucian values.

The End of the Manchu Empire

By the last years of the nineteenth century, the ancient civilization of China was beginning to collapse. In 1898, the young emperor and his advisers decided that China must follow the Japanese example and adopt Western ways. The experiment was short lived as the dowager empress led the faction of reaction. She imprisoned the emperor and gave support to the xenophobic Boxers, who were busy attacking mission stations and other Western interests across the country. When the embassy area of Peking was besieged, the Western powers replied by sending a combined army to relieve the city. Still the Manchu rulers clung to power, but they were threatened from two directions. The army warlords were now unreliable, and, outside the country, young foreign educated men plotted to overthrow the dynasty; in 1911–12 the two combined to bring down the Manchu Dynasty. The foreign educated Sun Yat-sen became president, but one year later he gave way to one of the country's military commanders.

Japan

The Tokugawa Shogunate

In 1603, at a time when the Imperial family had lost effective power, the military leader, or shogun, Tokugawa Ieyasu, established power over the whole of Japan. In the centuries that followed, the Tokugawa shogunate closed Japan off from the outside world. The Japanese were prohibited from travelling abroad; Jesuit missionaries were expelled and their converts persecuted; only a few Dutch traders were allowed to operate from the city of Nagasaki. For Japanese urban entrepreneurs, however, the cost was a small price to pay for the peace and prosperity brought by the powerful shoguns. Educational reforms created a high level of literacy and a vigorous free enterprise economy was permitted to flourish in the growing towns. The growing prosperity of the towns was not matched in the countryside, where both the traditional lords, and the peasants were becoming poorer.

The Opening of Japan

In 1854, US navy officer, Matthew Perry, was commissioned by the president of the USA to open up the Japanese market. His Treaty of Kanagawa brought the years of isolation to an end. The Tokugawa shogunate did not long survive it, and the young Emperor Meiji assumed direct power in 1868. There was now a fierce debate within Japan as to whether the country should adopt Western ways wholeheartedly, or follow the example of China and remain separate. The reformers were able to point to the disastrous results of conservative policies, as applied in China. The largest feudal families voluntarily surrendered their rights and the government systematically set about the modernization of their country. The changes were based on the solid structure bequeathed by the Tokugawa shogunate, but there remains no example in history of a comparable change in social life within a single generation. By 1900 an advanced system of state education had been constructed, Western experts were imported to train the people in engineering, and young Japanese students were sent to study overseas. At first the new industries, like textiles and shipbuilding, were faithful copies of Western prototypes, but they gained an increasing share in world markets. By the 1920s, Japan was a formidable industrial competitor to the European nations.

Japanese Expansionism

The era of peace had left the samurai caste deprived of employment. They bequeathed an aggressive nationalism to the new state. The Japanese also recognized that European world domination had been based on the use of force. The now popular motto 'Asia for the Asians' was intended as a Monroe Doctrine for a Japanese sphere of influence.

Russian power was particularly menacing. The transcontinental railway had now reached Vladivostok, and the Russians were showing interest in the newly independent Korea. In 1902, Japan concluded a treaty with Britain, which provided security against intervention and two years later she attacked Russian shipping in the Manchurian Port Arthur. The city fell in January of the next year and the Russian Baltic fleet was destroyed in the Tsushima Straits in May.

This victory of an Asian over an essentially European power in the Russo-Japanese War marked the end of the European military domination of the world that had survived since the fifteenth century. In the years that followed, Japan continued to build an empire, first by the annexation of Korea and then by the acquisition of wide tracts of Chinese land. These conquests were accepted as a *fait accompli* by the European powers at the Treaty of Versailles in 1919.

The Pacific

The Aborigines of Australia

Over 50,000 years ago, great ice caps in the polar regions made the world's seas lower than they are today. The Indonesian islands formed a great peninsula, and Australia was joined to Tasmania and New Guinea in a single land mass. At this time the ancestors of the Australian aborigines arrived in their isolated home. Despite the lower waters, they had still crossed a wide stretch of ocean, making them possibly the world's first seafaring people. These early settlers brought their dogs, but the animals already existing in Australia would have provided a strange sight to people accustomed to the fauna of Asia. In their new home, they adopted a hunter-gatherer lifestyle, delicately in balance with their unique environment.

The Polynesians

Much later, some three to four thousand years ago, a different race of people began to spread out across the islands of the Pacific Ocean. The methods by which they navigated their great canoes are little understood; they probably followed the paths of migrating birds, and it is suggested that they could feel the current off distant land masses on the surface of the water with their hands. Certainly they made successful voyages of up to 2000 miles to colonize unknown islands. It appears that they went via Fiji and Samoa to the remote Marquesas Islands, from where they fanned out, north to Hawaii, southeast to Easter Island and southwest to New Zealand, which they called Ao-te-roa, or Long White Cloud. The earliest settlers were probably fleeing from war, but in time warfare followed them to their new homes.

The Arrival of the Europeans

Australian aborigines and Polynesian islanders alike were long protected from European ships by unfavourable trade winds. In the seventeenth century, several Dutch sailors, operating from the East Indies, made voyages in the area, but they were not attracted by what they saw as the region offered no prospect of profitable trade. In 1770, the English Captain James Cook sailed along the east coast of Australia and landed at Botany Bay. He later commanded two more voyages through the Pacific Islands. The sailors found the Pacific island societies to be living examples of the 'noble savage' existence – as extolled by writers such as Rousseau – and bequeathed the devastations of syphilis to the islanders.

Australia

The Penal Colony

The war with the American colonies shut Britain off from the penal colonies of Georgia and the Carolinas, and so posed the British government with the problem of how to dispose of its surplus criminal population. As long as the war was in progress, convicts were kept in hulks moored in river estuaries.

One of those who had landed off Captain Cook's ship in Botany Bay was a geographer and scientist called Joseph Banks. In the years that followed, he had become the driving force behind an exploration movement, intended to open new areas of the world to British trade. Banks argued the case for establishing a penal colony in Botany Bay. The land was good, he argued, the climate mild and the natives few in number.

The first convoy sailed in 1787, under the command of Captain Arthur Phillip, with 571 male and 159 female convicts, supervised by over 200 marines. Most of those transported were hard-core criminals, but there were also a significant number of political prisoners, particularly from a rebellious Ireland. Large numbers of enforced immigrants suffered dreadfully on the long journey and in the penal settlements, and many continued to nurse resentment against the 'old country' and the forces of law and order.

Exploration

By the end of the century, it was established that New South Wales in the east and New Holland (an early name for Australia and then Western Australia) in the west lay within a single continent. In 1813, pioneers crossed the Great Dividing Range, which hemmed in the eastern coastal plain, to discover the broad grasslands of the interior. By 1859, the landmass of the continent had been divided into six colonies.

It is said that when these first white men appeared on the central plain, an aborigine scrambled into a tree and let out a long, high-pitched shriek. The establishment of European civilization in Australia was an immense achievement, but, yet again, a heavy price would be paid by the indigenous people in the age-old clash of interests between nomadic hunter-gatherers and settled agriculturalists.

Economic Growth

The earliest settlers did not readily find cash crops to make the colony self-sufficient. Lieutenant John Macarthur is credited with recognizing the immense potential of the interior for sheep farming. He developed new breeds that would flourish in the New South Wales grasslands and he was able to live in the style of an English country gentleman. His example was followed by emancipated convicts and a new generation of free settlers. The influx of cheap Australian wool to England stimulated the Yorkshire woollen industry at a time when woollen fabrics were gaining popularity in world markets. Towards the end of the nineteenth century, the development of refrigerated ships boosted the meat trade. Then, in the early years of the twentieth century, strains of wheat were developed to suit the dry climate.

Early on, it was also established that the Australian continent possessed great mineral wealth. Gold and copper mines were in operation by the middle of the nineteenth century, and the great Broken Hills complex was opened up in 1883. Despite such development in the interior, the country's cities proved to be the main beneficiaries. By 1901, 65 per cent of the population lived in the six capital cities.

Political Development

Progress with self-government in Canada encouraged the British government to devolve increasing political responsibility to its colonies. In 1901, the six Australian colonies became states to form the Commonwealth of Australia and the constitution of Australia came into being. Old links proved decisive when Australian soldiers fought with the British army in the wars of the twentieth century.

During the Second World War, however, Australia's leaders, recognizing that Britain could contribute little against an expansionist Japan, turned to the United States for support. Since then, extensive non-British immigration into Australia, and the increasing orientation of Britain towards Europe has further weakened traditional ties.

New Zealand

European Settlement

In 1814, a group of missionaries arrived in the land that had been described by Captain Cook. It is estimated that at that time there was a population of about a quarter of a million Maori people, who had lived in complete isolation for many centuries. In 1839, Edward Gibbon Wakefield established the New Zealand Association, with a view to buying land from the tribes and organizing settlements. The British government, hoping to control the movement, formally annexed the country in the following year.

The British proclaimed equality between Maori and European people, but practice never matched theory, and the colonists' land hunger provoked the Land War of 1845–48. After further settlers arrived, many from Scotland, war broke out again in the 1860s. By 1870, the Maori people had effectively lost control of their land.

Constitution and Economy

The country was granted a constitution in 1852 and became a self-governing dominion within the British Empire in 1907. Its dependence on agriculture, however, left it heavily dependent on the British economy. Early prosperity was based on wool and gold, but the introduction of refrigerated shipping in the last years of the nineteenth century favoured low-cost New Zealand farmers. Ties with Britain weakened in the second half of the twentieth century when migration patterns changed, and with most incomers coming from Asia and Pacific island states, New Zealand began to develop new markets closer to home, notable in Australia, the US and Japan and to play a more active role in Pacific affairs.

Japan and The United States

By 1914, Britain was withdrawing from direct involvement in the Pacific region but neither the emerging Australia or New Zealand were showing potential as a regional power. The Dutch still controlled the East Indies (modern Indonesia) but only at the cost of a series of major struggles against an emerging nationalism on Bali, Sumatra, and Java. Two powers now faced each other: the United States, with forward bases in Samoa, Guam and the Philippines, and the emerging power of Japan. The foundations of a major regional conflict were already laid.

North Africa

Egypt

In classical times, North Africa had been an integral part of Mediterranean civilization. After the early flowering of Islamic civilization, however, it became increasingly cut off from the countries on the northern, Christian shore of the inland sea. Egypt was for centuries isolated under Mameluke rule. When Napoleon led an army into Egypt in 1798, he took with him not only fighting men, but also scholars, who would be able to interpret the remains of the country's fabled ancient civilization.

French interest in the area survived the fall of Napoleon, and, when Muhammad Ali broke the power of the Mamelukes and established effective independence from Ottoman rule, French influence remained powerful. Under Muhammad Ali and his grandson, Ishmael, Egyptian power was taken south into the Sudan and along the Red Sea. Ishmael contracted with France for the construction of the Suez Canal, which was opened in 1869. He staved off financial collapse, however, by selling a controlling interest in the canal to Britain, who now controlled this lifeline to India. In 1881, the Egyptian government was threatened by a nationalist rising in Egypt and by the Mahdi in the Sudan, and Britain responded by sending a force to protect the canal. It was not intended as an army of occupation, but Britain became involved in a protracted war in the Sudan and in administering a protectorate over Egypt.

Algeria

The coast of Algeria to the west had long been the home of Barbary pirates. In the 1830s, France began a major advance into the area. The pirates were driven from their harbours, and the French moved south to the Atlas Mountains. Here they met fierce resistance, led by Abd al-Kadir, but they won control of the mountain passes. French military success was followed by an influx of French settlers into the coastal region.

Sub-Saharan Africa

An Unknown Continent

For centuries the interior of Africa had been viewed by the outside world as little more than a source of human merchandise. European merchants had shipped slaves by the million out of the west coast. Bedu and Tuareg tribesmen had driven them across the Sahara to the markets of North Africa; they had been carried across the Red Sea in dhows by Arab traders; they had been beaten into submission by Dutch settlers in the south. The slave trade had had a profoundly brutalizing effect on African life, far beyond the boundaries of foreign exploration.

Yet in the early nineteenth century, Africa had its own political movements. In the grasslands in the centre of northwestern Africa, an aggressive Islam was expanding in Hausaland under the Fulani Usman dan Fodio, and in Fouta Djallon, under El Hadj Umar Tall. In the south, the Bantu people were experiencing a period of unrest when Shaka founded the Zulu kingdom in 1818 and set neighbouring people on the move.

European Explorers and Missionaries

In the early days of the industrial revolution, there was a general view, vigorously fostered by Joseph Banks, that Africa was a land of unbounded wealth that offered untapped opportunities for trade. Since Britain had most to sell, British interests funded the early explorers, such as Mungo Park, who acted as commercial travellers, carrying samples of Lancashire textiles and other manufactures. Results were disappointing but some solid business was established on the coast in products such as palm oil.

By the middle of the century, European interest was increasingly focused on 'the dark continent', and explorers, such as David Livingstone and H. M. Stanley, became major celebrities. Livingstone maintained an interest in 'legitimate trade', which he hoped would displace the continuing traffic in slaves in Central Africa, but he travelled as a missionary. European civilization had now achieved an unassailable self-confidence. Romantic concepts of the noble savage were forgotten and it was readily assumed that Africa was in need of Christianity, Western customs, and post-industrial working practices that alone could provide the basis for economic advance.

Explorers, mainly following the routes of the great rivers, penetrated deep into the continent. They were followed by missionaries from a wide range of denominations from Europe and America, who were at times almost as much at competition with each other as they were with traditional practice. Expectation of life for explorers, traders and missionaries in malarial West Africa could be measured in months until quinine was introduced as a prophylactic in the 1840s and even afterwards the coast was still considered unfit for European settlement.

The Scramble for Africa

In 1880, active European political interest in Africa was limited to the French colony of Algeria in the north and the British Cape Colony in the south. The old Portuguese colonies, various ex-slaving trading outposts and settlements of freed slaves retained only tenuous links with Europe. By 1914, only Ethiopia in the whole continent was a truly independent nation. In the intervening decades, the continent was divided up between colonizing powers. Lines were drawn on maps in European capitals; boundaries often followed rivers, placing a village in one country and its farmland in another. The colonizing movement was in places the focus of national policy; elsewhere it was the product of adventurers or commercial companies working on their own initiative.

The British assumption of control in Egypt provoked the jealousy of other European countries. In particular, the French army was suffering from the bitter humiliation of its defeat in the Franco-Prussian War at Sedan in 1870. Africa offered a forum for the recovery of lost military prestige.

France and Britain were the main protagonists in the northern half of the continent. French colonization followed two thrusts: the first came south across the Sahara from Algeria into the grasslands of northwest Africa; the second went east from Senegal along the upper Niger to Lake Chad towards the Nile. The British also had a dual thrust, south from Egypt and north from South Africa. The imperialist, Cecil Rhodes, dreamed of establishing an unbroken chain of British possessions from the Cape to Cairo. French and British forces met where their thrusts intersected at Fashoda in the southern Sudan in 1898, when for a time it seemed likely that the two countries would be involved in a colonial war.

Meanwhile the British had also established West African colonies, based on their old slaving stations. The Germans were active in West , South West and East Africa. King Leopold of the Belgians gained control of the Congo as a private venture but it was taken over by the Belgian state in 1908. Spain won control of much of the northwestern Sahara and shared influence in Morocco with France. Italy belatedly joined the scramble by invading Libya in 1911.

In the early years, colonization was largely bloodless but the process became increasingly violent. Britain faced African revolts as far apart as the Gold Coast and Rhodesia, and France the Niger and Madagascar. The brutality of King Leopold's exploitation of the Congo was exposed in 1904. In the same year, a major rebellion broke out against the Germans in South West Africa, which ended when they drove the Herero people to virtual extinction in the desert. The Italian invasion of Libya was also conducted with widespread brutality. By the beginning of 1914, the redrawn map of Africa could be seen as a symbol of a dangerously aggressive and expansionist mood within Europe.

South Africa

The Great Trek

During the Napoleonic Wars, Britain occupied the Cape of Good Hope and in 1814 the territory was retained, as the Cape Colony, for its strategic value in controlling the sea routes to the East. At that time, however, there were no British settlers, the land being shared between nomadic Bushmen and Hottentots and Afrikaans-speaking Boers of Dutch and French Huguenot origin. Soon the government began to bring in thousands of British settlers. The Boers were angered when their black slaves were freed and laws were introduced that they considered to be unduly favourable to the previously subject black people. In 1835, some 10,000 Boers left their homes in the Cape and settled on land close to the Vaal and Orange rivers; more followed when the British annexed Natal. The Boer settlers create the new republics of Transvaal and the Orange Free State where they could live free from British interference.

The Boers' Great Trek north coincided with migrations of Bantu people, displaced by the Zulu kingdom. The two peoples clashed, but the main losers were the native Bushmen, who were driven to a precarious existence in the desert.

The Anglo-Boer Wars

Resentment between the Boers and the British continued to grow. The British briefly annexed the Transvaal, and, although they withdrew, this left the Boers feeling that they would never be left in peace. Then, in 1886, gold was discovered in the Transvaal, and, within a few years,the new city of Johannesburg had grown to a population of 100,000. Most of the newcomers were British, but they were excluded from the running of the republic. Angry that the great British Empire, the modern Rome, could be frustrated by a small number of intransigent Boer farmers, Cecil Rhodes provoked a confrontation. President Kruger of the Transvaal, an implacable opponent of British rule, responded with an ultimatum, and the Second Boer War broke out in 1899.

Liberal opinion in Britain and Europe saw the Boers as an oppressed minority, and, when they were finally defeated in 1902, there was pressure for a generous settlement. A few voices were raised in the British parliament to defend the rights of the black peoples, but these found no support. In 1910, the four territories were brought together into the self-governing Union of South Africa, which lost little time in passing laws that discriminated against the non-white peoples. In 1948, the Afrikaans-speaking people won power within the country and put in place the formal structure of apartheid.

12

The Nation State in Crisis

The Eastern Question

The Decline of Ottoman Power

In 1683, armies of the Turkish Ottoman Empire laid siege to the city of Vienna for the second time and Europe was threatened once more from the East. The armies withdrew, but the emperor at Istanbul, Sultan Mehmed IV, still controlled almost three quarters of the Mediterranean coastline – North Africa, the Arab lands of the Middle East, the homeland of Turkey, Greece and the Balkans.

By the eighteenth century, however, statesmen could recognize that the Ottoman Empire, like other empires before it, was in decline. Administration was clumsy, and the sultan had to rely on local rulers, whose loyalty was often in doubt. Also, the social military structure of the empire was becoming increasingly out of date.

Russian Objectives

Russian statesmen took the closest interest in the Ottoman decline. Peter the Great had won a warm-water port, but, for both trade and strategic reasons, the country still badly needed an outlet into the Mediterranean Sea. During 1768–74 Catherine the Great fought a successful war against the Turks and won the Crimea and other territory on the north bank of the Black Sea, along with rights of navigation into the Mediterranean. She also established that Russia had the right to act as the protector of Eastern Christians within the Turkish dominions.

Russia continued to make advances after the defeat of Napoleon. She won control of the ancestral Ottoman homeland in the grasslands east of the Caspian Sea, taking her empire as far as the mountain passes of the Himalayas. Still further east, she won the Pacific port of Vladivostok from the Chinese. Russian territorial ambitions were backed by huge military force, and other European powers perceived her as an aggressive imperial power.

Concern focused on the fate of the Turkish European territories. In a private conversation with the British ambassador, Tsar Nicholas I described Turkey as 'the sick man of Europe'. He implied that it would be better for the powers to consider how to share the sick man's possessions, rather than to wait and fight over them when he died. Other powers, however, preferred to support Turkey so that it could continue to act as a check on Russian ambitions in Eastern Europe.

In 1841, the European powers came together in the Convention of the Straits to guarantee Turkish independence. It was agreed then that the Bosphorus should be closed to all ships of war. This shut Russia out of the Mediterranean, and meant that she could not protect her merchant ships, now carrying increasing amounts of grain exports via the Black Sea.

The Crimean War

In 1851, Russia invaded Turkey's Danube lands, and in 1853 her navy sank the Turkish fleet, so winning back her outlet to the Mediterranean. Excitement ran high in Paris and London. Napoleon III was looking for a way of rebuilding the family's military prestige. Britain was concerned for her links with India, for, although the Suez Canal was not yet built, traffic was already following the Mediterranean route. In March 1854, the two powers declared war on Russia in support of Turkey. Combined forces were despatched to capture the Russian naval base at Sebastopol in the Crimea. The huge Russian army was unable to dislodge the invading force and in 1856 she was forced to accept peace on the terms that she would keep no fleet in the Black Sea and build no bases on its shores.

The battles of the Crimean War were made famous because the armies were followed by a journalist, who published detailed reports in the London *Times*. For the first time in history, the public was able to read first-hand reports of the sufferings of the soldiers. The modern profession of nursing dates itself from the work done by Florence Nightingale and her staff in this campaign.

Disintegration

Victory over Russia in the Crimean War could not long delay the final disintegration of the Ottoman Empire. France and Britain, who had fought as allies of the Turks, were happy to help themselves to territory in North Africa. Britain also occupied Cyprus and extended her influence in the Middle East. Russia continued her forward movement in the less sensitive territory to the east of the Caspian Sea. In Eastern Europe, Greece was already independent and in the half century after the end of the Crimean War, Serbia, Romania and Bulgaria would also break free. Russia, always ready to stand as protector of the oppressed Slav peoples, went to war with Turkey again in 1877. For a time Europe stood on the brink of another war as the powers prepared to shore up the tottering empire once again. However, in 1878, Russia, faced by the combination of Prussia, Austria and Britain, was forced to accept terms at the Congress of Berlin.

In 1907, rebellion broke out in Turkey itself. A group, who called themselves the Young Turks, demanded constitutional reforms, along European lines. In 1909, the long-reigning Abdul-Hamid II was deposed. The new rulers dressed their government as a constitutional monarchy, but it was effectively a dictatorship, dedicated to reviving Turkish power at home and in the remaining Ottoman lands of the Middle East.

Nationalism

Western Europe

The Napoleonic conquests and reactions against them had aroused fierce emotions of nationalism that were to influence European politics. Germany and Italy began their discovery of a national identity (Chapter 8), but the mood also affected smaller peoples, such as Belgians and Norwegians. Britain had her own problems in Ireland. The situation there was complicated by the fact that Westminster politicians had to reconcile two vocal nationalist groups. The majority Catholics considered themselves to be under a foreign power, discriminated against in their religion and insecure in their landholding. The minority Protestants in the north, mostly of Scots descent, used their political connections with English Conservatives to defend accustomed privileges. After 1848, however, concern on issues of nationality centred on Eastern Europe.

Poland

Russia might stand as the liberator of oppressed Slav peoples in the Balkans, but, on her own western frontier, she was the oppressor. The decline of Poland began with long wars against Sweden, which ended in 1709. Depopulated and weakened, with no natural frontiers, she stood between aggressive powers to the east and west. In the last decades of the eighteenth century, she was partitioned between Russia, Austria and

Prussia. A supposedly free Poland, created in 1815, was effectively a Russian colony. A series of nationalist rebellions were a failure and Russian administrators tried to eliminate all traces of Polish nationalism, insisting that even primary schoolchildren should be taught in the Russian language.

The Austro-Hungarian Empire

Metternich recognized very clearly that the new nationalism could undermine the whole structure of the Austrian Empire. The house of Habsburg ruled over different nationalities, speaking a wide range of languages. Defeat by Prussia and then the loss of Italy had pushed the western boundaries of the once great empire back to the Austrian heartland. Alone of all the major European powers, landlocked Austria was not in a position to participate in the scramble for colonial possessions. Any expansion had to be towards the east, and foreign policy now focused on the Danube and the Balkans.

The new nationalists of the region, however, saw Austria, as much as Turkey, as a threat to their aspirations. The Hungarians exploited the weakness of the empire after the Prussian victory at Sadowa to negotiate a new Covenant with Vienna. The Habsburgs now ruled a dual Austro-Hungarian Empire, in which military and foreign policy was coordinated, but in other ways the eastern part had virtual self-government. The new Hungarian section of the empire contained a number of national minorities, and trouble was never far from the surface.

In 1878, after the war between Russia and Turkey, Bosnia and Herzegovina were placed under Austrian administration, and in 1908 they were annexed by Austria. The independent Serbia, with Russian support, now stood as the focus of pan-Slavic aspirations, and so as protector of the nationalist movements in the two territories. The Austrian government, angry at this subversion, looked for an opportunity to crush Serbia.

Russia

Despotism

In the decades before the Crimean War, Russia was ruled by the autocratic Tsar Nicholas I. He tried to keep all Western ideas of liberalism and socialism at bay by a suffocating censorship. At the same time, the administration became ever more corrupt and inefficient. The repression of this period was primarily directed against the intelligentsia, who were traditionally close to developments in the West. Nicholas did recognize, however, that the position of the serfs had become such an anomaly that it endangered the Russian state. As in France before the Revolution, these poorest people had to carry by far the bulk of the taxation load. Nicholas declared a desire to make changes and he did make progress in codifying peasants' rights and bringing them within the legal system. He was unable, however, to tackle the medieval structure of serfdom, which tied the mass of the people to their villages, and left them as the virtual possessions of their masters.

Emancipation and Reform

Nicholas was succeeded by his son, Tsar Alexander II, during the Crimean War. The failure of the superior Russian armies and the humiliating nature of the peace, left no doubt that the state needed radical overhaul. Although conservative by nature, the new tsar supervised a major overhaul of the army, the law and the administrative system.

Most difficult, he put in train the process of emancipation for the serfs. 'Better,' he said, 'to abolish serfdom from above, than to wait till it begins to abolish itself from below.' Emancipation was pronounced in 1861, but problems still remained to be solved. Landlords needed to be compensated and a system established whereby the peasants could buy their own land. This took the form of a tax, which left many, in practice, worse off than they had been before emancipation.

The Prelude to Revolution

The first shot was fired at Alexander only five years after his emancipation decree; he was assassinated in 1881. The reforms of his reign were matched with a continued autocracy, which aroused profound frustration, particularly amongst the intelligentsia. The education system, in particular, was subject to the tightest control by a reactionary bureaucracy. Also during these years, individuals within government gave support to pogroms against the Jews. After the murder of Alexander II in 1881, government fell increasingly into the hands of the opponents of reform.

Opposition was divided between liberals, socialists and groups of nihilists, all of whose leaders were drawn from the intelligentsia. They appealed first to the suffering peasants, demanding a programme of land reform. Towards the end of the century, however, large numbers of peasants were leaving the land to make up the industrial proletariat of the long-delayed industrial revolution. Revolutionary activists now found it productive to work in the growing city slums, building up revolutionary cells of workers.

Success is the ultimate justification of autocratic government, and defeat by Japan in 1905 brought the Imperial government to the brink of collapse. The battleship *Potemkin* mutinied and terrorized the Black Sea. Massive strikes, particularly by railway workers, crippled the economy. In October 1905, the socialist groups organized themselves into the First Soviet, based on the principle of the cells that had been established in the factories. Nicholas II, like Louis XVI before him, was forced to attempt to rally national unity by calling a national parliament, or *duma*. Experiments in representative democracy were, however, halfhearted and failed. In the years that followed, the weak tsar shut himself off within his family circle, now increasingly dominated by the eccentric Rasputin. When the European First World War broke out in 1914, Russia was ill prepared for such a disaster.

The Armed Peace

The Alliances

In the years after 1871, there were two fixed points in European diplomacy. Austria and Russia faced each other over the control of the liberated Turkish lands in the Balkans. Fighting could break out at any time within the region, leading to the risk of 'superpower involvement'. France also, smarting from defeat at Sadowa and the occupation of Paris, was chronically hostile to Germany. She was, however, militarily weak and the autocratic powers of Austria and Russia looked on her as a threat, and so she remained isolated and impotent.

In previous centuries, alliances had been formed under the immediate threat of war, and they had disintegrated immediately after the threat was over. During these decades, however, the European powers began to form themselves into permanent alliances, committed to help each other in the event of war. By the beginning of the twentieth century, a new alignment of powers had become established: Germany allied with Austria, and they were later to be joined by Italy to form the Triple Alliance; to meet this threat, France and Russia joined to form the Dual Alliance. Britain was not a significant continental power, and as late as 1898 the two countries narrowly avoided a colonial war. In 1904, however, policy changed dramatically as Britain concluded a nonbinding *entente cordiale* with France, which was followed by a similar agreement with Russia. Hostility towards Germany increased as the German government set about a major naval construction programme, which was interpreted as a direct threat to Britain. The British government responded with its own programme, and a major arms race was under way.

Military Strategy

With Europe organized into armed camps, the generals considered strategy in the event of conflict. Failing to take account of the bloody attrition of the American Civil War, they assumed that events would be settled, as in Bismark's wars, by one swift, decisive campaign. Germany was faced with the prospect of fighting on two fronts. Strategists decided that, while the Russian war machine was massive, bureaucratic inefficiency would prevent rapid deployment of forces. They therefore developed a plan that, in the event of impending war, the German army would make a first strike to knock out France, so that it could then give its full attention to the eastern front.

In the early years of the century, there was a mood of militarism throughout Europe, fed by accounts of colonial wars and victories against non-European people. It was most evident in Germany, where theorists declared that war was the natural state of man, but it spread much wider. In Britain, for instance, metaphors of war and sport were subtly mingled in the public school education of the nation's élite.

The Outbreak of War

Austria and Serbia

By the summer of 1914, Serbian support for rebels in Bosnia and Herzegovina had brought relationships with Austria to a low state. On 28 June 1914, the heir to the Austrian throne, the Archduke Franz Ferdinand, and his wife were murdered in the Bosnian capital of Sarajevo. Encouraged by her ally, Germany, Austria used this as a pretext for invading Serbia on 28 July. On 30 July Tsar Nicholas II ordered mobilization, not only in the Balkans, but along the whole border.

First Strike

It appears that, at the last moment, Kaiser Wilhelm II of Germany may have had doubts about plunging Europe into war. The British foreign minister tried to gather support for a conference to localize the conflict, but the German war machine was now moving under its own impetus. On 3 August, Germany attacked France through undefended neutral Belgium. Italy declared that the conflict was none of her concern, so the central powers of Germany and Austria faced France and Russia. Britain had no treaty obligation to enter the war on behalf of France, but did consider herself bound by the guarantee made to Belgium after the 1830 uprising. Her formal position for taking up arms was therefore as defender of the rights of small nations. Italy later entered the war on the side of the Allies, as they were now called, while Turkey and Bulgaria aligned themselves with the Central Powers. Military enthusiasts forecast a short war, to be decided by Christmas, but the British foreign secretary, Sir Edward Grey, warned 'The lamps are going out all over Europe. We shall not see them lit again in our lifetime.'

War and Revolution

Stalemate

The German first-strike strategy involved high risk. Russia mobilized more rapidly than anticipated and the German army was defeated at Grumbinnen on 20 August. In early September the western offensive became bogged down on the Marne. Germany was fighting the war on two fronts, just as her generals had feared. On the western front, the opposing armies dug in for their long years of attrition. The new German navy remained in port as the British fleet set about sapping German resistance by blockade. Allied attempts to break the stalemate by offensives in the Dardanelles and Salonika, were unsuccessful.

The Russian Revolution

The huge open spaces of the eastern front kept war more mobile. Early Russian success was undermined by the failure of the political structure. In March 1917, a wave of unrest swept the tsar from power. The opposition was divided between liberal politicians, who now set up a provisional government and the socialist Soviet – itself divided between the moderates and a radical Bolshevik wing. The moderate provisional government pledged itself to continue the war but in April the Bolshevik, Vladimir Ilyich Lenin, returned from exile and announced the arrival of world revolution. Russian workers, he claimed, should not be dying in a bosses' war. The provisional government staked everything on a last great offensive, but this failed, and on 7 November, Lenin staged a Bolshevik coup d'état. In March 1918 he concluded peace between his newly born Soviet Union and the Central Powers at Brest Litovsk. In July of 1918 the tsar and his family were shot at Yekaterinburg.

American Intervention

Germany now had to fight on only one front, but, during this period, another, even more formidable enemy had been drawn into the war. Desperate at the success of the British naval blockade, the German navy mounted its own submarine blockade of Britain. To be successful it had to attack American ships that were carrying supplies to Britain. This brought the United States into the conflict in April 1917. The German High Command recognized that the intervention of American troops would tilt the battle against the Central Powers, but it staked everything on defeating Britain and France before the Americans arrived; 1917 and 1918 saw huge and costly offensives from both sides on the western front. In the autumn of 1918, Germany's allies, Austria and Bulgaria began to crumble, the German fleet mutinied and there was increasing unrest in German cities. Finally the kaiser abdicated and the generals sued for peace.

The World of Versailles

The Cost of War

All the major continental nations emerged weakened from the First World War: Russia, involved in civil war, was no longer a factor in international politics; France, although victorious, had suffered grievously; Austria was not a power of any significance. Germany, although defeated, was no longer surrounded by serious rivals. Loss of life had been severe in all the combatant nations, but wealth had also drained away. The United States was the main beneficiary of the war at a cost of fewer casualties than had been suffered by Australia. In the past, the USA had been a major debtor nation, but now she moved into a period of being the world's main creditor nation.

A New World

The war was also an emotional and intellectual landmark. It was as if the great optimism which had buoyed up a successful and expansionist Europe was suddenly pierced. The belief in an inevitable tide of progress, prevalent since the time of

Descartes, no longer seemed tenable in the face of sustained barbarity on European soil. Liberal thinkers, in disciplines such as theology as well as in politics, found themselves on the defensive. New absolutisms, of both left and right, emerged in confrontation, both threatening to overwhelm traditions of representative government.

The conflict had also brought permanent changes in the structure of society. Women, who had been mobilized to fill men's jobs, could no longer be denied political and a growing economic emancipation. The war brought technological advances in areas such as aeronautics and the development of motor vehicles. Output had increased to meet the demands of a technological war, and, in the process, labour unions had established a stronger position for themselves. Many felt threatened by the rapid social change, evident in almost every field of life.

In the years before the war, artists had already been working in strange and disturbing new forms. Stravinsky's *Rite of Spring* and Picasso's *Demoiselles d'Avignon* created scandal in their fields. In 1922, Joyce's *Ulysses* dispensed with the convention of the English novel. It seemed as though all recognizable values were now fractured as creative artists abandoned both classical and romantic forms to explore abstraction and inner life, now provided with a whole new vocabulary by the works of Sigmund Freud. The arrival of jazz from America, exploiting the interaction between African and European popular music, only served to heighten the alarm of traditionalists.

The Treaties

The Treaty of Versailles, ratified by Germany in July 1919, was the first of a series of treaties imposed on the defeated Central Powers. The leading architects of the new order were Woodrow Wilson, president of the United States, Georges Clemenceau, premier of France and David Lloyd George, prime minister of Britain. Clemenceau, recognizing the continuing potential of Germany, pressed for financial reparations, intended to retard industrial recovery, the return of Alsace-Lorraine to France, and the demilitarization of the Rhineland. The map of Eastern Europe was redrawn, with Poland, Hungary, Czechoslovakia and Yugoslavia created as new nations. In the north, Finland, which had won independence from Russia in 1917, was joined by the three newly independent Baltic States: Estonia, Latvia and Lithuania. The pattern of nationalities was, however, more complex than could be accommodated within national boundaries, and all these nations had substantial minorities. Of greatest significance for the future, large numbers of German-speaking people found themselves within Czechoslovakia and Poland. The treaties attempted to protect minority rights, but there was considerable movement of peoples across national boundaries. The largest movement came at the end of the war between Greece and Turkey from 1920 to 1922. In particular, Greek people left the coast of Asia Minor, where they had lived since ancient times. The two communities continued in uneasy coexistence in Cyprus. The treaties also changed the wider world. Germany's East and West African possessions were divided between Britain and France, while South West Africa (the future Namibia) was placed under the trusteeship of South Africa. The concept of trusteeship was also used to extend Western influence over the old Ottoman territories of the Middle East.

The League of Nations

President Wilson hoped that his country, with its democratic tradition, could take the lead in creating a new atmosphere of goodwill. He therefore proposed a League of Nations to be the guardian of world peace. Wilson was bitterly disappointed when his own Congress refused to let the United States join the new body. Unhappy about the way in which their country had been plunged into European affairs, the majority of Americans were anxious to return to their traditional isolationism. It became evident that the new body lacked credibility as early as 1920, when Poland successfully seized Vilna from Lithuania. Later incidents reinforced the fact that successful international collaboration to repel aggression could not be organized through the League. The Italian government took full advantage when, in Europe's final African venture, it launched an attack on Ethiopia in 1935.

Ireland

Attempts by prewar Liberal administrations to give home rule to Ireland had been frustrated by the collaboration of Ulster Protestants and Conservative politicians. Prime Minister Lloyd George now faced destructive guerilla warfare from the more extreme nationalists. In 1921, the moderate nationalists accepted partition of the island, which left a significant Catholic minority within the Protestant-dominated northern provinces. This led to civil war within the new Irish Free State of 1922, and laid the foundations of continuing strife in the north.

The World Economy

The Post-war Boom

During the 1920s, world trade appeared to be returning to its prewar vigour, but, even during these boom years, there were signs of problems ahead. The war had created an increased potential for production, but demand was stagnant. The Soviet Union was in no position to import goods from abroad, and new nations raised tariff barriers to protect fledgling industries. The United States now produced over half of all the world's manufactures, but American consumers, like the Japanese 70 years later, showed little desire to buy goods from abroad and domestic industry was protected by import duties.

As industry boomed, so the price of raw materials, including agricultural products, decreased, creating problems for primary producers. At the same time, the fact that workers did not have a share in the profits of their industries, brought outbursts of industrial unrest, such as the British General Strike of 1926.

The Great Depression

By 1928, world trade had become heavily dependent on American finance. In that year, Wall Street experienced 'the Great Bull Market' as the price of shares rose to unrealistic heights. Then, on 28 October 1929, the stock market crashed. American capital for investment dried up, leading to a rapid world wide collapse of industrial confidence. Governments took what action they could to protect their own industries against imports, so further inhibiting world trade. It is estimated that at the depth of the recession in 1932 industrial production in the United States and Germany was only half of what it had been three years earlier. Unemployment reached record levels in all the industrial countries, bringing times of great hardship.

The New Deal

In America, the parties divided over their political response to the problems. The Republicans, favouring a traditional *laissez-faire* approach, were defeated in the 1932 elections by a Democratic party, led by Franklin Roosevelt. He instituted a New Deal, based on substantial public investment, the showpiece of which was the publicly owned Tennessee Valley Authority, designed to provide an industrial infrastructure for one of the country's poorest regions. Roosevelt won great popularity, going on to win an unprecedented four presidential elections, but the improvement brought by the New Deal was as much psychological as practical, and real recovery had to await the stimulus of a second world war.

The Rise of the Dictators

Italy

In the elections of 1921, a new party won just 36 seats in the Italian parliament. Its leader, Benito Mussolini, had a background as a socialist, but he now proclaimed that he would save Italy from the menace of communism. The party appealed to ancient Rome in its extended arm salute and the symbol of the *fasces*, which gave the movement its name. The black-shirted Fascists used intimidation, first to come to power and then to eliminate all political opposition. Mussolini's rule achieved some legitimacy when, in 1929, he negotiated a treaty with the highly conservative papacy.

Germany

The Austrian-born Adolf Hitler became leader of the German National Socialist, or Nazi, party in 1921. Having failed in an early attempt to take control of the Bavarian government, he set about reorganizing his party as a military movement, not hesitating to purge his own followers. He directed his appeal to a German people who were frustrated by military defeat, humiliated by the loss of empire and European territory, and, in many cases, impoverished by hyperinflation. Hitler's philosophy was laid out in his early book *Mein Kampf*. This described both his military ambitions for Germany, and his obsessive hatred of the Jewish people.

The struggle appeared to lie between Hitler's new right, and the parties of the left; but the left was divided. The communists, taking their orders from Moscow, attempted, and sometimes succeeded, in fomenting revolution. The social democrats were therefore forced into alliance with conservative military leaders. Capitalizing on these divisions and on the economic problems brought by the Depression, Hitler took his Nazi party to power in 1933. He then quickly set up a reign of terror. While the Jews were his prime target, political opponents, gypsies, the handicapped, and anybody not considered to be of true Aryan descent also suffered. Despite this, his popularity remained high among most Germans. His armaments and other public works programmes appeared to be bringing a return of prosperity, while military success restored national pride.

The Soviet Union

The Bolshevik Revolution of 1917 was followed by three years of civil war, during which White Russian armies, supported by foreign troops, tried to overthrow the new communist state. Lenin and his followers emerged successful, but at a huge cost. It is estimated that some 13 million died in the civil war and through the famine it caused; economic life was at a standstill. In 1921, as an emergency measure, Lenin largely freed the economy and recovery followed rapidly.

Lenin died in January 1924, leaving two men contending the succession. Trotsky proclaimed that the new Russian society could only flourish within a communist world, and the prime task was therefore to export revolution. His opponent, Stalin, argued that the priority was to rebuild the Soviet Union by creating 'communism within one state'. When Stalin emerged victorious, it appeared as though the forces of moderation had prevailed.

Stalin assumed autocratic power and created a personality cult, not dissimilar to those constructed around the Fascist dictators. He set himself the objective of changing the Soviet Union from a largely medieval economy to a major modern state within a few decades. This involved the conversion of agriculture from its peasant structure by wholesale collectivization, and the rapid development of heavy industry. The programme was forced through at huge human cost. Industrially the results were dramatic. Production of coal, iron and steel and other basics increased many times over. The expansion of heavy industry was, however, bought at the expense of consumer goods, and the Russian people were constantly disappointed in the promised general improvement in living standards. Peasants on the collective farms, also resentful at being expected to produce low-cost food for the growing cities for little return, remained obstinately unproductive.

Stalin's increasingly paranoiac behaviour was now demonstrated in a series of show trials and purges. Virtually all the old political leaders and a high proportion of military officers were executed to ensure that nobody would be able to challenge for power. Millions more suffered and died in labour camps. The new administrators of the country were tied to Stalin by a common guilt, and by an increasing web of petty corruption.

Spain

By the 1930s, the days in which Spain had been a great European power were long past, and she had therefore avoided involvement in the First World War. In 1933, a right-wing government came to power, which provoked rebellion by national minorities. In early 1936, a left-wing government was elected with a large majority. General Franco, modelling himself on theFascist dictators, led a mutiny of the army in Morocco and invaded the mainland. The army, the political right and the Roman Catholic Church aligned with Franco, while left-wing groups and the national minorities aligned with the elected government. Franco received assistance from the Fascist states, while the government was supported by the Soviet Union and a variety of international volunteers. The bitter war lasted until 1939, when Franco achieved the position of dictator, which he held until his death in 1975.

The Second World War in the West

German Expansion

From the beginning, Hitler followed a programme for the creation of a German empire in central Europe. His first objective was to win back land lost at Versailles; he then planned to conquer the whole of mainland Europe, including European Russia, and create an empire in which 'lower' races, such as the Slavs, would be reduced to a servile status. He exploited the weakness of the League of Nations, American isolationism, and lack of unity among other European powers in a series of successes – the recovery of the Saarland by plebiscite, the remilitarization of the Rhineland, unification with Austria, and finally the dismemberment of Czechoslovakia. When Britain and France acquiesced to the last of these at Munich, it appeared as though no other power had the will to frustrate his ambitions.

In 1939, Hitler and Stalin concluded the Nazi–Soviet Pact to preserve Russian neutrality. The Soviet Union was awarded eastern Poland and took the opportunity to advance further into the Baltic States and Finland, where Russian armies were halted by fierce national resistance. Unlike Czechoslovakia, Poland was protected by treaty links with Britain and France, and the German invasion provoked a joint ultimatum then war. Mussolini took the opportunity of entering the war in support of Germany and invading Greece.

German Successes

After defeating Poland, in 1940 the German army repeated the 1914 tactic of invading France across Belgium. This time Paris fell and a puppet government was installed in southern France. After successful campaigns to the north and south, German troops occupied Denmark, Norway, Yugoslavia and Greece. In early 1941, the Afrika Corps landed in Libya and within two months was threatening Cairo and the Suez Canal. Britain, now rallied by its charismatic leader, Winston Churchill, held off an air offensive, intended to prepare the way for invasion, in the Battle of Britain.

On 22 June 1941, Hitler launched Operation Barbarossa against an unprepared Soviet Union. The invasion followed the logic of Hitler's master plan, but it dangerously overstretched German resources. The imbalance was made greater when the Japanese attack on Pearl Harbor brought the United States into the war in December of the same year. Stalin demonstrated his character as a national leader in rallying his people for a massively costly defence. The war turned in November 1942, when the Russians broke the German front at Stalingrad and a British army defeated the Afrika Corps at El Alamein. Once the Allies had re-established a western front with the Normandy landings of June 1944, the final defeat in 1945 was inevitable.

The years from 1939–45 gave a new and terrible meaning to warfare. The Germans mobilized conquered people for slave labour, and perpetrated mass genocide on European Jewry; the Russians deported whole national populations for alleged collaboration; residential areas of cities were targeted in indiscriminate bombing by both sides. Among the 52 million dead were an estimated 27 million Russians, 6 million Jews and 4½ million Poles.

Europe Divided

The Yalta Settlement

The future political shape of Europe was negotiated in February 1945 at a conference at Yalta in the Crimea attended by Stalin, Roosevelt and Churchill. Germany was to be partitioned and the countries of Eastern Europe were to form a zone of Russian influence. In the event, Austria and Greece – the latter after civil war – remained within the sphere of Western Europe.

The Recovery of Western Europe

At the end of the war, Western Europe was in a state of serious economic collapse. Once again, there were large movements of displaced people, and food shortages continued for years after the war. In June 1947, US Secretary of State, George Marshall, announced a major aid programme, directed 'not against any country or doctrine, but against hunger, poverty, desperation and chaos.' The Soviet Union was offered the chance of participating but turned it down. The Marshall Plan provided much needed capital for reconstruction.

The United Nations

During the last years of the war, thought was given to the reasons why the League of Nations had failed to preserve world peace. In 1945, representatives of the world's nations met in San Francisco to set up the new United Nations. In its constitution, great influence was given to the Security Council, which had five 'great powers' as permanent members and representatives of other nations. The right of veto was given to the great powers, but at least all the major powers were now involved in the organization, and debates were subject to the scrutiny of the world media.

The European Community

Some European leaders argued that the nation state was no longer capable of providing a secure structure for world peace. In particular, the long standing enmity between France and Germany was no longer acceptable. In 1958, the Federal Republic of Germany, France, Italy, Holland, Belgium and Luxembourg formed the European Economic Community. This was designed to be both a trading group, capable of competing with the new superpowers, and also a stabilizing influence on the volatile European political scene.

The Cold War in Europe

It soon became clear that European nationalism had run its destructive course, and the danger to world peace now lay in the confrontation between the United States and the Soviet Union. In the words of Winston Churchill, an 'iron curtain' had descended across Europe.

The Soviet Union emerged from the Second World War in control of a vast empire. It had inherited Imperial conquests, and had further added the Baltic Republics. It also now controlled puppet regimes in Eastern Europe, bound together in the Warsaw Pact, which maintained huge land forces on its western front. Stalin's policy was still primarily directed at preserving national security, which had been so devastatingly violated by Hitler's army. He and later Soviet leaders therefore felt threatened by American superiority in nuclear weapons. A crash nuclear programme was put in hand and advances in rocketry were clearly illustrated when, in April 1961, the Russian Yuri Gagarin became the first man to be launched into space.

America and her allies in the North Atlantic Treaty Organization (NATO) relied heavily on nuclear superiority. The Americans responded to the Russian space programme and, in July 1969, with a wondering world watching on television, men walked on the Moon.

Berlin, divided between the four occupying powers, lay exposed within the Russian area of influence and in 1948–49 conflict loomed as the Russians shut off Western communications with the city. A later crisis ended with the building of the Berlin Wall in 1961. This stood for the next 28 years as a potent symbol of the Cold War and the division of Europe into two hostile camps.

13

After Empire

The Expansion of Japan

The Beginnings of Aggression

The 1914–18 world war brought prosperity to the rising Japanese economy. European competition in Asian markets was reduced and Japanese factories were able to export to the combatants. During this period, heavy industries, such as shipbuilding, were able to build up a firm base. Competition returned in the post-war boom years, but Japan continued to export successfully. During the boom years, companies reinvested profits in preparation for more difficult times. Japanese industry, none the less, suffered badly in the Depression. With foreign markets closed and the home market as yet undeveloped, industry worked at only a fraction of capacity. The weakness was exacerbated by the country's lack of raw materials. Foreign policy therefore became directed at the winning control of the export markets and natural resources of East Asia. China was the first target for expansion.

China's Weakness

After the fall of the Manchu Empire in 1912, China plunged back into chaos. Sun Yat-sen's Nationalist (Kuomintang) party struggled for power with independent warlords. During this time Communist cells were coming into existence. Following Marxist orthodoxy, they initially concentrated on the cities, but later, under the influence of the rising Mao Zedong (Mao Tse-tung), they worked increasingly among the mass of the peasants, who had suffered greatly during the upheavals. Under his influence, the Communists built up communes in scattered and remote areas. Sun Yat-sen died in 1925, to be succeeded as Kuomintang leader by the more conservative Chiang Kai-shek. After a period of collaboration, Chiang attempted to exterminate the Communist opposition. Driven from their southern bases, the Communists only survived by coming together in the Long March of 1934–35 and establishing a new northern headquarters, based on Yenan.

War in the East

The Attack on China

Japan exploited the weakness and growing corruption of the Kuomintang government by strengthening its control over Manchuria and areas of the north in the early 1930s. In 1936, the Kuomintang and the Communists made common cause against the foreigners, but in the following year, Japan launched a major assault on China. In December 1937, the Japanese army captured the capital at Nanking and the Chinese government had to retreat to remote Szechwan, leaving the Japanese in control of the north, and most of the Pacific coast, including the major industrial cities.

Victory brought Japan into conflict with the Pacific colonial powers, and their concessionary ports were blockaded. The Americans and British responded by supplying Chiang Kai-shek along the Burma Road, and the United States renounced its commercial agreement with Japan.

Control of the Pacific

Japanese foreign policy was now set on winning control over the whole of the Pacific rim. With the outbreak of war in Europe, she allied herself with Germany. Then in 1941, as German troops were sweeping into Russia, she launched her first attack on French Indo-China. On 7 December 1941, her air force attacked the American navy in Pearl Harbor, Hawaii, and, at the same time, she launched assaults on the Dutch in Indonesia and the British in Malaysia and Burma. The campaigns were brilliantly successful and by mid-1942 both India and Australia were under threat.

Defeat and the Atom Bomb

The attack on Pearl Harbor put and end to isolationism and united Americans behind President Roosevelt. As the world's greatest industrial power became geared for war, the tide turned against Japan. In June 1942, the Japanese fleet suffered a reverse at the battle of Midway atoll, and thereafter a relentless American offensive drove them from their Pacific conquests, while the British also fought back through Burma. From November 1944 the Japanese cities came under direct air attack. The war ended with the use of the new atomic weapon on the cities of Hiroshima and Nagasaki in August 1945.

Decolonialization

The Japanese victories, and, in particular, the fall of Singapore on 15 February 1942, involved a profound loss of face for the colonizing powers. The invading armies were seen by many Asians as liberators from Western regimes. Many of those who had assumed control, under Japanese direction, now became prominent in independence movements. The United States handed over political control of the Philippines in 1946 after negotiating a continued military presence. The Dutch, themselves newly liberated, at first fought to preserve their possessions but in 1948 they accepted the independence of the Republic of Indonesia. The British fought a communist rebellion in Malaya before handing over to a more acceptable national government in 1957. The French became involved in a long war for Indo-China before being defeated in 1954.

China and her Neighbours

Communist China

The fall of Japan left the two forces of the Kuomintang and the Communists vying for the control of China. China's miseries continued when civil war broke out in 1946. In one battle, half a million men were engaged on each side. By 1949 the Communists had gained the upper hand and Chiang Kai-shek retreated from the mainland to the island of Taiwan with his government.

The new Communist government was faced by a huge task of reconstruction. According to Mao's estimate, some 800,000 'enemies of the people' were executed, largely from the old village landlord class. The Communists had long experience with the collectivization of agriculture within their own territories, and they did not follow Stalin's example of imposing it from above. Peasants were organized to control their own operations and, despite setbacks, the conditions of life for the mass of people improved.

Mao Zedong capitalized on the age-old Chinese respect for authority to provide a strong central government, which had for so long been lacking. He adapted Western Marxist ideology to traditional thought patterns, and showed a strong hostility to Western culture, which was given full rein in the Cultural Revolution, which he launched in 1966.

To Western eyes, China appeared now to be a part of a united Communist bloc, intent on achieving world dominance. In practice, however, Mao had largely rejected the Russian brand of communism. By the 1960s, acute strains were appearing in the relationship between the two countries. When China developed its own nuclear capability in 1964, it was primarily as a deterrent against potential Russian aggression. The Chinese reconquest of the old province of Tibet also led to a successful war with India in 1962.

The Korean War

In 1945, the Japanese colony of Korea was occupied by Russian troops from the north and Americans from the south. This led to partition, with both governments claiming the whole country. In 1950, the northern armies invaded the south. The United States and other Western nations, with the backing of a United Nations resolution, responded by sending forces to support the south.

For a time it appeared as though the north would be defeated, but China, concerned at her own security, sent an army across the border. American President Truman refused to become involved in a war on Chinese soil, and the war was concluded in 1953 by an armistice that perpetuated partition.

Conflict of Ideologies

American analysts saw the communist strategy in South East Asia as being a process of 'slicing the salami'. Territories were to fall to communism, not in one major conflict, but one by one. The communist uprisings, which faced almost every nation of South East Asia in the coming decades, were in fact little coordinated and variously owned allegiance to Moscow, Peking or neither.

American policy became dedicated to holding the line against communism in the region. This involved providing support to noncommunist regimes, including the Chinese nationalist government in Taiwan. The United States was therefore deeply involved in the politics of the region.

The French defeat in Indo-China left the new country of Vietnam divided, with a communist regime under the old nationalist Ho Chi Minh established in the north. The United States became increasingly involved in the struggle, supporting unstable non-communist administrations, based in the southern capital of Saigon. In 1965, faced with the possibility of the defeat, President Johnson authorized massive US involvement in the conflict but the weight of American fire-power proved ineffective against a highly motivated enemy. In 1973, the American government withdrew from the conflict. In the next two years the three countries of Indo-China fell to the communists, and the people of Cambodia, having experienced American bombing, now suffered from the worst aberrations of Marxism, as interpreted by the Pol Pot regime.

The Pacific Rim

Japanese Reconstruction

United States troops occupied Japan, in an enlightened manner, from 1945 until 1952. The first objective was to ensure that the expansionist phase was over. A new democratic constitution was established, the emperor renounced his divinity, and expenditure on defence and armaments was radically curtailed. As with Germany, industrial reconstruction followed fast. After the humiliation of defeat, both nations needed to experience success. Also, the imposed limitation of defence expenditure proved a powerful boost to the civilian economy.

The Technological Revolution

Soon Japan was no longer a low-cost economy and her heavy industries began to suffer some of the problems experienced in the West. By this time, however, the nation had developed skills that enabled it to take the lead in the third, technological phase of world industrialization. Automobile production boomed, winning markets in Europe and North America, and Japanese labour and management skills proved highly suitable for the detailed work involved in the production of hi-tech goods. Supported by a huge balance of payments surplus, she established a position of dominance in world markets in a wide range of product areas. However, the rapid expansion of the post-war years had by the 1990s run out of steam and the 1997 Asian financial crisis and bouts of recession precipitated major economic reforms. By 2003, there were signs of an upturn in her economy and Japan once again had a considerable role to play on the world stage.

An Area of Growth

In the last decade of the twentieth century it became clear that the region of the Pacific rim was established as a formidable competitor to the established industrialized regions of Western Europe and North America. It remained, however, a region of wide diversity. South Korea, Taiwan, Singapore and – at least until reunification with China in 1997 – Hong Kong, all participated in the economic prosperity pioneered by Japan. At the other extreme, peoples of many of the nations of South East Asia continued to survive on low per capita incomes. China herself emerged from the isolation of the Cultural Revolution to rebuild international links and become the world's fastest growing economy but the economic gap between her urban and rural populations remains among the largest in the world.

The Indian Subcontinent

The Independence Movement

Indian troops made a significant contribution to the Allied victory in the First World War, and in 1918, nationalist politicians looked to see their country start its progress towards the self-government that had already been given to the white dominions. In 1919, however, a British general ordered troops to fire on a demonstration in Amritsar, killing some four hundred people and injuring many more. Although the government disavowed the act, many British residents were loud in support, fuelling bitterness between the two communities. One of those radicalized by the Amritsar massacre was Mohandas Gandhi, known as Mahatma ('Great Soul'). During the next decades, he led a civil disobedience movement, based, if not always successfully, on nonviolent principles.

In the face of opposition at home, as well as from residents in India, the British government slowly moved towards accepting the principle of granting dominion status to India, and the Government of India Act of 1935 gave substantial power to elected representatives. The movement for complete independence, however, continued to grow. With the outbreak of the Second World War, some Indians sided with Japan in the hope of bringing down the colonial power.

Partition

The independence movement still faced the problem of reconciling the two major religious groupings of the subcontinent. Muhammad Ali Jinnah emerged as leader of the Muslim League, which now demanded that an independent state of Pakistan should be established at independence for the Islamic community. In 1945, a Labour government was returned in Britain and in March 1946 it made an offer of full independence. As disputes continued, it announced that Britain would withdraw not later than June 1948. Faced with this ultimatum, the Hindu leaders accepted partition – for which decision Gandhi was assassinated by an extremist Hindu.

The new state of Pakistan was established in two blocks in the northwest and northeast. The rulers of princely states on the border of the two nations were permitted to decide their allegiance, leaving Kashmir as a disputed territory, which it remains until this day. Independence was marked by communal rioting, which left some half a million dead, and the mass movement of peoples in both directions across the frontier.

Independence and After

Jinnah died in 1948, and a decade later the army took control of Pakistan. Leadership of India fell to Jawaharlal Nehru and later passed to his daughter Indira and grandson Rajiv Gandhi. The new country faced formidable problems. Independence was quickly followed by famine in 1951 and, with a rising population, it appeared as though Malthusian disaster was imminent. A combination of a reduction in the rate of population growth and an agricultural 'green' revolution improved the supply of food. The fragile ecology of eastern Pakistan, however, continued to bring disasters, and a cyclone in 1970 led to rebellion that, with Indian help, brought into being the separate Islamic state of Bangladesh.

Pakistan has experienced alternating periods of civilian and military rule in the last few decades and thousands have been killed since the violence in the 1980s between Sunni and Shia Muslims. Under military rule since 1999, the country has faced economic and law and order challenges but it has gained foreign acceptance after its stand against Islamic extremists in the wake of the terrorist attacks on the USA on 11 September 2001.

In India, Indira Gandhi was assassinated by discontented Sikh nationalists, and her son Rajiv by Tamils of the south. Mahatma Gandhi had allied himself with outcasts and hoped to see the end of the caste system, but this has been frustrated by a resurgence of Hindu fundamentalism. For all its problems, however, India remains the world's largest democracy and has emerged as a major world power since the late 1980s with economic reform and a large skilled workforce making it a popular choice for international companies seeking to outsource work. Now a nuclear weapons state, India launches its own satellites but many of its huge rural population remain illiterate and impoverished.

Sub-Saharan Africa

Decolonialization

British governments of both parties continued the policy, which had begun with India, of giving independence to her colonies. The sheer size of the British Empire had meant that expatriate manpower was spread thinly. The second layer of administration was already staffed by African personnel and the machinery of local government was in place. Riots in the Gold Coast in 1948 gave notice of a growing nationalist movement and in 1957, the Gold Coast became the first independent country within the British Commonwealth under its new name, Ghana. Three years later the much larger Nigeria became a sovereign state.

Across the continent, in Kenya and Rhodesia the problem was complicated by the presence of a white settler population, bitterly opposed to any move towards majority rule. The most serious challenge was posed by the Mau Mau disturbances in Kenya of 1952–56. Two years later the white minority government of Southern Rhodesia declared unilateral independence and seceded from the British Commonwealth. The British government failed to take effective action against this colonial rebellion and war continued between the white government and black nationalist groups, until the latter won and set up the state of Zimbabwe in 1976.

French governments, disillusioned by prolonged war in Indo-China and Algeria, gave independence at an even faster pace. In 1960, French sub-Saharan colonies were offered either complete separation, in which case, they would receive no continued assistance, or association with France, within a French Community.

The two largest African empires were therefore dismantled within a few years with comparatively little strife. Independence for the remaining colonies proved a more painful process. In 1960, the Belgians withdrew from the Congo, which became the state of Zaire. Until that time, Africans had held no positions of responsibility, and there was little preparation for the event. When the mineral-rich area of Katanga attempted to secede, the Cold War superpowers became involved in the ensuing civil war. The last African empire was also the oldest. The Portuguese colonies of Guinea-Bissau, Mozambique and Angola achieved independence only after prolonged struggle.

After Independence

The emergent nations faced formidable problems. Some new nations spent unwisely on military prestige projects, but, even where this was avoided, as, for instance, in Tanzania, falling world commodity prices led to a serious reduction in government revenue. Industrialization has proved almost unattainable, both through lack of capital and because it has proved hard for their products to break into the controlled markets of the developed world.

Independent African nations found themselves caught in the Malthusian nutcracker of increasing population and falling revenue. This led to a decline in already low living standards and a failure by governments to deliver the public health and education programmes expected within a newly liberated nation. This exacerbated traditional communal rivalries, which in turn frequently erupted into civil war, like the Nigerian Biafran War of 1967–70 and later struggles in the Sudan, Ethiopia and the Horn of Africa. In the Rwandan genocide of 1994, Hutu extremists massacred some 8000,000 Tutsis in the space of 100 days in the belief that their self-interests would be advanced if every one of Rwanda's one million Tutsis were annihilated.

Political instability led to the emergence of authoritarian, often military, regimes. From the early 1990s, aid to Africa often came with the proviso that democracy be adopted along with the legitimization of political parties and free elections. The overall trend among Africa's governments is towards greater legitimacy but the last few decades have brought much human misery to Africa with ongoing drought and famine, a devastating AIDS epidemic and ethnic conflict.

South Africa

The violently imposed apartheid system led to South Africa being increasingly ostracized from the world community. She withdrew from the British Commonwealth in 1961 and was later expelled from the United Nations. Economic sanctions imposed by the USA and a world sporting boycott had an effect, and in the early 1990s the legal apparatus of apartheid was dismantled. Following the country's first all-race elections, held in 1994 and won by the African National Congress (ANC) led by Nelson Mandela, South Africa re-entered the world fold.

Now regarded as Africa's superpower, South Africa has the continent's most successful economy with strong financial and manufacturing sectors. Having held successful national elections and local polls since the end of white rule, a democratic culture seems to be taking hold but many South Africans remain poor, unemployment is high and around six million South Africans are infected with HIV.

Latin America

Capital and Industrialization

In the years before the First World War there was heavy European involvement in the economy of Latin America. The war then led to a drying up of European capital and the United States became the main investor in the region.

The world Depression of the 1930s hit the region hard. The price of primary products, which were the mainstay of the economies, collapsed. After the Second World War, many of the larger nations instituted industrialization programmes, at times with a measure of success, but this was achieved only by borrowing the required capital, which left the nation with a heavy burden of debt and vulnerable to currency and interest rate fluctuations on the international market. Economic problems created political instability. The rural poor had always lived in conditions of poverty, but they did not pose the same immediate problem to political stability as the growing and highly volatile urban populations.

Political Structures

The economic problems of the region meant that reforming governments did not have the revenue to deliver the social programmes needed to combat deprivation. When reforms were attempted, they created inflation that weakened the economic base of society. Reforming democracies were therefore under constant pressure from more authoritarian systems of government. These took three broad forms – popularist leaders, military regimes and revolutionary governments.

The archetype popularist leader was Getulio Vargas, who came to power in Brazil in 1930, and the best known was Juan Peron, who ruled Argentina from 1943–55 and then returned briefly in 1973. Both drew comparison with European dictators, but they had wide support among the urban poor, who believed that they alone could take on powerful vested interests on behalf of the people. They depended, however, on army support, and both were vulnerable when this was withdrawn.

Cuba and Revolution

The revolutionary movement had early roots in Mexico, but it became focused on Cuba with the success of Fidel Castro's revolution in 1959. An attempt by the United States to undermine the revolution came to disaster at the Bay of Pigs in April 1961 when they were overwhelmed by Cuban troops. In the following years Cuba, now aligned with Russia, exported revolution into Latin America.

Che Guevara, a symbol to the new left across the world, was killed fighting with Bolivian guerillas in 1967. The United States became involved, supporting anti-communist regimes within the region, even when these had a poor human rights record. The democratic left-wing government of Salvadore Allende in Chile, for instance, was overthrown by the military in 1973 with American support. Contra rebels against the Cuban-inspired government of Nicaragua were funded from Washington, and the government of the island of Grenada was overthrown by an American invasion in 1983.

The Missile Crisis and Beyond

In 1962 Cuba was the focus of the most dangerous crisis of the Cold War. In October, intelligence reports showed that sites were being built on Cuba from which Russian missiles would be able to reach any city in the United States. President Kennedy demanded that all missiles in Cuba should be withdrawn and announced that ships bringing more would be intercepted. The superpowers stood poised for nuclear confrontation, but the Russian president, Khrushchev, broke the crisis by agreeing to withdraw the missiles. President Kennedy had successfully reasserted the Monroe Doctrine that the American continent would remain an area of United States influence, and the powers would not again come so close to open war.

At the beginning of the twenty-first century, Cuba is only just beginning to recover from the severe economic recession that followed in the years after the missile crisis – the result of both an ongoing US economic, commercial and financial embargo and the withdrawal of Soviet aid after the collapse of communism in Eastern Europe in 1990.

Debt and Deforestation

High inflation and huge foreign debt continue to be major problems for South America, despite free-market reforms and the increasing industrialization of some countries, such as Brazil and Argentina. In many instances, political instability hinders economic development. Efforts to combat the illegal drug trade have been largely ineffective but there has been a decrease in deforestation.

The Middle East and North Africa

The New Turkey

In 1918, a proposal was put forward that Turkey itself should be divided into French, British and Italian spheres of influence. The successful general, Mustafa Kemal, led resistance against Greek and French forces, and established independence for the new, smaller nation. He set about a process of modernization of the nation, which went as far as Westernizing its script and converting the country into a secular state. His people gave him the name of Ataturk – 'father of the Turks'.

Turkey at the beginning of the twenty-first century remains poor, with a large and overwhelmingly Muslim population. It has recently undergone many reforms to strengthen its democracy and economy in order to meet the terms for entry into the European Union. Most European countries welcome the country's eventual membership, despite issues of religion, immigration and integration, hoping that Turkey will provide a bridge between the cultures and religions of Europe and the Near East.

The Mandates

The old Ottoman lands of the Islamic Middle East, now finally separated from the Ottoman Empire, had acquired new strategic importance with the early development of oil reserves – although the scale and future importance of these were not as yet recognized. National boundaries were drawn up and the region was divided between France and Britain under the mandate of the League of Nations. This implied that the newly defined countries were destined to move towards self-governing status. France was awarded Lebanon and Syria, although she had to take possession of the latter by force, and continued to rule it with considerable oppression. Britain received Palestine, Iraq, and Trans-Jordan, and she also controlled the emirates of the Persian Gulf. In 1932, Britain largely withdrew from Iraq, but the Palestinian mandate turned out to be something of a poisoned chalice.

The Founding of Israel

The objective of founding a Jewish national home in Palestine was first put forward in a Zionism Congress as early as 1897. It was to be a refuge for Jewish people who were persecuted in the pogroms of Eastern Europe, and it also attracted many from minority Jewish communities within the Arab world. In 1917, the British government gave support to the project, with the contradictory provision that it should not interfere with the rights of the indigenous people. The movement was given further impetus by German persecution of the Jews under Hitler. In the post-war years, large numbers of European Jews sought entry, and the British authorities had the impossible task of reconciling the opposing interests. In 1947, the United Nations voted for the partition of Palestine in the face of opposition from the Arab states and in 1948 the British withdrew. In the ensuing war, large numbers of Arabs left their homes for refugee camps in neighbouring countries. The Arab states refused to accept the existence of a Jewish state in the Islamic heartland.

North African Independence

After the Second World War, the British presence in Egypt was restricted to a defensive force in the canal zone and by 1956 Libya, Tunisia and Morocco had shaken off foreign ties. Armed conflict centred on Algeria, where over one million French settlers resisted any move towards independence. The country was declared an integral part of metropolitan France and a bitterly fought dispute continued from 1954–62. When General de Gaulle finally decided to give the country its independence, colonists allied with army generals and France itself was taken to the brink of civil war.

Nasser and Pan-Arabism

In 1952, a group of army officers overthrew the monarchy in Egypt. Two years later, Gamal Abdel Nasser became president of the country. In 1956, he nationalized the company that administered the Suez Canal. In October, the Israelis invaded Egyptian territory, ostensibly to destroy guerilla bases and this was followed by a joint attack by the British and French on the Suez Canal zone. World opinion was outraged, and the American government applied pressure that forced the invaders to withdraw. The Suez fiasco left Nasser as the leading figure within the Arab world, but his attempts to take this towards political union were unsuccessful. In 1967, he closed the Straits of Tiran to Israeli shipping and the Israeli army launched a 'first strike' in what has become known as the Six Day War.

After a successful campaign, Israel controlled new territory, including, from Jordan, the whole West Bank of the River Jordan, and, from Syria, the tactically important Golan Heights. Jerusalem, a city of great symbolic importance to all three Semitic religions, now passed under full Israeli control. As Israel's neighbour, the Lebanon, collapsed into civil war, many Arabs resorted to international terrorism. In 2000, Israel withdrew unilaterally from southern Lebanon. Progress towards a permanent peace settlement including the Camp David Summit of 2000 has been undermined by ongoing Palestinian-Israeli violence. In 2005, Israel withdrew some settlers from the West Bank and all its settlers from the Gaza Strip which was then handed over formally to the Palestinian National Authority (established in 1994).

The Oil Crisis

In 1961, Britain withdrew from her interests 'east of Suez'. Much of the, now increasingly vital, oil production of the region, however, remained under the control of Western companies. A further outbreak of hostilities between Israel and her neighbours in 1973 led the Arab countries to 'play the oil card' by taking more direct control over their own reserves and withholding supplies from Israel's allies in the developed world. This led to an increase in price, which had a sharp effect on the world economy. The Arab nations, and other oil-producing nations, led by Saudi Arabia, now organized themselves into OPEC (Organization of Petroleum-Exporting Countries) with a view to controlling world prices. This was less successful than had been anticipated because the depression caused by the price rise restricted world demand, and Britain and Norway, opening new North Sea reserves, stood outside the cartel. In 1978 Nasser's successor, President Sadat, made peace with Israel under American sponsorship in the Camp David Accords. This did not end the conflict within the region, but rather took Egypt out of the mainstream of Arab politics.

Iran and Islamic Fundamentalism

With Egypt in the American sphere of influence after Camp David, the Soviet Union turned increasingly to the radical, though mutually hostile, governments of Syria and Iraq. The United States, looking for a buffer between the Soviet Union and the oil-rich Middle East, put heavy backing behind the conservative and corrupt administration of the Shah of Iran. In 1979 discontent erupted into revolution, and the shah was replaced by a fundamentalist regime, dominated by the Ayatollah Khomeni. This sparked a wave of Islamic fundamentalism that gave expression to pent-up Arab anger at the imposition of alien values by aggressive Western societies. Equally hostile to capitalist and to communist ideologies, Islamic fundamentalism threatened governments from Afghanistan to Algeria. Indeed, the failure of the 1979 Soviet invasion of Afghanistan in support of a crumbling Marxist regime demonstrated militant Islam to be a highly effective barrier against further Russian expansion in the region.

Iraq

In 1979 Iraq came under the full control of a determined and ruthless leader, Sadaam Hussein. He had ambitions to revive Nasser's pan-Arab vision, this time based on Iraqi military power. He received wide Western and Arab backing when he took his country to war with Iran, but he failed to achieve any of his war objectives. In 1990, he attacked and occupied Kuwait, provoking an international response in 1991, which left his country damaged, but his own power intact. However, his failure to comply with UN resolutions requiring a full accounting of its weapons of mass destruction and full cooperation with UN weapons inspectors, led to the controversial invasion of Iraq by Coalition forces led by the USA and Great Britain in 2003. The Coalition forces managed to topple Saddam Hussein and his government and capture the key cities of Iraq in 28 days but their efforts to establish a democratic state capable of defending itself proved a much more difficult task due to ongoing attacks by various insurgents demanding that the foreign forces leave the country. Elections and a new constitution have paved the way for a new government but with ongoing violence and foreign troops still in place, peace in the new Iraq remains elusive.

The Collapse of the Russian Empire

Cracks in the Structure

As early as 1953, the year that Stalin died, there were signs of unrest among the subject peoples of the Russian Empire. Yugoslavia, while remaining communist, had already loosened her ties with the Soviet bloc. Anti-Soviet riots in East Germany in 1953 and in Poland in 1955 were followed by rebellion in Hungary in 1956. The profound unpopularity of Russian domination and of the repressive puppet regimes continued to be demonstrated by a haemorrhage of refugees crossing from East to West Germany. In 1961, the East German authorities responded by building that ultimate symbol of the Cold War – the Berlin Wall. In 1968, a reforming communist government in Czechoslovakia was again overthrown by Soviet tanks. By this time, large Russian forces were also tied down on the eastern frontier to check an increasingly hostile China.

Meanwhile within the Soviet Union, the government was coming increasingly under strain. Khrushchev's denunciation of Stalin at the Twentieth Congress of the Soviet Communist Party and the termination of the worst excesses of the secret police enabled citizens to express dissatisfaction. Industrialization had been bought at the expense of the production of consumer goods. The corrupt and petty bureaucracy was increasingly exposed, and agriculture remained in the disastrous condition bequeathed by Stalin's collectivization. In 1985, President Gorbachev inherited a collapsing empire. Constricted by domestic pressures, he chose not to intervene when, in a few dramatic months of late 1989 and early 1990, communist governments of Eastern Europe collapsed under popular pressure and new regimes declared themselves independent of Soviet control. The tearing down of the Berlin Wall, and subsequent unification of Germany (3 October 1990) was the most powerful symbol of change. The situation was little better in the republics that constituted the Soviet Union. As one republic after another declared their sovereignty, the Russian Empire slowly unravelled. In August 1991, an attempt by communist hardliners to restore the old system in a coup d'état failed, leaving the central Soviet government stripped of any real power. Gorbachev was replaced by Boris Yeltsin and the Soviet Union was dissolved.

The Russian Federation claims to be the legal successor to the USSR on the world stage and Vladamir Putin, who succeeded Yeltsin as president, has vowed to modernize Russia. While some progress has been made in terms of a new political order and market economy, much still remains to be done including resolving the conflict with separatists in the Republic of Chechnya.

Europe United?

The European Union

In the aftermath of the Second World War, a number of leading European leaders became convinced that the only way to secure lasting peace between their countries was to unite them economically and politically. Belgium, West Germany, Luxembourg, France, Italy and the Netherlands formed the first of the organizations that were to become the European Union (EU). Joined over the years by Britain, Ireland Denmark, Greece, Portugal, Spain, Austria, Finland and Sweden, the European Union had twenty-five member states by 2004 when Estonia, Latvia, Lithuania, Poland, the Czech Republic, Hungary, Slovenia, Malta and Cyprus joined. This large increase was partly due to a desire to reunite Europe after the end of the Cold War as well as an effort to tie Eastern Europe firmly to the West to prevent it falling again into communism or dictatorship.

Economic and political integration between member states means that these countries have to take joint decisions on many matters so they have developed common policies in a very wide range of fields from agriculture to transport and trade to consumer affairs and the environment. Other countries are set to join in the next decade but there are concerns among some of the EU's citizens that European integration is speeding out of control and that individual countries are in danger of losing their sovereignty and national identity.

A Chronology of World History

BC

4000
- Meslim, King of Kish, becomes overlord of Sumeria (southern Babylonia).

3000
- Ur-Nina founds a dynasty at Lagash in Sumeria; builds temples and canals.
- Fourth Egyptian Dynasty founded by Snefru; later kings of the dynasty, Cheops, Chephren and Mycerinus, build the Great Pyramids at Gizeh.

2900
- Eannatum, King of Lagash: conquers Umma, Kish, Opis, Erech, Ur; repels the Elamites.

2850
- Fu-hi, first Emperor of China.

2800
- Urukagina, King of Lagash: a great reformer; Lagash defeated and destroyed by Lugai-Zaggisi, ruler of Umma and King of Erech, who becomes overlord of all Sumeria.

2650
- Sargon founds Akkadian Empire in Mesopotamia.

2600
- Naram-Sin, son of Sargon.
- Sixth Dynasty in Egypt ends the ancient empire: Pepy I conquers Palestine; Pepy II reigns 94 years, longest reign in the world's history.

2500–2000
- Legendary period of the Second City on the site of Troy; destroyed by fire.

2450
- Gudea, ruler of Lagash.

2400
- Dynasty of Ur in Sumeria established by Ur-Engur; he reigns for 18 years; Dungi, his son, reigns for 58 years, extends empire over all Babylonia and also conquers Elam.

2300
- Asshur, the oldest Assyrian city, founded not later than this date.
- Dynasty of Isin in Sumeria, established by Ishbi-Ura; overthrow of Ur because of Elamite invasion.

c.2200
- Early Minoan Age of Cretan civilization begins.

2100
- First Dynasty of Babylon established by Sumu-Abu after fall of Isin; the Sumerians finally give way to the Semites.

2000
- Twelfth Egyptian Dynasty begins, with Thebes as capital.

2000–1800
- Twelfth Egyptian Dynasty: Amenemhet I, Usertesen I, Amenemhet II, Usertesen II, Usertesen III (conquered Nubia), Amenemhet III, Amenemhet IV and Queen Sebknofru; all great builders.

2000–1700
- Proto-Mycenean civilization of the island of Thera (now Santorini) destroyed by volcanic upheaval.

173

1900–1850
- Middle Minoan Age in Crete.

1860
- Construction of Stonehenge begins in Britain.

1840
- Ismi-Dagan, oldest known ruler of Assyria.

1800–1600
- Late Minoan Age in Crete.

1800–1200
- Babylon ruled by Kassite invaders.

1800
- Hyksos rule in Egypt begins.
- Rise of Shang Dynasty in China.

1795–1750
- Hammurabi, the greatest king of the first Babylon Dynasty: noted for agricultural improvements and the Code of Hammurabi, the first written code of law.

***c.*1600–1000**
- Mycenaen civilization in Greece.

1700
- Assyria becomes independent of Babylonia around this time.

1600
- Amasis I finally drives the Hyksos from Egypt and founds the New Empire; conquers Palestine and Phoenicia.
- Babylon destroyed by Hittites.

1600–1100
- The Sixth City on the site of Troy (Homeric Troy).

1560
- Thutmosis I of Egypt completes conquest of Nubia.

1515
- Thutmosis III of Egypt: conquers Syria and penetrates to Assyria.

1450
- Amenophis III of Egypt: noted temple-builder.

1415
- Amenophis IV of Egypt: replaces the old religion by sun worship.

1410
- Conflict between Assyria and Babylonia begins.

1355
- Rameses I begins Nineteenth Dynasty in Egypt.

1350
- Sethos I of Egypt: wars against Libyans, Syrians and Hittites.

1340
- Rameses II, the most celebrated King of Egypt; wages long war with the Hittites, retains Palestine; greatest builder among the Egyptian kings.

1330
- Shalmaneser I, King of Assyria.

1300–1000
- Hellenic conquests in Greece.

1290
- Tukulti-ninib, King of Assyria: conquers Babylonia.

1273
- Meneptah, King of Egypt: wars against Libyans and Asiatic pirates.

1200
- Rameses III of Twentieth Egyptian Dynasty.

1120
- Tiglath-Pileser I, King of Assyria.

1100
- Herihor, high priest of Ammon, seizes throne of Egypt; deposed by a Tanite Dynasty.
- Chou Dynasty supplants Shang Dynasty in China.

1000
- David, King of Israel.
- Iron Age begins.
- *Rigveda*: one of the four Hindu religious texts known as the Vedas (India).

970
- Solomon, King of Israel.

950
- Sheshonk, Libyan King of Egypt: conquers Palestine.

935
- Hebrew kingdom is divided on death of Solomon: Jeroboam I becomes King of Israel in the north; Rehoboam, King of Judah in the south.

900
- Homer's *Iliad* and *Odyssey* date from about this time.

884
- Asurnasirpal III, King of Assyria.

875
- Ahad, King of Israel.

860
- Shalmaneser II, King of Assyria: subdues Babylon and Syria.

854
- Battle of Karkar: Benhadad of Damascus and Ahab of Israel defeated by Shalmaneser II.

842
- Jehu, King of Israel.

800
- Carthage founded as a Phoenician colony (traditional).

797
- Jehoash, King of Israel, successfully repels Syrian attacks.

782
- Jeroboam II, King of Israel: defeats Syria and increases prestige of Israel.

776
- The first Olympiad in Greece.

753
- Legendary date of the Foundation of Rome by Romulus.

745
- Tiglath-Pileser III raises Assyria to greatest power.

740
- Conquest of Messenia by Sparta (First Messenian War).

738
- Menahem, King of Israel.

734
- Ahaz, King of Judah.

729
- Tiglath-Pileser III subdues Babylon.

721–722

- Sargon, King of Assyria, takes Samaria and transports a large number of Israelites to Mesopotamia and Media; the northern kingdom of Israel never revives.
- Merodach-baladan ends Assyrian power in Babylon and reigns as king for 12 years.

720

- Hezekiah becomes King of Judah: noted religious reformer and skilful leader.

705

- Sennacherib, King of Assyria.

701

- Sennacherib fails in his attack on Jerusalem.

700

- Deioces founds the Medean monarchy; Midas, King of Phrygia; Gyges, King of Lydia.

685

- Second Messenian War; Messenians again defeated by Sparta.

683

- End of monarchy in Athens.

680

- Esarhaddon, King of Assyria.

670

- Esarhaddon defeats Taharka, Ethiopian King of Egypt and captures Memphis.

668

- Ashurbanipal, King of Assyria: Babylon again subdued; Elam overthrown.

660

- Psammetichus I, aided by Gyges of Lydia, makes Egypt independent again.

647

- Phraortes, King of Media.

637

- Josiah, King of Judah: noted religious and political reformer.

628

- Birth of Zoroaster around this time.

625

- Nabopolassar, King of Babylon.

624

- Cyaxares, King of Media.

621

- Legislation of Draco at Athens.

612

- Nineveh captured and destroyed by Nabopolassar of Babylon and Cyaxares of Media; end of the Assyrian Empire.

609

- Necho, King of Egypt.

608

- Battle of Megiddo; Josiah of Judah defeated and killed by Necho of Egypt.

605

- Battle of Carchemish; Egyptian power in Syria overthrown by Babylon.

604

- Nebuchadnezzar, King of Babylon.

598

- Jerusalem taken by Nebuchadnezzar; Jehoiachin, the king, Esekiel, the prophet and others taken to Babylon; Sedekiah made King of Judah.

594

- Psammetichus II, King of Egypt.

- Legislation of Solon at Athens.

588
- Apries (Hophra), King of Egypt.

587
- Zedekiah's revolt against Babylonian rule; Jerusalem destroyed by Nebuchadnezzar.

585
- Battle between Cyaxares of Media and Alyattes of Lydia stopped by eclipse of sun.
- Tyre taken by Nebuchadnezzar.

584
- Astyages, King of Media.

570
- Athens conquers island of Salamis.

569
- Amasis, King of Egypt.

568
- Buddha born in India.

561
- Evil-Merodach, King of Babylon.

560
- Croesus, King of Lydia: subdues Greek cities in Asia Minor.
- Pisistratus becomes Tyrant of Athens (expelled 555 BC).

555
- Nabonidus, King of Babylon.

551
- Confucius born in China.

550
- Sparta becomes supreme in the Peloponnesus.
- Cyrus conquers Media and founds the Persian Empire.
- Second Tyranny of Pisistratus at Athens (expelled 549 BC).

546
- Cyrus conquers Lydia.
- Asiatic Greek cities conquered by Persia.

540
- Pisistratus again Tyrant of Athens until his death (528 BC).

538
- Cyrus conquers Babylon.

CLASSICAL GREECE AND PERSIA

529
- Cambyses, King of Persia.

528
- Hippias and Hipparchus in power at Athens.

525
- Persian conquest of Egypt.

521
- Darius I, King of Persia.

520
- Persian conquest of Babylon.

515
- Dedication of the New Temple at Jerusalem after return from the Babylonian Captivity.

512
• Persian conquest of Thrace.
510
• Pisistratid Tyranny at Athens ends; Hippias expelled; Athens joins Peloponnesian League.
509
• Etruscan kings, the Tarquins, expelled from Rome (traditional).
508
• Treaty between Rome and Carthage.
507
• Reforms of Cleisthenes at Athens.
500
• End of monarchy at Rome: Republic founded.
499
• Asiatic Greeks revolt from Persia.
497
• Athenians assist in the burning of Sardis.
493
• First Secession of Plebeians at Rome; Tribunes of the Plebs first appointed.
492
• Persians conquer Thrace and Macedonia.
490
• Battle of Marathon: Persians defeated by Greeks under Miltiades; Aeschylus flourishes at this time.
486
• First Agrarian Law (Land Reform) at Rome passed by Spurius Cassius.
485
• Xerxes, King of Persia.
483–221
• Warring States period in China.
480
• Battle of Thermopylae: Persians defeat Greeks (Leonidas).
• Battle of Salamis: Athenians under Themistocles defeat Persians in naval battle.
• Battle of Himera: Carthaginian attack on Sicily repelled by Sicilian Greeks.
  DEATHS
  Buddha
479
• Battle of Plataea: Persians defeated by Greeks under Pausanias.
• Battle of Mycale: Greek naval victory over the Persians.
477
• Confederacy of Delos founded by Athens for defence against Persia.
471
• Lex Publilia passed at Rome; tribunes to be chosen by the Comitia Tributa.
465
• Battle of the Eurymedon: Persians defeated by Greeks under Cimon.
464
• Artaxerxes I, King of Persia.
463
• Democratic reform at Athens; powers of the Areopagus limited by Ephialtes.
462
• Influence of Pericles begins at Athens; Sophocles and Euripides flourish at this time.

458
• Long Walls to Piraeus built by Athens.
• Ezra returns with many Jews from Babylon to Jerusalem.
456
• Athens conquers Aegina.
  DEATHS
  Aeschylus, Greek dramatist.
454
• Athenian expedition to Egypt fails after initial successes.
453
• Treasury of Confederacy of Delos removed to Athens; Athenian Empire at its height.
452
• Decemvirs drew up laws of the Twelve Tables at Rome.
448
• Second Secession of the Plebeians at Rome; great increase in powers of Comitia Tributa.
447
• Battle of Coronea, Athens loses Boeotia.
• Building of Parthenon begins.
  DEATHS
  Pindar, Greek musician and poet.
445
• Lex Canuleia: law that legalizes marriage between Patricians and Plebeians, Rome.
• Nehemiah begins rebuilding walls of Jerusalem.
431
• Peloponnesian War: Athens and allies against Sparta and allies; Thucydides its historian.
  DEATHS
  Herodotus, Greek historian.
424
• Darius II, King of Persia.
422
• Battle of Amphipolis: Athenian defeat.
421
• Peace of Nicias between Athens and Sparta.
418
• Battle of Mantinea: Athenians defeated by Spartans.
413
• Athenian defeat at Syracuse.
405
• Battle of Aegospotami: naval victory of Sparta under Lysander over Athens.
406
• Death of Euripides and Sophocles.
404
• Peloponnesian War ends; Spartans enter Athens and set up the Thirty Tyrants.
• Artaxerxes II, King of Persia.
403
• Thirty Tyrants overthrown at Athens.
401
• Battle of Cunaxa: a force of Greeks help Cyrus in his rebellion against Artaxerxes II, among them Xenophon.
400
• Etruscan city of Veii captured by Romans.

399
• Socrates executed.
398
• First Punic War of Dionysius of Syracuse.
394
• Battle of Coronea: Spartans under Agesilaus defeat confederacy against them.
• Battle of Cnidus: Spartan fleet destroyed by a combined Persian and Athenian fleet.
390
• Rome burned down by Gauls under Brennus.
387
• Peace of Antalcidas between Sparta and Persia.
   DEATHS
   Aristophanes, Greek dramatist.
371
• Battle of Leactra: Sparta defeated by Thebes under Epaminondas.
366
• Licinian Laws passed at Rome; first Plebeian consul.
362
• Battle of Mantinea: Sparta defeated by Thebes (Epaminondas killed).
359
• Artaxerxes III, King of Persia.
• Philip II becomes King of Macedonia.
347
• Death of Plato.
343–340
• First Saminite War waged by Rome.
340–338
• Rome conquers Latium.
339
• Publilian Laws at Rome; decrees of Comitia Tributa to bind whole people; one censor to be a Plebeian.
338
• Battle of Chaeronea: Athens and Thebes defeated by Philip of Macedon, who becomes supreme in Greece.
• Arses, King of Persia.
336
• Philip II assassinated and succeeded by his son, Alexander the Great.

ALEXANDER THE GREAT

336
• Alexander the Great becomes King of Macedon.
• Praetorship at Rome thrown open to Plebeians.
• Alexander elected supreme general of the Greeks.
335
• Alexander's campaign in Thrace and Illyria.
• Alexander captures Thebes (in Boeotia) and destroys it, except the house of Pindar.
• Darius III, King of Persia.
• Aristotle begins teaching at Athens.
• Memnon of Rhodes opposes Alexander's lieutenant, Parmenio, in Asia Minor.
334
• Alexander crosses the Hellespont into Asia.

- Battle of the Granicus: Alexander defeats the Persians.
- Alexander captures Sardis and conquers Lydia.
- Capture of Ephesus.
- Siege and capture of Miletus.
- Siege and capture of Halicarnassus.

333

- Alexander at Gordion; cuts the Gordian knot.
- Battle of Issus: Alexander defeats Darius.

332

- Siege and capture of Tyre.
- Capture of Gaza.
- Alexander enters Egypt.

331

- Alexander founds Alexandria.
- Alexander visits the temple of Zeus Ammon.
- Battle of Arbela (Gaugamela): Darius again defeated.
- Babylon submits to Alexander.
- Alexander at Susa.
- Battle of Megalopolis: Spartans under Agis defeated by Macedonian regent Antipater.

330

- Alexander at Persepolis.
- Alexander at Ecbatana.
- Death of Darius III: end of the Persian Empire.

330–327

- Alexander conquers Hyrcania, Gedrosia, Bactria, Sogdiana.

327

- Alexander enters India.
- Second Samnite War between Rome and the Samnites begins.

326

- Alexander crosses the Indus near Attock.
- Battle of the Hydaspes: the Punjab conquered.

323

- Alexander dies at Babylon.

RISE OF ROME

323

- Ptolemy I founds the dynasty of the Ptolemies in Egypt; makes Alexandria the intellectual centre of the Hellenic world; Euclid flourishes in his reign.

322

- Lamian War: Antipater of Macedonia defeats insurgent Greeks at Battle of Crannon.

DEATHS

Aristotle, Greek philosopher.

321

- The Samnites capture a Roman army at the Caudine Forks.

312

- The Seleucid Dynasty in Asia founded by Seleucus I (Nicator).

304

- Second Samnite War ends.

301

- Battle of Ipsus determines distribution of Alexander's empire among his generals.

300
• Antioch founded by Seleucus Nicator as capital of his Syrian kingdom.
300
• Lex Ogulnia: law at Rome provides for Plebeian pontiffs and augurs.
300
• Zeno, founder of Stoicism, and Epicurus, founder of Epicureanism, flourish at this time.
298
• Third Samnite War begins.
295
• Battle of Sentinum: Romans defeat Samnites and allies.
295
• Pyrrhus becomes King of Epirus.
294
• Demetrius I becomes King of Macedonia.
290
• Third (and last) Samnite War ends: Rome ruler of central Italy.
287
• Third Secession of the Plebs at Rome.
286
• Lex Hortensia at Rome: law makes the Comitia Tributa the supreme legislative power.
285
• Ptolemy II, King of Egypt.
283
• Battle of Vadimonian Lake: Romans defeat Gauls and Etruscans and become rulers of northern Italy.
280
• Pyrrhus invades Italy; Romans defeated in Battle of Heraclea.
• Achaen League revived in Greece.
• Gauls invade Greece.
279
• Battle of Asculum: Pyrrhus again defeats Romans.
275
• Battle of Beneventum: Romans defeat Pyrrhus and drive him from Italy.
266
• Rome ruler of all Italy.
264
• First Punic War (Rome v. Carthage) begins.
262
• Battle of Agrigentum: Roman victory.
260
• Battle of Myloe: Roman naval victory.
256
• Romans invade Africa.
255
• Romans under Regulus heavily defeated by Carthaginians in Africa.
251
• Battle of Panormus: Romans defeat Carthaginians.
247
• Ptolemy III, King of Egypt.
• Hamiclar Barca assumes Carthaginian command in Sicily.

245
- Aratus becomes leader of the Achaean League.
- Agis IV attempts to reform Sparta.

241
- Battle of Aegates Islands: Roman naval victory over Carthage; First Punic War ends with cession of Sicily to Rome; Sicily becomes the first Roman province.

240
- Livius Andronicus, the first Roman poet.

239
- Rome seizes Sardinia and makes it a province.

237
- Carthage begins conquest of Spain.

236
- Cleomenes III, the last King of Sparta.

222
- Conquest of Cisalpine Gaul by Rome completed.
- Ptolemy IV, King of Egypt; beginning of Egypt's decline.
- Cleomenes III defeated by Achean League at Battle of Sellasia.

220
- Philip V, King of Macedon.

219
- Hannibal, the great Carthaginian leader, captures Saguntum in Spain.

218
- Second Punic War begins; Hannibal crosses the Alps into Italy.
- Battle of the Trebia: Hannibal victorious.

217
- Battle of Lake Trasimene: Hannibal victorious.

216
- Battle of Cannae: Hannibal victorious.

214
- First Macedonian War; Romans victorious over Philip V; war ends in 205.
- Great Wall of China constructed.

212
- Romans under Marcellus capture Syracuse.
  DEATHS
  Archimedes, Greek mathematician.

208
- Philopoemen becomes leader of the Achaean League.

207
- Hasdrubal, brother of Hannibal, crosses the Alps into Italy; defeated and killed in Battle of Metaurus.

206
- Conquest of Spain by Scipio.

205
- Ptolemy V, King of Egypt; period of anarchy.

204
- Scipio carries the war into Africa.

202
- Battle of Zama: Hannibal completely defeated near Carthage by the younger Scipio; end of Second Punic War.

200
- Roman poets, Ennius and Plautus, flourish at this time.

• Second Macedonian War begins.

197

• Battle of Cynoscephaloe: Roman victory ends Second Macedonian War.

196

• Romans proclaim freedom of Greece.

190

• Battle of Magnesia: Romans defeat Antiochus the Great of Syria.

181

• Ptolemy VI, King of Egypt.

175

• Antiochus IV becomes King of Syria.

171

• Third Macedonian War begins.
• Battle of Pelusium; Antiochus Epiphanes takes Memphis.

170

• Roman poet Terence flourishes at this time.

168

• Battle of Pydna: Perseus of Macedonia crushed; end of Third Macedonian War.

166

• Death of Mattathias, the Jewish priest who led revolt of Jews against Hellenizing policy of Antiochus Epiphanes; succeeded by his son, Judas Maccabaeus.

161

• Judas Maccabaeus killed at Elasa; succeeded by his brother Jonathan.

149

• Fourth Macedonian War.
• Third Punic War begins.

147

• Roman victory under Mummius at Corinth; Macedonia becomes a Roman province.

146

• Greece becomes a Roman province.
• Carthage destroyed; Roman province of Africa formed.
• Ptolemy IX, King of Egypt.

143

• Simon, a brother of Judas Maccabaeus, becomes leader of the Jews.

142

• Syrian garrison expelled from Jerusalem.

140

• Roman conquest of Lusitania (now Portugal).

135

• John Hyrcanus becomes leader of the Jews.

134

• Roman provinces in Spain are formed.
• Attalus III, King of Pergamom, bequeathes his dominions to Rome; province of Asia formed.

DECLINE OF THE ROMAN REPUBLIC

133

• Tiberius Gracchus, tribune of the Plebs at Rome, attempts to solve the land problem.

123

• Cais Gracchus, brother of Tiberius, becomes tribune of the Plebs; further land reform.

121
- Caius Gracchus killed in a riot.

120
- Roman province in Southern Gaul (hence Provence).

111
- War between Rome and Jugurtha, King of Numidia in Africa; Roman generals, Metellus and Marius.

106
- Jugurtha defeated and captured by Marius.

102
- Barbarian Teutones moving to invade Italy defeated by Marius at Aix.

101
- Barbarian Cimbri moving towards Rome defeated by Marius at Vercellae.

90
- Social War: revolt of the Italians Cities against Rome.

89
- Roman franchise granted to some Italians; soon afterwards to all.

88
- First Mithradatic War begins: Rome against Mithradates VI (the Great), King of Pontus, in Asia Minor; Sulla the Roman general.

88
- Civil War in Rome: Marius against Sulla; immediate occasion was rivalry for the command in Asia.

87
- Massacres in Rome by Marius and Cinna.

86
- Death of Marius.

84
- End of First Mithradatic War.

83–82
- Second Mithradatic War.

83
- Sulla returns to Rome; many citizens proscribed and executed.

82
- Sulla made Dictator of Rome; makes the constitution more aristocratic.

79
- Sula resigns (d.78).

76–71
- Pompey suppresses the rebellion of Sertorius, a follower of Marius, in Spain.

75
- Cicero, the orator, comes into prominence at Rome.

74
- Third Mithradatic War begins; Roman leaders Lucullus and Pompey.

73–71
- Revolt of gladiators and slaves under Spartacus.

64
- Pompey conquers Syria and makes it a Roman province.

63
- Pompey takes Jerusalem.
- The conspiracy of Catiline exposed and foiled by Cicero.

60
- First Triumvirate: Caesar, Pompey and Crassus.

58
- Caesar begins the conquest of Gaul; the Helvetii defeated at Bibracte; Ariovistus, the German leader, defeated.

55
- Caesar's first invasion of Britain.

54
- Caesar's second invasion of Britain.

53
- Battle of Carrhoe: Crassus defeated and killed by Parthians.

52
- Battle of Alesia: Vercingetorix, leader of the Gauls, defeated and captured by Cæasar.

50
- Conquest of Gaul complete.

49
- Caesar crosses the Rubicon and invades Italy.

48
- Battle of Pharsalia: Cæasar defeats Pompey; Pompey murdered soon afterwards in Egypt.

48–47
- Caesar in Egypt; under the influence of Cleopatra, Queen of Egypt.

47
- Battle of Zela: Caesar defeats Pharnaces, King of Pontus.

46
- Battle of Thapsus: the Republicans defeated by Caesar in Africa; Cato commits suicide rather than survive the Republic.
- Calendar reformed by Caesar.

45
- Battle of Munda: Pompey's sons defeated in Spain by Caesar.

44
- Caesar made Perpetual Dictator.
- Assassination of Caesar.

43
- The Second Triumvirate constituted: Octavius, Antony and Lepidus; Cicero executed.

42
- Battle of Philippi: Brutus and Cassius, the leaders of the revolt against Caesar, are defeated and they commit suicide.

40
- Virgil and Horace, the Roman poets, flourish about this time.

31
- Battle of Actium: Antony and Cleopatra defeated in naval battle by Octavius.

30
- Suicide of Antony and Cleopatra; Egypt becomes a Roman province.

29
- Temple of Janus closed, denoting a world at peace – the first time for 200 years; Livy, the great historian, flourishes at this time.

27
- The Senate gives Octavius the title of Princeps of the Roman State; beginning of the Principate, an empire under the forms of the old republic.
- Senate gives Octavius the title of Augustus.

ROMAN EMPIRE

27
• Beginning of Roman Empire with Augustus as Principate.
23
• Readjustment of the authority of Augustus.
20
• Restoration of Temple at Jerusalem begun by Herod the Great.
4
• Death of Herod the Great; Herod Antipas becomes tetrarch of Galilee and Perea; Herod Archelaus becomes ethnarch of Judaea, Samaria and Idumea.

AD

9
• Roman army under Varus defeated in Germany by Arminius: Teutonic civilization saved from absorption by Rome.
14
• Tiberius becomes Emperor.
17
• Death of Livy.
18
• Death of Ovid.
26
• Pontius Pilate becomes Roman Procurator of Judaea.
30
• Probable date of crucifixion of Jesus Christ.
31
• Sejanus, minister of Tiberius, executed.
37
• Caligula becomes Emperor.
41
• Claudius becomes Emperor.
• Herod Agrippa I recognized as King of Judaea and Samaria.
43
• Roman conquest of Britain begins under Aulus Plautius.
44
• Death of Herod Agrippa I; Judea governed afterwards by Roman procurators.
50
• St Paul begins missionary work in Europe.
54
• Nero becomes Emperor; last of the Caesar family.
• The philosopher, Senecca, flourishes at this time.
61
• Revolt of Boadicea, Queen of the Iceni in Britain; defeated and killed by Suetonius Paulinus.
61
• St Paul arrives in Rome.
63
• Death of St Paul at Rome.
64
• Great fire in Rome.

65
- First persecution of Christians at Rome.
  DEATHS
  Senecca, Roman philosopher.

68
- Death of Nero.

68
- Galba usurps the Empire.

69
- Otho murdered and displaces Galba.
- Vitellius proclaimed Emperor at Cologne; defeats Otho and accepted as emperor.

70
- Vespasian becomes Emperor by the defeat of Vitellius; first of the Flavian emperors.
- Jerusalem destroyed by Titus; Jewish revolt suppressed.

78
- Agricola begins his conquest of Britain.

79
- Titus, son of Vespasian, becomes Emperor.
- Tacitus flourishes at this time.
- Herculaneum and Pompeii destroyed by eruption of Vesuvius.

80
- Colosseum completed at Rome.

81
- Domitian, son of Vespasian, becomes Emperor.

84
- Agricola completes conquest of Britain.

86–90
- Dacians under Decebalus successful against Roman armies; bought off by Domitian.

90
- Domitian expels Epictetus the Stoic and other philosophers from Rome.

95
- Persecution of Christians.

96
- Domitian murdered.
- Nerva becomes Emperor.

98
- Trajan (a native of Spain) becomes Emperor.

106
- Conquest of Dacia completed by Trajan.

107
- Persecution of Christians.

114
- Trajan at war with Parthians; the Roman Empire reaches its greatest extent.

117
- Publius Aelius Hadrianus (Hadrian) becomes Emperor; visits all the provinces; abandons Trajan's conquests beyond the Euphrates.

122
- Hadrian orders the building of a wall from the Solway Firth to the Tyne to hold back the Celtic tribes who inhabited Scotland.

125
- Persecution of Christians.

131
- Revolt of Jews under Simon Bar Cochba.

136
- Jewish revolt suppressed; dispersion of the race.

138
- Antoninus Pius becomes Emperor.

140
- Lollius Urbicus builds Antonine Wall from the River Forth to the River Clyde.

155
- Polycarp, Bishop of Smyrna, suffers martyrdom.

161
- Marcus Aurelius becomes Emperor.

163
- Justin Martyr, one of the earliest Fathers of the Christian Church, suffers martyrdom at Rome.

165
- The Parthians defeated.

166
- The plague in Italy.

169
- War with the German tribes Quadi and Marcomanni.

174
- Aurelius defeats the Quadi ('The Thundering Legion').

177
- Persecution of Christians; Irenaeus, a Father of the Church at Lyons about this time.

180
- Death of Marcus Aurelius.

180
- Commodus, son of Marcus Aurelius, becomes Emperor.

192
- Commodus strangled; Pertinax becomes Emperor.

193
- Murder of Pertinax by the Praetorian Guards.
- The Roman Empire sold to Didius Julianus by the Praetorian Guards; general revolt in the provinces.
- Julianus executed: Septimius Severus becomes Emperor.

194
- Battle of Issus: Pescennius Niger, Severus's rival, defeated and killed.

197
- Battle of Lyons: Clodius Albinus, another rival of Severus, defeated after ruling in Britain over three years.

200
- Tertullian, Latin Father of the Church and Clement of Alexandria, a Greek Father, flourish around this time.

202
- Persecution of Christians.

204
- Origen, a Greek Father of the Church, begins teaching at Alexandria.

210
- Severus strengthens Hadrian's Wall across Britain.

211
- Death of Severus at York; his sons, Caracalla and Geta, become joint Emperors; Geta murdered in 212.

212
- Roman citizenship conferred upon all free men.

217
- Caracalla murdered; Macrinus becomes Emperor.

218
- Heliogabalus becomes Emperor; tries to establish worship of Syrian sun-god.

222
- Alexander Severus becomes Emperor after murder of Heliogabalus.

229
- Sassanid Empire begins in Persia with Ardashir I, who overthrew the Parthians; he re-establishes the Zoroastrian religion.

231
- Alexander Severus at war with Persia.

235
- Alexander Severus murdered; Maximinus becomes Emperor.

238
- The elder and younger Gordians proclaimed joint Emperors in Africa, acknowledged by the Senate; defeated and killed after 36 days' reign; Balbinus and Maximus proclaimed joint Emperors by the Senate and associated with the third Gordian; Maximinus murdered by his own troops; Maximus and Balbinus murdered, leaving the third Gordian sole Emperor.

243
- Battle of Resaena: Gordian defeats the Persians under Sapor I.

244
- Gordian murdered by his mutinous soldiers; Philip (an Arabian) becomes Emperor.

249
- Decius becomes Emperor, after defeating and killing Philip.

250
- Cyprian, Bishop of Carthage, Latin Father of the Church.
- Persecution of the Christians.

251
- Battle of Forum Trebonii: Decius defeated and killed in Moesia by Gothic invaders; Gallus becomes Emperor and buys off the Goths.

253
- Aemilianus routs the Goths and is proclaimed Emperor; Gallus murdered; Aemilianus defeated and overthrown by Valerian.

260
- Valerian defeated and taken prisoner at Edessa by Sapor, King of Persia; his son Gallienus becomes sole Emperor; the Goths ravage the east of the Empire; general disorder and revolt (the so-called Thirty Tyrants); Postumus establishes a so-called Gallic Empire.

266
- Odenathus, after raising Palmyra to a position of power and repelling the Persians, is murdered; his widow, Zenobia, rules on behalf of her son and makes extensive conquests.

268
- Claudius becomes Emperor.

269
- Battle of Naïssus: Claudius defeats the Goths and saves the Empire from destruction.

270
- Aurelian becomes Emperor; Dacia granted to the Goths.

270
- St Anthony, the first Christian Monk, becomes an ascetic in Egypt.

271
- Battle at Châlons: Tetricus defeated and the Gallic Empire ended.

272
- Aurelian destroys the power of Palmyra and takes Zenobia prisoner.

275
- Aurelian assassinated; Tacitus elected Emperor by the Senate.

276
- Probus becomes Emperor.

277
- Probus expels the Almanni from Gaul.

282
- Probus assassinated; Carus becomes Emperor.

283
- Carus succeeded by his two sons, Carinus and Numerian, as joint Emperors.

284
- Diocletian becomes Emperor; divides the Roman Empire into the Eastern Roman Empire and the Western Roman Empire.

286
- Maximian chosen by Diocletian as his colleague.
- Carausius appointed to protect British shore against Frank and Saxon pirates; proclaimed Emperor and recognized.

293
- Constantius Chlorus and Galerius created Caesars, with a share in governing the Empire: Rome ceases to be real capital, being replaced by the four towns of Nicomedia, Sirmium, Milan and Trier, one for each Augustus and Caesar; these four divisions afterwards become the Prefectures of the East, Illyricum, Italy and Gaul.
- Carausius murdered in Britain by Allectus.

296
- Allectus defeated and killed by Constantius Chlorus.

303
- Persecution of Christians.

304
- St Alban the first Christian martyr in Britain.

305
- Abdication of Diocletian and Maximian.

BARBARIAN INVASIONS

306
- Constantine the Great proclaimed Emperor at York, on the death of his father Constantius; Severus made joint Emperor by Galerius; Maxentius, son of Maximian, declared Emperor at Rome.

307
- Severus executed by Maximian; Licinius made joint Emperor by Galerius; Maximian also proclaimed Emperor; six Emperors at one time.

310
- Maximian executed by Constantine.

311
- Death of Galerius.

312
- Constantine invades Italy; Maxentius's army defeated in battle of Turin and in battle of Verona.

312
- Battle of the Milvian Bridge (at Rome): Constantine captures Rome; death of Maxentius.

313
- Licinius defeats Maximin; death of Maximin soon afterwards.
- Edict of Milan grants freedom to Christians.

314
- Death of Tiridates, King of Armenia, who had become a Christian.

315
- Battle of Cibalis: Constantine defeats Licinius.
- Battle of Mardia: Licinius is again defeated; a Treaty of Peace concluded.

320
- St Pachomius founds the first Christian monastery in Egypt.

322
- Constantine defeats the Goths in Dacia.

323
- Battle of Adrianople: Liciunius defeated by Constantine.
- Battle of Chrysopolis: Licinius is defeated by Constantine and he dies soon afterwards.

324
- Constantine sole Roman Emperor; he adopts Christianity.

325
- Council of Nicaea, the first General Council of the Christian Church; held in the presence of Constantine; the doctrines of Arius condemned, chiefly through the influence of Athansius.

328
- Constantine founds a new capital at Byzantium under the name of Constantinople or New Rome.

330
- Constantinople dedicated.

332
- Constantius, son of Constantine, defeats the Goths in Moesia.

337
- Death of Constantine; his sons, Constantius, Constantine II and Constans, divide the Empire.
- The Empire at war with Persia under Sapor II.

340
- Constantine II killed in attacking the territories of Constans.

341
- Ulfilas begins the conversion of his fellow Goths to Arian Christianity; his translation of the Bible in Gothic is the oldest Teutonic literary work.

348
- Battle of Singara: Romans defeated by Persians.

350
- Constans murdered in a revolt by Magnetius, who assumes the purple.
- Third Siege of Nisbis: Sapor II unsuccessful.
- Hermanric becomes King of the Goths and establishes a Gothic Empire in Central Europe.

351
- Battle of Mursa: Magnentius defeated by Constantius.

353
- Battle of Mount Seleucus: defeat of Magnentius, who then commits suicide; Constantius sole Emperor.

356
- Julian (the Apostate) begins campaign in Gaul against the Alamanni, Franks and others.

357
- Battle of Strassburg: Julian defeats the Alamanni.

359
- Amida captured by Sapor II.
- Julian subdues the Franks.

360
- Singara and Bezabde captured by Sapor II.

361
- Julian becomes Emperor; tries to restore Paganism as the state religion.

363
- Julian campaign against Persia leads to his death; Jovian Emperor.
- Jovian makes a humiliating peace with Persia.

364
- Valentinian I becomes Emperor; he divides the Empire into Eastern and Western following the pattern established by Diocletian, making Valens the Eastern Emperor.

365
- Revolt of Procopius against Valens.

366
- Procopius defeated and executed.
- Alamanni invade Gaul; defeated by Jovinus.
- War against the Visigoths under Athanaric begins.

368
- Valentinian defeats the Alamanni in the Black Forest and fortifies the Rhine.

369
- Theodosius drives back the Picts and Scots from southern Britain.

370
- Basil the Great, a pioneer of monasticism, becomes Bishop of Caesarea.

372
- St Martin, a pioneer of monasticism, becomes Bishop of Tours.
- Huns under Balamir begin westward movement from the Caspian steppes; they defeat and absorb the Alans.

373
- Theodosius suppresses revolt in Africa.

374
- Huns attack the Ostrogoths of Hermanric's kingdom and conquer them.
- War against the Quadi and Sarmatians.
- St Ambrose becomes Bishop of Milan.

375
- Huns attack Athanaric and the Visigoths.
- Gratian and Valentinian II, sons of Valentinian I, become Western Emperors.

376
- Visigoths under Fritigern permitted by Valens to settle in Thrace; they successfully revolt because of oppression.

378
- The Alamanni defeated by Gratian near Colmar.

379

- Battle of Adrianople: Romans defeated by Goths and Valens killed.
- Massacre of Gothics in Asia by the Romans.
- Gregory Nazianzen accepts the mission of Constantinople.

379

- Theodosius the Great becomes Eastern Emperor.

380

- Theodosius baptized in the Orthodox faith; suppresses Arianism in Constantinople and begins persecution of heretics.

381

- Second General Council of the Church, at Constantinople.

382

- Theodosius makes terms with the Goths and enlists them in his service.

383

- Revolt of Maximus in Britain; he invades Gaul and murders Gratian; treaty between Theodosius and Maximus, leaving the latter in possession of Gaul, Spain and Britain.

385

- Priscillian, a Spanish bishop, is executed by Maximus at Träves for heresy.
- St Jerome works on the Latin translation of the Bible (the Vulgate).

386

- Conversion of St Augustine.
- Ostrogoths defeated on the Danube.

387

- Sedition of Antioch severely punished by Theodosius.
- Maximus invades Italy; Valentinian flees to Theodosius.

388

- Maximus defeated and executed by Theodosius.

390

- Sedition of Thessalonica punished by massacre; Theodosius compelled by St Ambrose to do humble penance at Milan.
- Paganism prohibited under heavy penalties.

392

- Death of Valentinian II, strangled by Arbogast, a Frankish general in the Imperial service; Eugenius usurps Western Empire at the instance of Arbogast.

394

- Theodosius defeats Eugenius and becomes sole Emperor; Eugenius is killed and Arbogast commits suicide.
- Olympic Games finally abolished.

395

- Final division of the Empire into East and West: Honorius becomes Western Emperor and Arcadius, Eastern Emperor.
- Death of Theodosius the Great.

396

- Alaric, the Visigothic leader, invades Greece.

397

- Alaric defeated in Greece by Stilicho, master-general of the Western armies, of Vandal race.

398

- Alaric made master-general of Eastern Illyricum and also proclaimed King of the Visigoths.
- St Chrysostom becomes Archbishop of Constantinople.

399
- Revolt of Ostrogoths in Asia Minor under Tribigild: joined by Gainas, a Goth, who was military minister of the Eastern Empire.

400
- St Ninian begins to Christianize the Picts of Galloway in Scotland.
- Alaric invades Italy; Honorius flees from Rome.
- Claudian, the last of the Roman poets, celebrates Stilicho's victories.

401
- Gainas defeated by Fravitta, a loyal Goth; beheaded later by the Hunnish king.

402
- Battle of Pollentia: Stilicho defeats Alaric.

403
- Battle of Verona: Stilicho again victorious over Alaric.

404
- Honorious makes Ravenna his capital.
- Gladiatorial contests abolished.

405
- Italy invaded by a Germanic host under the Pagan Radagaisus: Florence is besieged; the invaders are defeated and their leader is killed by Stilicho.
- St Patrick begins the conversion of the Irish.

407
- Revolt of British army: Constantine declared Emperor.

408
- Constantine acknowledged in Gaul and Spain.
- Theodosius II, Eastern Emperor; government conducted first by Anthemius, then by Pulcheria, sister of the Emperor.
- Stilicho disgraced and assassinated.
- Alaric besieges Rome; bought off.

409
- Second Siege of Rome by Alaric; Ostia captured; Attalus made Emperor by Alaric, with himself as master-general of the West.
- Spain invaded by Suevi, Vandals, Alans, etc.

410
- Alaric degrades Attalus; Rome besieged and sacked; Italy ravaged; death of Alaric.
- Edict of Honorius calling upon Britain to defend itself; Britain sets up a provisional government, as does Armorica (Brittany).

411
- Constantius regains Gaul for Honorius.

413
- Heraclian invades Italy from Africa; defeated and executed.

414
- Atawulf, successor of Alaric, after conquering in Gaul, marches to Spain in order to recover it for the Empire; he is assassinated next year at Barcelona.

418
- Visigoths under Wallia reconquer Spain for the Empire.

419
- Visigoths granted lands in Aquitania under the Empire: Visigothic kingdom of Toulouse established.
- Theodoric I, King of the Visigoths.

422
- Eastern Empire successful against Persia.

423
- Death of Honorius; usurpation of the western Empire by John.

425
- Emperor John beheaded at Aquileia: Valentinian III becomes Emperor, with his mother Placidia as guardian.

427
- Chlodio first known King of the Franks, on the lower Rhine.
- Aëtius, a general of Valentinian III, deceives Boniface, another general of the Empire, into revolting in Africa.

428
- Boniface invites the Vandals to invade Africa.

429
- The Vandals under Gaiseric invade Africa from Spain.

430
- Boniface, repenting, opposes the Vandals unsuccessfully.

431
- Third General Council of the Church, at Ephesus.

437
- Burgundian kingdom on the Upper Rhine overthrown by Aëtius: the Burgundians granted lands in Savoy.

439
- Carthage taken by the Vandals.

440
- Leo I (the Great) Pope (d.461).

445
- Huns under Attila attack the eastern Empire.

446
- 'The Groans of the Britons': unsuccessful appeal of the Britons to Aëtius for help against the invading Saxons and others (traditional).
- Treaty between Attila and Theodosius.

448
- Meroveus King of the Franks – hence Merovingian dynasty.

449
- Jutes under Hengist and Horsa invade and settle in Kent.

450
- Marcian becomes eastern Emperor as husband of Pulcheria.

451
- Attila and the Huns, with Ostrogothic subjects, invade Gaul.
- Battle of Châlons or Troyes or the Catalaunian Fields or Maurica: Aëtius in alliance with the Visigoths under Theodoric I and the Franks under Meroveus repel Attila and save Western Europe from the Huns; Theodoric killed.
- Fourth General Council of the Church, at Chalcedon.

452
- Attila invades Italy and destroys Aquileia; the city of Venice originated with fugitives.

453
- Death of Attila and end of his Empire; the Ostrogoths free again.
- Theodoric II, King of the Visigoths.
- Aëtius murdered by Valentinian III.

455
- Valentinian III assassinated at the instance of Maximus; Maximus becomes Emperor.

- Gaiseric and the Vandals march against Rome; Maximus assassinated when attempting flight; Rome sacked by the Vandals.
- Avitus made Emperor by the Visigoths.

456

- Avitus deposed by Rikimer, a Goth in the service of the Empire who had defeated the Vandals by sea and land; he is recognized as Patrician of Rome.
- Sardinia occupied by the Vandals.
- Visigoths conquers most of Spain: Toledo becomes their capital.

457

- Rikimer makes Majorian Western Emperor; Leo I becomes Eastern Emperor.
- Childeric, King of the Franks.

460

- Majorian's great fleet for invasion of Africa destroyed by Gaiseric in the Bay of Carthagena, through treachery.

461

- Rikimer compels Majorian to abdicate and makes Libius Severus a purely nominal Emperor; Marcellinus revolts in Dalmatia and Aegidius in Gaul.

465

- Death of Severus; no Western Emperor for two years.

466

- Euric King of the Visigoths.

467

- Anthemius becomes Western Emperor.

468

- Leo's expedition against the Vandals fails.
- Sardinia recovered from the Vandals.

469

- The Vandals occupy Corsica.

472

- Olybrius made Western Emperor by Rikimer, who sacks Rome and massacres Athemius; deaths of Rikimer and Olybrius.
- Glycerius, Emperor for a brief period; Julius Nepos made Emperor by Leo I.

474

- Leo II, Eastern Emperor; succeeded by Zeno.

475

- The Patrician Orestes leads the barbarian confederates against Nepos in Ravenna; Nepos flees to Dalmatia.
- Romulus Augustulus, son of Orestes, proclaimed Western Emperor.
- Odoacer, a Goth, leads a revolt of the barbarian allies, who proclaim him King of Italy: besieges Orestes in Pavia and executes him.

476

- Romulus Augustulus forced to resign the Empire.
- Zeno, at the instance of the Senate, made Odoacer, Patrician of Italy.
- Odoacer obtains Sicily from the Vandals for tribute.

477

- South Saxons under Ella settle in England.

478

- Ostrogoths under Theodoric the Great invade Greece.

480

- Julius Nepos assassinated in Dalmatia; no successor appointed; end of the Western Empire.

THE GERMANIC KINGDOMS

481
- Dalmatia annexed by Odoacer.
- Clovis becomes King of the Franks; Tournai his capital.

484
- Sardinia recaptured by the Vandals.

485
- Death of Euric, King of the Visigoths; the Visigothic kingdom at its greatest extent.

486
- Battle of Soissons: Syagrius, son of Aegidius, Roman ruler of a kingdom with Paris at its centre, defeated by Clovis and his kingdom annexed.

488
- Theodoric the Great commissioned by the Emperor Zeno to recover Italy for the Empire.

489
- Battle of Aquileia: Theodoric defeats Odoacer.

489
- Battle of Verona: Theodoric defeats Odoacer.

490
- Odoacer again defeated by Theodoric.

491
- Clovis subdues the Thuringi.
- Anastasius I becomes Emperor at Constantinople.

492
- Isaurian War begins and occupies Anastasius till 496.

493
- Theodoric captures Ravenna and puts Odoacer to death; beginning of Ostrogothic kingdom of Italy.

495
- West Saxons settle in England under Cerdic and Cynric.

496
- Clovis subdues the Alamanni.

496
- Clovis converts from Paganism to Catholicism.

500
- Scots under Fergus Mor cross from Ireland to found kingdom of Dalriada in Scotland.
- Clovis defeats Gundobald, King of the Burgundians, near Dijon.

502
- War between the Roman Empire and Persia (ended 506).

504
- Theodoric's general, Pitzia, defeats the Gepids and makes them subject allies.

507
- Battle of Vouillé (near Poitiers): Clovis defeats the Visigoths and kills their king, Alaric II.

508
- Clovis made a Roman Consul by the Emperor Anastasius.
- Peace between Theodoric and the Empire after a short war arising out of the Gepid war of 504.

510
- Clovis annexes Aquitania from Visigoths.

- Theodoric checks Clovis, wins Provence for the Ostrogoths and saves a small part of Gaul for the Visigoths.
- Theodoric rules the Visigothic kingdom as protector of his grandson Amalaric: Gothic power at its height.

511
- Death of Clovis; the Frankish kingdom divided among his four sons, Thierry, Childebert, Chlodomir and Clotaire, with capitals at Metz, Paris, Orleans and Soissons.

516
- Battle of Mount Badon: Saxon advance in Britain is checked by the Britons.

518
- Justin I becomes Emperor.

520
- The dating of the Christian Era introduced about this time in Italy by Dionysius Exiguus.

522
- War between the Empire and Persia.

524
- Boethius the philosopher executed by Theodoric on a charge of treason.

525
- Symmachus, father-in-law of Boethius, executed by Theodoric the Great.

526
- Remorse and death of Theodoric the Great.

IMPERIAL REVIVAL UNDER JUSTINIAN

526
- Destructive earthquake at Antioch: great loss of life.
- East and Middle Saxons settle in England about this time.

527
- Accession of Justinian I to the Roman Empire.

529
- Justinian suppresses the Athenian Schools of Philosophy.
- Justinian's Code of Civil Law is prepared under the direction of Tribonian.

530
- Gelimer becomes King of the Vandals.

531
- Chosroes I becomes King of Persia.
- The Franks subdue the Thuringians in central Germany; also the Bavarians.

532
- The Nika at Constantinople: a destructive revolt due to the rivalry of the Blue and Green circus factions; Belisarius' troops massacre 30, 000 of the rebels.
- Peace concluded between Justinian and Persia.
- Franks invade Burgundy.

533
- War between the Empire and the Vandals: Carthage captured by Belisarius and Gelimer taken prisoner.
- Justinian's *Institutes* published; also the *Pandects* or *Digest*.

534
- Conquest of Burgundy by the Franks: end of the Burgundian kingdom.
- North Africa recovered for the Roman Empire; the Vandal kingdom at an end.
- Malta becomes a province of the Byzantine Empire.

535

- Moors defeated in Africa by Solomon, colleague of Belisarius.
- Amalasuntha, Queen of the Ostrogoths, strangled by Theodatus; a pretext for Justinian's invasion.
- Belisarius subdues Sicily.

536

- Belisarius invades Italy and takes Naples; Witigis becomes King of the Ostrogoths; Belisarius enters Rome.

537

- Justinian builds and dedicates the Cathedral of St Sophia in Constantinople.
- The Ostrogoths, under Witigis, besiege Belisarius in Rome; the siege fails.
- Belisarius deposes the Pope, Sylverius; the see sold to Vigilius.

538

- Siege of Rome raised.
- Burgundians destroy Milan; Franks invade Italy.
- Buddhism arrives at the court of the Japanese Emperor.

539

- Belisarius takes Ravenna.
- Bulgarian invasion of Macedonia and Greece; Slavs invade Illyricum and Thrace.

540

- Recall of Belisarius.
- Chosroes I invades Syria.
- The Goths revolt in Italy.

541

- Justinian ends the Roman consulship.
- Chosroes I captures Antioch and expels many of its people; Belisarius sent to defend Asia against him.
- The Goths victorious in Italy under Totila; Byzantine rule in Italy brought to an end.

542

- Plague in Europe.
- Belisarius drives Chosroes across the Euphrates.
- Battle of Septa: Visigothic invasion of Africa defeated.

543

- Rebellion of the Moors begins (ends 558).
- Death of St Benedict, organizer of western monasticism at Monte Casino (in Italy).
- Franks invade Spain and besiege Saragossa; heavily defeated by the Visigoths.

544

- Belisarius again in Italy.

545

- The Turks ascendant in Tartary.

546

- Totila captures Rome.

547

- Belisarius recovers Rome.
- English kingdom of Bernicia founded by Ida.

548

- Final recall of Belisarius from Italy.

549

- The Goths again take Rome; Sicily, Sardinia and Corsica captured; Greece invaded.
- Siege of Petra begins (ends 551).
- Beginning of Colchian or Lazic War (ends 556).

551
- Germanus leads an army to Italy against the Goths; he dies.
- End of the Roman Senate.
- Introduction of silk cultivation into Europe.

552
- Narses made commander against the Goths.
- Battle of Tadino: Totila defeated and killed.

553
- Narses recovers Rome.
- Battle of Mons Lactarius: the Goths under Teias defeated and Teias killed.

553
- Fifth General Council of the Church, at Constantinople.
- Invasion of Italy by Frankish and Alamanni forces under Lothaire and Buccelin.

554
- Battle of Casilinum: The Alamannic invaders defeated by Narses.
- Part of southern Spain recovered for the Empire by this date.
- End of the Ostrogothic kingdom; Italy becomes the Exarchate of Ravenna under the Empire.

558
- Avar embassy to Justinian: the Avars employed against the Bulgarians and Slavs.
- Clotaire I, sole King of the Franks.

559
- Bulgarians under Zabergan invade Macedonia and Thrace and threaten Constantinople; defeated by Belisarius.

560
- Kingdom of Deira founded in Britain by Aella.

561
- Frankish monarchy divided among the four sons of Clotaire I: Charibert I, Guntram, Sigebert I and Chilperic I (capitals, Paris, Orleans, Rheims and Soissons).

562
- Peace concluded between Justinian and Persia.
  DEATHS
  Procopius, Byzantine historian.

563
- St Columba lands in Iona to Christianize the Picts of Scotland.

565
- Death of Justinian.

RISE OF THE PAPACY

565
- Justin II becomes Emperor: the Empire becoming Greek instead of Latin.

566
- Avar embassy to Justin II.
- Lombards and Avars destroy the Gepid kingdom.

568
- The Lombards under Alboin begin to conquer in Italy and establish a kingdom.
- Leovigild becomes King of the Visigoths.

570
- Birth of Muhammad.
- The Persians conquer Yemen in Arabia.

- Beginning of the Avar Empire under Baian in the Danube lands vacated by the Lombards.
- St Asaph preaching Christianity in north Wales.

571

- The Lombards take Pavia and make it their capital; Italy now partly Imperial and partly Lombard.

572

- Renewal of war between Persia and the Empire.

573

- Alboin murdered at the instance of his wife, Rosamond; Clepho becomes King of the Lombards.

573

- Battle of Arderydd: Christian party gains the victory in the kingdom of the Strathclyde Britons.

574

- Clepho murdered; the Lombards ruled for ten years by a number of independent dukes.

575

- Synod of Drumceatt in Ireland: Columba gets Aidan recognized as independent King of Dalriada.

577

- Battle of Deorham: the West Saxons under Ceawlin defeat Britons; Saxon advance resumed.

578

- Tiberius II becomes Emperor.

579

- Hormuz succeeds Chosroes I as King of Persia.

581

- Slavs invaded Greece and Thrace: defeated by Priscus.

582

- Maurice becomes Emperor.

584

- Autharis becomes King of the Lombards, but the duchies of Spoleto and Beneventum in the centre and south remain practically independent; three invasions of Franks and Alamanni repelled.

585

- Visigoths conquer and absorb the Suevic kingdom in northwest Spain.
- St Columba leaves Ireland to convert Burgundy.

586

- Reccared becomes King of the Visigoths: under him the Visigoths abandon Arianism and become Catholic Christians.

588

- The kingdom of Northumbria formed by the union of Bernicia and Deira.

590

- Gregory the Great becomes Pope (till 604): greatly increases the powers of the bishop of Rome by taking advantage of the confusion and disunion of Italy.
- Revolt of Bahram in Persia; Hormuz deposed: Chosroes II becomes King of Persia, but has to flee to the Romans for help; Roman general, Narses (not the conqueror of Italy), defeats Bahram and recovers his kingdom for Chosroes II.

592

- Agilulf becomes King of the Lombards.

595
- The Emperor Maurice has to fight against the Avars (till 602).

597
- Augustine, sent by Gregory the Great, converts Ethelbert and the kingdom of Kent to Christianity; becomes first Archbishop of Canterbury.

601
- Death of St David, patron saint of Wales.

602
- Phocas becomes Emperor: Maurice executed.

603
- Death of Kentigern (or St Mungo), who converted the Strathclyde Britons.
- Battle of Degsastan: Northumbrians under Tethelfrith defeat Scots under Aidan.

609
- Muhammad preaches at Mecca.

610
- Heraclius overthrows Phocas and becomes Emperor; the Empire hard pressed by Persians, Avar and Slavs.

611
- Persians capture Antioch.

613
- Clotaire II, sole King of the Franks.
- Persians take Damascus and overruns Syria.
- Battle of Chester: Northumbrians under Ethelfrith defeat Welsh.

614
- St Gall, from Ireland, settles in east Switzerland.

616
- Persians take Alexandria and subdue Egypt.
- Asia Minor conquered by the Persians.

617
- Persians capture Chalcedon, opposite Constantinople.

621
- Swinthila becomes King of the Visigoths; recovers southern Spain from the Empire.

622
- Heraclius begins his great campaigns against the Persians under Chosroes II.
- The Hejira, or flight of Muhammad from Mecca to Medina.

626
- Constantinople unsuccessfully attacked by the Persians in league with the Avars.

627
- Battle of Nineveh: Heraclius's final victory over the Persians.
- Edwin, King of Northumbria, embraces Christianity under the influence of Paulinus, who becomes first Archbishop of York.

628
- Chosroes II deposed and murdered; peace between Persia and the Empire.
- Muhammad's message to all rulers calling upon them to embrace Islam.

629
- Submission of Mecca to Muhammad; first battle between Muslims and the Empire, near the Dead Sea.

630
- Dagobert I, sole King of the Franks.

632
- Death of Muhammad: Arabia conquered by the Muslims by this date.

The Advance of Islam

632
- Muhammad succeeded by Abubekr, the first Caliph; beginning of the Caliphate.
  DEATHS
  Muhammad, founder of Islam.

633
- Battle of Heathfield: Edwin, King of Northumbria, overthrown and killed by Penda, heathen King of Mercia, in alliance with Welsh under Caedwalla.

634
- Battle of Ajnadain (near Jerusalem): Muslims under Khaled defeat the army of Heraclius.
- Omar becomes Caliph.
- Battle of Hexham: Oswald defeats Caedwalla and becomes King of Northumbria.

635
- The Muslims capture Damascus.
- St Aidan goes to Lindisfarne from Iona to reChristianize Northumbria.

636
- Battle of Yermuk: Muslim victory over Imperial troops seals fate of Syria.
- Rotharis, King of the Lombards; a great legislator.

637
- Battle of Cadesia: Muslims defeat the Persians and conquer western Persian provinces.
- Muslims capture Ctesiphon in Persia.

638
- Muslims capture Jerusalem.
- Muslims capture Aleppo and Antioch.

639
- Death of Dagobert I, last notable Merovingian King of the Franks; Mayors of the Palace become the real rulers in Austrasia (eastern division of kingdom), Neustria (western division) and Burgundy; nominal kings called *rois fainéants* ('do-nothing kings').

640
- Muslims begin conquest of Egypt under Amru.

641
- Heraclius succeeded in the Empire by his sons, Constantine III and Heracleonas.
- Battle of Nehavend: Muslims defeat Persians and overthrow the Sassanid Dynasty; last Sassanid King, Yezdegerd III, dies a fugitive in 651.

642
- Constans II, Emperor.
- Muslims occupy Alexandria.
- Battle of Maserfeld (Oswestry): Oswald of Northumbria defeated and killed by Penda of Mercia.

644
- Othman becomes Caliph.

647
- Muslims begin conquest of Africa.

649
- Muslims conquer Cyprus.

653
- Aribert first Catholic King of the Lombards.

654
- Muslims conquer Rhodes.

655
- Great naval victory of Muslims over Greeks off Lycian coast.
- Battle of the Winwaed: Penda of Mercia defeated and killed by the Northumbrians under Oswy.

656
- Othman murdered; Ali becomes Caliph.

659
- Wulfhere becomes King of Mercia and restores Mercian power.

660
- Sect of Paulicians, followers of St Paul, founded in Armenia by Constantine.

661
- Ali murdered; Moawiya first of the Ommiade Caliphs, with seat at Damascus.

662
- Emperor Constans II goes to Italy and tries to recover part of it.

664
- Synod of Whitby: Oswy of Northumbria decides for Roman against Celtic Christianity.

668
- Constantine IV becomes Emperor, after Constans II is assassinated in Italy.
- Death of Samo, a Frank who had founded a Slav kingdom in the Danube valley, after a long reign.

669
- Theodore of Tarsus reaches England as Archbishop of Canterbury; introduces Greek learning and organizes the English Church.

670
- English poet, Caedmon, flourishes at this time.
- Aquitaine about this time breaks away from Frankish rule.

671
- Egfrith, King of Northumbria.

672
- Wamba the last great King of the Visigoths.

673
- First Arab siege of Constantinople begins.

675
- Slavs and Bulgars overrun Macedonia.

677
- Arabs abandon siege of Constantinople and agree to pay tribute; Greek fire used by defenders.

679
- Bulgarians under Isperich occupy Moesia and settle there.

680
- Sixth General Council of the Church, at Constantinople; continues into 681.

685
- Justinian II becomes Emperor.
- Battle of Nechtansmere: Egfrith of Northumbria defeated and killed by the Picts under Brude; Northumbria never recovers its power.

687
- Battle of Tertry: Pepin of Heristal, the Austrasian Mayor of the Palace, defeats the Neustrian Mayor of the Palace and becomes virtual ruler over the whole Frankish kingdom.

DEATHS
St Cuthbert, Bishop of Lindisfarne.

688
- Ine, first great King of Wessex.

689
- Pepin defeats the Frisians.

690
- St Willibrord, an Anglo-Saxon, becomes Bishop of Frisia, which he converts to Christianity.

693
- Battle of Sebastopolis: Greeks defeated by the Muslims.

695
- Leontius usurps the Empire.

697
- First Doge of Venice elected.

698
- Muslims capture Carthage.
- Tiberius III usurps the Empire.

705
- Justinian II recovers the Empire and perpetrates great cruelties.

709
- Pepin defeats the Alamanni.

  DEATHS
  St Wilfrid, Bishop of York.

710
- Muslim conquest of Africa complete.
- Muslims begin conquest of Transoxiana; they reach India.
- Roderick, King of the Visigoths.
- First Muslim invasion of Spain.

711
- Second Muslim invasion of Spain under Tarik; Visigoth kingdom overthrown in Battle of Xeres or Guadalete or Lake Janda; Toledo, the capital, captured; oppressed Jews welcome invaders.
- Justinian II executed; Philippicus becomes Emperor.

712
- Liutprand, King of the Lombards; aims at unifying Italy under the Lombard monarchy.

713
- Battle of Segoyuela: Muslims again victorious over Visigoths; King Roderick killed.
- Anastasius II usurps the Empire.

714
- Death of Pepin of Heristal.

716
- Theodosius III usurps the Empire.

717
- Leo III (the Isaurian) becomes Emperor.
- Second Arab siege of Constantinople begins by land and sea under Moslemah, brother of the Caliph Soliman; Muslims routed in 718 with the help of the Bulgarians and by means of Greek fire.
- Battle of Vincy: Charles Martel, son of Pepin of Heristal, defeats the Neustrians and becomes virtual ruler of the Franks.
- Church of Iona confirmed to Roman Catholicism.

718
- Charles Martel ravages the country of the Saxons (in north Germany).

720
- Muslims cross the Pyrenees and capture Narbonne.

721
- Muslim attack on Toulouse repelled by Eudes (Eudo), Duke of Aquitaine.

722
- St Boniface, an Anglo-Saxon, goes as a Papal missionary to Germany under the protection of Charles Martel.

724
- Charles Martel ravages Frisia.

725
- Muslims take Carcassonne and Nimes.
- Charles Martel fights the Bavarians.

726
- Leo III begins his campaign against the worship of images, promulgating the Iconoclastic controversy; he is opposed by Pope Gregory II.

731
- Pope Gregory III summons a council at Rome that condemns the Iconoclasts; this breach between the Pope and the Empire makes the Roman Republic virtually independent of the Empire but under Papal influence.
- Muslims under Abderrahman advance to conquer France.
- Bede's *Ecclesiastical History* completed.

732
- Battle of Tours or Poitiers: Charles Martel defeats and drives back the Muslims.

THE AGE OF CHARLEMAGNE

733
- Ethelbald of Mercia becomes ruler of Wessex.

737
- Angus MacFergus, King of the Picts, subdues the Scots of Dalriada.

739
- Pope Gregory III appeals to Charles Martel for help against the Lombards, who, under Liutprand, are besieging Rome.

740
- Constantine V becomes Emperor.

741
- Death of Charles Martel: Frankish kingdom divided between his sons, Pepin the Short and Carloman.

747
- Carloman becomes a monk, leaving Pepin sole master of the Franks.

750
- Umayyad Dynasty of Caliphs overthrown and replaced by the Abbasids.
- Cynewulf, Anglo-Saxon poet.

751
- Pepin the Short, with the consent of Pope Zacharias, is crowned King of the Franks at Soissons, superseding the nominal Merovingian Childeric III: beginning of the Carolingian Dynasty.
- Ravenna captured by the Lombards under King Aistulf: end of the Exarchate.

752
- Battle of Burford: Cuthred of Wessex defeats Ethelbald of Mercia.

754

- Pope Stephen II concludes an alliance with Pepin, whom he anoints as King of the Franks and Patrician of the Romans.
- Pepin invades Italy and repels the Lombards under Aistulf; he grants the lands of the Exarchate to Pope Stephen II; beginning of the temporal power of the Papacy.
- Iconoclastic Synod, Constantinople.

755

- Abderrahman founds the Emirate (afterwards Caliphate) of Cordova in Spain as a secession from the Abbasid Caliphate.

756

- Pepin again in Italy to subdue the Lombards.
- Strathclyde subdued by Angus, the Pictish King, and Eadbert of Northumbria.

757

- Offa becomes King of Mercia and makes himself overlord of England.

758

- Pepin fights heathen Saxons between the Rhine and the Elbe.

759

- Pepin takes Narbonne from the Muslims.

760

- Pepin begins conquest of Aquitaine; completed in 768.

766

- The Abbasids remove the Caliphate to Baghdad.

768

- Death of Pepin; Frankish kingdom divided between his sons, Charlemagne (Charles the Great) and Carloman.

770

- Dissolution of the monasteries by the Eastern Emperor.

771

- Death of Carloman; Charlemagne, sole King of the Franks.

772

- Charlemagne begins his wars against the Saxons.

773

- Desiderius, King of the Lombards, attacks Pope Adrian I, who appeals to Charlemagne.

774

- Charlemagne captures Pavia and overthrows the Lombard kingdom; he is crowned King of the Lombards; renews Pepin's donation of territory to the Pope.

775

- Leo IV becomes Emperor.

776

- Charlemagne again in Italy to repress the Lombards.

777

- Battle of Bensington: Offa of Mercia defeats Cynewulf of Wessex.

778

- Charlemagne invades Spain and takes Pampeluna; origin of the Spanish March (established 795); his rearguard cut to pieces by Basques at Roncesvalles and Roland killed.

780

- Constantine VI becomes Emperor, with his mother Irene as regent; the latter opposes the Iconoclasts.

781

- Eastern Empire abandons claims to the pontifical state in Italy.

782
- Alcuin, a British scholar, goes to Aachen (Aix-la-Chapelle) to organize the palace school of Charlemagne.
- The Eastern Empire pays tribute to the great Caliph Haroun-al-Raschid.

787
- Seventh General Council of the Church, at Nicaea.

788
- Charlemagne finally conquers Bavaria; Duke Tassilo is deposed.

789
- Constantin I, King of the Picts.

790
- Constantine VI proclaimed sole Emperor.

793
- First Viking raid on Britain, at Lindisfarne in Northumbria.

795
- First Viking raid on Ireland.

796
- Charlemagne conquers the Avars.

797
- Irene blinds Constantine VI and rules alone.

798
- Vikings raid the Isle of Man.

800
- Charlemagne crowned Holy Roman Emperor by Pope Leo III in St Peter's at Rome on Christmas Day.

801
- Charlemagne receives an embassy from Haroun-al-Raschid.

802
- Nicephorus I dethrones Irene and becomes Eastern Emperor.
- First Viking raid on Iona.

804
- Charlemagne completes the conquest of the Saxons and compels them to accept Christianity.
  DEATHS
  Alcuin, English scholar.

806
- The Vikings desolate Iona.

807
- The Vikings attack the west coast of Ireland.

810
- The Frisian coast is ravaged by Vikings.

811
- Nicephorus I killed in a war against the Bulgarians under Krum; Michael I becomes Eastern Emperor, after Stauracius reigned a few months.
  DEATHS
  Abu Nuwas, Arab poet.

812
- Michael I acknowledges Charlemagne as Western Emperor.

813
- Michael I defeated by Bulgarians and dethroned; Leo V becomes Eastern Emperor.

814
- Death of Charlemagne.

EMERGENCE OF FRANCE AND GERMANY

814
- Louis I of France becomes King of the Franks and Western Emperor on the death of his father, Charlemagne.

817
- Partition of Aachen: Louis I divides his kingdom among his sons.

818
- Bernard, King of Italy, nephew of Louis I, revolts; he is defeated and executed.

820
- Eastern Emperor Leo V murdered; Michael II becomes Eastern Emperor.
- Viking raids on Ireland.

824
- Iona raided by the Vikings for the third time.

825
- Battle of Gafulford: Egbert of Wessex conquers the West Welsh (in Cornwall).
- Battle of Ellandune: Egbert of Wessex defeats Beornwulf of Mercia; Kent conquered about same time and East Saxons submitted.

826
- Crete taken by the Muslims.

827
- Muslim conquest of Sicily begins.

829
- Theophilus becomesEastern Emperor.
- Egbert of Wessex conquers Mercia.

833
- The Field of Lies: Louis I compelled by his sons to abdicate.

834
- Viking raids in Britain: Sheppey attacked.
- Vikings sack Dorstadt and Utrecht.

835
- Louis I restored to his kingdom.

836
- Vikings sack Antwerp; attack Dorsetshire.

838
- Vikings under Thorgils capture Dublin, after desolating much of Ireland.
- Battle of Hengestesdun: Egbert of Wessex defeats Vikings and West Welsh.

839
- Ethelwulf becomes King of Wessex and England.

840
- Muslims make conquests in Southern Italy.
- Death of Louis I; Lothair I, the eldest son, becomes Western Emperor.

841
- Vikings under Oscar sack Rouen.
- Battle of Fontenoy: Louis the German and Charles the Bald, sons of Louis I, defeat their brother, Lothair I.

842
- Louis the German and Charles the Bald exchange the Oaths of Strassburg in Romance and German, the earliest document of the French and German languages.
- Muslims capture Bari in south Italy and make it their base.
- Michael III becomes Eastern Emperor under the guardianship of his mother, Theodora, who finally restores image-worship.

843
- Treaty of Verdun: the Frankish or Carolingian Empire partitioned between Louis the German (eastern or German part), Charles the Bald (western or French part); Charles II of France and Emperor Lothair I (Italy and a part between France and Germany): the beginning of France and Germany as distinct states.

844
- Vikings raid Spanish coast, but are driven off.
- Kenneth MacAlpin, King of the Scots as well as King of the Picts: beginning of Scottish kingdom.

845
- Malachy, King of Meath, defeats and kills Thorgils, Norse King of Northern Ireland.
- Vikings destroy Hamburg; Paris partly destroyed by Vikings under Ragnar.
- Battle of Ballon: Charles the Bald defeated by Bretons.

846
- Vikings defeated in Somerset.
- Muslims sack Rome.

848
- Vikings take Bordeaux.
- Vikings defeated in Ireland.
- Battle of Ostia: Muslims defeated in naval battle at mouth of Tiber, largely owing to Pope Leo IV.

850
- John Scotus (Erigena), an Irish scholar and theologian, flourishes about this time at court of Charles the Bald.

851
- Battle of Juvardeil: Bretons defeat Charles the Bald.
- Great Viking attack on England under Roric; Canterbury burnt; London plundered.
- Battle of Aclea: Ethelwulf of Wessex routs Vikings.

853
- Vikings land in Thanet.

855
- Death of Emperor Lothair I; his son, Louis II, becomes Emperor and King of Italy; another son, Lothair, becomes King of Lotharingia or Lorraine (the central kingdom of his father); and a third son, Charles, becomes King of Provence.

858
- Ethelbald becomes King of Wessex and England.
- Nicholas I becomes Pope; final breach between Eastern and Western Churches.

860
- Ethelbert becomes King of Wessex and England.
- Donald becomes King of Scotland.
- Vikings under Weland capture Winchester, capital of Wessex; then are defeated.

862
- Swedish invasion of Russia under Rurik; a state founded with Novgorod as capital, afterwards Kiev, the origin of Russia; Swedes become absorbed by the Slavs.

863
- Death of Charles, King of Provence; his kingdom falls mostly to Emperor Louis II, King of Italy.

864
- Boris, King of Bulgarians, baptized as a Christian.

865
- Russian attack on Constantinople.

866
- Robert the Strong, Count of Anjou, killed in battle against the Vikings.
- Ethelred I becomes King of Wessex and England.
- 'Great Army' of Vikings under Ingwar and Hubba in East Anglia.
- Emperor Louis II routs the Muslims.

867
- Michael III murdered; Basil I, Eastern Emperor; founding of Macedonian Dynasty.
- Vikings capture York: Northumbrian kingdom overthrown.
- Scotland ravaged by Vikings from Ireland under Olaf the White, King of Dublin.

868
- Muslims capture Malta.

869
- Death of Lothair, King of Lorraine.

870
- Treaty of Mersen: Lorraine divided between Charles the Bald and Louis the German; France and Germany conterminous.
- Vikings from Northumbria invade East Anglia; death of St Edmund, King of East Anglia, in Battle of Hoxne.
- Eighth General Council of the Church, at Constantinople.

    DEATHS
    Al-Kindi, Arabian philosopher.
    Gottschalk, German theologian and poet.

871
- Vikings invade Wessex; capture Reading; defeated in battle of Ashdown; successful in battle of Basing; battle of Marden is indecisive.
- Alfred the Great becomes King of Wessex and England.
- Battle of Wilton: Alfred is defeated by the Vikings, who winter in London.
- Olaf the White, from Ireland, invades Strathclyde and takes Dumbarton.
- Emperor Louis II captures Bari, the Muslim headquarters in south Italy, with naval help from Eastern Emperor Basil I.

872
- Battle of Halfsfjord: Harold Haarfager becomes sole King of Norway.

874
- Iceland colonized by Norwegians.
- Vikings defeat Mercian kingdom.

875
- Death of Emperor Louis II; Charles the Bald becomes Western Emperor.
- Norse Earldom of Orkney established by Harold Haarfager.
- Viking attacks on Wessex renewed.
- Thorstein the Red, son of Olaf the White, conquers a large part of Scotland.

876
- Death of Louis the German: Charles the Fat becomes German King.
- Battle of Andernach: Charles the Bald defeated.

877
- Death of Charles the Bald: his son, Louis II (the Stammerer), becomes King of France.
- Vikings divide up Mercia.
- Battle of Dollar: Constantin II of Scotland defeated by Vikings.
- Battle of Forgan: Constantin II defeated and killed by Vikings.

878
- Vikings under Guthrum attack Wessex.
- Battle of Ethandun: Guthrum defeated by Alfred.

- Treaty of Wedmore: peace between Alfred and the Vikings; Guthrum baptized as a Christian; England divided between the two peoples.
- Muslims take Syracuse, almost completing conquest of Sicily.

879
- Death of Louis II; Louis III and Carloman, his sons, become joint Kings of France.
- Boso becomes independent King of Burgundy or the kingdom of Arles.

881
- Charles the Fat crowned Emperor at Rome.
- Vikings sack Aachen.
- Battle of Saucourt: Louis III and Carloman defeat the Vikings.

882
- Death of Louis III; Carloman, sole King of France.
- Treaty of Elsloo: Charles the Fat reaches agreement with the Vikings.

884
- Death of Carloman, King of France: Charles the Fat chosen King of France; re-union of most of Charlemagne's Empire.

885
- Vikings under Rollo besiege Paris.

886
- Paris saved from the Vikings by Odo, Count of Paris.
- Leo VI becomes Eastern Emperor.
- Alfred recovers London from the Vikings; Danelaw established in England.

887
- Charles the Fat deposed; final break-up of Frankish Empire.

VIKING AND MAGYAR SETTLEMENTS

887
- On deposition of Charles the Fat, Arnulf becomes King of Germany and Odo, Count of Paris, King of West Franks.
- Louis the Blind succeeds Boso as King of Cisjuran Burgundy (Arles); Rudolph I founds kingdom of Transjuran Burgundy farther north.

888
- Berengar of Friuli, King of Italy.
- Third siege of Paris by Vikings; bought off by Odo.
- Odo defeats Vikings in Champagne.
- Muslims or Moors settle on Provençal coast and penetrate inland.

891
- Battle of Louvain: Arnulf, King of Germany, defeats the Vikings.
- Guido of Spoleto becomes Emperor and King of Italy after defeating Berengar.

893
- Civil War between Odo and the Carolingian, Charles the Simple; the latter admitted to a share in the kingdom.
- Simeon founds a great Bulgarian Empire, which falls to pieces after his death.
- Great Viking invasion of England under Hastings; Vikings defeated at Farnham and Bemfleet.

895
- Arnulf overthrows Guido and becomes King of Italy.
- Alfred the Great captures the Viking fleet.
- Magyars under Arpad invade Hungary, where they settle permanently.

896
- Arnulf crowned Emperor at Rome.

898
* Charles the Simple, King of France on the death of Odo.

899
* Arnulf succeeded as German King by Louis the Child.
  DEATHS
  Alfred the Great.

900
* Edward the Elder succeeds Alfred the Great.
* Constantin III, King of Scotland.

901
* Louis the Blind (of Provence) crowned Emperor as Louis III.

902
* Battle of the Holme: Edward the Elder defeats the Vikings of Northumbria.

903
* Magyars reach the Elbe.

904
* Sergius III becomes Pope; degradation of the Papacy under the influence of Theodora, wife of Theophylact, Consul of Rome and her daughter, Marozia.
* Constantin III of Scotland expels the Vikings.
* Muslims raid Salonica.

905
* Louis the Blind blinded by Berengar.

906
* Magyars complete conquest of Hungary.

907
* Magyars invade Bavaria.
* Russian fleet under Oleg attacks Constantinople.

908
* Magyars ravage Thuringia.

909
* Magyars ravage Suabia.
* Fatimite Caliphate founded in North Africa by Obaidallah.

910
* Battle of Augsburg: Louis the Child defeated by the Magyars.
* Battle of Tottenhall: Edward the Elder severely defeats the Vikings.
* Foundation of Cluny Abbey in eastern France; becomes the centre of a monastic reformation.

911
* Conrad I of Franconia succeeds Louis the Child as German King.
* Charles the Simple acquires Lotharingia or Lorraine.
* Muslims destroy the Greek fleet.
* Treaty of St Clair-sur-epte; the Vikings, under Rollo, allowed by Charles the Simple to settle in the land that becomes Normandy.

912
* Constantine VII becomes Eastern Emperor; his uncle, Alexander, being regent and joint Emperor.

913
* Kingdom of Leon founded.
* Magyars penetrate to Rhine.

914
* Bulgarians capture Adrianople.

915
- Berengar crowned Emperor.

916
- Battle of Garigliano: Muslims defeated by Romans under Theophylact and Alberic, husband of Marozia.
- Pope John X forms a league against the Moors in South Italy.
- Edward the Elder and his sister, Ethelfled, the Lady of the Mercians, recover eastern Mercia from the Vikings.
- Battle of Tempsford: Danes heavily defeated by Edward the Elder.
- Battle of Maldon: Edward the Elder victorious over the Danes; East Anglia recovered.

917
- Edward the Elder's victories over the Vikings continue; death of Ethelfled.

918
- Henry I (the Fowler) becomes the German King; beginning of Saxon line.

919
- Romanus I becomes co-Emperor in the East with Constantine VII.
- Edward the Elder receives the homage of all the northern kings in Britain.

922
- Charles the Simple displaced; Robert I, Duke of France, brother of Odo, crowned King of France.

923
- Battle of Soissons: Robert I, King of France, killed, though victorious over Charles the Simple's supporters; Hugh the Great becomes Duke of France and Rudolph I of Burgundy, King of France; Charles the Simple made prisoner.

923
- Muslim fleet destroyed at Lemnos.
  DEATHS
  Rhases, Arab physician.

924
- Nine years' truce between Henry I and the Magyars; Magyars ravage Italy.
- Berengar, Emperor and King of Italy, assassinated.
- Athelstan, King of England.

926
- Hugh of Provence becomes King of Italy.

927
- William Longsword succeeds Rollo as Duke of Normandy.
- Odo becomes Abbot of Cluny and starts the Cluniac reformation.
- Death of Simeon of Bulgaria.

928
- Henry I takes Brandenburg from the Slavs.

929
- Emirate of Cordova becomes a Caliphate; there now exist three Caliphates.
  DEATHS
  Al-Battani, Arab astronomer.

932
- Alberic, son of Marozia, expels Hugh of Provence from Rome and becomes head of the commune.

933
- Battle of Merseburg: Henry I defeats the Magyars.
- The two Burgundian kingdoms (Cisjuran and Transjuran) united.

934
- Haakon I becomes King of Norway.

936
- Otto I (the Great) becomes German King.
- Louis IV (d'Outremer) becomes King of France.

937
- Magyars invade Burgundy and Aquitaine.
- Battle of Brunanburh: Athelastan defeats a combination of Scots, Vikings and Northumbrians.

938
- Alan of the Twisted Beard expels Normans from Brittany.

939
- Otto I conquers Lorraine.

940
- Edmund becomes King of England.
- Harold Bluetooth, King of Denmark.

941
- Russian raid defeated by Byzantine fleet.

942
- Richard the Fearless becomes Duke of Normandy.
- Malcolm I becomes King of Scotland on Constantin III's abdication.

943
- Dunstan becomes Abbot of Glastonbury.

944
- Battle of Wels: Magyars defeated by Bavarians.
- Romanus I deposed.

946
- Eadred becomes King of England.
  DEATHS
  Tsuraguki, Japanese poet.

947
- Magyars again invade Italy and Aquitaine.

948
- Eadred suppresses a Northumbrian rebellion.

950
- Berengar of Ivrea becomes King of Italy.
  DEATHS
  Al-Farabi, Arab philosopher.

951
- Otto I invades Italy and makes Berengar do homage.

954
- Death of Alberic, the head of the Roman commune.
- Lothair, King of France.
- Malcolm I of Scotland killed in battle; succeeded by Indulph.

955
- Battle of Augsburg (Lechfeld): Otto I defeats Magyars and the Slavs; East Mark (afterwards Austria) refounded.
- Eadwig becomes King of England.

956
- Death of Hugh the Great; succeeded as Duke of France by his son, Hugh Capet.

958
- Romanus II, Eastern Emperor.

959
- Edgar becomes King of England.

960
- Dunstan becomes Archbishop of Canterbury.

961
- Otto I again in Italy; crowned King of Italy at Pavia.
- Nicephorus takes Crete from the Muslims.
- Haakon I of Norway killed in battle.

962
- Otto crowned Western Emperor at Rome: revival of Holy Roman Empire after a period of decline.

The Saxon Emperors

962
- Dubh becomes King of Scotland.
- Byzantine victories under Nicephorus over Muslims in Asia Minor.
- Mieczyslaw I becomes ruler of Poland; accepts Christianity in 966.

963
- Basil II, Eastern Emperor, with Nicephorus II (Phocas) and Constantine VIII as co-Emperors.

964
- Nicephorus Phocas begins conquest of Cilicia from the Muslims.

967
- Cuilean, King of Scotland.

968
- Nicephorus Phocas conquers Northern Syria.

969
- Nicephorus Phocas murdered by nephew, John Zimisces; he becomes co-Emperor.
- North African Fatamids conquer Egypt and found Cairo.

971
- John Zimisces drives back the Russians from Thrace and other Balkan lands.
- Kenneth II, King of Scotland.

972
- Death of Sviatoslav, the Russian ruler.

973
- Otto II becomes Emperor in the West.

975
- Edward the Martyr, King of England.

976
- Death of John Zimisces; Basil II comes into power.
- Samuel becomes King of Bulgaria; he makes extensive conquests and builds up a Bulgarian Empire.
- Otto II deposes Henry the Quarrelsome, Duke of Bavaria.

978
- Murder of Edward the Martyr; Ethelred II (the Unready) becomes King of England.
- Lothair of France invades Lorraine.

980
- Otto II goes to Italy; aims at conquering southern Italy.
- Vikings attack Southampton, Thanet and Chester.
- Vladimir I (St Vladimir) becomes Russian ruler.
- Battle of Tara: Malachy II, King of Meath, defeats the Vikings in Ireland.

982
- Greenland discovered by the Norwegians.
- Otto II heavily defeated in Italy by combined Byzantine and Muslim forces.

983
- Otto III becomes German King.

985
- Duke Henry of Bavaria restored.

986
- Death of Harold Bluetooth of Denmark; Sweyn Forkbeard becomes Danish King.
- Louis V, King of France.

987
- Death of Louis V; Hugh Capet, son of Hugh the Great, becomes King of France, with Paris as capital: founder of the long Capetian Dynasty.

988
- Russian Duke Vladimir becomes a Christian.

990
- Pax Ecclesiae, restricting private warfare, introduced in southern France.

991
- Olaf Tryggveson of Norway raids the British Islands (till 994).
- Battle of Maldon: Vikings bought off by Ethelred II.

992
- Boleslaus I becomes ruler of Poland.

993
- Vikings sack Bamborough.

994
- Sweyn Forkbeard and Olaf Tryggveson attack London but are driven off.

995
- Olaf Tryggveson becomes Olaf I, King of Norway; imposes Christianity on his people.
- Constantin IV, King of Scotland.

996
- Richard the Fearless succeeded by Richard the Good as Duke of Normandy.
- Robert II (the Pious) becomes King of France.
- Otto III crowned Emperor at Rome.

997
- Vikings again attack Wessex.
- Kenneth III, King of Scotland.
- Stephen I becomes ruler of Hungary.

998
- Battle of Veszprem: Stephen I of Hungary victorious over rebels; takes title of king, which the Pope confirms in 1001.
- Crescentius, Patrician of Rome, executed: Otto III, Master of Rome.

999
- Gerbert of Aurillac becomes Pope Silvester II.

1000
- Battle of Svold: Norwegians defeated in naval battle by combined Swedes and Vikings; Norway divided between the conquerors.
- Leif Ericsson discovers Vinland, part of Canada.
- Battle of Glenmama: Malachy II and Brian Boru, Irish rivals, combine and defeat the Vikings.
- Revival of legal studies at Bologna: celebrated university founded later.

1001
- Vikings again bought off from Wessex.

1002
- Henry II, son of Henry the Quarrelsome, becomes German King.
- Ardoin of Ivrea crowned King of Italy.
- The Muslims take Sardinia.
- Massacre of Vikings in England on St Brice's Day.

1003
- Boleslaus I of Poland conquers Bohemia.
- Sweyn of Denmark again invades England.

1004
- Ardoin overthrown in Italy: Henry II becomes King of the Lombards.

1005
- Malcolm II, King of Scotland.

1006
- Boleslaus I of Poland gives up Bohemia.

1007
- Vikings again bought off from England by Ethelred II.

1009
- Another Viking invasion of England.

1012
- Ethelred II again buys off Vikings.

1013
- Sweyn of Denmark again invades England; flight of Ethelred II; Viking conquest.

1014
- Death of Sweyn; his son, Canute, becomes King of England.
- Claf II (St Olaf) becomes King of Norway.
- Crushing defeat of Bulgaria by Basil II, followed by death of Samuel, King of Bulgaria; his empire collapses.
- Battle of Clontarf: Vikings heavily defeated in Ireland by Brian Boru, but Brian himself killed.
- Henry II crowned Emperor at Rome.

1015
- Death of Vladimir I of Russia.
- Duchy of Burgundy annexed to the French monarchy by Robert II.

1016
- Death of Ethelred II; Edmund Ironside fights against Canute, but defeated at Assandun; partition of kingdom arranged, but death of Edmund leaves Canute sole king.

1018
- Basil II, the Bulgar-slayer, completes the conquest of Bulgaria.
- Battle of Carham: Scotland annexes Lothian.

1022
- Catharist heretics burned at Orleans.

1024
- Death of Henry II.

THE FRANCONIAN EMPERORS

1024
- Conrad II elected German King: first of Franconian Emperors.

1025
- Constantin VIII, sole Eastern Emperor.
- Death of Boleslaus I, King of Poland.

1027
- Conrad II crowned Emperor at Rome.
- Truce of God, restricting private war, first proclaimed in southern France.

1028
- Romanus III, Eastern Emperor.
- Fall of Caliphate of Cordova.
- Ferdinand I (the Great), King of Castile.

1030
- Normans begin conquest of southern Italy or Apulia.
- Battle of Stiklestad: Norway overthrown and annexed by Denmark.
- Seljuk Turks begin aggression in Asia Minor.
- Henry I, King of France.

1032
- Lusatia recovered from Poland by Emperor Conrad II.
- Duchy of Burgundy bestowed on King Henry's brother, Robert: line lasts till 1361.

1033
- Kingdom of Burgundy annexed to Emperor by Conrad II.

1034
- Duncan, King of Scotland.
- Michael IV, Eastern Emperor.

1035
- William the Conqueror becomes Duke of Normandy.
- Canute's sons, Hardicanute and Harold, joint rulers of England.

1037
- Norway recovers its independence from Denmark.
- Harold, King of all England.
- Bretislav I, Prince of Bohemia; conquers Moravia, Silesia, much of Poland.
    DEATHS
    Avicenna, Arab physician and philosopher.

1038
- Ferdinand I of Castile acquires Leon.
    DEATHS
    Alhazen, Arab physicist.

1039
- Henry III, German King.

1040
- Macbeth, King of Scotland.
- Hardicanute, King of England.

1041
- Bohemia made subject to the Empire.
- Michael V, Eastern Emperor.

1042
- Edward the Confessor, King of England.
- Emperor Michael V deposed: Constantine IX, Eastern Emperor.

1043
- Unsuccessful Russian expedition against Constantinople.

1044
- Henry II defeats Hungarians.
- Seljuks capture Edessa.

1046
- Anarchy in Rome: three rivals for Papacy: Henry III called in and chooses Clement II, who crowns him Emperor.

- The Norman, Robert Guiscard, arrives in Italy.
1047
- Battle of Val-ès-Dunes: William of Normandy, aided by King Henry I, defeats rebel nobles.
1049
- Harold Hardrada, King of Norway.
1050
- Emund succeeds Anund as King of Sweden.
1051
- Fall of Earl Godwin in England.
- Emperor Henry III subdues Hungary.
1052
- Earl Godwin's triumphant return.
- Edward the Confessor founds Westminster Abbey.
1053
- Battle of Civitella: Robert Guiscard, the Norman, defeats Papal forces; makes agreement with Pope Leo IX.
1054
- Scotland invaded by Siward in support of Malcolm Canmore; Macbeth defeated at Dunsinane.
- Battle of Mortemer: William of Normandy defeats the French royal forces.
- Death of Yaroslav the Great, Grand Duke of Russia.
- Breach between Eastern and Western Churches complete.
- Theodora, Eastern Empress.
1055
- Seljuk Turks under Togrul Beg occupy Baghdad and restore authority of the Caliph.
1056
- Henry IV, German King.
- Michael VI, Eastern Emperor: last of the Macedonian Dynasty.
1057
- Malcolm III (Canmore), King of Scotland.
- Isaac I (Comnenus), Eastern Emperor after dethroning Michael VI: first of the Comneni.
1058
- Battle of Varaville: William of Normandy defeats the French royal forces.
- Boleslaus II, King of Poland.
1059
- Constantine (X) Ducas, Eastern Emperor.
- Method of Papal election settled.
- Robert Guiscard obtains title of Duke of Apulia and Calabria from Pope Nicholas II, subject to Holy See.
1060
- Norman invasion of Sicily begins under Count Roger: Messina taken.
- Philip I ,King of France.
- Steinkel succeeds Emund as King of Sweden.
1063
- William of Normandy conquers Maine.
1064
- Seljuk Turks conquer Armenia.
- Ferdinand I takes Coimbra from Portugal.
1065
- Alfonso VI succeeds Ferdinand I as King of Castile and Leon.

1066
- Battle of Stamford Bridge: Norwegian invasion defeated: Harold Hardrada killed.
- Haakon the Red, King of Sweden: Olaf Kyrre, King of Norway.
- Battle of Hastings: William of Normandy (William the Conqueror) defeats and kills Harold II and Norman conquest of England begins.

1067
- Michael VII and Romanus IV, Eastern Emperors.

1070
- Malcolm III of Scotland marries Margaret of the English royal family.
- Duchy of Bavaria given to Count Welf.

1071
- Battle of Manzikert: Seljuk Turks under Alp Arslan defeat forces of Romanus IV, who is captured: Asia Minor lost to Eastern Empire.
- Normans capture Bari, last Greek possession in Italy.
- Normans take Palermo.
- Norman conquest of England complete.

1072
- Malcolm III of Scotland pays homage to William the Conqueror.

1073
- Hildebrand becomes Pope Gregory VII.
- Saxon revolt against the Empire.

1074
- Peace of Gerstungen between Henry IV and the Saxons.

1075
- Seljuk Turks capture Jerusalem.
- Henry IV reduces the Saxons.
- Gregory VII issues his decrees on clerical celibacy and investiture of prelates.

1076
- Emperor Henry IV summons a synod of German bishops at Worms, which declares Gregory VII deposed; Gregory VII declares Henry IV deposed and excommunicated.
- Sancho Ramirez of Aragon becomes King of Navarre.

1077
- Humiliation of Emperor Henry IV by Gregory VII at Canossa in Tuscany; Rudolph of Suabia elected German King; civil war results.
- Ladislas I (St Ladislas), King of Hungary.

1078
- Nicephorus III, Eastern Emperor, after displacing Michael VII.

1080
- Rudolph of Suabia defeated and killed; Seljuk Turks capture Nicaea.

1081
- Alexius I (Comenus), Eastern Emperor; beginning of continuous dynasty of Comneni.
- Battle of Durazzo: Normans under Robert Guiscard defeat Emperor Alexius I.

1083
- Henry IV enters Rome.
- Battle of Larissa: Emperor Alexius I defeats Normans.

1084
- Alfonso VI recovers Toledo from the Moors.
- Carthusians founded at Chartreuse, near Grenoble, by St Bruno.
- Henry IV crowned Emperor in Rome by the anti-Pope, Clement III; Gregory VII saved by Robert Guiscard; Rome sacked.

1085
- Emperor Alexius I recovers Durazzo from Normans.
- Death of Gregory VII.

1086
- The Domesday Book, a survey of England commissioned by William I, is completed.
- Battle of Zalaca: Alfonso VI defeated by Almoravides under Yusuf.

1087
- William II (Rufus), King of England.

1088
- Bohemia under Vratislav is made a kingdom by the Emperor.

1090
- Count Roger of Sicily takes Malta from the Moors.

1091
- Norman conquest of Sicily completed.
- Emperor Alexius I defeats the Petchenegs.

1092
- William Rufus annexes southern Cumbria to England.
- Seljuk Empire broken up into parts on death of Malik Shah.

1093
- Donald Bane, King of Scotland.
- Anselm becomes Archbishop of Canterbury.
- Magnus Barefoot, King of Norway.

1094
- Duncan, King of Scotland, after overthrowing Donald Bane; overthrown and killed by Donald Bane and Edmund, who share the kingdom between them.
- Rodrigo Diaz, called El Cid, takes Valencia from the Moors.

1095
- Pope Urban II advocates a crusade, to recover the holy places, at Council of Clermont.
- Coloman, great reforming King of Hungary.
- Count Henry of Burgundy marries Theresa of Leon, receiving County of Portugal as dowry; beginning of Portuguese state.

1096
- First Crusade sets out: led by Godfrey of Bouillon, his brother Baldwin, Raymond of Toulouse, Bohemond of Otranto and a Tancred; preceded by popular forces under Peter the Hermit and Walter the Penniless.

1097
- Edgar, King of Scotland.
- Frankish County of Edessa founded in Syria.
- Anselm quarrels with William Rufus, leaves the kingdom.
- Crusaders capture Nicaea and win battle of Doryloeum.

1098
- Crusaders take Antioch: Principality of Antioch formed under Bohemond.
- Cistercians founded by St Robert at Citeaux, near Dijon.
- Magnus Barefoot invades Orkneys and Sudreys (Hebrides).

1099
- Crusaders take Jerusalem.
- Crusaders win battle of Ascalon.

1100
- Henry I, King of England.
- Baldwin I succeeds his brother, Godfrey of Bouillon, as ruler of Jerusalem and takes title of King.

1102
- Magnus Barefoot devastates Sudreys and conquers Isle of Man: Scottish king, Edgar, recognizes his claim to the western islands.
- Boleslaus III, King of Poland.

1103
- Death of Magnus Barefoot.

1104
- Revolt of Henry, son of Henry IV (afterwards Henry V).
- Alfonso I (the Battler), King of Aragon.
- Crusaders capture Acre.

1106
- Henry V, German King.
- Battle of Tinchebrai: Henry I of England defeats Robert, Duke of Normandy, and gains the duchy.
- Lothair of Supplinburg appointed Duke of Saxony.

1107
- Alexander I, King of Scotland.
- Battle of Durazzo: Emperor Alexius defeats the Normans under Bohemond.
- Council of Troyes.

1108
- Louis VI (the Fat), King of France.

1109
- Crusaders capture Tripoli (in Syria).
  DEATHS
  Anselm of Canterbury, philosopher.

1110
- Crusaders capture Beirut.

1111
- Henry V crowned Emperor at Rome.

1112
- Theresa rules alone over Portugal on death of Count Henry.

1114
- Saxon rebellion against Empire.

1115
- Peter Abelard begins teaching at Paris; St Bernard, Abbot of Clairvaux.
- Death of Countess Matilda of Tuscany: her estates left to the Papacy.

1116
- Henry V in Italy.

1118
- John II, Eastern Emperor.
- Alfonso I of Aragon captures Saragossa.

1119
- Order of Templars founded.
- Battle of Brenneville (Brémule): Louis VI defeated by the English under Henry I.

1120
- Knights of St John (or the Hospitallers) acquire a military character.
- Battle of Cutanda: Almoravides defeated by Alfonso I of Aragon.

1122
- Concordat of Worms settles the controversy between empire and Papacy about investiture of bishops.

1123
- Emperor John II defeats the Serbians and exterminates the Petchenegs.

- First Lateran Council of the Church.
  DEATHS
  Omar Khayyam, Persian poet and scientist.

1124
- David I, King of Scotland.
- Emperor John II defeats the Hungarians.
- Boleslaus III of Poland converts the Pomeranians.
- Christians, with help of Venice, captured Tyre.

1125
- Death of Emperor Henry V: end of Franconian line of emperors.

THE HOHENSTAUFEN EMPERORS

1125
- Lothair of Supplinburg elected German king as Lothair II.

1126
- Emperor John II successful against Seljuk Turks.
- Henry the Proud becomes Duke of Bavaria.
- Pierre de Bruys burned for heresy.

1127
- Death of Guilhem, Count of Poitiers, first of the Troubadour poets.
- Conrad of Hohenstaufen proclaimed German King in rivalry with Lothair II: flees to Italy.
- Roger II, Count of Sicily, becomes also Duke of Apulia.

1128
- Conrad crowned King of Italy.
- Theresa deposed in Portugal: Alfonso I becomes Count.

1130
- Roger II assumes style of King of Sicily as Roger I.

1133
- Lothair II crowned Emperor at Rome; beginning of alliance between kingdom of Jerusalem and Emir of Damascus.

1134
- Conrad yields to Lothair II.
- Battle of Braga: death of Alfonso I of Aragon and Navarre: Navarre and Aragon again separated.
- Sverker, King of Sweden: amalgamates Swedes and Goths.

1135
- Stephen, King of England.
- Alfonso VII, King of Castile and Leon.

1137
- Emperor John II defeats Armenians.
- Louis VII, King of France.
- Queen of Aragon marries Raymond, Count of Barcelona; Aragon greatly extended.
- Henry the Proud of Bavaria obtains Duchy of Saxony.

1138
- Battle of the Standard: defeat of the Scots.
- Conrad III elected German King, never actually crowned Emperor: first of the Hohenstaufen line.
- Normans capture Naples.

1139
- Pope Innocent II compelled to recognize Norman kingdom of Sicily and south Italy.

- Second Lateran Council of the Church.
- Henry the Lion becomes Duke of Saxony.
- Death of Boleslaus III; his Polish realm is divided into four principalities.
- Battle of Ourique: Alfonso I of Portugal defeats the Moors and takes title of King.
- Geoffrey of Monmouth's *History of the Britons*.

1140
- Beginning of Guelf versus Ghibelline contest in Germany about this time; later mostly in Italy.
- Vienna becomes capital of Austria.

1142
- Treaty of Frankfort between Conrad and his opponents: Henry the Lion confirmed in Duchy of Saxony, and Bavaria given to Henry Jasomirgott, Margrave of Austria.

  DEATHS

  Peter Abelard, French theologian and philosopher.

1143
- Manuel I becomes Eastern Emperor.
- Alfonso I of Portugal recognized by Peace of Zamora as independent of Spain.
- Democratic revolution at Rome against nobles and the Pope's temporal power.

  DEATHS

  William of Malmesbury, English historian.

1144
- Turks recapture Edessa (end of the Christian principality).

1145
- Anold of Brescia at Rome to direct the revolution.

1146
- Second Crusade inspired by St Bernard.

1147
- Emperor Conrad III and Louis VII of France set out on Second Crusade; France governed by Abbé Suger.
- Henry the Lion, Duke of Saxony, conquers lands beyond the Elbe.
- Alfonso I of Portugal captures Lisbon.
- King Roger of Sicily invades Greece.
- Arnold of Brescia supreme in Rome.

1148
- Failure of Second Crusade against Damascus.

1149
- Normans expelled from island of Corfu.

1150
- Carmelites (White Friars) founded about this time at Mount Carmel by Berthold.
- University of Salerno founded, based upon a much older medical school.
- Approximate date of *Nibelungenlied*.
- Albert the Bear becomes Margrave of Brandenburg, the precursor of Prussia.
- Eric IX, King of Sweden.

1151
- Henry of Anjou becomes Duke of Normandy.
- Henry the Lion becomes Duke of Bavaria.

1152
- Frederick I (Barbarossa), German King.
- Louis VII divorces Eleanor of Aquitaine; she marries Henry of Anjou and brings Aquitaine to him.

1153
- Malcolm IV, King of Scotland.
- Treaty of Wallingford: succession of Henry of Anjou to English throne assured.

1154
- Henry of Anjou becomes King of England as Henry II.
- Frederick Barbarossa invades Italy.
- Nureddin, Turkish ruler of Mosul, captures Damascus.
- William I (the Bad), King of Sicily and Naples.
  DEATHS
  Geoffrey of Monmouth, English churchman and historian.

1155
- Arnold of Brescia hanged and burned at the command of Pope Adrian IV, to whom he had been handed over by the Emperor.
- Frederick Barbarossa crowned Emperor in Rome by the Pope.

1156
- Bavaria confirmed to Henry the Lion; Austria created as a duchy.
- Franche-Comté (County of Burgundy) gained for the Empire by marriage.

1157
- Castile and Leon separated at death of Alfonso VII.
- Waldemar I, King of Denmark.

1158
- Bohemia finally made a kingdom under Vladislav II.
- Alfonso VIII, King of Castile.
- Second invasion of Italy by Frederick Barbarossa.

1159
- Peter Lombard, noted theologian and Bishop of Paris.
- Milan besieged by Frederick Barbarossa.

1160
- Chrétien de Troyes, French poet, flourishes at this time.
- Frederick Barbarossa excommunicated by Pope Alexander III.

1162
- Frederick Barbarossa destroys Milan.
- Alfonso II, King of Aragon.

1163
- Frederick Barbarossa invades Italy for the third time.

1164
- Somerled of the Isles invades southern Scotland: dies at Renfrew.

1165
- William I (the Lyon), King of Scotland.

1166
- Assize of Clarendon.
- Fourth Invasion of Italy by Frederick Barbarossa.
- William II (the Good), King of Sicily and Naples.

1167
- Oxford University founded.
- Lombard League formed against Frederick Barbarossa.
- Frederick Barbarossa enters Rome; forced to withdraw by plague.

1169
- Wendish pirates overthrown in Rügen.

1170
- Murder of Thomas à Becket, Archbishop of Canterbury.

- Waldensians founded in southern France by Peter Waldo.
- Invasion of Ireland by Strongbow.

1171
- Saladin becomes ruler of Egypt, superseding Fatimite Dynasty and founding the Ayyubite Dynasty.
- Henry II lands in Ireland and receives submission of many chiefs.

1173
- Frederick Barbarossa invades Italy for fifth time.
- Bela III made King of Hungary by the Emperor Manuel.

1174
- William the Lyon, King of Scotland, captured by England; released under Treaty of Falaise on doing homage for his kingdom.
- Ottoman Turks under Saladin take Damascus: Muslim power in Asia consolidated.

1176
- Battle of Legnano: Lombard League completely defeats Frederick Barbarossa.

1177
- Treaty of Venice: a truce between Frederick Barbarossa, the Pope and the Lombard League.

1179
- Third Lateran Council of the Church.

1180
- Marie de France, French poetess, flourishes at this time.
- War between Emperor Frederick and Henry the Lion; Duchy of Bavaria given to Otto of Wittelsbach.
- Alexius II, Eastern Emperor.
- Philip II (Augustus), King of France.
  DEATHS
  John of Salisbury, English scholar and cleric.

1182
- Banishment of Jews decreed in France.
- Canute VI, King of Denmark.
- Massacre of Latins in Constantinople.

1183
- Peace of Constance: definite agreement between emperor, Pope and Lombard League.
- Emperor Alexius murdered; Andronicus I becomes Eastern Emperor.
- Turkish ruler, Saladin, takes Aleppo.

1185
- Emperor Andronicus I overthrown: Isaac II (Angelus), Eastern Emperor.
- Sancho I follows Alfonso I as King of Portugal.
- William II of Sicily takes Salonica, but fails to keep it.

1186
- Guy of Lusignan, King of Jerusalem.
- Saladin completes consolidation of Turkish power.
- Bulgarians recover independence of the Empire.

1187
- Battles of Tiberias and Hattin: Saladin victorious over Christians; Jerusalem taken by Saladin.

1189
- Henry II of England invades France.
- Richard I, King of England: independence of Scotland bought back.
- Tancred, King of Sicily and Naples.

- Third Crusade begins: joined by Emperor Frederick, Philip Augustus and Richard I; Siege of Acre begins.

1190
- Henry VI, German King.
- Order of Teutonic Knights founded.
- Trouvères flourishes at this time at the court of Marie of Champagne.
  DEATHS
  Chrétien de Troyes, French court poet.

1191
- Henry VI crowned Emperor at Rome.
- Henry VI invades southern Italy: fails against Naples.
- Richard I takes Cyprus and sells it to the Templars; resold to Guy of Lusignan, King of Jerusalem.
- Crusaders take Acre: King Philip returned to France.

1192
- Agreement between Richard I and Saladin; Richard captured by Duke Leopold of Austria on his way home and handed over to the Emperor.

1193
- Death of Saladin.
- Philip Augustus attacks Normandy.

1194
- Richard I released.
- Henry VI conquers kingdom of Sicily and Naples (claimed in right of his wife) and annexes it to the Empire.

1195
- Emperor Isaac II deposed: Alexius III, Eastern Emperor.
- Cyprus becomes a kingdom under Guy of Lusignan's brother, Amaury.

1196
- Christians lose Jaffa.
- Peter II becomes King of Aragon.

1197
- Ottacar becomes King of Bohemia.

1198
- Philip Suabia and Otto IV of Brunswick, rival Emperors.
- Innocent III becomes Pope.
- Frederick, son of Henry VI, crowned King of Sicily.
  DEATHS
  Averroes, Arabian scholar.

1199
- John, King of England.

1200
- Mariner's compass known in Europe soon after this date.
- Saxo Grammaticus, Danish historian, flourishes at this time.
- Walter Map, English author, flourishes at this time.
- Cambridge University founded.
  DEATHS
  Chu-Hsi, Chinese philosopher.
  Procopius, Byzantine historian.

1201
- Philip of Suabia under Papal ban.
- Fourth Crusade starts from Venice.
- Knights of the Sword founded to convert the Letts.

- Denmark conquers Holstein and Hamburg.
  DEATHS
  Archbishop Absalon, Danish statesman.
  Reynaud de Coucy, French poet.

1202
- Crusaders take Zara on behalf of Venice, at instance of the Doge, Henry Dandolo.
- Waldemar II succeeds Canute VI as King of Denmark; captures Lübeck, Schwerin.

1203
- Wolfram von Eschenbach, German poet, flourishes at this time.
- Emperor Isaac II restored by Crusaders along with Alexius IV.

1204
- France conquers Anjou, Maine, Normandy from England.
- Alexius V is made Eastern Emperor, then replaced by Baldwin I of Flanders, the first Latin Emperor; beginning of Latin Empire of Constantinople.
- Crete given to Venice.
  DEATHS
  Moses Maimonides, Jewish religious philosopher.

1205
- Emperor Baldwin defeated and captured by Bulgarians at Adrianople, then executed.
- Andrew II, King of Hungary.

1206
- Walther von der Vogelweide, German poet, flourishes at this time: the greatest of the Minnesingers.
- Genghis Khan unites the Mongol tribes.

1208
- Innocent III places England under interdict.
- Philip of Suabia murdered: Otto IV, sole Western Emperor.
- Albigensian Crusade begins: first crusade against heresy.

1209
- Otto IV in Italy: crowned Emperor at Rome.
- King John excommunicated.
- Cambridge University founded.

1210
- Godfrey of Strassburg, German poet, flourishes at this time.
- University of Paris founded about this time.
- Franciscan Order (Grey Friars) founded by St Francis of Assisi.
- Otto IV is excommunicated by the Pope, but successfully completes conquest of Sicily.
- Genghis Khan, Mongol leader, invades China.

1211
- Alfonso II becomes King of Portugal.

1212
- Battle of Navas de Tolosa: Almohades is defeated heavily by a combination of all the Christian kings of Spain and Portugal under Castile.
- Children's Crusade.
- Frederick II crowned German King.

1213
- Villehardouin, French historian of the Fourth Crusade, dies about this time.
- King John surrenders to Innocent III and does homage for kingdom.
- Battle of Muret: defeat of the Albigenses; Peter II of Aragon killed.

- James the Conqueror becomes King of Aragon.

1214
- Alexander II, King of Scotland.
- Battle of Bouvines: Philip of France defeats John of England, Otto IV and others.
  DEATHS
  Alfonso VIII of Castile.

1215
- Dominican Order (Black Friars) founded at Toulouse by St Dominic.
- Magna Carta signed by King John.
- Fourth Lateran Council of the Church abolishes trial by ordeal.

1216
- Louis, heir of French king, called in by English barons against John; death of John; Henry III, King of England.

1217
- Fair of Lincoln: Prince Louis of France defeated.
- Ferdinand III (the Saint), King of Castile.
- Fifth Crusade led by Andrew of Hungary.
- Haakon IV, King of Norway.

1218
- Death of Otto IV; Frederick I, Western Emperor.
- Waldemar II of Denmark captures Reval.
- Ivan Asen II, Bulgarian King: conquers Albania, Epirus, Macedonia and Thrace; capital, Tirnovo.

1219
- Damietta taken by John de Brienne, King of Jerusalem.
- Genghis Khan turns his Mongol armies westward.

1220
- Frederick II crowned Emperor at Rome.
- Approximate date of the *Owl and Nightingale* and of the *Queste del St Graal*.
  DEATHS
  Hartmann von der Aue, German poet.
  Saxo Grammaticus, Danish historian.

1221
- Dominicans settle at Oxford.
- Crusaders abandon Damietta.

1222
- Golden Bull, the Great Charter of Hungary.

1223
- Louis VIII, King of France.
- Sancho II, King of Portugal.
  DEATHS
  Giraldus Cambrensis, Welsh writer.

1224
- Franciscans settle at Oxford and Cambridge.
- Mongols advance into Russia; Russians defeated in battle of Kalka.

1225
- English take Gascony.
- Frederick II assumes the title of King of Jerusalem in right of his wife.

1226
- Lombard League renewed against Frederick II.
- Louis IX (St Louis), King of France.

- Waldemar II of Denmark compelled to surrender most of Danish conquests.
  DEATHS
  Francis of Assissi

1227
- Battle of Bornhöved: Frederick II defeats Denmark.
- Ottoman Turks settle in Angora under Ertoghrul.
- Frederick II sets out on a crusade, then excommunicated.
  DEATHS
  Genghis Khan.

1228
- Frederick II sets out on Sixth Crusade.
- French King gives the County of Venaissin, near Avignon, to the Papacy.

1229
- Jerusalem ceded to Christians through Frederick II; crowned King of Jerusalem.
- James of Aragon conquers the Balearic Islands.
- Papal victory over Frederick II's troops in Italy.
- Treaty of Meaux: submission of the County of Toulouse and the Albignesians.

1230
- Franciscans in Paris.
- Teutonic Knights begins to settle in Prussia.
- Wenceslas I, King of Bohemia.
- Final Union of Castile and Leon.

1231
- Privilege of Worms: German princes recognized by Emperor as virtually independent.

1232
- Pope Gregory IX establishes the monastic inquisition.

1234
- Mongols invade and destroy northern China.

1235
- War against Lombard League.
- Bela IV, King of Hungary.

1236
- Cordova conquered by the Christians.

1237
- Battle of Cortenuova: Lombard League defeated by Frederick II.
- Ryazan sacked by Mongols under Batu Khan.

1238
- James of Aragon conquers Valencia.
- Mongols settle in Russia (the Golden Horde), with capital at Sarai; Kiev taken.

1239
- Frederick II excommunicated.

1240
- Mendovg, ruler of Lithuania.

1241
- Invasion of Hungary and Poland by Batu Khan: Silesian princes defeated in battle of Liegnitz; Pesth captured.

1242
- Mongols defeated at Olmütz and Neustadt.
- Battles of Taillebourg and Saintes: Louis IX defeats Henry III of England.

1244
- End of Albigensian Persecution.
- Christians finally lose Jerusalem.

1245
- First Church Council of Lyons.
- Frederick II excommunicated and declared deposed by Innocent IV.
  DEATHS
  Alexander of Hales, philosopher and theologian.

1246
- Provence joined to France.
- Henry Raspe, Landgrave of Thuringia, elected German King at the instigation of the Pope.

1247
- Frederick II besieges Parma (defeated 1248).
- Death of Henry Raspe; William II, Count of Holland, elected German King by Papal party.

1248
- Rhodes taken by Genoa.
- Earl Birger virtual ruler of Sweden; Stockholm founded.
- St Louis starts Seventh Crusade (it fails 1254).
- Christians conquer Seville.
- Alfonso III succeeds Sancho II of Portugal.

1249
- Alexander III, King of Scotland.
- St Louis of France takes Damietta; then defeated and captured at Mansourah; released on giving up Damietta.

1250
- Conrad IV, German King.
- Sorbonne founded in Paris.
- Beginning of Mameluke rule in Egypt.
- Manfred, natural son of Frederick II, regent of Naples and Sicily.

1251
- Emperor Conrad IV in Italy.
- Conrad and Manfred take Capua and Naples.
- Alfonso X, King of Castile.

1252
- Innocent IV approves torture for the discovery of heresy.

1253
- Struggle between Venice and Genoa begins.
- Ottacar II, King of Bohemia.
  DEATHS
  Robert Grosseteste, Bishop of Lincoln.

1254
- Death of Conrad IV; son, Conradin, proclaimed King of Sicily.
- St Louis returns to France.

1255
- League of Rhenish towns formed, supported by William of Holland.
- Bavaria divided into Upper and Lower.

1256
- St Bonaventura becomes general of the Franciscans.
- Death of William of Holland: double election to Empire of Richard of Cornwall and Alfonso X of Castile: the period 1256–73 of the Empire known as the Interregnum.
- First form of Hanseatic League.

1258
- Provisions of Oxford forced by barons on King Henry III.

- Manfred crowned King of Sicily.
- Mongols capture Baghdad and destroy the Abbasid Caliphate.

1259
- Treaty of Paris: peace between Louis IX and Henry III.
- Death of Ezzelino de Romano, tyrant who supported Frederick II in Italy.
- Second Tatar raid on Poland.

  DEATHS
  Matthew Paris, English monk and historian.

1260
- Battle of Montaperti: Florentine Guelfs defeated by Ghibellines of Sienna; Ghibellines supreme in Florence.
- Mongols take Aleppo and Damascus; Mamelukes defeat Mongols at Ain Jalut.
- Battle of Kressenbrunn: Ottacar II of Bohemia defeats Bela, King of Hungary, and obtains Carinthia, Istria.

1261
- Tatar invasion of Hungary repelled by Bela IV.
- Latin Empire of Constantinople overthrown: Michael VIII becomes Eastern Byzantine Emperor: beginning of the Greek Palaeologian Dynasty that ruled the Byzantine Empire till 1453.
- Charles of Anjou accepts the crown of Sicily from the Pope.

1262
- First Visconti lord of Milan.

1263
- Norwegian disaster at Largs: death of Haakon IV; succeeded by Magnus VI.
- Portugal reaches present limits and attains complete independence.

1264
- Mise of Amiens: Louis IX arbitrates between Henry III and the English barons, deciding in favour of former.
- Battle of Lewes: Henry III defeated by Simon de Montfort.
- Battle of Trapani: Venetian victory over Genoese fleet.

1265
- Burgesses first called to English Parliament by Simon de Montfort.
- Battle of Evesham: Simon de Montfort defeated and killed by the royal army under Prince Edward.
- Christians conquer Murcia; only Granada left to Moors in Spain.

1266
- Hebrides ceded by Norway to Scotland.
- Battle of Benevento: defeat and death of Manfred; Charles of Anjou becomes master of Sicily and Naples.
- Ghibellines expelled from Florence.

1268
- Christians lose Antioch.
- Battle of Tagliacozzo: Conradin defeated by Charles of Anjou and executed; end of Hohenstaufen line.

THE AGE OF DANTE

1270
- St Louis on Eighth Crusade: dies at Tunis; Philip III (the Bold), King of France.
- Stephen V, King of Hungary.

1271
- Prince Edward of England goes to Acre on Ninth Crusade (returned in 1272).

- Marco Polo, Venetian traveller, sets out on his journey to China.
1272
- Edward I, King of England.
- Ladislas IV, King of Hungary.
1273
- Rudolph of Hapsburg elected German King.
1274
- Dominicans settle at Cambridge.
- Second Church Council of Lyons: temporary union of Eastern and Western Churches.
  DEATHS
  St Thomas Aquinas, scholastic theologian.
1275
- Magnus Ladulas, King of Sweden.
1276
- Peter III, King of Aragon.
1277
- Edward I invades Wales.
1278
- Battle of Marchfield, (Dürnkrut): Ottacar II of Bohemia killed; Czech Empire dismembered; Wenceslas II, King of Bohemia.
  DEATHS
  Nicola Pisano, Italian sculptor.
1279
- Statute of Mortmain: to prevent land passing into the hands of the Church.
- Diniz becomes King of Portugal.
- Southern Sung Empire falls to Mongols under Kublai Khan.
1280
- Trouvère poetry comes to an end.
- Eric II becomes King of Norway.
  DEATHS
  Albertus Magnus, German scholastic philosopher.
1282
- England conquers Wales.
- Andronicus II, Eastern Emperor.
- Sicilian Vespers: massacre of French in Sicily; Sicily separated from kingdom of Naples and obtained by King of Aragon.
- Hapsburgs established in the Duchy of Austria.
1283
- Prussia subjugated by Teutonic Knights.
  DEATHS
  Saadi, Persian poet.
1284
- Battle of Meloria: Genoa crushes Pisa.
- Sancho IV King of Castile.
- Queen of Navarre marries the eldest son of Philip III of France: Navarre now joined to France till 1328.
1285
- Statute of Winchester and Second Statute of Westminster.
- Philip IV (the Fair), King of France.
- Charles II, King of Naples.
- Alfonso III, King of Aragon.

1286
- Margaret, Maid of Norway, Queen of Scotland.

1288
- Pope declares a crusade against Ladislas IV of Hungary.
- Osman I succeeds Ertoghrul as leader of Ottoman Turks.

1289
- Christians lose Tripoli.

1290
- Treaty of Brigham between Scotland and Edward I; death of the Maid of Norway.
- Statue to Quia Emptores.
- Expulsion of Jews from England.
- Ladislas IV of Hungary murdered.

1291
- Fall of Acre: end of Christian power in Syria and Palestine.
- Death of Emperor Rudolph of Hapsburg.
- Everlasting League of Uri, Schwyz and Unterwalden: start of the Swiss Republic.
- James II, King of Aragon.

1292
- John Baliol made King of Scotland by Edward I.
- Adolf of Nassau elected German King.

1294
- Boniface VIII becomes Pope.
- Death of Guiraut Riquier, last of the Troubadours.
- Guienne seized by France.
- Venetian fleet defeated by Genoa.
- King of Aragon abandons Sicily; under Frederick III, it refuses to be joined to Naples.
  DEATHS
  Roger Bacon, English philosopher and scientist.
  Kublai Khan, founder of Mongol dynasty in China.

1295
- Model English Parliament summoned by Edward I, first representative parliament.
- Beginning of Franco-Scottish Alliance.

1296
- Bull of Clericis Laicos issued by Boniface VIII: extravagant Papal claims.
- John Baliol renounces the kingdom of Scotland.
- Ferdinand IV, King of Castile.

1297
- Battle of Stirling: victory of Sir William Wallace over English.

1298
- Battle of Falkirk: Edward I defeats Wallace.
- Adolf of Nassau defeated and killed at Gelheim by Albert I, Duke of Austria, elected German king.

1299
- Battle of Curzola: Venice defeated by Genoa.
- Treaty between Venice and the Turks.
- Haakon V, King of Norway.

1300
- Wenceslas II of Bohemia becomes King of Poland, later also of Hungary.
- Boniface VIII proclaims a Jubilee.

1301
- Albert of Austria ravages the Palatinate and Mainz.

- Charles of Valois overthrows the Bianchi (White) Guelfs in Florence and drives Dante into exile.

1302
- End of the War of the Sicilian Vespers; Frederick III recognized as King of Sicily by the Peace of Caltabellotta.
- French States-General meet for the first time.
- Battle of Courtrai: Flemish victory over France.
  DEATHS
  Cimabue, Italian painter.

1303
- Edward I again conquers Scotland.
  DEATHS
  Pope Boniface VIII.

1305
- Betrayal and execution of Sir William Wallace.
- Wenceslas III, King of Bohemia.

1306
- Robert the Bruce crowned King of Scotland.
- Jews expelled from France.
- Wenceslas III of Bohemia murdered: end of dynasty.
- Vladislas I becomes Duke of Great Poland: reunites Great and Little Poland.

1307
- Edward II, King of England.
- Philip IV of France seizes the property of the Knights Templars.

1308
- Murder of Albert of Austria: Henry VII (of Luxemburg) elected German King; conquers Bohemia (1308–10).
  DEATHS
  Duns Scotus, scholastic philosopher and theologian.

1309
- Robert, King of Naples.
- Clement V begins residence in Avignon: beginning of Babylonish Captivity of Popes (till 1377).

1310
- Henry VII goes to Italy.
- Arpad Dynasty in Hungary succeeded by dynasty of Anjou in person of Charles I.
- Knights of St John or Hospitallers seize Rhodes.
- John of Luxemburg, son of Henry VII, elected King of Bohemia.

1311
- Church Council of Vienna.
  DEATHS
  Arnold of Villanova, Italian physician and alchemist.

1312
- Henry VII crowned Emperor at Rome.
- Abolition of Templars finally decreed by Pope Clement V, under pressure from Philip IV of France.
- France obtains the Lyonnais.
- Piers Gaveston, favourite of Edward II, is murdered near Warwick Castle.

1313
- Alfonso XI becomes King of Castile.

1314
- Louis X, King of France.

- Battle of Bannockburn: Scottish independence asserted by Robert the Bruce.
- Louis IV of Bavaria and Frederick, Duke of Austria, rival claimants of the Empire.

1315
- Battle of Morgarten: a great Swiss victory over Leopold, Duke of Austria.
- Gedymin, ruler of Lithuania: annexes Kiev, Chernigov.

1316
- Edward Bruce, King of Ireland.
- Philip V (the Tall), King of France.

1318
- Battle of Dundalk: Edward Bruce defeated and killed.
- Truce between Swiss and Habsburgs.

1319
- First Union of Sweden and Norway: Magnus VII, common King.

1320
- End of War between France and Flanders.
- Vladislas I revives royal dynasty in Poland.

1321
- Death of Dante Alighieri, Italian poet.

1322
- Battle of Mühldorf: Frederick of Austria defeated and taken prisoner by Louis of Bavaria.
- Battle of Boroughbridge; Edward II defeats his kinsman, Thomas of Lancaster.
- Charles IV (the Fair), King of France.

1323
- James I of Aragon conquers Sardinia from the Pisans.
- Emperor Louis IV, deposed and excommunicated by John XXII, appeals to a Council.

1324
- Death of Marco Polo, Venetian traveller.

1325
- Frederick of Austria relinquishes claim to Empire.
- Alfonso IV, King of Portugal.

1326
- First Scottish Parliament (at Cambuskenneth).
- Gunpowder known by this date.
- Scots College founded in Paris.
- Brussa taken by the Ottoman Turks and becomes their capital.
- Orkhan succeeds Osman as leader of the Ottoman Turks.

1327
- Edward II agrees to abdicate; Edward III, King of England; ex-King Edward II then murdered at Berkeley Castle.
- Orkhan takes Nicomedia.
- Alfonso IV, King of Aragon.
  DEATHS
  Eckhart, German mystic.

1328
- Treaty of Northampton: England recognizes the complete independence of Scotland.
- Andronicus III, Eastern Emperor.
- Philip VI, King of France: beginning of Valois Dynasty: Navarre separated.
- Battle of Cassel: Flemish insurgents under Jacob van Artevelde defeated by Philip VI.

- Louis IV is crowned Emperor at Rome and deposes Pope John XXII.

1329
- David II, King of Scotland.
- Battle of Pelekanon: Andronicus III defeated by Ottoman Turks.

1330
- Ottoman Turks take Nicaea: Janissaries organized.
- Battle of Kustendil: Bulgaria conquered by Serbia.
- Walachia begins to gain independence from Hungary.

1331
- King John of Bohemia in Italy.

1332
- Battle of Dupplin Moor: Scottish regent, the Earl of Mar, killed; Edward Baliol crowned King of Scotland.
- Lucerne joins the Swiss League.
- Battle of Plowce: Vladislas I defeats the Teutonic Knights.

1333
- Edward Baliol again invades Scotland; Scots defeated by Edward III at Halidon Hill.
- Casimir III (the Great), King of Poland: acquires Galicia.

1335
- Edward III invades Scotland.
- Zurich joins the Swiss League.

1336
- Peter IV, King of Aragon.
- Revolution in Japan.

1337
- Peter II, King of Sicily.
- Jacob van Artevelde forms a league of Flemish cities with Ghent as leader; they join England in the war against France.
  DEATHS
  Giotto, Italian painter.

THE HUNDRED YEARS' WAR

1338
- Hundred Years' War between France and England begins.

1339
- Edward Baliol driven from Scotland.
- Battle of Laupen: Nobels overthrown in Berne.

1340
- Battle of Sluys: English naval victory over France.
- Edward III claims throne of France.
- Emperor Louis IV reunites Bavaria.
- Battle of Rio Salado: Spanish and Portuguese repel an African invasion.
- Waldemar IV, King of Denmark.

1341
- John V, Eastern Emperor.
- Black Death first appears in China.

1342
- Louis the Great, King of Hungary.
- Duke of Athens appointed head of Florentine state (expelled 1343).

1343
- Joanna I, wife of Andrew of Hungary, becomes Queen of Naples.

- Charles I (the Bad), King of Navarre.
- Haakon VI, King of Norway.

1344
- Suabian League of Cities formed.

1345
- Order of the Garter founded about this date.
- Andrew of Hungary assassinated.
- Jacob van Arteveide assassinated.
- Emperor Louis takes possession of Holland.

1346
- Battle of Neville's Cross: Scots defeated and David II captured.
- Battle of Crécy: English victory over French; King John of Bohemia killed.
- Battle of Zara: Venetians defeat Hungarians.
- Charles, King of Bohemia.

1347
- English take Calais.
- John VI (Cantacuzenus) becomes co-Emperor in the East.
- Cola di Rienzi becomes Tribune in Rome.
- Corsica transferred from Pisa to Genoa.

1348
- Charles IV (of Bohemia), German King.
- Great Plague in Italy.
- Battle of Epila: Peter IV of Aragon establishes his power over the nobles.

1349
- Black Death in England.
- Bavaria again divided.
- Persecution of Jews in Germany.
- Fall of Rienzi.

  DEATHS
  William of Occam, nominalist philosopher.

1350
- The Black Death in Scotland.
- Dafydd ap Gwilym, greatest of Welsh poets, flourishes at this time.
- John, King of France.
- Peter the Cruel, King of Castile.
- Boccaccio's *Decameron*.

1351
- Statute of Labourers in England attempts to regulate wages.
- Statute of Provisors in England.
- Zurich joins the Swiss League.

1352
- Glarus and Zug join the Swiss League.

1353
- Statute of Praemunire places restraints on Papal authority in England.
- Berne joins the Swiss League.
- Battle of the Bosphorus: Venice defeated by Genoa.

1354
- New League of the Rhine.
- Rienzi killed in a riot.

1355
- Charles IV crowned Emperor in Rome.

- Death of Stephen Dushan, King of the Serbians: break-up of Serbian Empire.
- Conspiracy of Marino Faliero in Venice foiled.

1356
- Battle of Poitiers: English victory over France won by the Black Prince; King John of France a prisoner.
- The Burnt Candlemass: Edward III burns every town and village in Lothian, Scotland.
- The Golden Bull settles the mode of electing the Holy Roman Emperor.
- War between Venice and Hungary.

1357
- Pedro I, King of Portugal.

1358
- Turks under Suleiman take Gallipoli.
- Peace between Habsburgs and the Swiss League.
- Treaty of Zara: peace between Venice and Hungary: Venice makes large cessions.
- Revolution in Paris: Étienne Marcel, provost of Paris merchants, leads a reform movement.
- Battle of Sapienza: Venice defeated by Genoa.
- Jacquerie or Peasants' Revolt in France.

1359
- Amurath (Murad) I becomes Turkish Sultan.
- Turks cross the Hellespont.

1360
- Peace of Bretigny between England and France.
- Moldavia independent of Hungary by this date.

1361
- Battle of Adrianople: Ottoman Turks defeat the Emperor and capture the town.
- Waldemar IV of Denmark recovers Scania and conquers Gotland.
- Duchy of Burgundy expires with Philip de Rouvre.

1362
- Turks conquer Philippopolis.
- English becomes language of parliament and the law courts in England.
- *Piers Plowman*, English poem, attributed to William Langland.

1363
- The King of France creates his son Philip, the Bold Duke of Burgundy.
  DEATHS
  Ranulf Higden, English chronicler.

1364
- Charles V, King of France.
- Crete revolts against Venice.

1365
- Peter I of Cyprus takes Alexandria, Tripoli, but does not retain his conquests.
- Albert of Mecklenburg supersedes Magnus as King of Sweden.

1366
- Statue of Kilkenny: English attempt to suppress Irish nationality in Leinster.
- Peter the Cruel expelled from Castile by his brother, Henry of Trastamara.
- Amadeus VI of Savoy takes Gallipoli from the Turks and Varna from the Bulgarians.

1367
- Battle of Navarete (Najara): Henry of Trastamara defeated and Peter the Cruel restored to Castilian throne with the aid of the Black Prince.
- Mongols overthrown in China by new Ming Dynasty.

- Ferdinand makes Lisbon capital of Portugal.
- Adrianople becomes Turkish capital.

1368
- Battle of Montiel: death of Peter the Cruel; succeeded by Henry of Trastamara.
  DEATHS
  Orcagna, Italian painter, sculptor and architect.

1369
- Venetians repel Hungarian invasion.
- Charles V declares war against England.
- Flanders passes by marriage to the Duchy of Burgundy.

1370
- Limoges sacked.
- Louis of Hungary elected King of Poland.
- Tamerlane begins his conquest of Asia

1371
- Robert II, first Stewart King of Scotland.
- Turks defeat Louis of Hungary.

1373
- Charles IV gains Brandenburg and Lower Lusatia by treaty.
- Bertrand du Guesclin reduces Brittany.

1374
- Death of Petrarch, Italian poet and pioneer of humanism.

1375
- Waldemar IV of Denmark succeeded by Margaret.
  DEATHS
  Giovanni Boccaccio, Italian writer.

1376
- *The Bruce* composed by Scottish poet John Barbour.

1377
- King Edward III dies; Richard II, King of England: effective power lies with the royal council.
- John Wycliffe, English theologian and religious reformer, summoned before the Bishop of London.
- Pope Gregory XI returns to Rome.

1378
- Second Great Schism in the Papacy begins: Popes Urban VI and Clement VII both elected and strongly supported.
- Wencelsas IV, King of Bohemia.
- War of Chioggia between Venice and Genoa begins.

1379
- Battle of Pola: Venice defeated by Genoa; Chioggia taken.
- John I, King of Castile.

1380
- Gerhard Groot founds Brethren of the Common Life at Deventer.
- John Wycliffe begins to attack Roman Catholic doctrine of transubstantiation.
- Venice wins Chioggia back and captures Genoese fleet.
- Charles VI, King of France.
- Battle of Kulikovo: Russian victory under Dimitri Donskoi over Golden Horde.

1381
- First English Navigation Act.
- Peasants' Revolt in England under Wat Tyler.
- Charles of Durazzo conquers Naples: Queen Joanna murdered in 1382.

- League of German Free Cities.
- End of the war between Venice and Genoa.
- Treaty of Turin between Venice and Hungary: Venice cedes Dalmatia.

1382
- Earthquake Council in London condemns Wycliffe.
- Death of Louis the Great of Hungary; period of disorder follows.
- Battle of Roosebeke: Philip van Artevelde and the Flemish insurgents defeated by the French; Philip killed.
- Moscow taken by Mongols.
- Maillotin Revolt in Paris.

1384
- Union of Heidelberg: peace between Count of Würtemberg and the Suabian League.
  DEATHS
  John Wycliffe, English religious reformer.

1385
- Gian Galeazzo Visconti, sole ruler of Milan.
- Battle of Aljubarrota: Portuguese victory over Castilians.
- John I, King of Portugal.

1386
- Battle of Sempach: Swiss victory over Austria; Leopold of Austria killed.
- Charles VI of France declares war against England.
- Death of Charles III of Naples: anarchy follows.
- Vladislas II becomes both King of Poland and Grand Duke of Lithuania: beginning of Jagellon Dynasty.
- Alliance between England and Portugal confirmed by Treaty of Windsor.

1387
- English poet, Geoffrey Chaucer, begins *The Canterbury Tales*.
- John I, King of Aragon.
- Charles III (the Noble), King of Navarre.
- Sigismund, King of Hungary.

1388
- Battle of Otterburn: Scottish victory over English under Sir Henry Percy (Hotspur).
- Battle of Naefels: victory of Swiss canton Glarus over Austrians.
- Count of Würtemberg defeats the Suabian League.
- Rhenish Towns defeated at Worms by Elector Palatine Rupert.

1389
- Battle of Kossovo: Serbians overthrown by Turks; Amurath I killed; Bajazet I succeeds him and obtains from the   the title of Sultan.

1390
- Robert III, King of Scotland; Duke of Albany, Regent.
- Henry III, King of Castile.

1391
- Manuel II, Eastern Emperor.
- Massacre of Jews in Spain.

1393
- Great Statute of Praemunire in England.
- Turks capture Philadelphia, in Asia Minor; also Tirnovo, in Bulgaria.

1394
- Habsburgs recognize the independence of the Swiss League.

1395
- Gian Galeazzo Visconti obtains title of Duke of Milan from Emperor.
- Martin I, King of Aragon.

- Tamerlane conquers the Kipchaks on the Volga.
- Turks, after taking Salonica and Larissa, besiege Constantinople.

1396

- Turkish conquest of Bulgaria completed.
- Fight at the North Inch between the Chattan and Kay clans.
- Battle of Nicopolis: crusading army of Hungarians and others under King Sigismund, defeated by Turks.

1397

- Union of Kalmar between Norway, Sweden and Denmark: Eric VII (XIII of Sweden) recognized as King.

1398

- Tamerlane conquers Northern India.
- Rome submits to complete authority of the Pope, who is supported by Ladislas, King of Naples.

1399

- Richard II forced to abdicate: Henry IV chosen as King of England.

1400

- Revolt of Owen Glendower in Wales.
- Wenceslas of Bavaria is deposed: Rupert, Elector Palatine, elected German King.
  DEATHS
  Geoffrey Chaucer, English poet.

1401

- William Sawtrey burned in England for heresy under a new statute against heretics.
- German king, Rupert, fails in Italy.
- Compact of Vilna: partial separation of Poland and Lithuania.

1402

- Battle of Homildon Hill: Scots defeated by English under Sir Henry Percy.
- Battle of Angora: Tamerlane defeats Bajazet I and makes him prisoner; Turkish pressure on the Empire relieved.

1403

- Revolt of the Percy family in England; defeated in battle at Shrewsbury.

1404

- John the Fearless becomes Duke of Burgundy.

1405

- Death of Tamerlane; his empire falls apart.

1406

- James I of Scotland captured by England; proclaimed King.
- John II, King of Castile.

1407

- Duke of Orleans murdered by a Burgundian.
- Rome occupied by Ladislas of Naples.
  DEATHS
  John Gower, English poet.

1409

- Sicily joined to Aragon by marriage.
- Council at Pisa: both Popes deposed; Alexander V elected.

1410

- Battle of Tannenberg: Teutonic Knights overthrown by Poland and Lithuania.
- Ferdinand, the Catholic King of Aragon.
  DEATHS
  Jean Froissart, French historian.

1411
* Battle of Harlaw: Scottish Highlanders under Donald, Lord of the Isles, defeated by a Lowland force under the Earl of Mar.
* Sigismund of Hungary elected German King.
* Battle of Rocca Secca: Louis of Anjou defeats Ladislas of Naples.

1412
* Treaty between Habsburgs and Swiss League renewed.
* Jan Hus of Bohemia excommunicated.
* Battle of St Cloud: Burgundian party in France defeat Armagnacs (followers of Orleans); Treaty of Auxerre concluded.

1413
* Ladislas of Naples sacks Rome.
* Henry V, King of England.
* Muhammad I, Turkish Sultan.

1414
* St Andrews University founded in Scotland.
* Council of Constance met.
* Treaty of Arras between Burgundians and Armagnacs.

1415
* Battle of Agincourt: Henry V defeats French.
* Council of Constance condemns Jan Hus, who is burned; Bohemian nobles protest.
* Count Frederick of Hohenzollern obtains Brandenburg and title of Elector.
* Portugal takes Ceuta on north African coast.

1416
* Jerome of Prague, a follower of Huss, burned.
* Alfonso V (the Magnanimous), King of Aragon: also King of Sicily and Naples.
  DEATHS
  Owen Glendower, Welsh rebel.

1417
* Sir John Oldcastle, the Lollard leader, is burnt for heresy.
* Henry V captures Caen.
* End of Papal schism: Martin V, sole Pope.

1418
* End of Council of Constance, without touching the reform question.
* Burgundians capture Paris.

1419
* Henry V captures Rouen.
* War between Empire and Bohemia begins.
* Duke of Burgundy murdered at Montereau; Philip the Good succeeds; Burgundians join the English.
* Sigismund, King of Bohemia, but not accepted by the people.

1420
* Treaty of Troyes: Henry V of England recognized as heir to crown of France.
* Battle of Vysehrad: Bohemians defeat Sigismund.

1421
* Battle of Baugé: Scottish victory over English.
* Amurath II, Turkish Sultan.
* Sigismund declared deposed in Bohemia.

1422
* Henry VI, King of England on death of Henry V, and of France on death of Charles VI; Charles VII in France called 'King of Bourges'.

- Battle of Deutschbrod: Bohemian victory over Sigismund.

1423
- Sigismund crowned Emperor at Rome.
- *The King is Quair* by James I of Scotland.
- Battle of Crevant: French defeated by English.
- Francesco Foscari, Doge of Venice.

1424
- James I of Scotland set free.
- Battle of Verneuil: Duke of Bedford defeats the French.
- Treaty between Venice and Florence against Milan.

1425
- John VII, Eastern Emperor.

1426
- Dom Henrique of Portugal (Prince Henry the Navigator) charts the west coast of Africa and engages in slave trade.
- Battle of Aussig: Bohemian victory over the Empire.
  DEATHS
  Hubert van Eyck, Flemish painter.

1427
- Bohemians under Procopius completely defeat the Empire: Germany invaded.

1428
- Siege of Orleans by English.
- Turks take Salonica.

1429
- Siege of Orleans raised by Joan of Arc.
- Charles VII crowned at Rheims.
  DEATHS
  Masaccio, Italian painter.

1431
- François Villon, French poet, born.
- Joan of Arc burned by English at Rouen.
- Battle of Taus: Bohemian victory over Empire.
- Council of Basle begins.

1432
- Carmagnola executed by Venetians for treason in the war against Milan.

1433
- Sigismund crowned Emperor at Rome.

1434
- Battle of Lipan: conflict between different Hussite parties in Bohemia; Procopius killed.
- Cosimo de' Medici in power in Florence.
  DEATHS
  Vladislav II of Poland.

1435
- Treaty of Arras between Burgundy and Charles VII.
- Alfonso the Magnanimous reunites the Two Sicilies.

1436
- Charles VII regains Paris.
- Council of Basle practically concedes the demands of the Bohemians.
- Sigismund recognized as King of Bohemia.
- Charles VIII elected King of Sweden.

1437
- James II, King of Scotland.
- Council of Basle transferred by Pope to Ferrara.

1438
- Albert V of Austria becomes King of Hungary and Bohemia; elected also King of Germany as Albert II.
- Pragmatic Sanction of Bourges: Charles VII of France establishes independence of French Church.
- Amurath II invades Hungary; opposed by John Huniades.
- Alfonso V, King of Portugal.

1439
- Formal union of Greek and Latin Churches arranged by Council of Basle sitting in Florence.
- Pragmatic Sanction of Mainz.
- Eric VII of Denmark is deposed, Christopher III of Bavaria elected King.

1440
- Bruges crushed by Duke Philip.
- Frederick III, German King.
- Praguerie revolt in France: nobles against king.
- The Azores discovered.
- Ladislas V (Postumus), King of Bohemia and Hungary; Vladislas III of Poland a rival in Hungary.
- Invention of printing with movable types by Johan Gutenberg of Mainz.
- Frederick II, Elector of Brandenburg.
  DEATHS
  Jan van Eyck, Flemish painter.

1441
- Thomas à Kempis *De Imitatione Christi* about this date.

1443
- Turks defeated by Albanians under Scanderbeg.
- Battle of Nissa: Turks defeated by John Huniades.

1444
- Peace of Szegedin: Amurath II surrenders control of Serbia, Walachia and Bosnia to Hungary.
- Battle of Varna: Turkish victory over Hungary; King Vladislas III killed.

1446
- Death of Brunelleschi, Italian pioneer of Renaissance architecture.

1447
- Amurath II defeated by Scanderbeg.
- Casimir IV, King of Poland and Grand Duke of Lithuania.

1448
- Constantine XI, Eastern Emperor.
- French regain Anjou and Maine.
- End of the Union of Kalmar: Christian I, King of Denmark.
- Concordat of Vienna between the Emperor Frederick III and the Pope: obedience of German people to Rome pledged.
- Battle of Kossovo: John Huniades defeated by the Turks.

1449
- End of the Council of Basle.

1450
- Rebellion of Jack Cade in England.

- Francesco Sforza becomes Duke of Milan.
- Battle of Formigny: English defeated by French; Normandy recovered.
- Papal Jubilee.

1451
- Glasgow University founded.
- French recover Guienne.
- Muhammad II, Turkish Sultan.

1452
- Frederick III crowned Emperor by Pope Nicholas V in Rome: the last coronation of an Emperor at Rome.
- James II of Scotland murders Sir William Douglas.

1453
- Ottoman Turks capture Constantinople: end of the Eastern or Byzantine Empire.
- Austria created an Archduchy.
- Ladislas V of Hungary becomes King of Bohemia also.
- Battle of Castillon: English defeated; end of the Hundred Years' War.

THE BEGINNING OF MODERN EUROPE

1454
- Peace of Lodi between Venice and Milan.
- First known document printed from movable types, at Mainz.
- Prussia incorporated in Poland.
- Henry IV, King of Castile.

1455
- Wars of the Roses begin in England: first battle of St Albans, Yorkist victory.
- House of Douglas overthrown in Scotland.

  DEATHS
  Fra Angelico, Italian religious painter.
  Lorenzo Ghiberti, Italian sculptor.

1456
- Turkish attack on Belgrade repelled by John Huniades.

1457
- End of Foscari's dogeship: Venice begins to decline.
- Death of Ladislas V of Hungary and Bohemia.

1458
- Matthias Corvinus, son of John Huniades, elected King of Hungary; George Podiebrad elected King of Bohemia.
- Death of Alfonso the Magnanimous: Two Sicilies again separated.
- John II, King of Aragon; Ferdinand I, King of Naples.

1459
- Turks conquer Serbia.

1460
- William Dunbar, Scottish poet, born.
- James III, King of Scotland.
- Battle of Wakefield: Lancastrian victory.
- Turks conquers the Morea.
- Denmark obtains Schleswig and Holstein.

1461
- Empire of Trebizond destroyed by Turks.
- Second battle of St Albans: Lancastrian victory.
- Battle of Mortimer's Cross: Yorkist victory.

- Battle of Towton: Yorkist victory makes Edward IV, King of England.
- Louis XI, King of France.
- Ivan III (the Great), ruler of Moscow.
- Pragmatic Sanction of Bourges revoked.

1462
- Battle of Puck: Polish victory; Prussia conquered.

1463
- War begins between Venice and the Turks.
- Turks acknowledge Scanderbeg as ruler of Albania.

1464
- Turks conquer Bosnia.
- Death of Cosimo de' Medici of Florence: succeeded by his son, Piero.
  DEATHS
  Roger van der Weyden, Flemish painter.

1465
- League of Public Welfare formed by French nobles against Louis XI.

1466
- Treaty of Thorn between Poland and the Teutonic Knights; Poland dominant and master of Prussia.
  DEATHS
  Donatello, Italian sculptor.

1467
- Turks conquer Herzegovina.
- Charles the Bold, Duke of Burgundy.

1468
- Orkney Islands annexed to Scotland.
- War declared against Bohemia by Hungary.

1469
- Shetland Islands annexed to Scotland.
- Matthias Corvinus, King of Hungary, crowned King of Bohemia by Papal legate.
- Lorenzo de' Medici begins rule in Florence along with his brother, Giuliano.
- Marriage of Ferdinand of Aragon and Isabella of Castile.

1470
- Truce between Hungary and Bohemia.
- Turks take Negropont.
- Three northern kingdoms reunited under Christian I of Denmark.

1471
- Battle of Barnet: Yorkist victory.
- Battle of Tewkesbury: Yorkist victory.
- Death of George Podiebrad of Bohemia; Prince Vladislav of Poland elected King.
- Sixtus IV becomes Pope; notorious for nepotism and abuses.
- Ivan the Great conquers Novgorod.
  DEATHS
  Thomas à Kempis, author of the *Imitation of Christ*.

1472
- Philip de Comines joins Louis XI.

1473
- Venice obtains Cyprus.
- Charles the Bold consolidates Burgundian power in Netherlands.

1474
- Scutari successfully defended against Turks.
- Ferdinand, the Catholic King of Castile.

- Everlasting Compact: Swiss independence recognized.

1475
- First book printed in English language: *Recuyell of the Histories of Troy* by William Caxton at Bruges.
- Edward IV invades France to help Charles the Bold: Treaty of Pecquigny arranged with Louis XI.
- Battle of Racova: Stephen the Great of Moldavia defeats the Turks.

1476
- William Caxton sets up his printing press at Westminster.
- Battle of Granson: Swiss defeat Charles the Bold.
- Battle of Morat: Swiss defeat Charles the Bold.
- Battle of Toro: Portugal defeated by Ferdinand of Castile.

1477
- Battle of Nancy: Charles the Bold defeated and killed; end of Duchy.
- Mary, daughter of Charles the Bold, marries Maximilian, afterwards Emperor.

1478
- Plot of the Pazzi in Florence: Giuliano de' Medici killed; Lorenzo's position strengthened.
- Treaty of Olmütz between Hungary and Bohemia: Moravia, Silesia and Lusatia ceded to former.

1479
- Treaty of Brünn between Poland and Hungary.
- Treaty of Constantinople between Venice and Turkey.
- Ferdinand the Catholic becomes Ferdinand II of Aragon: Aragon and Castile united.
- Battle of Guinegate: French defeated by Maximilian.

1480
- Turks occupy Otranto for a short time; fail against Rhodes.

1481
- Spanish Inquisition established by Ferdinand the Catholic: Torquemada as its chief.
- John II becomes King of Portugal.
- Hand becomes King of Denmark.
- Bajazet II becomes Turkish Sultan.

1482
- Treaty of Arras between France and the Netherlands: Louis IX receives Duchy of Burgundy, Franche-Comté, Picardy, etc.
- Portuguese settle Gold Coast (Ghana).

1483
- Edward V murdered; Richard III, King of England.
- Charles VIII, King of France.

1485
- Battle of Bosworth: Richard III defeated and killed; Henry VII, King of England, first of the Tudor Dynasty.
- Matthias Corvinus takes Vienna.
- The Mad War in France.
- Partition of Leipzig: henceforward two Saxon lines.
- Sir Thomas Malory's *Morte D'Arthur*.

1486
- Frederick the Wise, Elector of Saxony.
- John becomes Elector of Brandenburg.

1487
- Revolt of Lambert Simnel against Henry VII.
- Matthias Corvinus, master of Austria, Styria and Carinthia.

1488
- Bartholomew Diaz discovers the passage around Africa at the Cape of Good Hope.
- Battle of Sauchieburn: death of James III and accession of James IV of Scotland.
- Venice obtains Cyprus.
  DEATHS
  Verrocchio, Italian sculptor.

1490
- Death of Matthias Corvinus, King of Hungary; Vladislav II of Bohemia elected; Hungarians expelled from Austrian duchies by Emperor Maximilian.
- Maximilian obtains Tirol.

1491
- Maximilian invades Hungary: Treaty of Pressburg.
- France obtains Brittany by marriage.

1492
- Christopher Columbus discovers the West Indies.
- Henry VII invades France: Treaty of Étaples.
- Ferdinand the Catholic conquers Granada: end of Moorish power in Spain.
- Expulsion of Jews from Spain.
- Alexander VI becomes Pope: scandalous reign.
- Death of Casimir IV of Poland.
  DEATHS
  Lorenzo de' Medici.

1493
- Maximilian I becomes German King.
- End of the Lordship of the Isles.
- Pope Alexander VI divides newly explored lands between Spain and Portugal.
- Treaty of Senlis: France gives Artois and the County of Burgundy to Maximilian.

1494
- Aldus Manutius printing at Venice.
- Ottoman Turks driven out of Styria.
- The Medici expelled from Florence.
- Charles VIII of France invades Italy.
- Treaty of Tordesillas between Spain and Portugal.
- Sir Edward Poynings, Lord Deputy of Ireland.
- Poynings' Law passed: Parliament of Ireland made entirely dependent on that of England.
  DEATHS
  Hans Memling, Flemish painter.
  Pico de Mirandola, Italian painter.

1495
- Manuel, King of Portugal.
- Charles VIII conquers Naples.
- Battle of Fornovo: French advance in Italy checked.
- Holy League against France between Ferdinand, the Pope, the Emperor, etc.

1496
- Magnus Intercursus: a commercial treaty between England and Netherlands.
- Philip, son of Emperor Maximilian I and Mary of Burgundy, marries Juana, daughter of Ferdinand and Isabella of Spain.

1497
- John Cabot discovers Labrador and Newfoundland.
- Perkin Warbeck, pretender to the English throne, captured.
- Turks devastate Poland.

1498
- Girolamo Savonarola executed in Florence.
- Erasmus at Oxford.
- Vasco da Gama reaches India by sea.
- Louis XII, King of France.

1499
- Vicente Pinzon and Amerigo Vespucci reach America.
- Battle of Sapienza: Venetian fleet totally defeated by Turks.
- Louis XII conquers Milan; Ludovico il Moro overthrown.
- War between Ivan the Great and Alexander of Lithuania.
- Peace of Basle: Swiss League virtually recognized as independent of the Empire.

1500
- Battle of Vedrosha: Lithuanians routed by Russians.
- Poedro Cabral discovers Brazil.
  - *DEATHS*
  - Robert Henryson, Scottish poet.

1501
- France and Spain arrange joint conquest and partition of the kingdom of Naples; then fall out over the spoils.
- Alexander King of Poland: final union with Lithuania.

1502
- Massacre of the Orsini at Rome by Pope Alexander VI and his son, Caesar Borgia.

1503
- Marriage of James IV of Scotland to Margaret Tudor, daughter of Henry VII.
- Battle of Garigliano: French defeated by Spanish in Italy.
- Julius II becomes Pope; Caesar Borgia overthrown.

1504
- Treaty of Blois between Louis XII and Maximilian I.
- Portuguese establish a permanent base in India at Cochin.

1505
- Almeida, Portuguese Viceroy in India.
- Basil III, Tsar of Moscow.

1506
- Sigismund I, King of Poland.
- Philip, husband of Juana, recognized as King of Castile: dies same year.
  - *DEATHS*
  - Chrisopher Columbus.
  - Andrea Mantegna, Italian painter.

THE REFORMATION

1507
- Machiavelli in power at Florence.
- Margaret, daughter of Maximilian, becomes Governor-General of Netherlands.
- Louis XII takes Genoa.

1508
- Maximilian assumes the title of Roman Emperor elect at Trent, without waiting for coronation at Rome.
- League of Cambrai formed against Venice: France, Empire and Pope Julius II.
- *Romance of Amadis de Gaul* published.
- Michelangelo and Raphael working at Rome for Julius II: culmination of Renaissance Art.

1509
- Spaniards under Cardinal Ximenes defeat Barbary pirates and take Oran.
- Henry VIII, King of England.
- Battle of Agnadello: Venetians defeated by French.
- Florence finally subdues Pisa.
- Great earthquake in Constantinople.
- Emperor Maximilian fails to take Padua.

1510
- Venice reconciled to the Pope.
- Albuquerque captures Goa in India for Portugal.
- Erasmus begins lecturing on Greek at Cambridge.
  DEATHS
  Sandro Botticelli, Italian painter.

1511
- Albuquerque takes Malacca.
- Holy League of Pope, Venice and Spain: joined by Henry VIII.

1512
- Selim I becomes Sultan.
- Imperial Diet at Cologne: last reforming Diet.
- Battle of Ravenna: Gaston de Foix victorious against Holy League but killed; artillery first decides a battle.
- Holy League restores the Medici in Florence.
- League between the Pope and the Emperor.

1513
- Leo X (de' Medici) becomes Pope.
- Franco-Venetian League renewed.
- Maximilian allies with Henry VIII against France.
- Battle of Novara: Swiss defeat the French.
- Battle of Guinegaste: English defeat the French.
- Battle of Flodden: English victory over Scots: James IV killed; James V becomes King of Scotland.
- Christian II, King of Denmark.
- Vasco Núñez de Balboa discovers the Pacific Ocean.
- Machiavelli's *The Prince*.

1514
- Greek New Testament of Erasmus.
  DEATHS
  Donato Bramante, Italian architect.

1515
- Francis I becomes King of France.
- Charles, grandson of Maximilian, becomes Governor of the Netherlands.
- Navarre incorporated with Castile.
- Congress of Vienna: marriage treaties between Maximilian and Vladislav of Hungary.
- Battle of Marignano: French defeat Swiss and recovered Milan.
- Cardinal Wolsey becomes Lord Chancellor of England.

1516
- Church Concordat between Francis I and Leo X.
- Death of Ferdinand the Catholic: Charles I (afterwards Emperor Charles V) becomes King of Castile, Aragon and other regions.
- Louis II becomes King of Hungary.
- Barbarossa, the pirate leader, captures Algiers.

- Treaty of Noyon: between France, Spain and the Holy Roman Empire.
- Everlasting League between the Swiss and France.
- Sir Thomas More's *Utopia*.
  DEATHS
  Hieronymus Bosch, Dutch painter.
1517
- Ottoman Turks occupy Cairo and overthrow the Mamelukes: Turkish Sultan henceforth Caliph.
- Treaty of Rouen between Scotland and France.
- Martin Luther publishes his '95 Theses' at Wittenberg: beginning of Reformation.
1518
- Melanchthon becomes Professor of Greek at Wittenberg.
- Zwingli becomes People's Priest at Great Minster of Zurich.
1519
- Death of Emperor Maximilian: Charles V elected King of the Romans.
- Ferdinand Magellan starts on voyage round the world (completed in 1522).
  DEATHS
  Leonardo da Vinci, Italian artist.
1520
- Suleiman the Magnificent becomes Sultan.
- Luther excommunicated.
- The Meaux Preachers pioneer the Reformation in France; Zwingli leads Reformation in Switzerland.
- Field of the Cloth of Gold: interview between Henry VIII and Francis I.
- Christian II of Denmark, having overthrown Sten Sture, crowned King of Sweden.
- Stockholm Bath of Blood.
- Hernando Cortés conquers Mexico.
1521
- Luther at Diet of Worms: placed under the ban of the Empire.
- Battle of Villalar: Spanish revolt crushed by Charles V.
- Ferdinand, brother of Charles V, given government of Austrian Habsburg dominions.
- Treaty of Bruges between Emperor Charles V and Henry VIII.
- Milan occupied by the troops of Charles V and the Pope.
- Turks capture Belgrade.
1522
- Adrian VI becomes Pope: last non-Italian Pope until 1978.
- Henry VIII created Defender of the Faith for answering Luther.
- Battle of the Bicocca (near Milan): French defeated by Imperialists and compelled to evacuate Lombardy; Francesco Sforza set up in Milan.
- Turks conquer Rhodes.
- Treaty of Windsor: between Charles V and Henry VIII.
- The Knights' War: Franz von Sickingen, a German Lutheran knight, fails to capture Trier.
1523
- Revolt against Christian II causes his flight from Denmark: Frederick I becomes King.
- Franz von Sickingen defeated and killed.
- Gustavus Vasa King of Sweden (Gustavus I): Union of Kalmar ends.
- Albert of Brandenburg, last Grand Master of Teutonic Order, becomes Lutheran.
- Charles Brandon, Duke of Suffolk invades France.
- French invasion of Lombardy (Bayard killed).
- Clement VII (of the Medici family) becomes Pope.

1524
- Catholic Swiss League formed.
- Beginning of Peasants' Revolt in Germany.
- Invasion of France by Duke of Bourbon; fails to take Marseilles; pursued to Italy.
- 'Erection' of James V in Scotland.
- Order of Theatines founded.

1525
- Clement VII's agreement with Francis I.
- Battle of Pavia: Francis I defeated by Charles V and made prisoner; hand firearms triumphant.
- Lefèvre's French New Testament condemned to be burned.
- Mass abolished at Zürich.
- Massacre of Weinsberg by rebelling German peasants: rebels crushed in several fights.
- Peace between England and France.
- Albert of Brandenburg makes his dominions the hereditary Dukedom of Prussia.

1526
- Treaty of Madrid between Charles V and Francis I: Francis set free.
- Lutheran Alliance completed, with Landgrave Philip of Hesse as its moving spirit.
- League of Cognac against Emperor by Francis I, Pope, Florence, Venice and others.
- Milan surrenders to the Imperialists.
- Beginning of Danish breach with Rome.
- Battle of Mohács: Hungary overthrown by the Ottoman Turks: King Louis II drowned.
- John Zapolya and Ferdinand of Austria both elected King of Hungary: Zapolya defeated by Ferdinand at Tokay.
- Ferdinand elected King of Bohemia.
- Order of Capuchins founded.
- Battle of Panipat: Muslim conquest of India by Babur begun; Mughal Empire founded in northern India.

1527
- Alliance between Henry VIII and Francis I.
- Sack of Rome by Imperialist troops of Holy Roman Emperor Charles V.
- Second expulsion of Medici from Florence.
- Västeras Recess: beginning of official Swedish Reformation.
- French under Lautrec invade Italy.

1528
- England and France declare war against the Holy Roman Empire.
- Patrick Hamilton burned for heresy in Scotland.
- Naples besieged by French and Genoese.
- Genoese under Andrea Doria desert French, capture Genoa and establish a republic.

1529
- Diet of Speir: protest against its decisions by Lutheran Princes and cities, hence name of Protestant.
- Berquin burned for heresy in France.
- Zurich declares war on Lucerne and Catholic allies: Peace of Kappel arranged.
- Treaty of Barcelona: between Pope and Emperor.
- Peace of Cambrai: between Francis I, Emperor and England: France abandons Italy, Flanders and Artois; Malta and Tripoli to Knights of St John.
- Conference of Marburg between Luther and Zwingli: failure.
- Unsuccessful siege of Vienna by Ottoman Turks led by Suleiman I (the Magnificent).
- Henry VIII's divorce trial begins: transferred to Rome by the Pope.
- Fall of Cardinal Wolsey.
- Reformation Parliament in England (till 1536).

The Counter-Reformation
1530
- Compact between Charles V and Clement VII: Charles crowned Emperor by Pope at Bologna; the last to be crowned Emperor.
- Diet of Augsburg: Melanchthon prepares the anti-Zwinglian Confession of Augsburg.
- Tetrapolitana Confession (Zwinglian) prepared by cities of South Germany under influence of Bucer.
- Florence surrenders to the Medici after a long siege.
- Schmalkaldic League of Protestant German Princes formed.
- The Grisons League obtains the Valtelline.
1531
- Battle of Kappel: Catholic Swiss cantons victorious over Protestant: Zwingli killed.
- Second Peace of Kappel between the two religious parties in Switzerland.
- Spanish conquistador, Francisco Pizarro, invades gold-rich Inca Empire.
1532
- 'Submission of the Clergy' to Henry VIII in England.
- Agreement of Nuremberg: Protestants guarantee peace till next Diet of General Council.
- End of Florentine Republic: Alessandro de' Medici made Duke.
- Francisco Pizarro conquers Peru.
- College of Justice founded by James V.
- Ariosto's *Orlando Furioso*.
1533
- Thomas Cranmer becomes Archbishop of Canterbury.
- Death of Frederick I of Denmark: disputed succession.
- Anne Boleyn publicly named Queen of Henry VIII; Cranmer declares Catherine of Aragon's marriage null; Anne Boleyn crowned; Henry VIII excommunicated by Pope.
- Treaty of Peace between Turkey and Austria.
- Ivan IV (the Terrible) becomes Tsar of Russia.
1534
- Anabaptist revolution in Münster under John of Leyden (soon suppressed).
- Geneva adopts the Reformation.
- First Voyage of Jacques Cartier to Canada.
- Revolution in Lübeck under Wullenwever.
- Battle of Lauffen: Philip of Hesse, leader of the Schmalkaldic League, defeats Ferdinand's forces in Württemberg.
- Barbarossa II captures Tunis.
- Paul III becomes Pope.
- The Paris Placards against the mass: severe persecution.
- Luther's German Bible completed.
- Grevefeide or Count's War in Denmark.
1535
- Barbarossa II defeated and Tunis taken by Emperor Charles along with Andrea Doria, Venice, Knights of Malta and others.
- Act of Supremacy in England: Henry VIII, Supreme Head of the English Church.
- Execution of Bishop Fisher and Sir Thomas More.
- The English Bible of Miles Coverdale (first complete one).
- Thomas Cromwell becomes Vicar-General for Henry VIII.
1536
- Treaty between Francis I and Suleiman I.
- Dissolution of the monasteries ordered by Henry VIII in England.
- Savoy conquered by French.

- Calvin's *Institutes of the Christian Religion.*
- Anne Boleyn beheaded; Jane Seymour, Queen of Henry VIII.
- Concord of Wittenberg between Luther and Zwinglians.
- Calvin at Geneva.
- Imperialists invade Province, but repelled.
- Christian III enters Copenhagen as King.
- Pilgrimage of Grace in England led by Robert Aske.
- William Tyndale burned for heresy in the Netherlands.

DEATHS

Erasmus of Rotterdam, humanist scholar.

1537

- Christian III takes possession of Norway.
- A Papal Commission reports on reform.
- Suleiman I devastates Corfu in his war with Venice.
- End of Lübeck attempt at city-Empire: Wullenwever executed.

1538

- Defensive League against the Turks between the Emperor, Pope, Ferdinand and Venice.
- Calvin expelled from Geneva.
- Catholic League of Nürnberg.
- Truce for ten years between Francis I, Charles V and the Pope.
- Suleiman I annexes part of Moldavia.
- Turkish fleet sails against India; Yemen captured.
- Naval flight in the Ambracian Gulf: Barbarossa defeats forces of Emperor, Pope, Venice and Genoa.

1539

- Act of the Six Articles against heresy in England.
- Society of Jesus (Jesuits) founded by Ignatius Loyola.

1540

- Charles V punishes Ghent severely for rebellion.
- Severe Edict of Fontainebleau against heresy.
- Thomas Cromwell executed.
- Peace between Venice and the Turks.
- Jacques Cartier exploring in the St Lawrence.

1541

- Religious Conference at Ratisborn: failure.
- Suleiman I virtually annexes Hungary.
- Hernando De Soto discoverers the Mississippi.
- Henry VIII given the title King of Ireland by the Irish Parliament.
- Calvin finally settles in Geneva.
- Failure of Spanish attack on Algiers

1542

- Roberval attempts to found a French colony in Canada.
- French attack Artois and Flanders.
- Brunswick lands overrun by the Schmalkaldic League's forces.
- Imperialist forces under Joachim of Brandenburg fail to take Pesth from the Turks.
- Council of Trent opened.
- Battle of Solway Moss: English defeat Scots.
- Mary Stewart, Queen of Scotland: Earl of Arran, Regent.
- Inquisition set up in Rome.

DEATHS

Sir Thomas Wyatt, English poet.

1543

- Suleiman I takes Gran, Stuhlweissenburg and others.
- Vesalius, the anatomist, publishes his chief work.
- Barbarossa and the French fleet capture Nice city, but not the citadel.
- Charles V victorious in his war against Duke William of Cleves.

DEATHS
Nicolas Copernicus, Polish astronomer.

1544

- Edict calling upon all subjects in the hereditary Habsburg lands to accept Confession of Louvain.
- Battle of Ceresole: French defeat Spanish forces in Lombardy.
- Earl of Hertford invades Scotland; Edinburgh burned.
- Bologne taken by English.
- Peace of Crépy: between Emperor, England and France.

1545

- Battle of Ancrum Moor: Scottish victory.
- Massacre of the Waldenses.
- Brunswick territories appropriated by Schmalkaldic League.
- Council of Trent again opened.

1546

- Religious conference at Ratisbon: futile.
- George Wishart burned as a heretic in Scotland.
- Cardinal Beaton murdered to avenge Wishart and St Andrews Castle captured.
- Diet of Ratisbon: Protestants repudiate Council of Trent and demand a National Council.
- Anne Askew tortured and burned for heresy in London.
- Ban of the Empire against Philip of Hesse and the Elector, John Frederick of Saxony.
- Execution of the Fourteen of Meaux in France.
- Ernestine Saxony invaded and occupied by Maurice of Albertine Saxony, and Ferdinand: Elector John Frederick recovers his territory and invades that of Maurice.

DEATHS
Martin Luther, German religious reformer.

1547

- Brittany united to French kingdom.
- Failure of revolt against Andrea Doria of Genoa.
- Earl of Surrey executed for treason.
- Edward VI becomes King of England: Earl of Hertford (created Duke of Somerset) becomes Protector of the Realm.
- Practically all South German cities subdued by Emperor Charles V by this date; Duke Henry regains Brunswick; Catholicism re-established in Cologne.
- Council of Trent removed to Bologna by the Pope.
- Execution of Jaime de Enzines at Rome: first Italian death for heresy.
- Henry II, King of France.
- Battle of Mühlberg: Charles V defeats Elector John Frederick and takes him prisoner; the electoral dignity transferred to Maurice of Albertine Saxony.
- Philip of Hesse surrenders to Charles V.
- Capitulation of St Andrews: John Knox a French galley-slave.
- Inquisition established in Portugal.
- Battle of Pinkie: Somerset's victory over the Scots.
- Chambre Ardente created in France.
- Somerset repeals the English laws against heresy.
- English replaces Latin in English Church services.

1548
- Suleiman I victorious against Persia.
- Sigismund II (Augustus), King of Poland.
- The Bohemian Brethren, expelled from Bohemia, settle in Poland.
- Interim religious compromise drawn up by a committee chosen by Charles V and proclaimed as an Edict.
- Mary Queen of Scots lands in France.

1549
- First Book of Common Prayer sanctioned by English Parliament.
- First Act of Uniformity in England.
- Edward Seymour, Duke of Somerset, institutes social reforms in England: Enclosures Commission appointed.
- Ket's rebellion in eastern England suppressed.
- France declares war against England.
- Fall of Somerset: Warwick (afterwards Duke of Northumberland) in power.
- Parliament declares enclosures legal.

1550
- Julius III becomes Pope.
- Persecution of Catholics and heretics in England.
- Peace established between France and England: Boulogna given back to France.
- Dragut the Corsair defeated by Charles and headquarters in Tunisia taken.
- Severe placard against heresy in the Netherlands.

1551
- Council of Trent resumed at Trent.
- Turks capture Tripoli from Knights of St John.
- Turco-Hungarian War renewed after a truce.
- Magdeburg capitulates to the Elector Maurice.

1552
- Somerset executed.
- Treaty of Chambord between Henry II and the Protestant German Princes.
- French invade and occupy Lorraine.
- Council of Trent suspended.
- Charles V's flight from Maurice of Saxony across the Brenner Pass.
- Treaty of Passau: Protestant position secured.
- Second Act of Uniformity in England.
- Second Book of Common Prayer.
- Kazan annexed by Ivan IV.

1553
- Sir Hugh Willoughby and Richard Chancellor set out in search of northeast passage.
- Death of Edward VI of England: Lady Jane Grey proclaimed Queen of Northumberland; Mary Tudor also proclaimed; Northumberland executed and Mary victorious.
- Battle of Sievershausen: Elector Maurice defeats Albert Margrave of Brandenburg, but killed.
- Battle of Steterburg: Albert of Brandenburg defeated by Duke Henry of Brunswick.
- Michael Servetus, an anti-Trinitarian, burned for heresy in Geneva by Calvin.
  DEATHS
  François Rabelais, French writer.

1554
- Sir Thomas Wyatt leads a rebellion in Kent.
- Execution of Lady Jane Grey and her husband; also of Suffolk and Wyatt.
- Mary of Lorraine, Regent of Scotland.

- Battle of Schwarzach: Albert of Brandenburg defeated by Duke Henry of Brunswick and driven as a fugitive to France.
- Mary Tudor marries Philip, heir of Charles V.
- Cardinal Pole arrives in England: Parliament decides in favour of returning to Roman Catholicism.
- Astrakhan annexed by Ivan IV.

1555
- John Rogers burned for heresy in England; many others follow.
- Marcellas II becomes Pope; dies a few months later; Paul IV succeeds; Counter-Reformation in the Papal chair.
- Vaudois become Calvinists.
- Union of Bohemian Brethren and Calvinists in Poland.
- Latimer and Ridley burned in England.
- Religious Peace of Augsburg: Cujus regio, ejus religio.
- Charles V abdicates sovereignty of Netherlands at Brussels: Philip II succeeds.

1556
- Charles V abdicates sovereignty in Spain and Italy: Ferdinand I, Emperor.
- Peace of Vaucelles between Philip and France.
- Thomas Cranmer burned at the stake.
- Battle of Panipat (second): Mughal conquest of India made secure.
- Akbar becomes Mughal Emperor in India.
  DEATHS
  Nicholas Udall, English playwright.

1557
- War declared between England and France.
- Battle of St Quentin: French defeated by Spanish under Duke of Savoy and Egmont.
- Colloquy of Worms: no result.
- First Bond of Lords of the Congregation: organization of Scottish Protestantism.
- Portuguese establish a trading base at Macao off the Chinese mainland.

1558
- Beginning of the Livonian War: Russia invades Livonia.
- English expelled from Calais by the French.
- Mary Queen of Scots marries the French Dauphin Francis.
- Battle of Gravelines: Egmont again defeated by the French.
- Deaths of Mary Tudor and Cardinal Pole; Elizabeth I becomes Queen of England.

1559
- Death of Christian III of Denmark: Frederick II succeeds.
- Colloquy of Westminster.
- Treaty of Cateau-Cambrésis: a European settlement (the Empire, France and England).
- Acts of Uniformity and Supremacy in England.
- John Knox returns to Scotland.
- Auto-da-fé at Valladolid: first one against heresy.
- Francis II, King of France.
- First Papal Index of Prohibited Books: great opposition.
- Pius IV, Pope.
- Philip leaves the Netherlands: Margaret of Parma, Regent.

THE WARS OF RELIGION

1560
- Treaty of Berwick between Duke of Norfolk and the Scottish Lords of the Congregation.

- Tumult of Amboise.
- Elizabeth I sends Lord Grey with an army to help the Scottish Lords of the Congregation.
- Death of Mary of Lorraine, the Scottish Regent.
- Treaty of Edinburgh: French forces to quit Scotland.
- A Scottish Parliament abolishes Roman Catholicism in Scotland.
- Death of Gustavus Vasa, King of Sweden: succeeded by Erik XIV.
- Charles IX, King of France.
- First Book of Discipline in Scottish Church.

1561
- Abortive Protestant Conference at Naumberg: Lutherans and Calvinists irreconcilable.
- Vaudois rebellion suppressed by Savoy.
- Reval becomes Swedish.
- Mary Queen of Scots lands in Scotland.
- The Colloquy of Poissy: a form of French National Church Council.
- Teutonic Order submits to Poland.

1562
- Edict of January: first legal recognition of Protestantism in France.
- Council of Trent resumes at Trent.
- Massacre of Vassy: First War of Religion in France begins.
- Huguenots take Orleans.
- Treaty of Hampton Court between Elizabeth and the Prince of Condé.
- Treaty of Prague between Emperor Ferdinand and Suleiman I (the Magnificent).
- English forces land to assist the Huguenots in France: Le Havre is occupied.
- French Royalists occupy Rouen.
- Battle of Corrichie: Earl of Huntly defeated by Moray and killed.
- Battle of Dreux: indecisive Royalist victory in France.
- Emmanuel Philibert of Savoy obtains Turin and makes it his capital.

1563
- Duke of Guise murdered in a suburb of Orleans.
- Edict of Amboise ends First War of Religion.
- Swedes defeat Danes off Bornholm.
- Havre evacuated by the English.
- Northern Seven Years' War declared by Denmark.
- Charles IX declared of age in France.
- End of Council of Trent: the Counter-Reformation complete.

1564
- Papal Decree confirming Decrees of Council of Trent.
- Tridentine Index of Prohibited Books.
- Cardinal Granville recalled from the Netherlands.
- Treaty of Troyes between France and England.
- Maximilian II becomes Emperor.
- Philip orders Decrees of Trent to be enforced in the Netherlands.
- Anti-Trinitarians in Poland.
- Calvinism established in Palatinate by the Elector, Frederick III.
- Treaty of Lausanne adjusts boundaries between Berne and Savoy.
  DEATHS
  John Calvin, French theologian.

1565
- Failure of Turkish attack on Malta.
- Bayonne Conference between France and Spain.
- Mary Queen of Scots marries Henry Darnley; Moray flees to England.

- Trent Decrees and Placards against heresy begin to be enforced in Netherlands.
- Revival of Catholicism in Poland.
- First punishments of Puritans in England.

1566
- 'The Compromise' signed by many Netherland nobles, pledging them to oppose the Inquisition.
- Murder of David Riccio, confidential secretary to Mary Queen of Scots, at Holyrood Palace.
- 'The Request' presented to a Netherlands assembly by Lewis of Nassau and Brederode, embodying the principles of the 'Compromise'.
- The Culemberg Banquet in Brussels: Vivent les Gueux first heard.
- Iconoclastic outbreaks in the Netherlands.
- Conference at Dendermonde between William the Silent, Lewis of Nassau, Egmont, Horn; Egmont and Horn not prepared to resist Philip.
- Death of Suleiman the Magnificent in Hungary: Selim II succeeds as Sultan.
    DEATHS
    Nostradamus, French astrologer.

1567
- Murder of Lord Darnley.
- Rout of John de Marnix at Austruweel.
- Valenciennes taken by Royal forces.
- William of Orange goes into exile.
- Mary Queen of Scots marries James Hepburn, Earl of Bothwell.
- Shane O'Neill defeated and killed in Ireland.
- Murder of the Sture by Erik XIV of Sweden.
- Mary Queen of Scots taken prisoner at Carberry Hill, imprisoned in Lochleven Castle and compelled to abdicate.
- Arrest of Egmont and Horn after Alva had arrived in Netherlands as Captain-General; Council of Troubles created; Alva becomes Regent and Governor-General.
- Enterprise of Meaux.
- John Casimir, second son of Elector Palatine Frederick, leads a force into France to help the Huguenots.
- Battle of Saint Denis between Huguenots and Catholics: indecisive.
- Scottish Parliament declares Mary guilty of murder and to have forfeited the crown: James VI, King of Scotland.

1568
- William of Orange proclaimed an outlaw.
- La Rochelle opens its gates to the Huguenots.
- Condé raises the siege of Orleans.
- Peace between the Emperor and the Turks.
- Peace of Longjumeau ends the Second War of Religion in France.
- Mary escapes from Lochleven: defeated by Moray at Langside; flees to England.
- Battle of Heiligerlee: Lewis of Nassau defeats Spanish.
- Execution of Egmont and Horn.
- Revolt of Moriscos in Granada: suppressed with great slaughter.
- Douay College founded by Father Allen.

1569
- Erik XIV deposed by Swedish Diet: John III becomes King.
- Spanish treasure ships seized at Falmouth and Southampton.
- States-General summoned at Brussels: Alva fails to get all his taxes.
- Beggars of the Sea first appear.
- Battle of Jarnac: Huguenots routed; Condé captured and shot dead.

- Union of Lublin: Poland and Lithuania incorporated.
- Cosimo de' Medici created Grand Duke of Tuscany by the Pope.
- Battle of Moncontour: Huguenot defeat.

1570
- Assassination of Regent Moray; Lennox becomes Regent of Scotland.
- Peace of Saint-Germain ends Third War of Religion; La Rochelle becomes Huguenot headquarters.
- Concensus of Sadomir: Union of Bohemian Brethren, Lutherans and Calvinists in Poland.
- Queen Elizabeth declared deposed by Pope.
- Northern Seven Years' War ended by Peace of Stettin.

1571
- Triple Alliance of Spain, Venice and Pope against Turks.
- Turks land in Cyprus.
- Beggars of the Sea forbidden to use English ports.
- Ridolfi conspiracy discovered by William Cecil.
- Thirty-nine Articles enacted in England.
- Beginning of penal legislation against Catholics in England.
- Battle of Lepanto: Don John of Austria wins naval victory over Turks.
- Regent Lennox murdered in Scotland: Earl of Mar, Regent.
- Khan of Crimea invades Russia and burns Moscow.

1572
- Death of Sigismund II of Poland.
- Beggars of the Sea capture Brill; also Flushing, etc.
- Defensive alliance between France and England.
- Lewis of Nassau invades the Netherlands from France; takes Valenciennes and Mons.
- Edict of Rochelle ends Fourth War of Religion.
- William the Silent invades the Netherlands from the east: takes Roermond; Brussels shut against him.
- States of Holland at Dort recognize William the Silent as Stadtholder.
- Henry of Bourbon becomes King of Navarre.
- St Bartholomew's Day Massacre: Admiral Coligny murdered.
- Alva recovers Mons.
- Death of Regent Mar in Scotland: Morton succeeds.
- Sack of Malines, Zutphen and Naarden by Spanish troops.
- Siege of Haarlem begun by Don Frederick of Toledo.

1573
- Compact of Warsaw secures absolute religious liberty in Poland.
- Pacification of Perth.
- Edinburgh Castle surrendered by Kirkcaldy of Grange and Maitland of Levington.
- Venice cedes Cyprus to Turks.
- Duke of Anjou elected King of Poland.
- Surrender of Haarlem.
- Siege of Alkmaar: dykes cut; siege raised.
- Battle of Enckhuysen: Spanish fleet defeated by Dutch.
- William the Silent declares himself a Calvinist.
- Alva recalled from the Netherlands: Don Luis Requesens succeeds.

1574
- Huguenot rising begins Fifth War of Religion.
- Battle of Bergen: Dutch naval victory.
- Spaniards surrender Middelburg.

- Battle of Mookerheide: Lewis of Nassau killed.
- Plot of Vincennes.
- Henry III, King of France.
- Flight of Anjou from Poland.
- Relief of Leyden after long siege.
- The Gerusalemme Liberata of Tasso.
- Murad III becomes Sultan.

1575

- Anjou declared deposed in Poland: Maximilian II elected by Senate, Stephen Bathory by Diet; latter victorious.
- Escape of Monsieur to join Huguenots.
- Battle of Dormans: Huguenot defeat.
- John Casimir again in France.

1576

- Henry of Navarre escapes to the Huguenots and abjures Catholicism.
- Death of Requesens: Don John of Austria, Governor of Netherlands.
- Union of Holland and Zeeland completed.
- Edict of Beaulieu ends Fifth War of Religion (Peace of Monsieur).
- Rudolph II, Emperor.
- The League formed by French Catholics.
- Pacification of Ghent.
- Revolt of Spanish troops in Netherlands: sack of Antwerp and 'Spanish Fury'.

1577

- French King repudiates Edict of Beaulieu: Sixth War of Religion begins.
- Union of Brussels.
- 'Perpetual Edict': agreement between Netherlands and Don John of Austria.
- Don John seizes Namur.
- Peace of Bergerac: Edict of Poitiers; end of Sixth War of Religion.
- William the Silent enters Brussels.
- Francis Drake's voyage round the world begins.

1578

- State entry of Archduke Matthias into Brussels as Governor, with William the Silent as Lieutenant-General.
- Battle of Gemblours: Alexander of Parma's victory.
- Duke of Anjou accepts title of 'Defender of the Liberties of the Netherlands'.
- Battle of Alcazat-Kebir: King Sebastian of Portugal killed in Morocco; Henry succeeds.
- Battle of Verden: Poles and Swedes defeat Russians.
- Alexander of Parma becomes Governor of Netherlands.
- Morton resigns the Regency of Scotland, but afterwards takes possession of the King.
- Fausto Sozzini (Socinus) in Transylvania and Poland.

1579

- League of Arras for protection of Catholic religion in Hainault, Douay and Artois.
- Union of Utrecht: Dutch republic formed.
- Edmund Spenser's *Shepherd's Calendar*.
- John Lyly's *Euphues*.

1580

- Philip of Spain obtains Portuguese crown on death of King Henry.
- Seventh War of Religion begins; ends in same year by Peace of Fleix.
- Robert Parsons and Edmund Campion, Jesuit missionaries, arrive in England.
- First collection of the *Essays* of Montaigne.

- Charles Emmanuel succeeds Emmanuel Philibert as Duke of Savoy.
  DEATHS
  John Heywood, English dramatist.

1581
- Philip puts a price on the head of William the Silent, Prince of Orange.
- Morton executed in Scotland.
- William the Silent provisionally accepts the title of Count of Holland.
- Philip II abjured by Brabant, Flanders, Utrecht, Gelderland, Holland and Zeeland.
- Poles and Swedes take Narva.
- Battle of Terceira: naval victory of Santa Cruz over Don Antonio.
- The *Apology* of William the Silent.
- Second Book of Discipline in Scotland.

1582
- Peace between Poland and Russia: former gained Livonia, etc.
- Anjou inaugurated at Antwerp as Duke of Brabant.
- Pope Gregory XIII introduces new style in dating by Bull.
- Anjou accepted as Lord of Friesland, Duke of Gelderland and Count of Flanders.
- Raid of Ruthven: James VI of Scotland a prisoner (till June 1583).
  DEATHS
  George Buchanan, Scottish scholar and historian.

1583
- 'French Fury' at Antwerp.
- Sir Humphrey Gilbert's voyage to found a colony in Newfoundland.
- Truce of Pliusa between Russia and Sweden.
- John Whitgift becomes Archbishop of Canterbury to suppress Puritanism.
- Execution of the rebel Earl of Desmond.
- William the Silent accepts the hereditary Countship of Holland and Zeeland.

1584
- William the Silent assassinated at Delft by Gérard.
- Association formed to protect Elizabeth.
- Episcopacy established in Scottish Church by James VI.
- Death of Ivan IV: succeeded by Theodore I, with Boris Godunoff as real ruler of Russia.

1585
- Treaty of Joinville against Henry of Navarre: between Spain and the Catholic League.
- Sixtus V becomes Pope.
- Treaty of Nemours between Henry III and the Catholic League: latter victorious; Eighth War of Religion (War of the Three Henrys) follows.
- Papal Bull against Henry of Navarre and Condé.
- Drake commissioned for reprisals in West Indies.
- English Act against Jesuits, seminary priests, etc.
- Earl of Leicester lands in Holland with a force.

1586
- Leicester made Governor-General of United Provinces.
- Thomas Babington's Catholic plot exposed by Walsingham.
- Alliance between Elizabeth and James VI for the defence of Protestantism.
  DEATHS
  Sir Philip Sidney, English writer and soldier.

1587
- Execution of Mary Queen of Scots.
- Drake's expedition to Cadiz to delay sailing of Spanish Armada.

- Alexander of Parma captures Sluys.
- Leicester leaves Holland.
- Sigismund, son of John III of Sweden, elected King of Poland.
- Battle of Coutras: victory of Henry of Navarre.

1588

- Duke of Guise enters Paris: Henry III flees.
- Spanish Armada sets sail from Lisbon (20 May); defeated by English fleet on 29 July.
- Duke of Guise murdered in Henry III's antechamber; his brother, the Cardinal, executed; other Leaguers arrested.
- Martin Marprelate tracts attacking Anglican bishops begin.
- Christian IV, King of Denmark.

1589

- Duke of Aumale declared Lieutenant-General of France; occupies Paris.
- Truce between Henry III and Henry of Navarre.
- Failure of Drake's expedition against Portugal.
- Henry III assassinated: Henry of Navarre becomes king as Henry IV; beginning of Bourbon Dynasty.
- Battle of Arques: Henry IV victorious.
- Galileo experiments with falling objects at leaning tower of Pisa.

1590

- Dutch capture Breda.
- Battle of Ivry: Henry IV triumphant.
- Savoyard forces invade Provence: Duke of Savoy enters Aix.

1591

- Torgau Alliance of Protestant Princes to aid Henry IV.
- Henry IV excommunicated by the Pope.
- Dutch under Maurice and William Lewis of Nassau take Zutphen; then Deventer and Nimeguen.
- Murder of Tsarevitch Dimitri in Russia.
- Francis Vieta of Paris founds modern algebra.

1592

- Clement VIII, Pope.
- Death of Alexander of Parma: Archduke Ernest succeeds in Netherlands.
- Sigismund, King of Poland, becomes King of Sweden also; Charles, Regent of Sweden.
- Presbyterianism fully established in Scotland.
  DEATHS
  Michel de Montaigne, French author.

1593

- Upsala Council: Swedish Reformation.
- Maurice of Nassau takes Geertruidenburg.
- Henry IV's conversion to Catholicism: 'Paris vaut une messe.'
- Anti-Puritan Statute in England: many flee to Holland.
- English Acts against Popish recusants.
  DEATHS
  Christopher Marlowe, English playwright.

1594

- French invade Savoy.
- Henry IV enters Paris.
- Shakespeare's *Comedy of Errors* and *Titus Andronicus*: earliest of his plays.
  DEATHS
  Tintoretto, Italian painter.

1595
- Henry IV declares war on Spain.
- Death of Archduke Ernest, Governor of Netherlands.
- Peace of Teusin between Sweden and Russia.
- Battle of Groenloo: Maurice of Nassau's victory.
- Henry IV absolved by the Pope.
- Peasant insurrection in Upper Austria.
  DEATHS
  Torquato Tasso, Italian poet.

1596
- Archduke Albert made Governor of Netherlands.
- Archduke Albert captures Calais.
- Henry IV takes La Fère.
- Triple Alliance between England, France and United Provinces.
- English expedition to Cadiz: Cadiz captured.
- Muhammad III defeats Archduke Maximilian in a three days' battle.
- Sir Robert Cecil becomes Secretary of State in England.
- Edmund Spenser's *Faerie Queene*.

1597
- Battle of Turnhout: Maurice of Nassau's victory.
- Spaniards take Amiens (soon recovered).
- Polish suzerainty over Moldavia recognized by Sultan.
- Sully becomes Finance Minister of France.
- Serfdom introduced in Russia.
- Richard Hooker's *Ecclesiastical Polity*.

1598
- Edict of Nantes ends French Wars of Religion: Protestant liberties secured in France.
- Netherlands erected by Philip II into a sovereign state under Archduke Albert; Albert marries Philip's daughter Isabel.
- Peace of Vervins between France and Spain.
- Philip III becomes King of Spain.
- Battle of Stangebro: Charles of Sweden defeats Sigismund.
- Death of Theodore I: Boris Godunoff becomes Tsar.

1599
- Earl of Essex becomes Lord Deputy of Ireland: disgraced on his return.
- Sigismund deposed in Sweden: Charles IX becomes King.
- Sweden conquers Finland.
  DEATHS
  Edmund Spenser, English poet.

1600
- Giordano Bruno, Italian philosopher, burned for heresy.
- Esthonia seeks the protection of Charles IX.
- Battle of Nieuport: Maurice of Nassau's desperate victory.
- Charles IX invades Livonia.
- Gowrie Conspiracy in Scotland.
- East India Company founded in England.
- Dr William Gilbert's *De Magnete*, pioneering work on magnetism.

1601
- Valladolid becomes capital of Spain (till 1606).
- Rebellion and execution of Essex.
- Treaty of Lyons between France and Savoy: Savoy keeps Saluzzo, but cedes other territory.

- Siege of Ostend begun by Spinola (surrendered 1604).
- Poland reconquers Livonia.
- English Poor Law Act passed.
- Spanish invasion of Ireland.
  ### Deaths
  Tycho Brahe, Danish astronomer.
  Thomas Nashe, English poet and dramatist.

1602
- Dutch East India Company set up.
- Battle of Kinsale: Spaniards and Irish rebels defeated.
- Execution of Marshal Biron.
- Treaty between France and the Grisons regarding the Valtelline.
- Arminius becomes a professor at Leyden: rivalry with Gomarus.
- Savoy fails to take Geneva.
- Shakespeare's *Hamlet*.

1603
- Death of Elizabeth: James VI of Scotland becomes James I of England; Union of the Crowns.
- Earl of Tyrone submits: Ireland conquered.
- The False Dimitri appears in Poland to claim Tsardom.

1604
- Hampton Court Conference fails to reach agreement between Puritans and Anglican High Churchmen.
- Maurice of Nassau takes Sluys.
- Peace between England, Spain and the Netherlands.
- The False Dimitri invades Russia.

1605
- Paul V becomes Pope.
- The False Dimitri accepted as Tsar on death of Boris.
- Battle of Kirkholm: Poles defeat Charles IX of Sweden.
- Gunpowder Plot to blow up English Parliament discovered.
- Cervantes's *Don Quixote*.

1606
- Treaty of Venice between the Austrian Archdukes: Archduke Matthias becomes head of House of Austria.
- Venice under Papal Interdict.
- The False Dimitri killed: Vasili Shuiski becomes Tsar.
- Peace of Zsitva-Torok between Empire and Turks: Imperial tribute to Turks abolished.
- Grand Remonstrances of Sandomir against Sigismund of Poland: its supporters suppressed.
  ### Deaths
  John Lyly, English novelist and dramatist.

1607
- Battle of Gibraltar: Heemskerk destroys Spanish fleet.
- Earls of Tyrone and Tyrconnel leave Ireland forever with their families.
- London Company colonizes Virginia.
- Swedish power begins to be restored in Esthonia.

1608
- Alliance of Pressburg: Hungarian and Austrian Estates united against Emperor Rudolph.
- Evangelistic Union is formed by German Protestant Princes, headed by Christian of Anhalt.

- Emperor Rudolph cedes Hungarian crown and territorial dominion in Austria and Moravia to Archduke Matthias.
- Quebec founded by French under Champlain.

1609

- Alliance between Charles IX and Tsar against Poland.
- Death of Duke John William of Jülich and Cleves.
- Twelve Years' Truce between Spain and Holland: Spain concedes freedom of Indian trade.
- Rudolph's Letter of Majesty in Bohemia about religious freedom.
- Catholic Union (or League) formed at Munich under Maximilian of Bavaria.
- Edict against the Moriscos in Spain.
- Barbary Corsairs defeated at Tunis by Spain and France.
- Johannes Kepler begins publishing his astronomical laws.
- Galileo invents the telescope about this time.

1610

- James I and VI dissolves his first Parliament: constitutional struggle begins.
- Assassination of Henry IV of France: succeeded by Louis XIII.
- Battle of Klutsjino: Russians defeated by Poles and Tsar overthrown; Wladislav, son of Sigismund of Poland, crowned Tsar.
- Plantation of Ulster with English and Scottish colonists begins.
- Maurice of Nassau takes Jülich.
- Frederick V becomes Elector Palatine.
- Dutch bring tea to Europe (from China) for first time.
  DEATHS
  Michelangelo Caravaggio, Italian painter.

1611

- War of Kalmar between Denmark and Sweden begins.
- Matthias crowned King of Bohemia and Emperor Rudolph resigns Bohemian crown.
- Order of Baronets created.
- Gustavus Adolphus becomes King of Sweden: Oxenstierna, his chief statesman.
- The Authorized Version of the Bible published.

1612

- Death of Emperor Rudolph II: Matthias elected Emperor.
- Evangelical Union of Princes conclude treaty with England.
- Turks recover Moldavia.
- James VI establishes Episcopacy in Scotland.
- English factory founded at Surat in India.

1613

- Peace of Knäred ends the War of Kalmar.
- Michael Romanoff becomes Tsar: beginning of the Romanoff Dynasty in Russia
- Frederick V, Elector Palatine, marries Elizabeth, daughter of James I and VI.

1614

- Last meeting of French States-General till 1789.
- Alliance between Sweden and United Provinces.
- Jülich and Cleves divided between the two claimants by Treaty of Xanten.
- Addled Parliament in England.
- John Napier introduces logarithms.

1615

- Treaty between Empire and Turks.
- Sir Thomas Roe becomes resident English ambassador at court of Great Mughal in India,

- The Spanish Marriages: double alliance of French and Spanish royal families.
- Charles Emmanuel of Savoy defeated in Lombardy by Spanish Viceroy.
- First newspaper appears (in Germany).
- Dutch destroy Spanish fleet in East Indies and gain command of Moluccas.

1616
- Edict of Inquisition against Galileo.
- Fall of Somerset: Buckingham in power.
- Cardinal Richelieu becomes French Foreign and War Minister.
- Dutch bring coffee to Europe (from Arab port of Mocha) for the first time.
  DEATHS
  William Shakespeare, English poet and dramatist.

1617
- Peace of Stolbova between Sweden and Russia: Russia renounces Esthonia and Livonia; Sweden surrenders Novgorod.
- Richelieu out of office: Luynes in power.
- Ferdinand of Styria crowned King of Bohemia.
- Peace of Madrid between Austria and Bohemia.
- Treaty of Pavia between Savoy and Spain relating to Lombardy.
- War between Sweden and Poland.
- Henry Briggs introduces decimal notation.

THE THIRTY YEARS' WAR

1618
- Ferdinand of Styria proclaimed King of Hungary.
- Bohemian Protestants set up a provisional government.
- Failure of Osuna's conspiracy against Venice.
- Fall of Cardinal Klesl.
- Duke of Prussia added to Electorate of Brandenburg.
- The Five Articles of Perth accepted by a pseudo-General Assembly.
- Sir Walter Raleigh executed.
- Synod of Dort: the Arminian Remonstrants crushed in the United Provinces.

1619
- Death of the Emperor Matthias: Ferdinand II elected.
- Batavia founded as capital of Dutch East Indies.
- Execution of Oldenbarnveldt, the Dutch statesman.
- George William becomes Elector of Brandenburg.
- Emperor Ferdinand declared deposed from Bohemian throne and Elector Palatine Frederick V elected King of Bohemia.
- Bethlen Gabor of Transylvania, in alliance with Bohemians, occupies most of Upper Hungary.
- Agreement between Emperor Ferdinand and Maximilian of Bavaria.
- Slavery introduced in Virginia.
  DEATHS
  Nicholas Hilliard, English painter.

1620
- Frederick V ordered to quit the Emperor's dominions.
- Massacre of Protestants in the Valtelline.
- Tilly, the General of the Catholic League, enters Upper Austria.
- Spinola invades the Palatinate.
- Battle of the White Hill: Tilly defeats Christian of Anhalt and Thurn; Prague is taken.

- Battle of Cécora: Poles heavily defeated by Turks when attempting to recover Moldavia.
- Huguenots formulate their demands at La Rochelle: war follows.
- The Pilgrim Fathers set sail for New England.
- Francis Bacon's *Novum Organum.*

1621

- Philip IV becomes King of Spain, with Olivarez as chief minister.
- Treaty of Madrid between Spain and France: the Valtelline restored to Grisons.
- Evangelical Union of Princes dissolved.
- Riga taken by the Swedes.
- End of Twelve Years' Truce between Spain and United Provinces.
- English Parliament attacks monopolies; dissolved after Protestation of Rights.
- Five Articles of Perth passed by Scottish Parliament.
- Fall of Francis Bacon.
- Dutch West India Company founded.

1622

- Articles of Milan: Grisons renounce the Valtelline.
- Battle of Wimpfen: Tilly victorious.
- Battle of Höchst: Tilly defeats Christian of Halberstadt.
- Battle of Fleurus: victory of Mansfeld and Christian of Halberstadt.
- Treaty of Lindau: Austrian supremacy in the Valtelline strengthened.
- First English newspaper appears.
- Treaty of Montpellier between Louis XIII and Huguenots.

1623

- Ratisbon Conference: Maximilian gets Frederick's electoral dignity.
- Treaty of Paris: France, Venice and Savoy unite to restore the Valtelline.
- Prince Charles and Buckingham in Madrid.
- Expulsion of Protestant clergy from Bohemia.
- Battle of Stadtlohn: Tilly defeats Christian of Halberstadt.
- Dutch conquer Formosa.
  DEATHS
  William Byrd, English composer.

1624

- Monopoly Act in England: patents protected.
- Dutch take Bahia in Brazil from Portugal (soon recovered); Dutch settle New Amsterdam (later New York).
- Richelieu becomes Chief Minister of France.
- Massacre of Amboina.
- Protestants deprived of all rights in Bohemia.
- French occupy the Valtelline.

1625

- Huguenots seize Blavet and the royal ships.
- Charles I, King of England, Scotland and Ireland.
- Frederick Henry, Prince of Orange.
- Wallenstein becomes Imperialist Commander-in-Chief: enters Lower Saxony.
- English Parliament gives Charles I tonnage and poundage for one year only.
- Spinola takes Breda.
- Montmorency seizes islands of Ré and Oléron.
- Treaty of Southampton between England and the United Provinces.
- Swedes overrun Livonia.
- Failure of English expedition to Cadiz.
- Triple Alliance between England, Denmark and Holland.

- French colony of Cayenne founded; French also colonize St Kitts.

1626
- Battle of Wallhof: victory of Gustavus Adolphus, King of Sweden, over the Poles.
- English Treaty with Huguenots.
- Battle of Dessau Bridge: Wallenstein defeats Mansfeld.
- Treaty of Monzon between France and Spain regarding the Valtelline.
- Impeachment of Duke of Buckingham.
- Swedish invasion of Prussia.
- Tilly takes Göttingen.
- Battle of Lutter: Tilly defeats Christian IV of Denmark.
- Forced loan in England; Sir John Eliot and others imprisoned.
- Peace of Pressburg between Wallenstein and Bethlen Gabor.
- English settlement of Barbados.
  DEATHS
  Francis Bacon, English philosopher and statesman.

1627
- War between England and France.
- Treaty of Alliance between France and Spain.
- Duke of Buckingham's expedition to La Rochelle in aid of Huguenots.
- Wallenstein occupies Schleswig and Jutland.
- Disputed succession in Mantua.

1628
- Treaty between Sweden and Denmark.
- Unsuccessful siege of Stralsund by Imperialist troops under Arnim.
- Petition of Right passed by Parliament and receives Royal Assent.
- Murder of Duke of Buckingham.
- Hein, Dutch naval leader, captures Spanish treasure fleet.
- Capitulation of La Rochelle: final failure of the Huguenot cause.
- William Harvey's *On the Circulation of the Blood*.

1629
- Charles I dissolves Third Parliament; begins eleven years of personal rule.
- French invasion of Italy in support of Duke of Nevers's claim to Mantua.
- Edict of Restitution in Germany.
- Peace between England and France.
- Peace of Lübeck between Wallenstein and Denmark.
- Frederick Henry of Orange reduces Bois-le-Duc.
- Six-year truce between Sweden and Poland: Sweden gains Livonia and other territories.
- Spinola at war in Lombardy.
  DEATHS
  Cardinal Pierre de Berulle, French theologian.

1630
- Dutch take Pernambuco.
- French invasion of Savoy: death of Charles Emmanuel.
- Gustavus Adolphus lands in Germany: conquers Pomerania.
- Mantua and Casale captured by Spain.
- Dismissal of Wallenstein.
- Treaty of Madrid between England and Spain.

1631
- Treaty of Bärwalde between France and Sweden.
- Protestant Convention at Leipzig.
- Gustavus Adolphus takes Frankfort-on-the-Oder.

- Spain's ignominious peace with France.
- Fall of Magdeburg to Imperialists.
- Battle of the Slaak: Dutch destroy Spanish fleet.
- Alliance between Gustavus Adolphus and John George of Saxony.
- Battle of Breitenfield: Tilly defeated by Gustavus Adolphus.
- Gustavus Adolphus conquers Franconia and takes Mainz.
- Saxons invade Lusatia and occupy Prague.
- Treaties of Cherasco: settlement of Mantuan succession.
  DEATHS
  John Donne, English poet.

1632
- Mannheim taken by Bernard of Weimar (in Swedish service).
- Gustavus takes Nürnberg.
- Battle of the Lech: Gustavus defeats Tilly, who is mortally wounded.
- Gustavus takes Augsburg and Munich.
- Wallenstein resumes command and recaptures Prague.
- Frederick Henry of Orange reduces Maestricht.
- Battle of Lützen: Gustavus victorious but killed: Pappenheim mortally wounded.
- Christina, daughter of Gustavus, becomes Queen of Sweden.
  DEATHS
  George Herbert, English poet.

1633
- Alliance of Heilbronn: Palatinate restored to heir of Frederick V.
- Sir Thomas Wentworth (Earl of Strafford) becomes Lord Deputy of Ireland.
- French occupy Lorraine.
- Bernard of Weimar takes Ratisbon.
- Wallenstein invades Brandenburg and then Bavaria.
- Southern Netherlands reverts to Spain on death of Isobel.
  DEATHS
  Philaret, Russian monk-statesman.

1634
- Wallenstein deposed (murdered soon after).
- King Ferdinand of Hungary recaptures Ratisbon.
- Battle of Nördlingen: Imperialist victory; Heilbronn Alliance broken up.
- Ship-money begins to be demanded by Charles I.
- Treaty of Paris between France and Sweden: Oxenstierna, Swedish Chancellor, against it.
- French Academy founded.
- William Prynne, English Puritan pamphleteer, condemned for his *Histriomastix*.

1635
- Alliance between France and the United Provinces.
- Treaty of Compiègne between France and Sweden.
- War declared by France against Spain.
- Treaty of Prague between the Emperor and Saxony widely accepted: Sweden and France isolated.
- Battle of Livigno: Duke of Rohan's victory over the Austrian and Spanish forces in the Valtelline.
- Battle of Mazzo: Rohan's victory in the Valtelline.
- Compact at Stuhmsdorf between Sweden and Poland.
- Saxony declares war on Sweden.
- Compact between France and Bernard of Weimar.

- Imperialists take Mainz.
- Battle of Goldberg: Banér and Torstensson keep the Saxons out of Mecklenburg.
- Pierre Corneille's *Medea*.
  DEATHS
  Lope de Vega, Spanish dramatist.

1636
- Brandenburg declares war on Sweden.
- Treaty of Wismar between France and Sweden.
- Battle of Wittstock: Banér's victory over Saxons and Imperialists.
- Pierre Corneille's *Le Cid*.

1637
- Death of Ferdinand II; Ferdinand III elected Emperor.
- Rising of Grisons against France.
- William Laud's *Liturgy* published in Scotland: popular indignation.
- Frederick Henry of Orange recaptures Breda.
- Dutch conquests from Portuguese in West Africa.
- Descartes's *Discours de la Méthode*.
  DEATHS
  Ben Jonson, English dramatist.

1638
- War declared by France against Austria.
- Battles of Rheinfelden (two): victories of Bernard of Weimar.
- Battle of Wittenweier: Bernard's victory.
- The National Covenant signed in Scotland.
- The Glasgow Assembly meets.
- Bernard of Weimar takes Breisach.

1639
- First Bishop's War: ended by Pacification of Berwick.
- 'Perpetual Peace' of Milan between Austria and the Grisons.
- Maarten Tromp destroys a Spanish armada in the Battle of the Downs.

1640
- The Short Parliament in England (April–May).
- Catalonia revolt against Spain.
- Second Bishops' War begins: ended by Treaty of Ripon; a parliament is called.
- Long Parliament meets (November).
- Braganza proclaimed King of Portugal as John IV; Portugal re-establishes its independence from Spain.
- Impeachment of Archbishop William Laud.
- Frederick William, the 'Great Elector', becomes ruler of Brandenburg.
- Van Diemen conquers Malacca.
  DEATHS
  John Ford, English dramatist.
  Peter Paul Reubens, Flemish painter.

1641
- Spanish royal forces repelled from Barcelona.
- Execution of Strafford.
- Truce of Stockholm between Brandenburg and Sweden.
- Charles I sets out for Scotland.
- Rebellion in Ulster.
- Grand Remonstrance voted and published by English Parliament.

1642
- Attempt to seize the Five Members of the Commons.

- Parliament seizes Hull: English Civil War begins.
- Conspiracy of Cinq-Mars against Richlieu discovered: Cinq-Mars executed; Richelieu dies shortly afterwards.
- Charles I raises his standard at Nottingham.
- Portsmouth surrenders to Parliament.
- Battle of Edgehill: drawn.
- General Assembly of Confederated Catholics in Kilkenny.
- Battle of Breitenfield: Torstensson defeats the Imperialists.
- Abel Tasman's voyage begins.
- Richard Lovelace's *To Althea, from Prison*.

1643
- Fall of Olivarez.
- English Parliament abolishes Episcopacy.
- Battle of Ross: Irish rebels defeated by Ormond.
- Louis XIV becomes King of France.
- Battle of Rocroi: D'Enghien's victory.
- John Hampden killed at Chalgrove.
- Battle of Adwalton Moor: Parliamentary forces under the Fairfaxes defeated.
- Westminster Assembly begins its sessions.
- Battle of Roundway Down: Waller's Parliamentary army destroyed.
- Royalists under Prince Rupert storm Bristol.
- French take Thionville.
- Severe defeat of Spanish fleet by French off Carthagena.
- Solemn League and Covenant: agreement between English Parliament and the Scots.
- Battle of Newbury: drawn; Falkland killed.
- Battle of Winceby: victory of Sir Thomas Fairfax and Oliver Cromwell.
- Torstensson, Swedish general, invades Denmark.
  DEATHS
  John Pym, Parliamentary leader.

1644
- Scots enter England under Alexander Leslie, Earl of Leven.
- Battle of Copredy Bridge; defeat of Waller.
- Battle of Kolberg Heath; defeat of Christian IV of Denmark in naval battle.
- Battle of Marston Moor: Parliamentary victory due to Cromwell, aided by Scots.
- Parliament captures York.
- French take Gravelines.
- Battle of Tippermuir: Montrose victorious.
- Battle of Freiburg: D'Enghien and Turenne defeat Imperialist General Mercy.
- Capitulation of Parliamentary army under Essex at Lostwithiel.
- Battle of Newbury (second): Parliamentary success.
- Turenne takes Mainz.
- Manchu Dynasty established in China.

1645
- Execution of Archbishop Laud.
- Battle of Inverlochy: Montrose's victory.
- Uxbridge negotiations between Charles I and Parliament.
- New Model Army organized under Sir Thomas Fairfax.
- Battle of Jankau: Torstensson's victory.
- Battle of Auldearn: Montrose's victory.
- Battle of Herbsthausen: Mercy defeats Turenne.
- Royalists sack Leicester.
- Battle of Naseby: victory of Fairfax and Cromwell over Charles I and Rupert.

- Battle of Allerheim: D'Enghein and Turenne defeat Mercy (latter killed).
- Battle of Alford: Montrose's victory.
- Battle of Kilsyth: Montrose's victory.
- Peace of Brömsebro between Sweden and Denmark and United Provinces.
- Fairfax takes Bristol.
- Swedish General Wrangel takes Bornholm.
- Battle of Philiphaugh: Montrose defeated by David Leslie.
- French conquests in Catalonia.

1646
- Fairfax takes Exeter and Oxford.
- Charles I surrenders to the Scottish army.
- D'Enghiem (Condé) takes Dunkirk.

1647
- Charles I handed over to English Parliament.
- William II succeeds Frederick Henry of Orange in United Provinces.
- Cornet Joyce abducts Charles I.
- Masaniello heads revolt in Naples against Spain.
- Quakers founded by George Fox.
- 'Heads of the Proposals' prepared by Henry Ireton.
- Army marches on London.
- 'The Agreement of the People' prepared by the Levellers.
- Charles I escapes to Carisbrooke Castle.
- 'The Engagement' between Charles I and the Scots.

1648
- Commons passes 'Vote of No Addresses'.
- Naples revolt suppressed by Don Juan of Austria.
- Frederick III, King of Denmark.
- Battle of Zusmarshausen: Wrangel and Turenne defeat the Imperialists.
- Second Civil War begins in England.
- Assembly of the Hall of St Louis to discuss French situation.
- Battle of Preston: Cromwell defeats the Scots under Hamilton.
- Battle of Lens: Condé defeats the Spaniards.
- Rising in Paris.
- Fairfax takes Colchester.
- Peace of Westphalia ends Thirty Years' War; Treaty of Münster ends Eighty Years' War or Dutch Revolt.
- Declaration of Saint-Germain: demands of the Fronde granted.
- Failure of Newport negotiations between Parliament and Charles I.
- Charles I declines terms offered by the army.
- Pride's purge of Parliament.

THE AGE OF CROMWELL

1649
- First War of the Fronde in France (quickly ended by Treaty of Rueil).
- Execution of Charles I.
- Charles II proclaimed King of Scotland.
- English Parliament abolishes the House of Lords and the Monarchy.
- Cromwell storms Drogheda and captures Wexford.
- Sorbonne condemns Jansenism.

1650
- Arrest of Condé and other princes in France.
- Montrose captured by Davis Leslie and executed.

- Agreement of Breda between Charles II and the Scots.
- Cromwell leaves Ireland, leaving Ireton in command.
- Battle of Dunbar: Cromwell defeats the Scots under Leslie.

1651
- Charles II crowned at Scone.
- Parliament of Paris votes the release of Condé and the Princes and demands dismissal of Mazarin; Princes released; Mazarin flees.
- Condé in revolt.
- Battle of Worcester: Cromwell defeats Charles II.
- Navigation Act passed by English Parliament.
- William III succeeds William II in United Provinces.

1652
- General Monck subdues Scotland.
- First War between England and Holland begins.
- Battle of Saint-Antoinne: Turenne against Condé.
- Provisional Fronde government in Paris: soon overthrown.
- Act for Settling of Ireland.
- English Admiral Robert Blake defeats De Ruyter in naval battle off coast of Kent.
- Capitulation of Barcelona.
- Maarten Tromp defeats Blake off Dungeness.
- Dutch settlement at Cape of Good Hope.
- France surrenders Dunkirk and Gravelines.
- Nukon, an ecclesiastical reformer, becomes Patriarch of Moscow.
  DEATHS
  Inigo Jones, English architect.

1653
- Mazarin returns to Paris.
- Maarten Tromp defeated by Blake off Portland.
- Rupert's Royalist fleet destroyed.
- Rump Parliament dissolved by Cromwell.
- Monck and Blake defeat Dutch off the Gabbard.
- Barebones Parliament meets.
- Monck defeats Dutch off the Texel: Maarten Tromp killed.
- John De Witt, Grand Pensionary of Holland: the Orange family excluded.
- Cromwell accepts the Instrument of Government and becomes Protector.

1654
- Peace between England and Holland.
- Abdication of Christina of Sweden: Charles X, King.
- Dutch lose Brazil to the Portuguese.

1655
- Jamaica taken from Spaniards by Penn and Venables.
- Sweden declares war on Poland.
- Charles X takes Warsaw and Cracow.
- Treaty of Westminster between France and England.

1656
- Treaty of Königsberg between Charles X and Frederick William of Brandenburg; also Treaty of Marienburg later and that of Labiau still later in same year.
- Warsaw recovered by Poles.
- Battle of Valenciennes: Turenne defeated by Condé and Don Juan.
- Battle of Warsaw: Poles defeated by Swedes and Brandenburgers; Warsaw recaptured.
- Blake captures the Plate fleet.
- Muhammad Kiuprili becomes Vizier of Turkey.

1657
- Cromwell accepts the Humble Petition and Advice and assumes the title of Lord Protector after refusing that of King.
- Brief Anglo-Scottish parliamentary union: annulled after the restoration of Charles II to the throne in 1660.
- Treaty of Paris between England and France.
- Death of Emperor Ferdinand III: Leopold I elected next year.
- Blake destroys Spanish fleet at Tenerife.
- Alliance between Austria and Poland.
- Denmark declares war against Sweden.
- Charles X invades Holstein.
- Treaty of Wehlau: Brandenburg joins Austria and Poland.

1658
- Swedes conquer most of Denmark.
- Peace of Roeskilde between Sweden and Denmark.
- Battle of the Dunes: Turenne defeats Condé and Don Juan and captures Dunkirk and Gravelines.
- League of the Rhine formed, including France.
- Second Danish War of Charles X.
- Death of Cromwell: Richard Cromwell, Protector.
- Copenhagen relieved by the Dutch.
- Muhammad Kiuprili conquers Transylvania.
- Aurangzeb becomes Mughal Emperor in India.

1659
- Battle of Elvas: Portuguese defeat the Spaniards.
- Rump Parliament reassembled.
- Concert of the Hague: Holland, France and England against Sweden.
- Abdication of Richard Cromwell.
- Peace of the Pyrenees between France and Spain.
- Dutch take Nyborg and capture a Swedish force.
- English Parliament resumed.

1660
- Long Parliament dissolved and a new parliament called.
- Restoration of Charles II.
- Death of Charles X of Sweden.
- Peace of Oliva ends Swedo-Danish wars.
    - *DEATHS*
    - Velásquez, Spanish artist.

THE AGE OF LOUIS XIV

1661
- Death of Mazarin: Louis XIV assumes role of own minister.
- Savoy Conference fails to make agreement between Puritans and other churchmen.
- Treaty between England and Portugal: England obtains Tangier and Bombay as a marriage dowry.
- Peace between Holland and Portugal.
- Episcopacy established in Scotland by decree.
- Peace of Kardis between Sweden and Russia.
- Corporation Act: first of a series of statutes against Puritans.

1662
- Alliance between France and Holland.
- Press Act in England.

- Act of Uniformity in England: leads to ejection of many clergy; beginning of English Nonconformity.
- Patronage restored by Scottish Parliament.
- Royal Society incorporated.
- Treaty between England and Holland.
- Act for the Settlement of Ireland.
- Dunkirk sold to France.
  DEATHS
  Blaise Pascal, French philosopher and scientist.

1663
- Battle of Amegial: Spaniards under Don Juan defeat the Portuguese and their English allies.
- Turks begins war against Austria.

1664
- French East India Company founded.
- Battle of St Gothard: Turks under Ahmed Kiuprili defeated by Imperialists under Montecuculi.
- Jean Baptiste Colbert becomes chief minister under Louis XIV.
- Treaty of Vasvar between Turks and the Empire.
- First Conventicle Act in England.
- English expedition seizes New Netherland on east coast of North America and New Amsterdam becomes New York.

1665
- Battle of Lowestoft: English naval victory over Dutch.
- Battle of Montes Claros: Portuguese defeat Spaniards.
- Great Plague in London.
- Charles II becomes King of Spain.
- Five Mile Act.
  DEATHS
  Nicolas Poussin, French painter.

1666
- Louis XIV declares war against England.
- Monck and Rupert defeated by De Ruyter in Four Days' Naval Battle.
- Dutch fleet defeated by Monck and Rupert.
- Great Fire of London.
- Quadruple Alliance: Holland, Brandenburg, Denmark and Brunswick-Lüneburg.
- Battle of Rullion Green: Scottish Covenanters defeated.

1667
- Act of English Parliament against Irish cattle trade.
- Dutch conquer Surinam and Tobago.
- Secret Treaty between Charles II and Louis XIV.
- War of Devolution in regard to Spanish Netherlands.
- Dutch fleet in the Thames.
- Peace of Breda between England and Holland.
- Lille taken by French.
- Fall of Clarendon in England: the Cabal ministry takes over.

1668
- Spain recognizes independence of Portugal.
- France conquers Franche-Comté.
- Triple Alliance: England, Holland and Sweden.
- Peace of Aix-la-Chapelle between France and Spain.
- Abdication of John Casimir of Poland.

1669

- Michael Korybut Wisniowiecki becomes King of Poland.
- Turks conquer Crete.
- Ormond recalled from Ireland: restored in 1667.
- Secret Treaty between Louis XIV and the Elector of Brandenburg.
  DEATHS
  Rembrandt, Dutch painter.

1670

- Christian V becomes King of Denmark.
- Treaty between Holland and Brandenburg.
- Second Conventicle Act.
- Secret Treaty of Dover between Charles II and Louis XIV.

1671

- Leaders of a Hungarian Conspiracy executed.

1672

- Stop of the Exchequer in England.
- First Declaration of Indulgence issued.
- England declares war against Holland.
- Treaty between Sweden and France; also one between Sweden and England.
- War between France and Holland.
- Battle of Southwold Bay: De Ruyter defeats an Anglo-French fleet under the Duke of York.
- Alliance between the Emperor and Brandenburg.
- John de Witt resigns post of Grand Pensionary of Holland.
- Murder of John and Cornelius de Witt.
- Alliance between Emperor and Holland.

1673

- Test Act passed, barring Roman Catholics from holding public office.
- Charles II cancels Declaration of Indulgence.
- Battles of Schooneveld: De Ruyter against Rupert; both drawn.
- Battle of Kykduin: De Ruyter defeats Anglo-French fleet.
- Death of King Michael of Poland.
- Battle of Khoczim: John Sobieski defeats Turks.
- William of Orange takes Bonn: French have to evacuate Netherlands.
  DEATHS
  Molière, French playwright.

1674

- Peace between England and Holland.
- John Sobieski elected King of Poland.
- Franche-Comté conquered by France.
- Battle of Sinsheim: Turennne defeats the Imperialists and devastates the Palatinate.
- Battle of Seneff: indecisive conflict between William of Orange and Condé.
- Battle of Enzheim: Turenne's victory.
- Sweden at war with Brandenburg.
- Pondicherry founded by French in India.
- Sivaji crowns himself an independent Mahratta sovereign in India: wars with Aurangzeb.
  DEATHS
  John Milton, English poet.

1675

- Battle of Calmar: Turenne defeats the Great Elector and conquers Alsace.
- Battle of Fehrbellin: Great Elector's decisive victory over Sweden.

- Turenne killed.
- Shaftesbury organizes an opposition in English Parliament: beginning of Whig Party.
- Letters of Intercommuning in Scotland against Covenanters.
- Battle of Lemberg: Sobieski defeats the Turks.
- War of Scania begins between Sweden and Denmark.

1676
- Battle of Öland: Swedish naval disaster.
- Danes conquer Scania.
- Treaty of Zurawna between Turkey and Poland.
- Kara Mustafa succeeds Ahmed Kiuprili as Vizier of Turkey.
- Theodore II, Tsar of Russia.
- French found Chandernagore in India.

1677
- Battle of Landskrona: Charles XI victorious over Danes.
- Marriage of William of Orange and Mary, daughter of James, Duke of York.
- Turkey at war with Russia.
- Stettin capitulates to the Great Elector.
  DEATHS
  Benedict Spinoza, Dutch philosopher.

1678
- Treaty between England and Holland.
- Peace between France and Holland.
- Titus Oates and the Popish Plot against King Charles II.
- Murder of Sir Edmund Berry Godfrey.
- Swedes expelled from Germany.

1679
- Archbishop Sharp murdered by Scottish Covenanters.
- Exclusion Bill introduced by English Parliament.
- Battle of Drumclog: Scottish Covenanters defeat Graham of Claverhouse.
- Battle of Bothwell Bridge: Covenanters defeated by Duke of Monmouth.
- Treaty of St Germain between Brandenburg and Sweden.
- Treaty of Fontainebleau between Denmark and Sweden.
- Peace of Nimeguen: treaties between France, Spain, Holland and Empire.
- The Great Elector makes an alliance with France.

1680
- Petitioners and Abhorrers for and against Exclusion Bill: beginnings of English political party system.
- House of Lords reject Exclusion Bill.
- Sanquhar Declaration: Charles II disowned by strong Covenanters.
- Battle of Aird's Moss, Ayrshire, Scotland: Covenanter, Richard Cameron, killed.

1681
- French occupy Strassburg.
- Donald Cargill executed in Scotland.
  DEATHS
  Pedro Calderon de la Barca, Spanish dramatist.

1682
- Revolt of Hungary.
- Death of Theodore II: Tsarevna Sophia becomes Regent for Ivan and Peter.

1683
- City of London Charter forfeited.
- Rye House Plot against King Charles II discovered.
- Siege of Vienna by Turks under Kara Mustafa: relieved by John Sobieski.

- Battle of Parkány (7 Oct): Turks defeat Poles.
- Battle of Parkány (9 Oct): Turks defeated by Austrians and Poles; Gran captured.
- Kara Mustafa executed.
- Execution of English plotters, Algernon Sidney and Russell.

1684

- Holy League against Turks between Austria, Poland and Venice.
- French take Luxemburg.
- Truce of Ratisbon between Louis XIV and Emperor Leopold.

1685

- Accession of James VII of Scotland and II of England.
- Alliance between Great Elector and Holland.
- Duke of Monmouth proclaims himself King.
- Battle of Sedgemoor: defeat of Monmouth.
- Judge Jeffreys and the Bloody Assizes in England.
- Execution of Monmouth.
- Execution of Earl of Argyle.
- Venetians under Francesco Morosini begin conquest of Morea.
- Battle of Gran: Charles of Lorraine defeats the Turks.
- Buda captured from the Turks.
- Revocation of Edict of Nantes in France: great emigration of the Huguenots.

1686

- Tyrconnel, Commander-in-Chief in Ireland.
- Second Treaty between Frederick William and the Emperor.
- Augsburg Alliance to maintain Treaties of Westphalia and Nimeguen.
- Frances annexes Madagascar.

1687

- Tyrconnel, Viceroy of Ireland.
- Second Declaration of Indulgence.
- Venetians capture Corinth
- Battle of Mohács: Imperial victory by Charles of Lorraine and Lewis of Baden over Turks.
- Venetians take Athens.
- Muhammad IV supplanted by Suleiman II.

1688

- Frederick III, Elector of Brandenburg.
- Acquital of Seven Bishops for opposing James II's policy of religious toleration.
- Invitation to William of Orange.
- Belgrade taken by the Elector of Bavaria.
- William of Orange lands in England; flight of James II to France; the 'Glorious Revolution'.
  DEATHS
  John Bunyan, English author.

1689

- House of Commons declare the English throne vacant: William and Mary declared joint sovereigns.
- The Palatinate devastated by forces of Louis XIV.
- Ex-King James II lands in Ireland.
- Louis XIV declares war against Spain.
- Scottish Parliament declare that James II has forfeited the Scottish crown: William and Mary chosen.
- Siege of Derry: ultimately relieved.
- Toleration Act in England.

- Battle of Killiecrankie: Claverhouse, Viscount Dundee, killed in hour of victory.
- Battle of Newtown Butler: James II's army defeated.
- Bill of Rights in England.
- Sophia's rule overthrown in Russia.

THE SPANISH SUCCESSION

1690
- Battle of the Boyne: James defeated and flees to France; Schomberg killed.
- Battle of Fleurus: French victory by Luxembourg over Dutch and allies.
- Battle of Beachy Head: French naval victory by Tourville over England and Holland.
- First Siege of Limerick.
- Belgrade recaptured by the Turks.
- Scottish Parliament abolishes the Lords of the Articles and Lay Patronage, re-establishes Presbyterianism: Scottish Parliament becomes a real power in Scotland.

1691
- French take Mons.
- Athlone taken by Ginkel.
- Battle of Aughrim: Ginkel defeats St Ruth (who is killed).
- Galway surrenders to William's forces.
- Second Siege of Limerick: capitulated.
- Battle of Szalankemen: Turks defeated by Lewis of Baden.

1692
- Massacre of Glencoe.
- Battle of La Hogue: Russell's naval victory over French.
- Louis XIV takes Namur.
- Battle of Steinkirke:Luxembourg defeats William of Orange.

1693
- Battle of Neerwinden: Luxembourg defeats William of Orange.
- Battle of Marsaglia: Duke of Savoy defeated by Catinat.
- Dutch take Pondicherry.
- National Debt created in England by Charles Montagu.

1694
- Bank of England founded by William Paterson.
- Triennal Act in England.
  DEATHS
  Queen Mary (England).

1695
- William III takes Namur.
- Freedom of the press established in England.
- Fénelon becomes Bishop of Cambrai.
- Darien Scheme proposed by Paterson.
- Anti-Catholic legislation in Ireland.
- Mustafa II, Sultan.

1696
- Recoinage Act.
- Assassination Plot against William III discovered.
- Russia takes Azoff.
- Death of Ivan V: Peter the Great rules alone.
- Duke of Savoy joins France.

1697
- Charles XII, King of Sweden.
- Irish Parliament refuses full ratification of the Articles of Limerick.

- Elector of Saxony elected King of Poland as Augustus II.
- Battle of Zenta: Turks defeated by Prince Eugene.
- Peace of Ryswick between France, England, Holland, Spain and the Empire.
  DEATHS
  John Aubrey, English author.

1698

- Revolt of the Strieltzy in Russia suppressed.
- First Treaty of Partition (of Spanish dominions) between Louis XIV and William III.
- New East India Company founded in England.

1699

- Treaty of Carlowitz between Austria, Venice, Poland and Turkey: Austria gains Hungary, Poland Podolia, Venice Dalmatia and Morea.
- Death of Joseph Ferdinand of Bavaria: Spanish Succession reopened.
- Second Partition Treaty.
- English legislation against Irish woollen industry.
- Frederick IV, King of Denmark.
- Convention between Denmark and Russia.
- Alliance of Denmark and Poland against Sweden.
- Russia signs treaty with Poland for partition of Sweden.
  DEATHS
  Jean Racine, French dramatist.

1700

- Act of Resumption in Ireland.
- Thirty Years' Truce between Russia and Turkey.
- Great Northern war begins: Russia and Poland against Sweden.
- Peace of Traventhal between Denmark and Sweden.
- Last will of Charles II of Spain makes Duke Philip of Anjou his heir.
- Death of Charles II of Spain: Louis XIV accepts the dead king's will; War of Spanish Succession begins.
- Battle of Narva: Charles XII defeats Russians.
  DEATHS
  John Dryden, English poet.

1701

- Brandenburg erected into the kingdom of Prussia: Frederick III, first King as Frederick I.
- Prince Eugene invades Italy.
- Battle of Dünamunde: Charles XII defeats Russians and Saxons; Courland occupied.
- Battle of Chiari: Eugene defeats Villeroi.
- Grand Alliance concluded between England, Holland and the Holy Roman Emperor.
- Act of Settlement in England.

1702

- Battle of Errestièr: Swedes defeated by Russians.
- Eugene raids Cremona and captures Villeroi.
- King William III dies in a riding accident; Anne becomes Queen of Britain.
- Charles XII at Warsaw.
- The Troops of the Grand Alliance take Kaiserswerth.
- Battle of Hummelshof: Swedes defeated by Russians.
- Battle of Klissow: Charles XII defeats the Poles and Saxons: Cracow is captured.
- Failure of English attack on Cadiz.
- English admiral, Sir George Rooke, destroys Plate fleet in Vigo.
- Battle of Friedlingen: Lewis of Baden defeated by Villers.

- English general, Marlborough, takes Liège.
- Camisard Rebellion (Huguenot) in central France.

1703
- Battle of Scharding: Austrians defeated by Bavarians.
- Battle of Pultusk: Charles XII defeats Saxons.
- Methuan Treaty between England and Portugal; later in same year, another Methuan Treaty (commercial).
- Marlborough takes Bonn.
- Battle of Höchstädt: Villars defeats Germans.
- Savoy joins Grand Alliance.
- Battle of Speyerbach: Grand Alliance army defeated by Tallard.
- St Petersburg founded by Peter the Great.
- Act of Security in Scotland.
  DEATHS
  Samuel Pepys, English diarist.

1704
- Alien Act in England.
- Marlborough's victory at Donauwörth.
- Stanislaus Leszczynski made King of Poland by Charles XII.
- Russians take Dorpat and Narva.
- Rooke captures Gibralter.
- Battle of Blenheim: Marlborough and Eugene defeat Tallard and the Elector of Bavaria.
- Battle of Malaga: drawn naval battle between Rooke and Toulouse.
- Warsaw recaptured from Charles XII.
- Marlborough occupies Trier.

1705
- Death of Leopold I: Joseph I elected Emperor.
- Battle of Gemaurhof: Swedes defeat Russian attempt on Coutland.

1706
- Battle of Fraustadt: Swedish victory.
- Grand Alliance forces take Madrid (soon evacuated).
- Battle of Ramillies: Marlborough crushes Villeroi.
- Marlborough takes Ostend.
- Battle of Turin: Eugene defeats the investing army: French evacuate Piedmont.
- Peace of Altranstädt between Saxony and Sweden: Stanislaus recognized as King.
- Execution of Patkul.
- Battle of Kalisch: Swedes defeated by Russians and Saxons.
  DEATHS
  Pierre Bayle, French philosopher.

1707
- Convention of Milan: France abandons North Italy.
- Battle of Almanza: British defeated in Spain by Berwick.
- Treaty of Union between Scotland and England.
- Eugene abandons attempt on Toulon.
- Perpetual Alliance between Prussia and Sweden.
- Death of Aurangzeb: Mughal Empire in decline.

1708
- Whig Ministry in England.
- Battle of Holowczyn: Charles XII defeats Russians.
- Battle of Oudenarde: Marlborough defeats Vendôme.
- Battle of Lyesna: Swedes under Levenhaupt defeated by Russians.

- Leake and Stanhope take Minorca and Sardinia.
- Cossack leader, Mazepa, joins Charles XII.
- Lille taken by the Allies.
- Union of the two British East India Companies.

1709
- Battle of Pultawa: Charles XII defeated by Peter the Great and flees to Turkey.
- Alliance between Denmark and Augustus of Poland and Saxony.
- Battle of Malplaquet: victory of Marlborough and Eugene.
- Allies take Mons.
- New League against Sweden is formed between Augustus and Peter the Great.
- First Barrier Treaty between Britain and Holland.
- Danish invasion of Scania.

1710
- Battle of Helsingborg: Danes are defeated and driven out of Sweden.
- Russians take Viborg, Riga, Pernau and Reval.
- Battle of Almenara: defeat of Spaniards by Starhemberg.
- Impeachment by English Parliament of Dr Henry Sacheverell for a sermon against religious toleration.
- Battle of Saragossa: Spaniards defeated by Starhemberg.
- Madrid again occupied by Allies.

1711
- War between Russia and Turkey.
- Death of Emperor Joseph: Charles VI elected Emperor.
- Peace of the Pruth between Russia and Turkey.
- Marlborough dismissed.

1712
- Peers created in British Parliament to pass peace clauses.
- Battle of Denain: Dutch defeated by Villars.
- Lay Patronage restored in Scottish Church against Scottish opinion.
- Battle of Gadesbusch: Swedish victory over Danes.

1713
- Second Barrier Treaty between Britain and Holland.
- Charles XII's defence against Turks at Bender.
- Death of Frederick I of Prussia: Frederick William I succeeds.
- Treaty of Utrecht ends War of Spanish Succession: Acadia, Newfound land and other territories, ceded by France to Britain; Victor Amadeus of Savoy becomes King of Sicily.
- Pragmatic Sanction of Charles VI to settle Austrian Succession.
- Swedish forces capitulate at Oldenburg.
- Peace of Adrianople between Russia and Turkey.
- Papal Bull Unigenitus condemns Jansenism.

THE AUSTRIAN SUCCESSION

1714
- Treaty of Rastadt (Rastatt) between Austria and France (later confirmed by the Treaty of Baden) ends hostilities in the War of Spanish Succession.
- Accession of George I in Britain: beginning of Hanoverian Dynasty.
- Peter the Great conquers Finland.

1715
- Louis XV becomes King of France.
- Jacobite rebellion in Scotland and northern England.
- Battle of Preston: Jacobites defeated and their army surrenders.

- Battle of Sheriffmuir between Jacobites and Royalists: indecisive
- Denmark cedes Bremen and Verden to Hanover.
- Third Dutch Barrier Treaty.
- Commercial treaty between Britain and Spain.

1716
- Commercial treaty between Britain and Holland.
- Prussia captures all Swedish Pomerania.
- Battle of Peterwardein: Turks defeated by Prince Eugene.
- John Law establishes Banque Générale in France.
- Treaty of Westminster between Britain and the Emperor.
- Septenniel Act in Britain, life of Parliament extended from three to seven years.
- Triple Alliance: France, Britain and Holland.
- Turks conquer Morea.
  DEATHS
  Gottfried Wilhelm Leibnitz, German philosopher.

1717
- John Law founds the Louisiana Company.
- Spanish conquest of Sardinia.
- Bangorian controversy.
- Battle of Belgrade: Turks defeated by Prince Eugene.

1718
- Peace of Passarowitz between the Empire and the Turks.
- Charles VI joins Triple Alliance, making it a Quadruple Alliance.
- Battle of Cape Passaro: Byng destroys the Spanish fleet.
- Death of Charles XII of Spain.
- Victor Amadeus of Savoy becomes King of Sardinia instead of King of Sicily.
- Britain declares war against Spain.

1719
- France declares war against Spain.
- Treaty of Vienna between George I, Austria and Saxony.
- Treaty of Stockholm between Hanover and Sweden.
- Fall of the Spanish minister, Alberoni.
- Daniel Defoe's *Robinson Crusoe*.
  DEATHS
  Joseph Addison, English essayist.

1720
- Quadruple Alliance joined by Spain, Denmark and Poland.
- Failure of Law's Banque Générale in France.
- Outbreak of plague in Marseilles and southern France.
- South Sea Bubble.
- Francis Atterbury's plot to restore the Stuarts to English throne.
- Treaties between Sweden and Prussia and between Sweden and Denmark.

1721
- Treaty of Madrid between Spain and France.
- Sir Robert Walpole becomes Prime Minister.
- Peace of Nystad between Peter the Great and Sweden: Sweden ceases to be a top power.

1722
- Peter the Great takes Baku.

1723
- Ostend East India Company chartered by Charles VI.
  DEATHS
  Christopher Wren, English architect.

1724
- Abdication of Philip V of Spain; the short reign of his eldest son, Luis, is followed by his re-accession.
- Jonathan Swift begins publication of his *Drapier's Letters*.

1725
- First Treaty of Vienna between Austria and Spain.
- Alliance of Hanover between Britain, France and Prussia.
- Catherine I succeeds Peter the Great in Russia.

1726
- Alliance of Hanover joined by Sweden and Denmark.
- Treaty of Wusterhausen between Austria and Prussia.

1727
- Spain declares war against Britain.
- Peter II, Tsar of Russia.
- George II, King of Britain.
- First Indemnity Act for Nonconformists in England.
  ### DEATHS
  Isaac Newton, English scientist.

1728
- Convention of Pardo ends war between Spain and Britain.

1729
- Beginning of Methodist revival in Britain.
- Treaty of Seville between Britain, France and Spain.
- The Ostend Company abolished.
  ### DEATHS
  William Congreve, English dramatist.

1730
- Anne becomes Tsarina of Russia.
- Victor Amadeus, King of Sardinia, abdicates: succeeded by Charles Emmanuel.
- Christian VI becomes King of Denmark.

1731
- Spain denounces the Treaty of Seville.
- Britain and Holland guarantee the Pragmatic Sanction.
- Second Treaty of Vienna: Emperor ratifies Treaty of Seville; Spain accedes.

1733
- Death of Augustus II of Poland: Stanislaus Leszczynski elected King, also Augustus III; War of Polish Succession follows.
- Battle of Bitonto: Spanish victory in Italy over Austrian forces.
- Treaty of Turin between France and Sardinia.
- Treaty of the Escurial: First Family Compact between France and Spain.
- Prime Minister Sir Robert Walpole compelled to withdraw Excise Bill.
- Invention of flying shuttle by John Kay.
- Jethro Tull's *The Horse-Hoeing Husbandry* encourages improved agricultural techniques.

1735
- Abdication of Stanislaus Leszczynski: Augustus III elected King of Poland.
- War begins between Russia and Turkey.

1736
- Porteous Riots in Edinburgh.

1737
- Third Treaty of Vienna ends War of the Polish Succession: Don Carlos established as King of Naples.

1738
- Parties of Hats and Caps first appear in Sweden.

1739
- Peace of Belgrade: Austria sacrifices all the achievements of Peace of Passarowitz to Turks.
- Treaty of Constantinople ends Russo-Turkish war.
- War between Britain and Spain.
- Portobello in West Indies captured by Vernon.

1740
- Frederick II (Frederick the Great) becomes King of Prussia.
- Ivan VI becomes Tsar of Russia.
- Death of Charles VI: War of Austrian Succession begins, to prevent accession of his daughter, Maria Theresa.
- Invasion of Silesia by Frederick the Great.
- Samuel Richardson's *Pamela*.

1741
- Battle of Mollwitz: Frederick the Great's victory over Austrians.
- Treaty of Breslau between France and Frederick the Great.
- Sweden declares war against Russia.
- Battle of Vilmanstrand: defeat of Swedes.
- Convention of Klein-Schnellendorf: Maria Theresa abandons Lower Silesia to Frederick.
- Frederick's allies capture Prague and Frederick invades Moravia.
- Elizabeth becomes Tsarina of Russia.
- Handel's *Messiah*.
- Thomas Arne's *Rule, Britannia!*

1742
- Fall of Sir Robert Walpole.
- Charles VII elected Emperor.
- Battle of Chotusitz: Austrians defeated by Frederick the Great.
  Deaths
  Edmund Halley, English astronomer.

1743
- Battle of Campo Santo: Spanish defeat.
- Treaty of Worms between Austria, Britain and Sardinia.
- Battle of Dettingen: George II defeats the French.
- Peace of Berlin between Austria, Prussia and Saxony.
- Peace of Abo between Sweden and Russia.
- Treaty of Fontainebleau: Second Family Compact between France and Spain.

1744
- Union of Frankfort between Prussia, Hesse-Cassel and Elector Palatine.
- Henry Pelham ministry in Britain.
- Invasion of Bohemia by Frederick the Great.
- War declared between Britain and France.
- Britain captures Louisburg from America.
  Deaths
  Alexander Pope, English poet.

1745
- Death of Charles VII: Francis I, husband of Maria Theresa, elected Emperor.
- Treaty of Füssen between Austria and Bavaria.
- Jacobite rebellion in Britain.
- Battle of Prestonpans: Prince Charles Edward victorious.

- Battle of Fontenoy: defeat of British by Marshal Saxe.
- Alliance between Austria and Russia.
- Battle of Hohenfriedberg: Frederick the Great victorious.
- Battles of Sohr and Hennersdorf: Frederick the Great victorious.
- Battle of Kesselsdorf: Prussian victory over Austrians and Saxons.
- Battle of Basignano: French and Spanish victory in Italy; Milan captured.
- Treaty of Dresden between Prussia and Austria.
  ### DEATHS
  Jonathan Swift, English author.

1746
- Battle of Falkirk: Prince Charles victorious.
- Franco-Sardinian Alliance.
- Milan retaken from the French and Spaniards with aid of Charles Emmanuel of Sardinia: all Piedmont and Lombardy recovered.
- Brussels taken by Marshal Saxe.
- Frederick V, King of Denmark
- Franco-Danish Alliance.
- Battle of Culloden: Jacobites finally crushed.
- Battle of Piacenza: Austrian victory.
- Treaty of St Petersburg between Russia and Austria.
- Britain takes Cape Breton.
- Ferdinand VI, King of Spain.
- Battle of Roucoux: Marshal Saxe defeats the Allies; Netherlands secured.
- France captures Madras.

1747
- William IV, Stadtholder of United Provinces.
- Treaty between Prussia and Sweden.
- Battle of Lauffeldt: French victory.

1748
- French take Bergen-op-Zoom.
- Treaty of Aix-La-Chapelle: War of Austrian Succession ended.

THE RISE OF THE BRITISH EMPIRE

1749
- Commercial Treaty of Aquisgran between Britain and Spain.
- Dupleix makes the Carnatic, French.
- Henry Fielding's *Tom Jones*.

1750
- Bill for the Prohibition of Colonial Manufactures before Parliament.
- Joseph becomes King of Portugal.
  ### DEATHS
  Johann Sebastian Bach, German composer.

1751
- Seizure and defence of Arcot by Clive.
- The *Encyclopédie* begins to appear in France.

1752
- Treaty of Aranjuez between Spain and Austria regarding Italy.
- Britain adopts the Gregorian calendar.

1755
- Convention of St Petersburg between Britain and Russia.

- Great Lisbon earthquake.
- Forces of English general, Edward Braddock, destroyed by French and Indians in America.

1756
- Convention of Westminster between Britain and Prussia.
- Devonshire and Pitt (afterwards Earl of Chatham) form a ministry.
- Treaty of Versailles between France and Austria.
- France captures Minorca.
- Britain declares war against France: Seven Years' War begins.
- Surajah Dowlah seizes Calcutta; the Black Hole of Calcutta, in which many British prisoners are suffocated.
- Battle of Lobositz: Frederick the Great against the Austrians; indecisive.
- Russia adheres to Treaty of Versailles.

1757
- Clive captures Calcutta and Chandernagore.
- New Treaty of Versailles between France and Austria.
- Battle of Plassey: Clive's victory over Surajah Dowlah.
- Battle of Prague: Frederick defeats the Austrians.
- Battle of Kolin: Frederick defeated by Austrians under Daun.
- Battle of Hastenbeck: Hanoverians under Duke of Cumberland beaten by French.
- Battle of Gross-Jägerndorf: Prussians defeated by Russians.
- Convention of Klosterzeven: Hanoverian army to be disbanded.
- Battle of Rossbach: Frederick defeats the French.
- Battle of Breslau: Prussians defeated by Austrians.
- Battle of Leuthen: Prussian victory over the Austrians.

1758
- British capture Louisburg.
- Robert Clive becomes Governor of Bengal.
- Battle of Zorndorf: drawn between Frederick and the Russians.
- Battle of Hochkirch: Frederick defeated by Austrians.

1759
- Battle of Kay: Prussians defeated by Russians.
- Battle of Minden: French defeated by Ferdinand of Brunswick: Hanover saved.
- Battle of Kunersdorf: Frederick defeated by Russians.
- Battle of Quebec: Britain captures Quebec from French; Wolfe and Montcalm killed.
- Charles III, King of Spain.
- Jesuits expelled from Portugal and Brazil.
- Battle of Quiberon Bay: Hawke destroys French fleet.

1760
- Battle of Wandewash: Sir Eyre Coote defeats French in India; Pondicherry taken following year.
- Battle of Landshut: Prussian force annihilated; fall of Glatz.
- Battle of Leignitz: Frederick defeats the Austrians.
- Russians occupy Berlin.
- George III, King of Britain.
- Capitulation of Montreal: Britain in control of Canada.
- Battle of Torgau: Frederick defeats the Austrians.

1761
- Battle of Panipat: Mahrattas defeated by Afghans in India: the Mughal Empire now only a shadow.
- Spaniards invade Portugal.

- Treaty of San Ildefonso: Third Family Compact between France and Spain.
- Fall of Prime Minister William Pitt the Elder.
- Earl of Bute becomes Prime Minister.

1762
- Britain declares war against Spain.
- Peter III becomes Tsar of Russia; Catharine II, Tsarina soon afterwards.
- Prussia concludes peace with Russia and Sweden: alliance between Russia and Prussia.
- Martinique, Havana, Manila and other territories, captured by Britain.
- Battle of Wilhelmsthal: British and Hanoverian victory over France.
- Battle of Lutternberg: British and Hanoverians defeat the French.
- Battle of Freiberg: Prussians defeat the Austrians.
- Jean Jacques Rousseau's *Du Contrat Social*.

1763
- Seven Years' War ended by Peace of Hubertusburg between Prussia, Austria and Saxony.
- Peace of Paris between France, Spain and Britain: Britain gains Canada and other territories.
- Lord Bute resigns office in Britain: Granville ministry formed.
- Whiteboy outbreaks in Ireland.

THE RISE OF THE UNITED STATES

1764
- John Wilkes expelled from House of Commons for attacks on the British monarchy.
- Stanislaus Poniatowski elected King of Poland.
- Jesuits expelled from France.
- Battle of Buxar: Britain gains Oude and other territories in India.
- Invention of spinning jenny by James Hargreaves.

1765
- Stamp Act passed by British Parliament.
- Joseph II becomes Emperor.

1766
- Repeal of Stamp Act, but Declaratory Act passed declaring Britain's right to tax the colonies.
- France annexes Lorraine.
- Oliver Goldsmith's *Vicar of Wakefield*.

1767
- Spain expels the Jesuits.
- Treaty of alliance between Prussia and Russia.
- Tea and other duties imposed by British Parliament on America.

1768
- Corsica bought by France from Genoa.
- Renewal of alliance between Russia and Prussia.
- Confederation of Bar formed in Poland.
- Russia invades Poland.
- Turks declare war against Russia.
- Royal Academy established.
- The water frame invented by Richard Arkwright.
- James Cook sets off on his first voyage to the Pacific.
  ### DEATHS
  Laurence Sterne, English novelist.

1769
- Russians defeat Turks and occupied Moldavia and Bucharest.

1770
- Lord North becomes British Prime Minister.
- The 'Boston Massacre'.
- Spaniards attack Falkland Islands.
- Battle of Tchesmé: Turkish fleet destroyed by Russia.
- James Cook discovers New South Wales.
- Edmund Burke's *Thoughts on the Present Discontents*.
  DEATHS
  Thomas Chatterton, English poet.

1771
- Parliament of Paris exiled.
- Gustavus III, King of Sweden.
- Russia occupies the Crimea.
  DEATHS
  Tobias Smollet, Scottish novelist.

1772
- First Partition of Poland between Russia, Austria and Prussia.
- Royal Marriage Act in Britain.
- Gustavus III re-establishes absolutism in Sweden.
- Struensee, Danish reforming statesman, executed: Guldberg in power.

1773
- Alliance between France and Sweden.
- Jesuit Order suppressed by Pope Clement XIV.
- Indian Regulating Act passed.
- Warren Hastings becomes first Governor-General of Bengal.
- Pugachoff's insurrection in Russia.

1774
- 'Boston Tea Party' riot: retaliatory legislation by British Parliament.
- Louis XVI becomes King of France.
- Turgot becomes Finance Minister of France.
- Quebec Act passed.
- Battle of Shumla: Russians rout Turks.
- Treaty of Kutchuk-Kainardji between Russia and Turkey.
- Oxygen discovered by Joseph Priestley.
- Chlorine discovered by Karl Wilhelm Scheele.

1775
- Battle of Lexington: American victory; start of the American War of Independence.
- George Washington becomes Commander-in-Chief of American forces.
- Battle of Bunker Hill: Americans defeated.
- Spaniards attack Algiers.

1776
- Spaniards attack Sacramento.
- Parliament passes a Prohibitory Act against American commerce.
- Declaration of Independence by American colonies.
- Edward Gibbon begins *Decline and Fall of the Roman Empire*.
- Adam Smith's *Inquiry into the Nature and Causes of the Wealth of Nations*.
  DEATHS
  David Hume, Scottish philosopher.

1777
- Maria I, Queen of Portugal, along with Pedro III.
- Necker becomes Finance Minister of France.
- General Burgoyne capitulates to Americans at Saratoga.

1778
- Treaty of Paris between France and America.
- Treaty of the Pardo between Spain and Portugal.
- Bavarian War of Succession begins.
- Treaty between Holland and America.
- Saville's Roman Catholic Relief Act.
  DEATHS
  Giambattista Piranesi, Italian etcher and architect.
  Voltaire, French writer.

1779
- Treaty of Teschen between Austria and Russia ends War of Bavarian Succession.
- Spain declares war against Britain.
- Siege of Gibraltar begins (relieved following year).
- The spinning mule invented by Samuel Crompton.
  DEATHS
  David Garrick, English actor.

1780
- Joseph II, sole Emperor, on death of Maria Theresa.
- Holland declares war against Britain.
- Armed Neutrality formed against Britain by Russia and Prussia.
- Alliance of Austria and Russia against Turkey.
- Hyder Ali conquers Carnatic.
  DEATHS
  Bernardo Canaletto, Italian painter.

1781
- French attack on Jersey defeated by Pierson.
- Rodney's victories in West Indies.
- French admiral, De Grasse, captures Tobago.
- Patent of Tolerance issued by Joseph II.
- Battle of Porto Novo: Sir Eyre Coote defeats Hyder Ali.
- Capitulation of Cornwallis in Yorktown to Americans.
- Serfdom abolished by Joseph II.

1782
- French capture Minorca and various West Indian islands.
- Spain suppresses rebellion in Peru.
- Evacuation of Barrier fortresses by Dutch.
- Rodney's victory over De Grasse in West Indies saves Jamaica.
- Declaration of Rights by Grattan: Irish legislative independence.
- Relief of Gibraltar by Howe.
- British inventor James Watt patents his steam engine.

1783
- Treaty of Versailles between Britain, France and America.
- Britain recognizes independence of American colonies.
- Coalition ministry of Fox and North.
- William Pitt the Younger in power in Britain.
- Catherine II annexes the Crimea.

1784
- Bernstorff in power in Denmark.
- India Act of William Pitt.
- Treaty of Constantinople between Russia and Turkey: Crimea finally passes to Russia.

1785
- Sweden declares war against Russia.
- Battle of Hogland: Russian naval victory over Sweden.
- The Fürstenbund (League of Princes) formed by Frederick the Great.
- Danish attack on Sweden.
- Treaty of Fontainebleau abrogates Barrier Treaty of 1715.
- The Diamond Necklace Affair in France.
- Power loom invented by Edmund Cartwright.
  DEATHS
  Samuel Johnson, English lexicographer.

1786
- Death of Frederick the Great: succeeded by Frederick William II.
- Commercial Treaty between Britain and France.
- Robert Burns's *Poems Chiefly in the Scottish Dialect*.

1787
- Impeachment of Warren Hastings begins: Edmund Burke the leader.
- Disturbances in Austrian Netherlands.
- Invasion of Holland by Prussia.
- Assembly of Notables meet in France.
- Austria and Russia declare war against Turkey.

1788
- Triple Alliance between Britain, Holland and Prussia.
- First motion in House of Commons for abolition of slave trade.
- War between Sweden and Russia.
- Convention of Uddevalla: Danes evacuate Sweden.
- Charles IV, King of Spain.
- Russians take Ochakoff from the Turks.
- British penal colony founded at Botany Bay, Australia.

THE FRENCH REVOLUTION

1789
- Bread Riots in France.
- Gustavus III makes Swedish monarchy virtually absolute.
- States General meet in Versailles (4 May).
- Third Estate declares itself a National Assembly (17 June).
- Joseph II cancels the liberties of Brabant.
- Oath of the Tennis Court.
- Union of the Three Estates.
- Committee of the Constitution appointed.
- Fall of Necker.
- Fall of the Bastille (14 July).
- Battle of Focsani: Turks defeated by Austrians and Russians.
- King Louis XVI recalls Necker.
- Great reforming session of National Assembly on 4 August.
- Declaration of the Rights of Man.
- Battle of Rimnik: Turks defeated by Austrians and Russians.
- Émeute in Paris: mob marches to Versailles: King and National Assembly go to Paris (October).
- Austrians take Belgrade.
- Church lands nationalized by National Assembly (November).
- Assignats first issued (December).

- George Washington elected first President of the US.
- Selim III becomes Sultan of Turkey.

1790
- Belgian Republic constituted (January): suppressed in November.
- Alliance between Prussia and Turkey.
- French National Assembly deprives monastic vows of force and suppresses religious orders.
- Leopold II, Emperor.
- Convention of Reichenbach: ends war between Austria and Turkey and Russia; war between Prussia and Austria averted.
- Suppression by France of a revolt in San Domingo.
- Treaty of Werelå between Russia and Sweden.
- Civil constitution of the clergy enacted in France.
- Resignation of Necker in France.
- Nootka Sound Convention between Britain and Spain.
- National Assembly issue a decree imposing an oath on the clergy.
- Edmund Burke's *Reflections on the French Revolution*.

1791
- National Assembly decrees abolition of slavery in West Indies.
- New Polish constitution granted by Stanislaus Poniatowski: throne made hereditary.
- Flight of Louis XVI to Varennes.
- Massacre of the Champ de Mars.
- Treaty of Sistova between Austria and Turkey.
- Conference of Pillnitz between Emperor and Prussian King to arrange for support of Louis XVI.
- Fresh slave revolt in San Domingo.
- New French Constitution enacted (September).
- Union of Avignon and the Venaissin to France decreed.
- Louis XVI takes the oath to the new Constitution.
- End of National Assembly (30 September): Legislative Assembly begins next day.
- Treaty of Drottningholm between Sweden and Russia.
- Decree against the émigrés: vetoed by Louis XVI.
- Decree against non-juring priests: vetoed by Louis XVI.
- Joseph Priestley's house in Birmingham burned down by mob.
- Wolfe Tone founds the Society of United Irishmen.
- Constitutional Act for Canada.
- Slave revolt in Haiti.
- Thomas Paine's *Rights of Man*: reply to Edmund Burke's *Reflections*.
  DEATHS
  Mirabeau, French political writer.
  Wolfgang Amadeus Mozart, German composer.

1792
- Treaty of Jassy: ends war between Russia and Turkey: Russia obtains Crimea.
- Tipu surrenders Seringapatam to the British: end of Second Mysore War.
- Alliance between Austria and Prussia.
- Francis II becomes Emperor.
- Assassination of Gustavus III of Sweden: Gustavus IV succeeds.
- A Jacobin ministry in power in France.
- 'Society of the Friends of the People' founded in Britain.
- France declares war against Austria (20 April).
- Russia invades Poland and Lithuania.
- Insurrection in the Tuileries at Paris: the Tuileries later taken by the mob.

- Longwy taken from the French by the Allies: then Verdun.
- September Massacres in Paris.
- Battle of Valmy: Dumouriez defeats Prussians.
- National Convention replaces Legislative Assembly (21 September).
- Monarchy abolished in France.
- French take Nice, Spires and Mainz.
- Battle of Jemappes: Dumouriez defeats Austrians; Brussels occupied by French.
- National Convention offers its protection to all nations struggling for freedom.
- Opening of Scheldt to commerce.
- Trial of Louis XVI begun.
- Outbreak of the bubonic plague in Egypt kills 800, 000.
- Mary Wollstonecraft's *Vindication of the Rights of Women*.
- Rouget de Lisle's *La Marseillaise*.
  ### DEATHS
  Robert Adam, Scottish architect.
  Sir Joshua Reynolds, English painter.

1793
- Committee of General Defence in France.
- Execution of Louis XVI (21 January).
- Second Partition of Poland.
- British government declares war against France.
- France declares war against Britain and Holland.
- Royalist insurrection in the Vendée.
- French take Aix-la-Chapelle.
- Revolutionary Tribunal created in Paris.
- Battle of Neerwinden: French defeated by Austrians; Brussels evacuated by French.
- French evacuate the Netherlands.
- Dumouriez deserts to the Austrians.
- First Committee of Public Safety.
- The Girondists proscribed.
- Vendéans fail to take Nantes.
- Battle of Chatillon: Republican forces defeated in west of France by rebels.
- Second or Great Committee of Public Safety: more extreme; the Reign of Terror.
- Assassination of Marat by Charlotte Corday.
- Prussians take Mainz.
- Allies take Valenciennes.
- Toulon surrenders to Admiral Hood.
- French relieve Dunkirk.
- End of the Lyons revolt.
- Battle of Wattignies: French under Jourdan victorious over Austrians.
- Battle of Cholet: defeat of Vendéans.
- Execution of Marie Antoinette (16 October).
- Battle of Château Gontier: western French rebels victorious under La Rochejaquelin.
- Lyons massacres.
- The Girondists executed.
- Notre Dame consecrated to the worship of Reason.
- Diet of Grodno agrees to partition of Poland; revokes the new Polish constitution.
- New Republican Calendar comes into force in France.
- Battle of Kaiserslautern: Hoche fails against the Austrians in a three days' battle.
- Law of 14 Frimaire makes Committee of Public Safety supreme in France.
- Battle of Le Mans: Vendéans crushed.
- French recover Toulon: Napoleon Bonaparte distinguishes himself.

- Battle of Savenay: Kléber finally defeats the Vendéans.
- British take Tobago from the French.
- William Godwin's *Political Justice*.

1794
- Hoche, Master of the Palatinate.
- Execution of the Hébertists.
- Manifesto of Kosciusko in Poland against Prussia and Russia.
- Battle of Raslawice: Kosciusko defeats Russians.
- Execution of Dantonists.
- Russians evacuate Warsaw.
- Battle of the First of June: Howe defeats the French fleet.
- Jourdan takes Charleroi.
- Battle of Rawka: Poles defeated by Prussians.
- Feast of the Supreme Being in Paris organized by Robespierre.
- Law of 22 Prairial strengthens Revolutionary Tribunal.
- Prussians take Cracow.
- Battle of Fleurus: hard-won victory by Jourdan over Austrians under Coburg.
- The Ninth Thermidor: fall of Robespierre.
- Execution of Robespierre, Saint-Just and others.
- French capture Fuenterrabia.
- Britain captures Corsica.
- Battle of Maciejowice: Kosciusko routed and taken prisoner by Russians; Russians recapture Warsaw.
- Jacobin Club closed in Paris.
- French conquer all the North Catalonian fortresses.
- British capture Martinique, St Lucia and other territories.
  Deaths
  Antoine Laurent Lavoisier, French chemist.

1795
- Treaty between Emperor and Catherine the Great of Russia for partition of Turkey, Venice, Poland and Bavaria.
- Peace of La Jaunaie with Royalist rebels in western France.
- British capture Ceylon and Malacca from Dutch.
- Insurrection of 12 Germinal in Paris: 'Bread and the Constitution of 1793'.
- Treaty of Basle between France and Prussia: Holland and Spain accede later.
- Insurrection of 1 Prairial in Paris.
- Revolutionary Tribunal abolished in France.
- 'White Terror' in southern France.
- Death of the French Dauphin in prison.
- Bilbao taken by French.
- Cape Town taken by British from Dutch.
- Orange Society founded in Ireland.
- Triple Alliance of Britain, Austria and Russia.
- Constitution of the Year III proclaimed (23 September).
- Belgium incorporated in France.
- Insurrection of Vendémiaire in Paris suppressed.
- The Directory installed in France (3 November).
- Battle of Loano: French victory over Austrian and Sardinian forces.
- Abdication of Stanislaus Poniatowski in Poland.
- French troops conquer Holland and establish the Batavian Republic.
- French recapture St Lucia.

James Boswell, Scottish author.

1796
- Napoleon Bonaparte appointed to command the army of Italy.
- Armistice of Cherasco: neutrality of Sardinia.
- Conspiracy of Babeuf frustrated in Paris.
- Battle of Lodi: Bonaparte defeats Austrians.
- French occupy Milan, but abandon siege of Mantua.
- Battle of Solferino: Bonaparte defeats Austrians under Wurmser.
- Treaty of San Ildefonso between France and Spain.
- Archduke Charles defeats Jourdan in Bavaria and drives him across the Rhine.
- Cispadane Republic founded by Bonaparte: includes Modena, Bologna and Ferrara.
- Battle of Arcola: Bonaparte's desperate victory over Austrians under Alvintzy.
- Paul I, Tsar of Russia.
- British evacuate Corsica.
- Battle of Lonato: Austrians defeated by French under Augereau.
- British reconquer St Lucia from French and take Demerara from the Dutch.
- John Quincy Adams elected President of US.

DEATHS
Robert Burns, Scottish poet.

1797
- Failure of Hoche's attempted invasion of Ireland.
- Third and Final Partition of Poland.
- Bonaparte takes Mantua.
- Battle of Cape St Vincent: Spanish fleet defeated by Jervis.
- Pope submits to Bonaparte.
- Mutiny in British fleet at Spithead: demands granted.
- Rising against French in Verona.
- Battle of Neuwied: Austrians defeated by Hoche.
- Preliminaries of peace at Loeben between Austria and Bonaparte.
- Mutiny in British fleet at the Nore: special legislation against it.
- French enter Venice.
- Genoa becomes Ligurian Republic under French influence.
- Cisalpine Republic established by Bonaparte in Lombardy.
- Cispadane Republic unites to Cisalpine Republic.
- Treaty between France and Portugal.
- Coup d'état of 18 Fructidor in France.
- Battle of Camperdown: Dutch fleet under De Winter defeated by Duncan.
- Peace of Campo Formio: Venice given to Austria; Ionian Islands to France; Austria surrenders Netherlands and recognizes Cisalpine Republic.
- Valtellines annexed to Cisalpine Republic.
- Frederick William III, King of Prussia.
- Paul I made Protector of the Knights of Malta.
- Congress of Rastatt.
- Britain takes Trinidad from Spain.

1798
- Roman Republic declared, with aid of France: temporal power of Pope overthrown.
- French occupation of Bern: Swiss Confederacy replaced by Helvetic Republic.
- Fall of Godoy in Spain.
- Sieyès elected a French Director.

- Bonaparte's Egyptian expedition sets sail: Malta taken.
- Bonaparte takes Alexandria.
- French occupy citadel of Turin.
- Battle of the Pyramids: French victory in Egypt; Bonaparte enters Cairo.
- Battle of the Nile: Nelson destroys French fleet under Brueys.
- France at war with Turkey: Russian fleet in Mediterranean to help Turks.
- Conscription introduced in France.
- Rebellion in Cairo.
- Paul I made Grand Master of the Knights of Malta.
- Ferdinand IV of Naples enters Rome: retaken by French.
- Abdication of Charles Emmanuel IV of Savoy.
- Flight of Ferdinand of Naples.
- Alliance between Russia and Turkey: soon joined by Britain.
- Pitt introduces an Income Tax.
- *Lyrical Ballads* of English poets, William Wordsworth and Samuel Taylor Coleridge.
- Thomas Malthus's *Essay on Population*.

1799

- French occupation of Naples: Parthenopean Republic created.
- Bonaparte's Syrian campaign begins: Jaffa taken.
- Austria declares war against France.
- Siege of Acre by French fails.
- Battle of Stockach: Jourdan defeated by Archduke Charles.
- British storm Seringapatam: Tipu killed.
- Congress of Rastatt ends without result.
- Milan taken by Russians and Austrians under Suvóroff.
- Allies enter Turin.
- Battle of Modena: French under Macdonald defeat Austrians.
- Naples capitulates to Bourbons.
- Suvóroff defeats Macdonald and overthrows the Italian republics.
- Battle of Aboukir: French victory in Egypt over Turks.
- Allies take Mantua.
- Battle of Novi: French routed; Joubert killed.
- British force lands in Holland under Duke of York.
- Battle of Bergen: British and Russians defeated in Holland.
- Battle of Zürich: Russians defeated by Masséna: Suvóroff driven out of Switzerland.
- Bonaparte deserts Egyptian army, leaving Kléber in command and lands in France.
- Convention of Alkmaar: Britain to evacuate Holland.
- 18 Brumaire: directory overthrown by Bonaparte.
- Consulate established in France: Bonaparte, Cambacérès and Lebrun, Consuls.
- British take Surinam from Dutch.
- Repressive legislation in Britain against combinations and corresponding societies.
  DEATHS
  Joseph Black, Scottish chemist.
  George Washington, first President of the USA.

NAPOLEON

1800

- Robert Owen establishes model industrial community in New Lanark, Scotland.
- Treaty of El Arish between Kléber and the Turks: French to evacuate Egypt.
- Pius VII becomes Pope.
- Battle of Heliopolis: Kléber defeats the Turks.

- Godoy restored in Spain at instance of Napoleon.
- Napoleon crosses the Great St Bernard Pass into Italy: occupies Milan.
- Masséna capitulates in Genoa.
- Assassination of Kléber in Egypt.
- Battle of Marengo: Austrian victory turned into French victory by Desaix, who is killed.
- Battle of Hochstädt: Moreau defeats Austrians under Kray.
- British capture Malta.
- Battle of Hohenlinden: Moreau defeats Austrians under Archduke John.
- Second Armed Neutrality: Russia, Sweden, Denmark and Prussia.
- Union of Britain and Ireland: abolition of Irish Parliament.
- Thomas Jefferson elected US President.

  DEATHS
  William Cowper, English poet.

1801
- British embargo on Russian, Danish and Swedish vessels in British ports.
- Toussaint L'Ouverture, Master of San Domingo.
- William Pitt the Younger resigns as Prime Minister.
- Peace of Lunéville between France and Austria: France gains Belgium, Luxemburg, Piedmont and other territories.
- Kingdom of Etruria founded by Napoleon in Tuscany.
- Treaty of Florence between France and Naples.
- Battle of Alexandria: Abercromby defeats French, but killed; Cairo surrenders to British; French evacuate Egypt.
- Paul I murdered: Alexander I, Tsar.
- Danish embargo on British ships in Danish ports.
- Battle of Copenhagen: Parker and Nelson destroy Danish fleet.
- Constitution of Malmaison imposed on Switzerland by France.
- Treaty of Badajos between Spain and Portugal: Napoleon angry.
- Treaty of St Petersburg between Russia and Britain.
- Denmark accepts Russo-British Treaty.
- Chateaubriand's Génie de Christianisme: a Catholic revival.

1802
- Cisalpine Republic called Italian Republic.
- Peace of Amiens.
- Sweden accepts Anglo-Russian treaty.
- Concordat between Napoleon and the Pope.
- Legion of Honour created.
- Constitution of the Year X: Napoleon, First Consul for Life (4 August).
- France annexes Piedmont.
- Treaty between France and Russia.
- French Marshall Ney sent to crush Switzerland.
- First British Factory Act.
- First practical steamboat: the *Charlotte Dundas of* British engineer, William Symington.

1803
- Act of Mediation replaces Helvetic Republic with a Swiss Confederation.
- Britain declares war against France.
- Robert Emmet, Irish rebel, hanged.
- United States purchases Louisiana from Napoleon, who had taken it from Spain.

1804
- Napoleon's legislation of the Civil Code, alternatively called the Napoleonic Code or the Code of Napoleon, which sought to make French law completely uniform.

- Duc d'Enghien shot.
- William Pitt again Prime Minister.
- Empire established in France: Napoleon, Emperor.
- Execution of Cadoudal and others for conspiracy in Paris.
- Napoleon makes Spain declare war against Britain.
- First Serbian uprising against Ottoman Turks: Karageorge (Karadjordje) leader.

  DEATHS

  Immanuel Kant, German philosopher.

  Joseph Priestly, English chemist.

1805

- Napoleon crowns himself King of Italy at Milan.
- Ligurian Republic annexed to France.
- Battle of Finisterre: Franco-Spanish fleet under Villeneuve defeated by Calder.
- Russo-Austrian Treaty.
- Parma and Piacenza annexed to France.
- Capitulation of Austrian general, Mack, in Ulm.
- Battle of Trafalgar: Nelson destroys the Franco-Spanish fleet, but is killed.
- Napoleon enters Vienna.
- Battle of Austerlitz: Napoleon defeats Austro-Russian army.
- Treaty of Vienna between France and Prussia: Prussia to get Hanover.
- Peace of Pressburg between France and Austria: Bavaria and Württemberg become kingdoms; Austria loses Venice and Tyrol.
- Sir Walter Scott's *Lay of the Last Minstrel*.

  DEATHS

  Friedrich von Schiller, German writer.

1806

- Death of William Pitt: so-called 'Ministry of All the Talents' formed under Grenville and including Fox.
- New treaty between France and Prussia.
- Venetia annexed to kingdom of Italy.
- Joseph Bonaparte declared King of the Two Sicilies.
- Prussia annexes Hanover.
- Prussia excludes British ships from Prussian ports: Britain declares war against Prussia.
- Louis Bonaparte becomes King of Holland.
- British occupy Buenos Aires, but forced by citizens to surrender.
- Battle of Maida: British defeat French in South Italy.
- Confederation of the Rhine formed by Napoleon: the confederated states secede from the Empire.
- Francis II resigns the Empire and becomes Francis I, Emperor of Austria: end of Holy Roman Empire.
- Death of Fox.
- Prussian ultimatum to Napoleon.
- Battle of Jena: Napoleon defeats Prussia.
- Battle of Auerstädt: Davout defeats Prussia.
- French occupation of Berlin: Prussia subdued.
- Napoleon's Berlin Decrees against Britain: the Continental System.
- Murat occupies Warsaw.
- Treaty of Posen: Saxony joins Confederation of the Rhine and becomes a kingdom.
- Russia suppresses Bucharest.

  DEATHS

  George Stubbs, English painter.

1807
* British Order in Council in reply to Berlin Decrees.
* Battle of Eylau: Napoleon against the Russians; indecisive.
* Bill passed by British Parliament abolishing the slave trade.
* Selim III of Turkey dethroned: Mustafa IV, Sultan.
* Britain accedes to Convention of Bartenstein to help Prussia and Sweden.
* Battle of Friedland: Napoleon defeats the Russians.
* Treaty of Tilsit between France and Russia.
* British bombardment of Copenhagen: Danish fleet surrenders.
* Serfdom abolished in Prussia.
* Convention of Fontainebleau between Napoleon and Spain for partition of Portugal.
* Russian breach with Britain.
* French troops cross into Spain.
* Flight of Portuguese royal family to Brazil.
* British capture Montevideo.
* Kingdom of Westphalia founded by Napoleon for Jerome.

1808
* French seize Pampeluna and Barcelona.
* Russia invades Finland.
* Joachim Murat becomes King of Naples.
* Charles IV of Spain abdicates: Ferdinand VII becomes King.
* French under Murat in Madrid.
* National insurrection in Spain.
* Etrurian kingdom annexed to France.
* Papal States partly annexed to kingdom of Italy.
* Joseph Bonaparte made King of Spain.
* Palafox's defence of Saragossa: French repelled.
* French fail against Valencia.
* Capitulation of French at Baylen.
* Mahmud II, Sultan of Turkey after murder of Mustafa IV.
* Joseph evacuates Madrid.
* British force lands in Portugal under Wellington.
* Battle of Vimiero: Wellington defeats Junot.
* Convention of Cintra: French evacuate Portugal.
* Convention of Erfurt: Napoleon and Russia.
* Napoleon takes Madrid.
* Frederick VI, King of Denmark.
* Second siege of Saragossa (surrendered following year).
* James Madison elected US President.
* Goethe completes first part of *Faust*.

1809
* Peace of the Dardanelles between Britain and Turkey.
* Battle of Corunna: Moore defeats Soult, but is killed.
* Soult takes Oporto.
* Battle of Medellin: French under Victor defeat Spanish.
* Deposition of Gustavus IV of Sweden: Charles XIII succeeds.
* Battle of Abensberg: Napoleon defeats Austrians.
* Austrians occupy Warsaw for a time.
* Battle of Eckmühl: Napoleon defeats Archduke Charles.
* Wellington drives Soult out of Portugal.
* Napoleon in Vienna.

- Napoleon annexes Rome and Papal States to French Empire: Pius VII a prisoner.
- Battle of Aspern: Napoleon defeated by Archduke Charles; Lannes killed.
- Andreas Hofer and the Tyrolese take Innsbruck.
- Battle of Wagram: Napoleon defeats Austrians.
- Battle of Talavera: French under Victor defeated by Wellington.
- British Walcheren expedition: a failure.
- Revolts in Quito and other places in Spanish South America.
- Treaty of Fredrikshamn: Sweden cedes Finland to Russia.
- Peace of Schönbrunn between France and Austria.
- Battle of Alba de Tormes: Spaniards defeated.
- French take Gerona after long siege.
- Treaty of Jonköping ends war between Sweden and Denmark.
- Spencer Perceval becomes British Prime Minister.
- French naturalist, Lamarck, originates theory of evolution.

  DEATHS

  Thomas Paine, Anglo-American author.

1810
- Treaty between Sweden and France: Sweden adopts Continental System.
- Napoleon divorces Josephine.
- Soult takes Seville.
- Andreas Hofer shot.
- Caracas Junta appointed in South America.
- Revolution in Buenos Aires.
- Holland annexed to France.
- Ney takes Ciudad Rodrigo.
- Masséna invades Portugal.
- Battle of Busaco: Wellington defeats Masséna.
- Coimbra with its garrison taken by British.
- Wellington retires behind the lines of Torres Vedras.
- Fontainebleau Decrees by Napoleon against British goods.
- France annexes northwestern Germany.

1811
- French take Tortosa.
- France annexes Duchy of Oldenburg: leads to breach with Russia.
- Soult takes Badajoz.
- Masséna retreats from Portugal.
- Battle of Fuentes d'Oñoro: Masséna fails against Wellington.
- Wellington takes Almeida.
- Battle of Albuera: Beresford defeats Soult.
- Caracas Congress proclaims independence of Spain.
- Battle of Sagunto: Suchet defeats Spaniards.
- Massacre of the Mamelukes: Muhammad Ali supreme in Egypt.
- Chilian revolution.

1812
- French take Valencia.
- Napoleon occupies Swedish Pomerania.
- Wellington takes Ciudad Rodrigo.
- Caracas destroyed by earthquake.
- Wellington takes Badajoz.
- Assassination of Spencer Perceval: Lord Liverpool becomes Prime Minister.
- Treaty of Bucharest between Russia and Turkey.
- Napoleon invades Russia (24 June).

- Revolutionists capitulate under Miranda in Caracas.
- Battle of Salamanca: Wellington defeats Marmont.
- Wellington enters Madrid.
- Battle of the Borodino: Napoleon against the Russians under Kutusoff; drawn.
- Napoleon enters Moscow (14 September): city in flames.
- Napoleon evacuates Moscow (18 October).
- Crossing of the Berezina (26 November).
- Napoleon in Paris (19 December) ahead of the remnant of his army.
- War between Britain and US.

1813
- Russians invade Germany.
- Alliance between Russia and Prussia.
- Treaty of Stockholm between Sweden and Britain.
- Battle of Gross-Görschen: Napoleon defeats Russians and Prussians.
- Battle of Bautzen: Napoleon defeats the Russians and Prussians.
- Armistice of Pläswitz concluded at instance of Napoleon.
- Treaty of Reichenbach.
- Battle of Vittoria: Wellington defeats Jourdan and Joseph Bonaparte.
- French take Vilna.
- Battles of the Pyrenees: Wellington defeats Soult.
- Bolivar enters Caracas as Liberator.
- Austria declares war against Napoleon (12 August).
- Battle of Gross-Beeren: French defeated by Prussians.
- Battle of Katzbach: Blücher defeats Napoleon.
- Battle of Dresden: Napoleon defeats the Allies.
- Battle of Kulm: Allies defeat French.
- Battle of Dennewitz: Prussians defeat Ney.
- Turks reconquer Serbia: Karageorge flees.
- Wellington takes San Sebastian.
- Battle of Leipzig or Battle of the Nations (16–19 October): Napoleon defeated by the Allies; Leipzig taken.
- Wellington takes Pampeluna.
- Battles of the Nive: Wellington defeats Soult.
- Treaty of Valençay: Napoleon gives crown of Spain to Ferdinand.
- Wellington invades France (22 December).

1814
- Battle of La Rothière: Blücher defeats Napoleon.
- Treaty of Kiel: Denmark surrenders Norway to Sweden.
- Battle of Orthez: Wellinton defeats Soult.
- Battle of Laon: Allies defeat Napoleon.
- Treaty of Chaumont between Russia, Austria, Prussia and Britain.
- Allies occupy Paris (31 March).
- Battle of Toulouse: Wellington defeats Soult (10 April).
- Abdication of Napoleon (11 April).
- Treaty of Fontainebleau accepted by Napoleon: banished to Elba (13 April).
- Louis XVIII enters Paris (3 May).
- Ferdinand of Spain issues proclamation against the Constitution: Liberal deputies arrested.
- First Peace of Paris (30 May).
- Fall of Montevideo.
- Bolivar heavily defeated: abandons Caracas.
- Society of Jesus reconstituted by Pope Pius VII.

- Congress of Vienna opens.
- Peruvian invasion overthrows Chilian republic.
- Hetairia Philike founded at Odessa: Greek national movement begins.
- Treaty of Ghent ends war between Britain and the United States.
- Britain acquires Cape Colony in South Africa from the Dutch.
- Sir Walter Scott's *Waverley*.

  DEATHS
  Marquis de Sade, French writer.

1815
- Napoleon lands in France (5 March): the Hundred Days begin.
- William I of Holland becomes King of the Netherlands.
- Louis XVIII flees from Paris (19 March) and Napoleon enters next day.
- Second Serbian uprising, under Milos Obrenovic, against Ottoman Turks.
- Spanish forces land at Cumaná in South America under Morillo.
- Brazil declared a separate kingdom.
- Battle of Tolentino: Murat overthrown in Italy.
- Revolt in the Vendée.
- Battle of St Gilles: Vendéans defeated and La Rochejaquelin killed.
- Final Act of Congress of Vienna (9 June).
- Battle of Quatre-Bras: Wellington defeats Ney (16 June).
- Battle of Ligny: Blücher defeated after hard fight (16 June).
- Battle of Waterloo: Napoleon defeated by Wellington and Blücher (18 June).
- Abdication of Napoleon (22 June).
- Allies enter Paris (7 July): Louis XVIII restored next day.
- Richelieu, Prime Minister of France.
- Napoleon surrenders to the British (15 July), and is sent to St Helena.
- Holy Alliance between Russia, Austria and Prussia.
- Concert of Europe established between Britain, Russia, Prussia and Austria.
- Alexander I grants a Polish constitution.
- Morillo invades New Granada: Bolivar flees.
- First Corn Law passed in Britain.

THE AGE OF METTERNICH

1816
- Death of mad Queen Maria I of Portugal: John VI proclaimed King of Portugal, Brazil and the Algarves.
- Independence of the Argentine provinces proclaimed.
- Radical meeting at Spa Fields broken up.
- Luddite anti-machinery riots.
- James Monroe elected US President.

1817
- Battle of Chacabuco: San Martin defeats the Royalists in South America.
- Seditious Meetings Act in Britain passed by Castlereagh, suspending Habeas Corpus Act.
- Simon Bolivar captures Angostura.
- Serbian autonomy recognized by Turkey.
- Ali Pasha of Janina at the height of his power.
- Acquittal of William Hone, arrested for publishing radical political and religious pamphlets.
- David Ricardo's *Principles of Political Economy*.

  DEATHS
  Jane Austen, English novelist.

1818
- Battle of Maipú: Chilian independence.
- Charles XIV (Bernadotte) becomes King of Sweden and Norway.
- Prussia becomes a free trade area.
- Bavaria obtains a constitution: also Baden.
- Congress of Aix-la-Chapelle: France admitted to the Concert.
- Decazes, Chief Minister in France.
- End of last Mahratta War in India: Mahratta power completely destroyed.

1819
- Radical meeting at Bonnymuir dispersed.
- Treaty of Frankfort completes work of Congress of Aix-la-Chapelle.
- Peterloo Massacre near Manchester.
- Carlsbad Decrees: reaction in Germany.
- The Six Acts in Britain restricting right of meeting, etc.
- Bolivar occupies Bogotá.
- Britain establishes a trading post at Singapore.

1820
- Spanish Revolution breaks out.
- George IV becomes King of Britain.
- Murder of the Duke of Berry in France.
- Fall of Decazes in France: Richelieu again Chief Minister.
- Cato Street Conspiracy against the Cabinet discovered: Thistlewood and others executed.
- Ferdinand of Spain decides to adopt the Constitution of 1812.
- Revolt in Naples.
- Congress of Troppau: Britain and France dissent from the reactionary protocol.
- Failure of George IV's Divorce Bill.
- Democratic insurrection in Lisbon.
- The Missouri Compromise on the slavery issue in the US.

1821
- Congress of Laibach.
- Prince Ypsilanti invades Moldavia to rouse the Greeks against Turkey.
- Battle of Rieti: Neapolitan constitutionalists defeated by Austrians.
- Revolt in Piedmont.
- Greek revolt in the Morea.
- Patriarch Gregorius and two bishops hanged by Turks.
- John VI returned from Brazil to Lisbon.
- Death of Napoleon (5 May).
- Greeks under Ypsilanti defeated in Wallachia.
- San Martín enters Lima and proclaims independence of Peru.
- Battle of Carabobo: Bolivar defeats the Royalist forces and occupies Caracas.
- Richelieu resigns in France: Royalist reaction under Villèle.
- Iturbide declares for an independent Mexican Empire.
- Muhammad Ali begins conquest of Soudan.

  DEATHS

  John Keats, English poet.

1822
- Massacre in Scio by the Turks.
- Lima occupied by the Royalists.
- Battle of Pichincha: Sucre frees Quito.
- Iturbide proclaimed Emperor of Mexico.
- US recognizes national independence of Colombia, Chile, Buenos Aires and Mexico.

- Dom Pedro proclaimed Emperor of Brazil.
- Suicide of Robert Stewart, Viscount Castlereagh: George Canning succeeds him.
- Brazil declared as an independent Empire.
- Congress of Verona: Britain dissents from coercion of Spain.
- Ali Pasha surrenders to the Turks and is murdered.
- Liberia founded on the west coast of Africa for freed American slaves.
  DEATHS
  Antonio Canova, Italian sculptor.
  Percy Bysshe Shelley, English poet.

1823
- France, Russia, Austria and Prussia demand the abolition of 1812 Constitution in Spain.
- Louis XVIII declares war against Spanish rebels.
- Britain recognizes the Greeks as belligerents.
- The French invade Spain and enter Madrid.
- Bolivar enters Lima.
- Leo XII becomes Pope.
- President Monroe's message: beginning of Monroe Doctrine.
- Iturbide abdicates in Mexico owing to military revolt of Santa Anna.

1824
- Muhammad Ali takes part against the Greeks.
- Dom Miguel assumes government of Portugal; compelled by the Powers to withdraw.
- Conference of St Petersburg on Eastern Question between Russia and Austria.
- Battle of Junin: Bolivar victorious.
- Charles X, King of France.
- Battle of Ayacucho: Sucre decisively defeats Royalists.
- Laws against combinations repealed in Britain.
- John Quincy Adams elected US President.
  DEATHS
  George Gordon, Lord Byron, English poet.

1825
- Britain recognizes independence of Buenos Aires, Colombia and Mexico.
- Ibrahim, son of Muhammad Ali, lands in Morea to help Turkey.
- Consecration of Charles X at Reims.
- Nicholas I becomes Tsar.
- December rising in Russia suppressed.
- Financial crisis in Britain.
- Navigation Laws partly repealed.
- Stockton and Darlington Railway opened.

1826
- Death of John VI of Portugal.
- Russian ultimatum to Turkey demanding evacuation of principalities of Moldavia and Wallachia.
- Protocol of St Petersburg regarding Greece: between Britain and Russia.
- End of defence of Missolonghi.
- Revolt of the Janissaries in Constantinople crushed.
- Chief Decembrists hanged in Russia.
- Massacre of the Janissaries in Constantinople.
- Jesuits return to France.
- Treaty of Akkerman: Turkey agrees to Russian demands.

1827
- George Canning becomes Prime Minister: Whig coalition.
- Press censorship established in France.

- Treaty of London regarding Greece: between Britain, Russia and France.
- Death of Canning: Goderich, Prime Minister.
- Battle of Navarino: Turkish fleet destroyed by allied fleet under Codrington.
- Martignac, Chief Minister in France.
- Turkey denounces Treaty of Akkerman.
  DEATHS
  Ludwig van Beethoven, German composer.
  William Blake, English poet and artist.

1828
- Capodistrias elected Greek President.
- Wellington becomes Prime Minister.
- Dom Miguel lands at Lisbon as Regent.
- Russia invades Turkey.
- Dom Miguel takes title of King of Portugal: reign of terror.
- Protocol of London: Britain, France and Russia.
- Ibrahim evacuates the Morea.
- Repeal of Test and Corporation Acts.
- O'Connell elected for Clare.
- Andrew Jackson elected US President.

1829
- Pius VIII becomes Pope.
- Polignac becomes Chief Minister in France.
- Catholic Emancipation Act passed in Britain.
- Treaty of Adrianople between Russia and Turkey: Greece recognized as independent; Serbian autonomy secured; Danubian principalities practically independent states.
- Fourth marriage of Ferdinand of Spain (to Maria Christina of Naples): beginning of Carlist movement.
- William Lloyd Garrison begins the abolitionist movement in US.
- The Rainhill locomotive trials: victory of George Stephenson's *Rocket*.
  DEATHS
  Sir Humphry Davy, English chemist.

1830
- William IV becomes King of Britain.
- The July Revolution in Paris: Louis Philippe becomes King.
- Belgian revolt against Holland: Belgian provinces proclaim their independence.
- Wellington succeeded by Earl Grey as Prime Minister.
- French begin conquest of Algeria.
- Insurrection in Poland, Italy and Germany.
- Milos Obrevonic becomes a hereditary Prince of Serbia.
- Conference of London recognizes Belgian independence.
- Victor Hugo's *Hernani*.
  DEATHS
  William Hazlitt, English author.

1831
- Polish Diet declares the Romanoffs excluded from the sovereignty.
- Gregory XVI becomes Pope.
- Revolution in the Papal States.
- Battle of Grochov: Russians defeat Poles.
- Casimir Périer ministry in France.
- Second Reading of first Reform Bill carried in House of Commons by majority of 1 (21 March); hostile amendment carried (April); Parliament dissolved (22 April); majority for reform elected.

- Austrian troops help Pope to suppress rising in Bologna.
- Abdication of Pedro I in Brazil: Pedro II succeeds.
- Leopold of Saxe-Coburg elected as Leopold I, King of the Belgians.
- French squadron in the Tagus: Portuguese fleet surrenders.
- Dutch invasion of Belgium.
- Assassination of Capodistrias.
- Polish revolution crushed: the kingdom ended.
- House of Lords rejects first Reform Bill in its second form (8 October).
- Muhammad Ali invades Syria: siege of Acre.
- Charles Albert becomes King of Sardinia.
- Young Italy founded by Giuseppe Mazzini.

  DEATHS

  Georg Wilhelm Friedrich Hegel, German philosopher.

1832

- Kingdom of Greece erected by Convention of London: Otho of Bavaria becomes King.
- Ibrahim takes Acre.
- First Reform Act passed (7 June).
- Ibrahim takes Damascus.
- Pedro's expedition lands in Portugal.
- Ibrahim conquers all Syria.
- The Pope condemns the teaching of Lamennals.
- Soult ministry in France, including the doctrinaires (Guizot, Thiers, etc).
- Antwerp capitulates to French.
- Battle of Konich: Ibrahim defeats Turks.
- General Election: Whig triumph.
- Crete placed under Egypt.

  DEATHS

  Jeremy Bentham, English philosopher.
  Johann Wolfgang von Goethe, German writer.
  Sir Walter Scott, Scottish novelist.

1833

- Russian squadron in the Bosphorus.
- Convention of Kutaya: Muhammad Ali recognized by Turkey as Pasha of Syria, etc.
- Battle of Cape St Vincent: Napier destroys the Miguelist fleet.
- Treaty of Unkiar Skelessi: alliance between Russia and Turkey.
- Terceira defeats Miguelists near Lisbon.
- Siege of Oporto raised by Miguelists.
- Dom Pedro enters Lisbon.
- Death of Ferdinand of Spain: succeeded by his daughter, Isabella II.
- Convention of Münchengrätz between Russia, Austria and Prussia in aid of Turkey (secret).
- Abolition of Slavery Act abolishes slavery throughout the British Empire.
- Treaty of Berlin between Austria, Prussia and Russia.
- Thomas Carlyle's *Sartor Resartus*.

  DEATHS

  Edmund Kean, English actor.

1834

- Treaty between Britain, Spain, Portugal and France: Austria, Russia and Prussia become Carlist.
- Battle of Asseiceira: Miguelists finally defeated by Pedroists in Portugal; Maria II established as Queen.

- Poor Law Act in England.
- The Veto Act passed by the Scottish General Assembly.

1835
- Ferdinand I becomes Emperor of Austria.
- Carlists failed to capture Bilbao.
- Municipal Reform Act.
- Electric telegraph invented.
  - **DEATHS**
    James Hogg, Scottish poet.
    John Nash, English architect.

1836
- Thiers ministry in France: then Guizot ministry.
- Bilbao again relieved by Espartero from Carlist attack.
- Orange Lodges dissolved.
- Beginning of Chartist movement.
- Beginning of Great Trek of Boers away from British territory in South Africa.
- Martin Van Buren elected US President.

1837
- Molé ministry in France.
- Reign of Queen Victoria begins.
- Rebellion in Canada under Papineau and Mackenzie.
- Charles Dickens's *Pickwick Papers*.
  - **DEATHS**
    John Constable, English painter.
    Giacomo Leopardi, Italian poet.
    Alexander Sergeievich Pushkin, Russian poet.

1838
- Massacre of Boers by Zulu Chief, Dingaan.
- People's Charter published.
- Anti-Corn Law League founded by William Cobden and John Bright.
- Battle of Blood River: Boer revenge on Zulus,
- National Gallery opened.

1839
- Durham's Report on Canada submitted to British Parliament.
- War again between Sultan of Turkey and Muhammad Ali: Sultan's army invades Syria.
- Soult ministry in France.
- Treaty of London: final adjustment of Belgian frontiers and recognition by Holland.
- Battle of Nezib: Ibrahim's decisive victory over the Turks.
- Abdul Mejid becomes Sultan of Turkey.
- Prince Milos abdicates in Serbia.
- French conquest of Algeria completed.
- First Afghan War begins (ends 1842).
- Christian VIII, King of Denmark.

1840
- Penny postage introduced in Britain.
- Treaty of Waitangi between Captain Hobson and Maori chiefs establishes British sovereignty over New Zealand.
- Thiers ministry in France.
- O'Connell revives the Repeal Association.
- End of the Carlist War in Spain.
- Frederick William IV, King of Prussia.
- Convention of London: four Powers to Act against Muhammad Ali.

- Reactionary constitution imposed in Hanover.
- Beirut bombarded by Sir Charles Napier.
- Christina abdicates the Regency in Spain.
- Resignation of Thiers.
- Crete restored to Turkey.
- Acre taken by an allied fleet, mainly British.
- Union Act for Canada: responsible government granted.
- End of convict transportation to New South Wales, Australia.
- First Opium War between Britain and China on question of the opium trade.
- Abdication of William I in Holland: William II succeeds.
- William Henry Harrison elected US President.
- David Livingstone begins his work in Africa.

1841
- Muhammad Ali submits to Sultan: becomes hereditary Pasha of Egypt.
- Espartero becomes Spanish Regent.
- John Tyler becomes President of US on death of Harrison.
- Hong Kong ceded to Britain by China.
- James Baird discovers hypnosis.

1842
- Death of Duke of Orleans: Regency Act in France.
- Alexander Karageorgevic becomes Prince of Serbia.
- Treaty between Britain and China ends First Opium War: several ports opened.
  DEATHS
  Thomas Arnold, English educator.
  Stendhal, French novelist.

1843
- Entente Cordiale between France and Britain.
- Natal declared British.
- Battle of Miani: Napier conquers Sind.
- Counter-revolution in Spain: flight of Espartero; Narvaez in power.

1844
- Oscar I King of Sweden and Norway.
- France annexes Tahiti.
- Otto compelled to grant a constitution in Greece.
- Railway Act.
- Bank Charter Act.
- James Knox Polk elected US President.

1845
- Catholic Sonderbund formed in Switzerland.
- Failure of the potato crop in Ireland.
- First Sikh War.
- Texas annexed by the US.

1846
- Pius IX becomes Pope.
- Repeal of the Corn Laws.
- Entente Cordiale (Britain and France) broken off on question of Spanish marriages.
- Austria absorbs Cracow.
- War between US and Mexico, due to annexation of Texas by former.

1847
- Austrian occupation of Ferrara.
- Federal Diet in Switzerland declares dissolution of Sonderbund.
- Swiss Federal general, Dufour, takes Fribourg and Lucerne; crushes the Sonderbund.

- Ten Hours Act in Britain.
- Mexico occupied by US troops.
- French defeat and capture Abd-el-Kader in Algeria.
- William Makepeace Thackeray's *Vanity Fair*.

1848

- Austrians crush disturbances in Milan.
- Rising in Palermo: Sicily soon freed, except fortress of Messina.
- Constitutional edict in Naples.
- Frederick VII, King of Denmark.
- Orange River Sovereignty named by Sir Harry Smith.
- Demand for a German National Parliament formulated in Baden Chamber.
- Constitution granted in Tuscany.
- February Revolution in Paris: Republic proclaimed; Lamartine a leader.
- Guizot dismissed.
- Louis Philippe abdicates.
- Neuchâtel proclaimed a Republic.
- Constitution granted in Piedmont.
- Insurrection in Vienna: resignation and flight of Metternich; end of Absolutist Reaction.
- Constitution granted in Rome: Republic proclaimed, with Mazzini at its head.
- Hungary gains the People's Charter: virtual autonomy.
- Successful insurrection in Berlin.
- Successful revolution in Milan.
- Venice proclaimed a Republic.
- Charles Albert invades Lombardy (25 March).
- Tuscany declares war against Austria.
- Chartist demonstration in London a fiasco.
- Tuscan forces invade Lombardy.
- Pope disclaims the Italian cause.
- Prussia occupies Schleswig and invades Jutland.
- Neapolitan constitution dropped.
- Flight of Emperor Ferdinand.
- German National Assembly at Frankfort.
- Battle of Goito: Piedmontese victory over Austrians.
- Radetzky overruns Venetia.
- National Workshops in Paris: soon abolished.
- Cavaignac suppresses a Paris insurrection.
- Archduke John elected Reichsverweser by Frankfort Assembly.
- Reichstag meets at Vienna.
- Battle of Custozza: Charles Albert defeated by Radetzky.
- Union of Venetia and Piedmont declared: soon overthrown.
- Radetzky reoccupies Milan.
- Salasco armistice.
- Truce of Malmoe between Denmark and Prussia.
- Battle of Boomplaats: Boers defeated by Sir Harry Smith.
- New Swiss Federal constitution.
- Hungary invaded by Jellachich, Ban of Croatia.
- Austria declares war against Hungary.
- Vienna again in revolution.
- Battle of Schwechat: defeat and retreat of Hungarian army.
- Vienna falls to Windischgrätz.
- New Dutch constitution.

- Flight of Pius IX to Gaeta.
- Ferdinand forced to abdicate: Francis Joseph becomes Austrian Emperor.
- Prince Louis Napoleon Bonaparte elected President of France for four years.
- Second Sikh War erupts in India: Punjab annexed.
- Transportation of leaders of Young Ireland.
- Treaty of Guadalupe Hidalgo cedes New Mexico, California and Texas from Mexico to the US.
- Gold discovered in California.
- Zachary Taylor elected US President.

REVOLUTION AND NATIONALISM

1849

- Battle of Kápolna: Hungarians defeated in bloody battle.
- William III, King of Holland.
- Battle of Novara: Radetzky defeats Charles Albert.
- Battle of Chilianwala: Gough defeats the Sikhs.
- Battle of Gujrat: Gough crushes the Sikhs.
- Punjab annexed to British India.
- Charles Albert abdicates in favour of Victor Emmanuel II.
- Frankfort Assembly chooses King of Prussia as German Emperor: King of Prussia declines.
- Schleswig-Holstein War reopened.
- Twenty-eight German states accept Frankfort Constitution of the Empire.
- Hungary declares itself a republic, at instance of Kossuth.
- Prussia rejects the Frankfort Constitution.
- French under Oudinot land in Italy to suppress Roman Republic: Garibaldi repels them at first, but Rome falls.
- Russia helps Austria to suppress Hungarian revolution.
- Revolt in Bavarian Palatinate.
- Prussians suppress revolt in Dresden.
- Revolt in Baden: provisional government formed.
- Sicilian revolution crushed by Naples.
- Haynau's brutality at Brescia.
- Austrians enter Florence.
- Garibaldi repulses the Neapolitans.
- Hungarians under Görgei take Budapest.
- Windischgrätz suppresses the Prague insurrection.
- Austrians take Budapest.
- Prussians suppress Baden revolution.
- Battle of Segesvár: Hungarians under Bem routed.
- Death of Muhammad Ali: Abbas I succeeds in Egypt.
- Battle of Szöreg:Haynau defeats Hungarians.
- Battle of Temesvar: Hungarians defeated.
- Abdication and flight of Kossuth.
- Surrender of Görgei and a Hungarian army at Világos.
- Venice surrenders to Austrians.
- Flight of Pope to Gaeta.
- Complete repeal of Navigation Laws in Britain.
  DEATHS
  Edgar Allan Poe, US author.

1850
- Erfurt Parliament called by Prussia.
- Saxony and Hanover withdraw from the Three Kings' League.
- Pius IX returns to Rome.
- Dispute between Greece and Britain over Don Pacifico.
- Peace of Berlin ends Schleswig-Holstein War.
- Cavour, Prime Minister in Piedmont.
- Olmütz 'Punctuation': Austria and Prussia adjust Hesse-Cassel question.
- Millard Fillmore becomes US President on death of Taylor.
- Tennyson's *In Memoriam*.
  DEATHS
  Sir Robert Peel, British statesman.

1851
- Secret Alliance between Austria and Prussia.
- First Australian goldfield opened.
- Louis Napoleon's coup d'état in France: victorious on a plebiscite.
- Palmerston dismissed from Foreign Office for unauthorized recognition of the French coup d'état.
- Austrian constitution abolished.
- Catholic hierarchy restored in Britain and Holland.
- Start of the T'ai-p'ing Rebellion in China.
- The Great Exhibition in London.
  DEATHS
  William Turner, English painter.

1852
- Sand River Convention: Britain recognizes independence of Transvaal in South Africa.
- Hereditary Empire restored in France: Louis Napoleon becomes Napoleon III.
- Enrico Tazzoli hanged in Italy: 'Mantuan Trials'.
- Annexation of Lower Burma by Britain.
- Fall of Derby ministry.
- Franklin Pierce elected US President.
- Harriet Beecher Stowe's *Uncle Tom's Cabin*.

1853
- Montenegrins defeat Turkish expedition against them.
- American naval commander, Perry, in Japan.
- Pedro V, King of Portugal.
- Orange River Sovereignty abandoned by Britain.

1854
- German Zollverein practically complete.
- Orange Free State established in South Africa.
- British and French troops occupy the Piraeus.
- Said Pasha, ruler in Egypt.
- Revolt in Madrid: Espartero becomes Premier.
- British and French troops land in the Crimea: beginning of Crimean War.
- Battle of the Alma: Russians defeated.
- Siege of Sebastopol begins.
- Battle of Balaklava: 'Charge of the Light Brigade'; drawn.
- Battle of Inkerman: Russians defeated.
- Missouri Compromise repealed in US.

1855
- Sardinia joins Britain and France in Crimean War.

- Alexander II, Tsar of Russia.
- Fall of Sebastopol.
  DEATHS
  Charlotte Brontë, English novelist.

1856
- Treaty of Paris ends Crimean War.
- Annexation of Oude to British India.
- James Buchanan elected US President.
  DEATHS
  Heinrich Heine, German poet.

1857
- *Arrow* incident in China leads to Second Opium War: Palmerston defeated in Parliament; appeals to the country and obtains a majority.
- Outbreak of Indian Mutiny at Meerut.
- Prussia relinquishes control over Neuchâtel.
- Massacre of Cawnpore.
- Havelock's relief of Lucknow.
- British take Delhi Palace.
- Campbell relieves Lucknow.
- Bank Charter Act suspended.
  DEATHS
  Honoré de Balzac, French novelist.

1858
- Orsini's attempt on life of Napoleon III.
- Occupation of Lucknow.
- Treaty of Aigun: Russia obtains from China a large part of Amur basin.
- Cavour and Napoleon III meet at Plombières.
- Sir Hugh Rose takes Gwalior.
- Harris Treaty: US trade treaty with Japan.
- Government of India transferred to the Crown: title of Viceroy given to Lord Canning.

1859
- Milos restored as Prince of Serbia.
- War between Austria and Piedmont: Austria invades Piedmont.
- Battle of Montebello: Austrians defeated by Piedmontese.
- Battle of Palestro: Austrians defeated by Piedmontese.
- Battle of Magenta: French defeat Austrians and free Milan.
- Battle of Melegnano: French defeat Austrians.
- Battle of Solferino: Austrians defeated by French and Piedmontese.
- Peace of Villafranca between France and Austria; Italy gains Lombardy.
- The duchies declare for union with Piedmont.
- Union of Moldavia and Wallachia under Prince Cuza: joint state becomes known as Romania.
- Spain at war with Morocco.
- Treaty of Zürich completes the Villafranca peace.
- Charles XV, King of Sweden and Norway.
- John Brown's attack on Harper's Ferry.
- Charles Darwin's *Origin of Species*.
  DEATHS
  Thomas de Quincey, English author.
  Alexis de Tocqueville, French author.

1860
- Commercial treaty between Britain and France negotiated by Richard Cobden.
- Tuscany and Emilia declare for union with Piedmont.
- Treaty of Turin between France and Piedmont: France given Nice and Savoy.
- Revolution in Sicily: Garibaldi lands.
- Battle of Calatafimi: Garibaldi's victory.
- Garibaldi enters Palermo.
- Battle of Milazzo: Garibaldi victorious.
- Garibaldi invades Italy: enters Naples, from which Francis II had fled.
- Piedmontese army in kingdom of Naples.
- Naples and Sicily voted for annexation to Piedmont.
- Meeting of Garibaldi and Victor Emmanuel II: former salutes latter as King of Italy.
- Marches and Umbria vote for annexation to Piedmont.
- The Liberal Decrees in France.
- Michael becomes Prince of Serbia.
- Treaty of Tientsin ends Second Opium War in China: more ports opened.
- Abraham Lincoln elected US President.
- Secession of Southern States: American Civil War begins.
- John Ruskin's *Modern Painters*.

1861
- William I becomes King of Prussia.
- Confederate States constituted in southern US: Jefferson Davis, President.
- Fall of Gaeta.
- First manifesto of serf emancipation in Russia.
- Kingdom of Italy proclaimed (17 May).
- Fort Sumter capitulates to the Confederates: first shots in American Civil War.
- Lebanon constitution.
- Battle of Bull Run: Northern Union army defeated by Confederates.
- Abdul Aziz becomes Sultan of Turkey.
- France, Britain and Spain intervene in Mexico.
- Luiz I, King of Portugal.

  DEATHS
  Elizabeth Barrett Browning, English poet.
  Count Camillo Cavour, Italian statesman.

1862
- Battle of Shiloh: Confederates defeated by Halleck.
- French troops enter Mexico: Maximilian of Austria proclaimed Emperor.
- Seven Days' Battles: Confederate victories; great loss of life on both sides.
- Garibaldi at Palermo.
- *The Alabama* sets out from Britain.
- Cotton famine in Lancashire.
- Garibaldi invades southern Italy.
- Battle of Aspromonte: Garibaldi defeated and taken prisoner.
- Second Battle of Bull Run: Confederates under Lee defeat Union army.
- Montenegrin war ended by Convention of Scutari.
- Speke and Grant discover sources of the Nile.
- Bismarck becomes Prussian minister.
- Battle of Antietam: Confederates under Lee and Union army under McClellan; drawn.
- Lincoln's first Emancipation Proclamation.
- King Otho deposed in Greece.

- Battle of Fredericksburg: Union army under Burnside completely defeated.
  DEATHS
  Henry David Thoreau, US author.

1863
- Battle of Murfreesborough: Confederates defeated by Rosecrans.
- Uprising in Poland against Russia.
- Ismail Pasha succeeds in Egypt.
- New constitution proclaimed for Schleswig and Holstein: indignation in Germany.
- Prince William of Schleswig-Holstein elected King of Greece as George I.
- Battle of Chancellorsville: Lee defeats Union army under Hooker; Stonewall Jackson killed.
- Battle of Gettysburg: Lee defeated by Union army under Meade.
- Vicksburg captured for the North by Ulysses S. Grant.
- Battle of Chickamauga: Union army defeated in fierce battle.
- Christian IX, King of Denmark.
- Battle of Chattanooga: Confederates defeated by Grant.
- Saxon and Hanoverian troops invade Holstein.
- Fenian Secret Society founded in Ireland to set up Irish republic.
  DEATHS
  Ferdinand Delacroix, French painter.
  W. M. Thackeray, English novelist.

1864
- War declared against Denmark by Prussia and Austria.
- Battles of the Wilderness and Spotsylvania: indecisive struggles between Lee and Grant.
- Britain cedes the Ionian Islands to Greece.
- Battle of Cold Harbour: Grant defeated by Lee.
- Russia completes subjugation of the Caucasus.
- Geneva Convention regarding sick and wounded in war.
- End of T'ai-p'ing Rebellion in China.
- Danish government hands over Schleswig and Holstein to Prussia and Austria.
- Atlanta captured by Union troops under Sherman.
- Pius IX issued the Bull Quanta Cura and the Syllabus: Papal war against modern enlightenment and progress.
- Battle of Franklin: Confederates under Hood crushingly defeated.
- Battle of Nashville: Hood defeated by Union army under Thomas.
- Sherman captures Savannah for the North.
- International Working Men's Association founded in London.
  DEATHS
  John Clare, English poet.

1865
- Richmond evacuated by the Confederates.
- Lee surrenders at Appomattox: end of American Civil War.
- Assassination of Lincoln: Andrew Johnson becomes US President.
- Convention of Gastein between Prussia and Austria.
- Thirteenth Amendment of US Constitution abolishes slavery.
- Leopold II, King of the Belgians.
- Russia acquires Tashkent.

1866
- Habeas Corpus Act suspended in Ireland.
- Treaty between Prussia and Italy.

- Austria declares war against Prussia.
- Italy declares war against Austria.
- Battle of Custozza: Italians defeated by Austrians.
- Battle of Lissa: naval defeat of Italians by Austrians.
- Hanoverians capitulate to Prussia.
- Battle of Königgrätz (Sadowa): Austrians under Benedek defeated by Prussians.
- Preliminaries of Nikolsburg between Austria and Prussia.
- Treaty of Prague between Prussia and Austria ends Seven Weeks' War.
- Treaty of Vienna between Austria and Italy: Italy obtains Venetia.
- Prince Charles becomes ruler of Romania.
- French withdraw from Rome.
- First Atlantic cable successfully laid.

1867
- Turkey agrees to withdraw her garrisons from Serbia.
- French withdraw from Mexico.
- British North America Act creates Dominion of Canada.
- Luxemburg made neutral.
- Title of Khedive granted by Sultan to the Viceroy of Egypt.
- Maximilian shot in Mexico.
- North German Confederation formed.
- Russia sells Alaska to US.
- Battle of Mentana: French help to defeat Garibaldi.
- Second Reform Act passed in Britain.
- Fenian outrages in London, Manchester, etc.
- Karl Marx's *Das Kapital*.
- Louisa May Alcott's *Little Women*.

  DEATHS
  Charles Pierre Baudelaire, French poet.
  J. A. D. Ingres, French painter.

1868
- Shogunate abolished in Japan: Mikado resumes the government.
- Benjamin Disraeli becomes British Prime Minister.
- Prince Michael of Serbia assassinated: Milan becomes Prince.
- Treaty between Russia and Bokhara giving Samarkand to former.
- Isabella II dethroned in Spain.
- Liberal triumph in British general election: William E. Gladstone, Prime Minister.
- President Andrew Johnson impeached in US: Ulysses S. Grant elected President.
- Hungarian autonomy established.

1869
- Suez Canal opened.
- Disestablishment and disendowment of Irish Church.

  DEATHS
  Hector Berlioz, French composer.

1870
- Ollivier ministry in France.
- Bulgarian Exarchate established.
- Leopold of Hohenzollern accepts offer of Spanish crown: candidature soon withdrawn: France insists on promise not to renew it.
- Bismarck modifies the Ems telegram.
- France declares war (14 July): beginning of Franco-Prussian War.
- Battle of Wörth: Macmahon defeated by Crown Prince Frederick.

- Battle of Spicheren: French defeated.
- Battle of Colombey: German failure; battle drawn.
- Battle of Vionville: drawn.
- Battle of Gravelotte: Bazaine defeated.
- French troops finally abandon Rome: Rome occupied by Italian troops and becomes capital of the kingdom of Italy.
- Battle of Sedan: capitulation of French army under Macmahon: the Emperor a prisoner.
- Republic proclaimed in France.
- Revolution in Paris: provisional government of National Defence.
- Capitulation of Bazaine in Metz.
- Russia denounces Black Sea clauses of Treaty of Paris.
- Germans driven out of Orleans, but reoccupy it later.
- Irish Land Act.
- Education Act for England and Wales.
- Prim assassinated in Madrid.
- Amadeo I, King of Spain.
- Red River Rebellion in Canada under Louis Riel: suppressed by Wolseley.
  DEATHS
  Charles Dickens, English novelist.

RELATIVE PEACE AND STABILITY

1871
- German Empire created at Versailles.
- Conference of London modifies Treaty of Paris of 1856.
- Bombardment of Paris: capitulation.
- Battle of Le Mans: Germans defeat Chanzy.
- Armistice between France and Germany.
- Bourbaki's army disarmed in Switzerland.
- National Assembly at Bordeaux: ratifies peace and deposes Napoleon III.
- Paris Commune set up: notable buildings destroyed.
- Treaty of Frankfort between France and Germany.
- Treaty of Washington: Alabama claims submitted to arbitration.
- Paris Commune suppressed with great cruelty.
- Thiers becomes President of the French Republic.
- Beginning of legislation legalizing trade unions in Britain.

1872
- League of the Three Emperors: informal alliance between Austria-Hungary, Germany and Russia.
- Oscar II, King of Sweden and Norway.
- Geneva award in Alabama case.
- Education Act for Scotland.
- Ballot Act passed.
- Rebellion against Spain in the Philippines.
- Self-government in Cape Colony.
  DEATHS
  Grillparzer, Austrian dramatist.
  Samuel F. B. Morse, US inventor.

1873
- Abdication of Amadeo in Spain: Republic proclaimed.
- Russia takes Khiva.
- The Kulturkampf in Germany.

- Macmahon President in France.
- German troops evacuate France after indemnity had been paid.
  DEATHS
  David Livingstone, Scottish explorer.

1874
- Disraeli, Prime Minister after general election.
- New Federal Constitution for Switzerland.
- Treaty between Germany and Russia.
- Patronage Act repealed in Scotland.
- Alfonso XII, King of Spain.

1875
- Insurrection in Herzegovina.
- Britain annexes the Fiji Islands.
- Russia obtains Sakhalin.
- Treaty between Japan and Korea.
- Telephone invented by Alexander Graham Bell.

1876
- Disraeli buys Khedive's shares in Suez Canal for Britain.
- International control begins in Egypt.
- Russia annexes Khokand.
- Bulgarian massacres.
- Serbia declares war against Turkey.
- Murad V, Sultan on deposition of Abdul Aziz: soon replaced by Abdul Hamid II.
- Rutherford Hayes elected US President.
  DEATHS
  George Sand, French author.

1877
- Queen Victoria proclaimed Empress of India.
- Russo-Turkish War begins.
- Romania declared independent.
- Siege and capture of Plevna.
- Britain annexes Transvaal in South Africa.
- Satsuma rebellion in Japan.
- Porfirio Diaz becomes President of Mexico.
- Great Indian famine.
- Sir Henry Morton Stanley explores the Congo.
  DEATHS
  Gustave Courbet, French painter.

1878
- Humbert I, King of Italy.
- Russians take Adrianople: Montenegrins take Antivari, Dulcigno, etc.
- Leo XIII becomes Pope.
- Austria occupies Bosnia and Herzegovina.
- Treaty of San Stefano between Russia and Turkey.
- Treaty of Berlin replaces Treaty of San Stefano: Serbia and Romania independent; Bulgaria autonomous; Macedonia restored to Turkey.
- Cyprus placed under British administration.
- Second Afghan War begins (ends in 1880).

1879
- Anglo-Zulu War.
- Prince Alexander, first Prince of Bulgaria.
- Dual control in Egypt: Britain and France.

- Alliance of Austria and Germany.
- Grévy, President in France.
- Henry George's *Progress and Poverty*.

1880
- Gladstone, Prime Minister after a general election.
- Britain recognized Abdurrahman as Amir of Afghanistan.
- Turkey cedes part of Thessaly to Greece.
- Montenegro obtains Dulcigno.
- Revolt of Boers in the Transvaal leads to first Anglo-Boer War.
- James Garfield elected US President.
    DEATHS
    Jacques Offenbach, French composer.

1881
- Battle of Majuba Hill: British defeated by Boers; end of first Anglo-Boer War.
- Murder of Tsar Alexander II: Alexander III succeeds.
- France occupies Tunis.
- Transvaal independence recognized.
- Irish Land Act.
- Murder of President Garfield: Chester Arthur becomes President of US.
- Gambetta, Chief Minister in France.
- Romania declares itself a kingdom.
- Revolt of the Mahdi in the Sudan.
- French protectorate on Upper Niger.
    DEATHS
    Fyodor Mikhailovich Dostoyevsky, Russian novelist.

1882
- Triple Alliance formed: Austria, Germany and Italy.
- Serbia declares itself a kingdom.
- War between Serbia and Bulgaria.
- Phoenix Park murders in Dublin.
- Arabi Pasha, Egyptian Minister: national revolt against misgovernment.
- British fleet bombard Alexandria; followed by British occupation of Egypt.
- Battle of Tel-el-Kebir: Wolseley defeats Arabi Pasha.
    DEATHS
    Ralph Waldo Emerson, US poet.
    Henry Wordsworth Longfellow, US poet.

1883
- Destruction of Egyptian army under Hicks Pasha near El Obeid.
- French protectorate in Annam.
- Germany begins national insurance.
    DEATHS
    Gustave Doré, French artist.
    Edouard Manet, French painter.
    Ivan Turgenev, Russian novelist.
    Richard Wagner, German composer.

1884
- Sir Evelyn Baring (Lord Cromer), Consul-General in Egypt.
- Three Emperors' League revived.
- Gordon in Khartoum: besieged.
- Russia annexes Merv.
- Germany and Britain appropriate parts of New Guinea; Germany also acquires African colonies.

- French in Tonkin.
- Berlin Conference of the Powers regarding Africa.
- Convention of London between Britain and the Transvaal: Boer independence strengthened.
- Third Reform Act.
- Stephen Grover Cleveland elected US President.

1885

- Fall of Khartoum: Gordon killed: British and Egyptians evacuate the Sudan.
- Congo Free State constituted by the signatory powers at the Berlin Conference.
- Russians and Afghans in conflict at Penjdeh.
- Treaty of Tientsin between France and China.
- Regency of Maria Christina in Spain.
- Italians occupy Massowah.
- Bulgaria absorbs eastern Roumelia.
- Indian National Congress formed.
- 3rd Marquis of Salisbury, Prime Minister.
- Serbia declares war against Bulgaria and suffers defeat.
- Second Rebellion in Canada under Louis Riel: Riel executed.
- Daimler invents his petrol engine.

1886

- William Gladstone becomes Prime Minister.
- Alfonso XIII born to be King of Spain.
- Gladstone introduces his first Home Rule Bill for Ireland: defeated in Commons.
- The Plan of Campaign in Ireland.
- Treaty of Bucharest settles Serbo-Bulgarian War.
- Abdication of Prince Alexander in Bulgaria: Stambuloff, the leading statesman.
- Britain annexes Upper Burma; Upper and Lower Burma united under British India.
- Royal Niger Company formed.
- Canadian Pacific Railway completed.
- Gold discovered in the Transvaal.
- East Africa divided between Germany and Britain.

1887

- Jubilee of Queen Victoria.
- First Colonial Conference.
- Prince Ferdinand elected ruler of Bulgaria.
- Treaty between France and China.
- Marie François Carnot, President in France.

1888

- Frederick III, German Emperor: soon succeeded by William II.
- British protectorate declared over parts of Borneo.
- Treaty between Russia and Korea.
- County councils created in Britain.
- Parnell Commission.
- William Henry Harrison elected US President.

1889

- Abdication of Milan in Serbia: Alexander becomes King.
- Flight of General Boulanger: end of Boulangism in France.
- Franco-Russian entente.
- British South Africa Company formed.
- Pedro II deposed in Brazil: Brazil becomes a Republic.
- Carlos I, King of Portugal.

- Treaty between Italy and Abyssinia.
  DEATHS
  Robert Browning, English poet.

1890
- Wilhelmina Queen of Holland.
- Fall of Bismarck.
- Britain cedes Heligoland to Germany.
- British protectorate over Zanzibar.
- French protectorate over Madagascar.
- First Japanese Parliament.
- Sherman Anti-Trust Act in US.

1891
- Trans-Siberian Railway begun.
- Agreement between Britain and Portugal regarding East Africa.
- Great famine in Russia.
  DEATHS
  Georges Seurat, French painter.

1892
- Abbas II becomes Khedive of Egypt.
- Panama scandals in France.
- France annexes the Ivory Coast.
- Indian Councils Act.
- Gladstone, Prime Minister after a general election.
- Cleveland again elected US President.
  DEATHS
  Alfred, Lord Tennyson, English poet.

1893
- Matabele War in Rhodesia.
- Natal granted responsible government.
- Gladstone's second Home Rule Bill rejected by the Lords.
- New Zealand adopts women's suffrage.
- Behring Sea arbitration between Britain and the US.

1894
- Nicholas II becomes Tsar.
- Gladstone resigns: Rosebery becomes Prime Minister.
- Murder of President Carnot in France: Casimir-Périer elected successor.
- Trial and condemnation of Dreyfus in France.
- Armenian massacres.
- First Sino-Japanese War between Japan and China: latter easily defeated.
- Return of King Milan in Serbia.
- British protectorate over Uganda.
- Motor vehicles become common.
  DEATHS
  Oliver Wendell Holmes, US author.
  Christina Rossetti, English poet.

1895
- Franco-Russian alliance.
- Salisbury again Prime Minister: Conservative victory at general election.
- Jameson Raid in South Africa fails.
- François Félix Faure, President in France.
- Murder of Stambuloff in Bulgaria.
- British ultimatum to the Transvaal.

- Armenian massacres.
- X-rays discovered by Röntgen.

1896
- Franco-British treaty regarding Siam.
- France annexes Madagascar.
- Insurrection in Crete: international intervention.
- Battle of Adowa: Italians heavily defeated in Abyssinia.
- Outbreak of plague in India.
- William McKinley elected US President.
- Guglielmo Marconi perfects wireless telegraphy.
  DEATHS
  Edmund de Goncourt, French author.

1897
- Queen Victoria's Diamond Jubilee.
- Massacre in Crete: international occupation.
- War between Greece and Turkey: Turkey victorious.
- Autonomy proclaimed for Crete.
- Revolt of tribes on Indian north-west frontier.
- Germany seizes Kiao-chow in China.
- Philippine revolt against Spain.

1898
- US declares war against Spain.
- Egyptian army under Kitchener take Omdurman and reconquer the Sudan.
- The French under Marchand at Fashoda.
- Dargai stormed: Indian frontier rebellion ended.
- Treaty of Paris between Spain and US: Spain loses her American possessions and also the Philippines.
- Russia obtains Port Arthur from China.
- Britain obtains Wei Hai Wei and Hong Kong New Territories on lease from China.
- US annexes Hawaii.
- Prince George of Greece, High Commissioner in Crete.
- Irish Local Government Act.
- Radium discovered.
- Oscar Wilde's *The Ballad of Reading Gaol*.
- Henry James's *The Turn of the Screw*.
- H. G. Wells's *The War of the Worlds*.
  DEATHS
  Lewis Carroll, English author.
  Aubrey Beardsley, English illustrator.

1899
- Loubet, President in France.
- First Peace Conference at The Hague.
- End of Dreyfus affair in France.
- Outbreak of Second Anglo-Boer War.
- Ladysmith, Mafeking and Kimberley besieged by Boers.
- Germany and the US annexe and share Samoa Islands.
- Venezuela boundary question settled.
- Gold discovered in Klondyke.
- The Khalifa defeated and killed in the Sudan.
- Battle of Modder River: Boers defeated by Lord Methuen.
- Battle of Stormberg: Boers defeat Gatacre.
- Battle of Magersfontein: Boers defeat Methuen.

- Battle of the Tugela: Boers defeat Buller.
- United Irish League formed.
- Wladyslaw Reymont's *The Promised Land*.
- Edward Elgar's *Enigma Variations*.
  DEATHS
  Robert Bunsen, German chemist.
  Alfred Sisley, French painter.

1900

- Boer War: Boers attack Ladysmith (6 January); Field Marshal Lord Roberts takes command of British forces (10 January); relief of Kimberley (15 February); relief of Ladysmith (28 February) and Mafeking (17 May); British annexe Orange Free State (26 May) and Transvaal (25 October).
- Nigeria becomes British protectorate.
- Boxer Rebellion against Europeans in China begins.
- Victor Emmanuel III, King of Italy after assassination of Humbert I.
- British archaeologist, Sir Arthur Evans, begins excavation of Knossos on Crete.
- Ramsay MacDonald named as Secretary of newly organized Labour Representation Committee.
- World Exhibition opens in Paris.
- William McKinley re-elected as US President.
- Russia annexes Manchuria.
- Conservative Party returned to power with large majority in 'Khaki Election'.
  DEATHS
  Gottlieb Daimler, German motor-car designer.
  Sir Charles Grove, British musicologist.
  Casey Jones, US railway engineer.
  Friedrich Nietzsche, German philosopher.
  Sir Arthur Sullivan, British composer.
  Oscar Wilde, British author.

1901

- Commonwealth of Australia founded.
- Queen Victoria dies and is succeeded by Edward VII.
- Philippine revolt suppressed by US.
- Student rioters in St Petersburg dispersed by Cossacks.
- William McKinley assassinated; Theodore Roosevelt becomes US President.
- Peking Treaty ends Boxer Rebellion in China.
- Britain's first submarine launched.
- Trans-Siberian Railway opened.
- Marconi transmits telegraphic signal across the Atlantic from Cornwall to Newfoundland.
- Invention of the vacuum cleaner by Hubert Cecil Booth.
- First Nobel Prizes awarded in fields of literature, chemistry, physics, peace and medicine.
  DEATHS
  Henri de Toulouse-Lautrec, French painter.

1902

- Anglo-Japanese Alliance.
- Treaty between China and Russia over Manchuria.
- Treaty of Vereeniging ends Second Anglo-Boer War.
- Arthur Balfour becomes Prime Minister.
- Aswan Dam completed in Egypt.

DEATHS

Friedrich Krupp, German steel magnate.

Cecile Rhodes, British statesman.

Émile Zola, French writer.

1903

- Pius X becomes Pope.
- King Alexander I and Queen Draga of Serbia murdered: Peter I becomes King.
- Anti-Semitic pogroms in Russia.
- Mrs Emmeline Pankhurst forms Women's Social and Political Union to agitate for votes for women.
- US recognizes Panama as independent republic and leases Canal Zone.
- Turkish troops massacre Bulgarians in Macedonia.
- Orville and Wilbur Wright fly heavier-than-air aircraft at Kitty Hawk.
- Commander Robert Scott and Lieutenant Ernest Shackleton travel further towards the South Pole than any previous expedition.

DEATHS

Dr Richard Gatling, US rapid-fire gun inventor.

Paul Gaugin, French painter.

Herbert Spencer, English philosopher.

James McNeill Whistler, US painter.

Camille Pissarro, French artist.

1904

- Russo-Japanese War begins.
- US occupation of Cuba ends.
- Rebellious tribesmen massacre German settlers in South West Africa.
- Anglo-French Entente signed: aimed at solving all outstanding grievances.
- Theodore Roosevelt wins US presidential election.
- British military expedition to Tibet captures Lhasa (3 August); Anglo-Tibetan Treaty signed giving Britain exclusive trading rights (7 September).

DEATHS

Frederic Bartholdi, French sculptor.

Anton Chekhov, Russian writer.

Antonin Dvoràk, Czech composer.

Theodor Herzl, Hungarian-born Zionist.

Paul Kruger, Boer leader.

Henri Fantin-Latour, French painter.

Friedrich Siemens, German industrialist.

Sir Henry Morton Stanley, British explorer.

1905

- Russo-Japanese War: Japanese capture Port Arthur (5 January); Russians routed by Japanese at Battle of Mukden (10 March); Battle of Tsushima, Russian navy destroyed (28 May); Japanese capture Sakhalin (31 July); Treaty of Portsmouth ends conflict (5 September).
- Russian Grand Duke Sergei killed in bomb attack.
- Earthquake in India claims 10,000 victims.
- Norway separated from Sweden: Haakon VII becomes King of Norway.
- Riots in St Petersburg crushed by Tsarist police (22 January); first workers' soviet formed; sailors mutiny on battleship 'Potemkin' (27 June); revolt by students and workers in Moscow crushed by Tsarist troops (30 December).
- Sinn Fein founded in Dublin.
- Liberal leader, Henry Campbell-Bannerman, becomes Prime Minister.

- Automobile Association founded.

  DEATHS

  Thomas John Bernado, Irish-born doctor and philanthropist.

  Sir Henry Irving, British actor.

  Jules Verne, French writer.

1906

- First Duma (elected parliament with limited powers) convened in Russia.
- San Francisco destroyed by earthquake and fire.
- General election in Britain results in Liberal landslide victory: first Labour MPs returned to Parliament.
- Algeciras Conference on Franco-German crisis over Morocco: dispute settled in favour of France.
- Self-government granted to Transvaal in South Africa.
- Mount Vesuvius erupts leaving hundreds dead.
- Armand Fallières, President in France.
- Frederick VIII, King of Denmark.
- Simplon Tunnel opened for railway traffic.
- Campaign for women's suffrage gathers strength.
- Vitamins discovered by Frederick G. Hopkins.

  DEATHS

  Pierre Curie, French physicist.

  Henrik Ibsen, Norwegian playwright.

  Albert Sorel, French historian.

1907

- Earthquake devastates Kingston in Jamaica.
- Orange River Colony in South Africa becomes independent as Orange Free State.
- Lawyer, Mahatma Gandhi, leads civil disobedience movement ('Satyagraha') in South Africa.
- Second Hague Peace Conference.
- New Zealand gains Dominion status within the British Empire.
- Boy Scouts founded by Sir Robert Baden-Powell.
- Belgian Parliament votes to annexe the Congo and end absolute rule over the central African territory by King Leopold.
- Gustavus V succeeds Oscar II as King of Sweden.
- Cunard ship, the *Mauretania*, the world's largest liner, leaves Liverpool on her maiden voyage.

  DEATHS

  Edvard Grieg, Norwegian composer.

  William Howard Russell, British journalist.

  Dmitri Mendeleev, Russian chemist.

  William Thomson, Lord Kelvin, British physicist.

1908

- Carlos I of Portugal and Crown Prince Luiz assassinated: Manuel II becomes King.
- Herbert Henry Asquith becomes Prime Minister after resignation of Sir Henry Campbell-Bannerman.
- Old age pensions introduced in Britain.
- King Edward VII is first British monarch to visit Russia.
- Mass demonstration of suffragettes in Hyde Park, London.
- Young Turks revolutionary movement forces Sultan Abdul Hamid II to restore the Turkish constitution.
- Bulgaria declares independence from Ottoman Empire.
- Austria annexes Bosnia-Herzegovina.

- Over 200,00 people killed in earthquake in southern Italy and Messina in Sicily, the most violent tremor ever recorded in Europe.
- William Howard Taft elected US President.
- Ford Motor Company produces first 'Model T' motor car.
- In Paris, Henri Farman makes the first aeroplane flight with a passenger.
- Franco-British Exhibition opens in London.

DEATHS

Henri Becquerel, French physicist.

Joel Chandler Harris, US author.

Nikolai Rimsky-Korsakov, Russian composer.

Rev. Benjamin Waugh, founder of the National Society for the Prevention of Cruelty to Children.

1909

- Chancellor of the Exchequer, Lloyd-George, introduces radical 'People's Budget' (April); vetoed by the House of Lords (November).
- Japanese statesman, Prince Hirobumi Ito, assassinated.
- North Pole reached by US explorer, Commander Robert E. Peary.
- Louis Blériot crosses the English Channel for the first time in an aeroplane.
- Young Turks celebrate as Turkish Parliament forces Sultan Abdul Hamid to abdicate in favour of reformist Muhammad V.
- US store, Selfridge's, opens branch in Oxford Street, London.
- The first bra is announced in American *Vogue*; it is patented in 1914 by Mary Phelps Jacob.

DEATHS

Geronimo, Apache chief.

George Meredith, British writer.

John Synge, Irish playwright.

1910

- Liberals cling on to power in general elections in January and December as crisis over the Budget and the power of the House of Lords escalates.
- Labour exchanges established in Britain.
- Edward VII dies and is succeeded by George V.
- Union of South Africa formed.
- Japan annexes Korea.
- Montenegro declares itself a Kingdom.
- King Manuel overthrown in Portugal: Republic proclaimed.
- Captain Robert Scott sets out on expedition to South Pole.
- Girl Guides founded by Sir Robert Baden-Powell.

DEATHS

Henri Dunant, Swiss founder of the Red Cross.

William Holman Hunt, British painter.

Julia Ward Howe, US women's campaigner.

Robert Koch, German bacteriologist.

Samuel Langhorne Clemens (Mark Twain), US writer.

Florence Nightingale, British nursing pioneer.

Henri Rousseau, French painter.

Count Leo Tolstoy, Russian writer.

1911

- Armed troops and police besiege Anarchist hideout in house in Sidney Street, London.
- James Ramsay MacDonald elected Chairman of the Labour Party to succeed Keir Hardie.

- French move to suppress revolt in Morocco.
- Mexican dictator, Porfirio Diaz, deposed by rebels.
- Parliament Act reduces the power of the House of Lords.
- Payment of MPs begins in Britain.
- Coronation of George V.
- Assassination of Peter Stolypin, the Russian Premier.
- Italy declares war against Turkey over Italian claim on Tripoli: Tripoli annexed by Italy.
- Chinese revolution: Manchu Dynasty overthrown (October); Dr Sun Yat Sen elected president of the new Chinese Republic (December).
- Andrew Bonar Law chosen to succeed Balfour as leader of the Conservative Party.
- Franco-German Treaty recognizes French demand for protectorate in Morocco.
- Norwegian explorer, Roald Amundsen, beats Captain Robert Scott to the South Pole.
  DEATHS
  Sir William Gilbert, librettist.
  Gustav Mahler, Austrian composer.

1912
- Mass rallies in Ulster to protest at proposals for home rule for Ireland (January); Third Home Rule for Ireland Bill passed by Commons (May); 'Solemn Covenant' to oppose home rule signed at mass rally of Ulster Loyalists led by Sir Edward Carson (September).
- Militant suffragettes riot in the West End of London.
- Coal Mines Act establishes principle of a minimum wage.
- The *Titanic* sinks in the Atlantic with the loss of 1,513 lives.
- Yoshihito becomes Emperor of Japan.
- Right of France to establish a protectorate over Morocco ceded in Fez Treaty.
- Peace of Ouchy between Italy and Turkey signed in Switzerland: Italy acquires Tripoli.
- War between Turkey and the Balkan States: Bulgarian and Serbian forces inflict a series of defeats on Turkey.
- Democrat Woodrow Wilson elected US President.
  DEATHS
  General William Booth, founder of Salvation Army.
  Joseph, Lord Lister, British pioneer of antiseptic.
  August Strindberg, Swedish playwright.
  Samuel Coleridge-Taylor, British composer.
  Jules Massenet, French composer.
  Wilbur Wright, US pioneer aviator.

1913
- Young Turks depose government of Grand Vizier Kiamil Pasha in Turkey.
- Bodies of explorers Captain Robert Falcon Scott and companions discovered in the Antarctic.
- Suffragette Emily Davison dies after throwing herself in front of the King's horse during the Derby.
- Raymond Poincaré elected President of French Republic.
- King George I of Greece murdered: Constantine I succeeds.
- Treaty of Bucharest settles Balkan wars: increases of territory to Serbia, Greece, Montenegro, Bulgaria and Romania; Turkey loses Macedonia, part of Thrace, Albania and most of the islands; Albanian kingdom founded.
- Panama Canal completed.
  DEATHS
  Alfred Austin, British poet.
  Rudolf Diesel, German engineer.

First World War

1914

- Irish Home Rule Act creates a separate parliament in Ireland with some MPs in Westminster.
- June: Murder of Archduke Franz Ferdinand, heir to Austrian throne, in Sarajevo, capital of Bosnia (28).
- July: Austria-Hungary declares war against Serbia (28).
- August: Germany declares war against Russia (1); Germany declares war against France (3); German invasion of Belgium (4); Britain declares war on Germany (4); British Expeditionary Force under Sir John French suffers heavy casualties at Battle of Mons (20–31); Japan declares war on Germany (23); Russians routed at Battle of Tannenberg on eastern front (31).
- September: Germans capture Rheims (5); Battle of the Marne (5–9); trench warfare begins on Aisne salient (16); three British cruisers sunk by a U-boat (22).
- October: First Battle of Ypres (12 Oct–11 Nov).
- November: Britain declares war against Turkey (5).
- December: Royal Navy destroys German squadron off the Falkland Islands (8); British protectorate over Egypt proclaimed (17).

  Deaths

  Henri Alain-Fournier, French writer.

  August Macke, German painter.

  Sir John Tenniel, British artist.

1915

- January: Turkish army surrenders to Russians in Central Asia (5); German Zeppelin raid on Norfolk towns (19); British sink German battleship *Blucher* in North Sea (24).
- February: German submarine blockade of Britain begins (2); Imperial troops repulse Turkish attack on Suez Canal (2); French begin offensive in Champagne on Western Front (12).
- March: Britain declares blockade of German ports (1); Battle of Neuve Chapelle (10–13); Naval attack on Dardanelles aborted (22).
- April: Second Battle of Ypres (22 April–25 May); Germans use gas for first time on Western Front (22); British, ANZAC and French troops land at Gallipoli (25).
- May: Sinking of the Cunard liner *Lusitania* (7); Battle of Aubers Ridge (9–25); Italy declares war on Austria (22); British coalition government formed (26).
- June: British pilot, Reginald Warneford, awarded VC for destroying a Zeppelin (8); Austrians retake Lemburg, capital of Galicia, from the Russians (23).
- July: Germans advance farther into Poland (3); General Botha accepts surrender of all German forces in South West Africa (9).
- August: Allied forces meet stubborn resistance at Gallipoli (13); Italy declares war on Turkey (20); Brest-Litovsk falls to the Germans (30).
- September: Allies breech German lines at Champagne and at Loos in Flanders (26); Turks defeated at Kut-el-Amara in Mesopotamia (28).
- October: Russia begins campaign against Bulgaria (8); British nurse, Edith Cavell, executed by Germans as a spy (12).
- November: Italians suffer heavy losses at Isonzo River (10); Serbia occupied by German-Austrian and Bulgarian forces (28).
- December: Sir Douglas Haig replaces Sir John French as British Commander on Western Front (15); French and British troops occupy Salonika (13); Allied troops begin evacuation of Gallipoli (20).

  Deaths

  Rupert Brooke, British poet.

Paul Ehrlich, German doctor and discoverer of diptheria antitoxin.

(James) Keir Hardie, British politician.

Alexander Skryabin, Russian composer.

1916

- January: conscription introduced, Britain (6); Montenegro captured by Austrians (20).
- February: Allies complete occupation of German colony of Cameroons (18); Battle of Verdun begins (21).
- March: US troops defeat Mexican rebels led by Pancho Villa (31).
- April: Easter Rising by Sinn Fein in Dublin (24); British forces surrender to Turks after fall of Kut-el-Amara (29).
- May: Battle of Jutland, only major sea battle of the war, in which both sides claim victory (31).
- June: Lord Kitchener drowned as cruiser *Hampshire* struck by a mine off the Orkneys (5); Arab revolt against Turkish rule (21); Russians led by General Brusilov capture Galicia from the Austrians (23).
- July: Battle of the Somme (1 July–13 Nov); Russians rout Turkish army at Erzinjan (27).
- August: Sir Roger Casement hanged in London for high treason (3); Italians capture Gorizia (10); Field Marshall Paul von Hindenburg appointed Chief of German General Staff (27); Romania declares war against Austria and Germany (27).
- September: Tanks first used by British on Western Front (15); Allies launch new offensive in Balkans (18).
- October: Allies occupy Athens (16); Captain T. E. Lawrence arrives in Jeddah to offer British support for Arab Revolt against Turkey (16); Second Battle of Verdun begins (24).
- November: Austro-Hungarian Emperor Franz Josef dies (21); Woodrow Wilson re-elected US President.
- December: General Joffre replaces General Robert Nivelle as head of French forces on the Somme (3); Lloyd George forms war cabinet as new Prime Minister (7); 'Mad Monk' Gregory Rasputin murdered by Russian nobles (30).

DEATHS

Sir Joseph Beecham, British pharmaceuticals manufacturer.

George Butterworth, British composer.

Henry James, US-born author.

Jack London, US author.

Henrik Sienkiewicz, Polish writer.

1917

- February: Unrestricted submarine warfare begins (1).
- March: In Russia, Tsar Nicholas II abdicates and provisional government established (16); British defeat Turks near Gaza (27).
- April: US declares war on Germany (6); Battle of Arras (9–14); Vimy Ridge captured by Canadian troops (10); German government helps Bolshevik leader, Vladimir Lenin, return to Russia (16).
- June: Messines Ridge taken by British (7); German aircraft carry out first bombing raid on London (14); first US troops land in France (26); General Edmund Allenby assumes Palestine command (29).
- July: Russian provisional government crushes Bolshevik uprising (16); Alexander Kerensky appointed Russian Prime Minister (22); Third Battle of Ypres begins (31).
- August: French break German lines at Verdun on 11-mile front (20).
- September: Kerensky proclaims Russia a republic (15); Germans expel Russians from Riga (17); the ex-Tsar and his family are moved to Siberia (30).

- October: British victory on Passchendaele Ridge (4); French victory on the Aisne (23); Italians routed by Austrians at Battle of Caporetto (24).
- November: Passchendaele captured by British (6); Bolshevik Revolution, Kerensky overthrown (7); Balfour Declaration recognizing Palestine as Jewish national home (8); Hindenburg lines smashed on 10-mile front (20).
- December: British take Jerusalem (9); Russo-German armistice (15); Bolsheviks open peace talks with Germans at Brest-Litovsk (22).

DEATHS

Colonel William F. Cody ('Buffalo Bill').
Edgar Degas, French painter.
Scott Joplin, US ragtime pianist and composer.
Auguste Rodin, French sculptor.

1918

- January: President Wilson outlines US war aims to Congress in his Fourteen Points (9); Lenin creates Red Army (28).
- February: Demoralized Russian army attacked by Germans in Estonia as Brest-Litovsk peace talks stall (20).
- March: Treaty of Brest-Litovsk (3); German offensive against British on the Somme opens (21); Battle of Arras (21 March–4 April).
- April: Second German offensive against British (9–25); General Ferdinand Foch appointed Commander of Allied armies (14); British naval raid on Belgian ports of Zeebrugge and Ostend (23).
- June: Conflict between Bolshevik Red Army and anti-Bolshevik White forces begins.
- July: Last German offensive against the French (15); ex-Tsar and his family shot by Bolsheviks in cellar in Ekaterinburg (16).
- August: Allied offensive near Amiens results in German collapse (8).
- September: Turkish army destroyed at Megiddo (19); Bulgarians sign armistice (29); Allied breakthrough along the whole Western Front (30).
- October: T. E. Lawrence leads Arabs into Damascus (1); Germany accepts President Wilson's Fourteen Points (23); Italian advance (24); surrender of Turkey (30).
- November: Austria accepts peace terms (4); Socialist Republic declared in Bavaria (7); Kaiser abdicates and escapes to Holland (9); Armistice signed by Germany (11).
- December: British women over 30 allowed to vote for first time.

DEATHS

Guillaume Apollinaire, French poet.
Claude Debussy, French composer.
Gustav Klimt, Austrian painter.
Wilfred Owen, British poet.
Egon Schiele, Austrian painter.

1919

- Peace Conference in Paris; Germany signs Treaty of Versailles; Treaty of St Germain leads to dissolution of the Austro-Hungarian Empire; kingdom of Serbs, Croats and Slovenes established, consisting of Serbia, Montenegro and former regions of the Austro-Hungarian Empire (Croatia, Slovenia and Bosnia-Herzegovina).
- Interned German fleet scuttled at Scapa Flow.
- Communist 'Sparticist' uprising suppressed in Berlin, leaders Rosa Luxemburg and Karl Liebknecht arrested and then killed.
- Third International founded in Moscow.
- Benito Mussolini founds Fascist party (Fasci de Combattimento) in Italy.
- Jan Christian Smuts, Prime Minister of South Africa after death of Louis Botha.
- President Wilson suffers a stroke.

- Red Army close to victory over White forces in the civil war in Russia.
- Nationalist uprisings in Egypt against British occcupation.
- Nancy Astor elected as first woman MP in Britain.
- Lloyd-George announces plan for the partition of Ireland.
- John Alcock and Arthur Brown fly nonstop across the Atlantic.

  DEATHS

  Andrew Carnegie, Scottish-born US philanthropist.
  Auguste Renoir, French artist.

THE TWENTIES AND THIRTIES

1920
- Peace Treaty ratified in Paris.
- First meeting of League of Nations in Paris: Germany, Austria, Russia and Turkey excluded; US Senate votes against US membership of League.
- French troops occupy the Ruhr.
- 18th Ammendment to US Constitution banning sale of alcohol goes into force: beginning of Prohibition.
- Treaty of Sévres concludes peace with Turkey and dissolves Ottoman Empire.
- Communist Party of Great Britain founded.
- Rebel leader Pancho Villa surrenders to Mexican government.
- Roscoe 'Fatty' Arbuckle charged with rape and murder of actress Virginia Rappe in Hollywood; later acquitted.
- 'Bloody Sunday': IRA kill 14 British soldiers in Ireland.
- Civil war in Russia ends with triumph of the Bolshevik Red Army.
- Warren G. Harding elected US President.
- King Constantine of Greece returns to Athens.

  DEATHS

  Amedeo Modigliani, Italian artist.

1921
- Spanish Prime Minister, Eduardo Dato, assassinated.
- First Indian Parliament opens.
- Anti-Bolshevik mutiny of Russian sailors at Kronstadt naval base.
- Lenin's New Economic Policy introduces limited free enterprise in Soviet Union.
- Reparations Commission fixes Germany's liability at 200 billion gold marks (£10 billion).
- British troops sent to quell rioting in Egypt.
- Japanese Premier, Takashi Hara, assassinated.
- Crown Prince Hirohito named Regent of Japan.
- Anglo-Irish Treaty establishes Irish Free State.
- Eduard Benes, Prime Minister of Czechoslovakia.
- British Broadcasting Company founded.

  DEATHS

  Enrico Caruso, Italian opera singer.
  John Boyd Dunlop, British inventor of the pneumatic tyre.
  Georges Feydeau, French playwright.
  Engelbert Humperdinck, German composer.

1922
- Cardinal Achille Ratti, Archbishop of Milan, elected Pope Pius XI.
- Four Power Pacific Treaty ratified by US Senate.
- Treaty of Rapallo between Germany and USSR restoring full diplomatic relations.
- Walter Rathenau, German foreign minister, assassinated.
- Irish Free State comes into force.

- King Constantine of Greece abdicates: succeeded by George II.
- Andrew Bonar Law is Prime Minister after resignation of Lloyd-George.
- Friedrich Ebert re-elected German President.
- Mussolini's 'March on Rome': Fascist government formed.
- Egypt achieves independence.
- Tomb of Tutankhamun discovered.
- James Joyce's *Ulysses*.

DEATHS

Alexander Graham Bell, inventor of the telephone.
Alfred Harmsworth, Lord Northcliffe, British newspaper proprietor.
Marcel Proust, French author.
Sir Ernest Shackleton, British Antarctic explorer.

1923

- Japanese earthquake: 300,000 dead in Tokyo and Yokohama.
- Miguel Primo de Rivera, dictator in Spain after army coup.
- French troops occupy the Rhineland to secure reparations.
- King George II deposed by Greek army.
- Stanley Baldwin becomes Prime Minister.
- Calvin Coolidge, President of US after death of Harding.
- Teapot Dome oil scandal in US.
- Turkish Republic proclaimed with Mustapha Kemal as first President.
- Failed attempt by Hitler attempts to overthrow the Weimar Republic in Munich (the 'Beer Hall Putsch').
- Catastrophic inflation in Germany: mark drops to 4 trillion to US dollar.

DEATHS

Sarah Bernhardt, French actress.
Gustav Eiffel, French engineer.
Jaroslav Hasek, Czech writer.
Katherine Mansfield, New Zealand-born writer.
Wilhelm Roentgen, pioneer of X-rays.

1924

- Vladimir Ilyich Lenin, founder of the USSR, dies.
- First Labour government elected (January): Ramsay MacDonald, Prime Minister.
- Britain recognizes USSR.
- Dawes Plan for restructuring the payment of German reparations to the Allies agreed at the London Conference; French and Belgians agree to the evacuation of the Ruhr.
- Greece proclaimed a Republic: King George II deposed by Greek Parliament.
- Publication of the Zinoviev letter allegedly from the Communist International inciting British communists to start a revolution.
- Mussolini's Fascists gain convincing victory in Italian general election.
- Stanley Baldwin is Prime Minister after Conservative victory in general election (October).
- J. Edgar Hoover appointed Director of the Federal Bureau of Investigation.

DEATHS

Frances Hodgson Burnett, British author.
Joseph Conrad, Polish-born British author.
Gabriel Fauré, French composer.
Anatole France, French author.
Franz Kafka, German author.
Edith Nesbit, British children's author.
Giacomo Puccini, Italian composer.

1925
- Field Marshall Paul von Hindenburg elected President of Germany.
- Treaty of Locarno signed in London.
- Cyprus becomes a British colony.
- Rheza Khan, King of Persia.
- Tennessee school teacher, John T. Scopes, found guilty of teaching evolution in a state school and fined $100.
- Queen Alexandria, widow of King Edward VII, dies.
- Adolph Hitler's *Mein Kampf.*
- F. Scott Fitzgerald's *Great Gatsby.*
  ### DEATHS
  William Jennings Bryan, US Democratic politician.
  H. Rider Haggard, British author.
  John Singer Sargent, US artist.

1926
- General Strike in Britain disrupts industry for nine days.
- Abdul Aziz ibn Saud proclaimed King of the Hejaz: he names the province, Saudi Arabia.
- British troops end occupation of the Rhineland.
- Hitler Youth founded in Germany.
- Ali Reza Khan crowned Shah of Persia with title, King Pahlavi.
- Jósef Pilsudski stages coup and seizes power in Poland.
- Germany admitted to the League of Nations.
- Hirohito succeeds his father, Yoshihito, as Emperor of Japan.
  ### DEATHS
  Eugene Debs, US socialist leader.
  Harry Houdini (Ernst Weiss), Hungarian-born US escapologist.
  Claude Monet, French artist.
  Annie Oakley, US sharpshooter.
  Rainer Maria Rilke, Austrian poet.
  Rudolph Valentino, Italian-born US film star.

1927
- Canberra inaugurated as new capital of the Australian Commonwealth.
- Allied military control of Germany ends.
- Tomas Masaryk re-elected President of Czechoslovakia.
- In Chinese civil war, Nationalist forces under Chiang Kai-shek conquer Shanghai.
- Leon Trotsky and Grigori Zinoviev expelled from the Soviet Communist Party by Stalin.
- Italian-born anarchists, Sacco and Vanzetti, executed in US for armed robbery despite worldwide protests of their innocence.
- Captain Charles Lindbergh makes first solo nonstop flight across the Atlantic.
- Al Jolson stars in first talking film, 'The Jazz Singer'.
  ### DEATHS
  Isadora Duncan, US dancer.
  Jerome K. Jerome, British writer.

1928
- Earthquake destroys Corinth in Greece.
- Kellog-Briand Pact, renouncing war, signed in Paris by 65 states.
- Chinese Nationalist forces led by Chiang Kai-shek take Peking (July); Chiang Kai-shek becomes President of Republic of China (October).
- Women entitled to vote on same basis as men (age 21) in Britain.
- Herbert Hoover elected US President.

- First Five Year Plan begins in USSR.
- Hirohito crowned Emperor of Japan.
- Amelia Earhart is the first woman to fly the Atlantic.
- Professor Alexander Fleming of St Mary's Hospital in London discovers penicillin.
- Otto Frederick Rohwedder of Battle Creek, Michigan, invents sliced bread.
- D. H. Lawrence's *Lady Chatterley's Lover.*
  DEATHS
  Thomas Hardy, English novelist and poet.
  Leos Janacek, Czech composer.
  Emmeline Pankhurst, suffragette leader.
  Sir George Trevelyan, British statesman and historian.

1929
- Kingdom of Serbs, Croats and Slovenes changes its name to Yugoslavia; King Alexander I declares himself dictator.
- St Valentine's Day Massacre in Chicago.
- Mussolini signs Lateran Treaty with Pope Pius XI establishing independent Vatican City.
- Trotsky expelled from the USSR.
- Ramsay MacDonald forms second Labour government.
- Aristide Briand, Premier of France.
- Wall Street Crash causes slump in US economy: Great Depression begins.
- Airship *Graf Zeppelin* flies around the world in 21 days.
- Ernest Hemingway's *A Farewell to Arms* is published.
  DEATHS
  Carl Benz, German engineer.
  Sergei Diaghilev, Russian impresario.
  Wyatt Earp, US marshal.
  Lillie Langtry, British actress.
  Gustav Stresemann, German statesman.

1930
- Stalin's collectivization of agriculture in USSR accelerated at enormous human cost.
- Ras Tafari becomes Emperor Haile Selassie of Ethiopia.
- Treaty between Britain, US, France, Italy and Japan on naval disarmament.
- Last French troops withdraw from the Rhineland.
- Unemployment in UK reaches 2 million.
- Nazis come second in German general election.
- Mandate policy in government White Paper on Palestine suggests halting Jewish immigration.
- *R.101* disaster: world's biggest airship explodes in France on maiden flight to India killing 48 people.
- Uruguay wins first World Cup football competition.
- Planet Pluto discovered by C. W. Tombaugh.
- Nylon discovered in US by Wallace Carrothers of the Du Pont company.
  DEATHS
  Lon Chaney, US actor.
  Sir Arthur Conan Doyle, British author.
  D. H. Lawrence, British author.

1931
- Sir Oswald Mosley founds the New Party along Fascist lines in Britain.
- King Alfonso abdicates and Spain is declared a republic.
- Mutiny over pay cuts at Invergordon naval base.
- Coalition government formed under Ramsay MacDonald.

- Britain abandons the gold standard and devalues the pound.
- US gangster, Al(phonse) Capone, jailed for income tax evasion.
- Empire State Building completed in New York.
  DEATHS
  Bix Beiderbecke, US jazz musician.
  Arnold Bennett, British writer.
  Thomas Alva Edison, US inventor.
  Anna Pavlova, Russian ballerina.

1932
- Japanese capture Shanghai.
- Manchukuo, Japanese puppet regime, established in Manchuria.
- Kidnappers abduct Charles Lindbergh's baby son.
- Second Five Year Plan begins in USSR.
- Paul von Hindenburg narrowly defeats Hitler in German presidential contest; Nazis win majority of seats in Reichstag (July); Hitler fails to become Chancellor (August).
- Assassination of French President, Paul Donner; replaced by Albert Lebrun.
- Eamon de Valera elected President of Ireland.
- Olivier Salazar elected Premier of Portugal.
- Franklin D. Roosevelt elected US President in landslide victory.
- Sydney Harbour Bridge opened in Australia.
- Aldous Huxley's *Brave New World*.
  DEATHS
  George Eastman, US industrialist.
  John Philip Sousa, US musician.
  Edgar Wallace, British crime writer.

1933
- Adolf Hitler appointed Chancellor of Germany (January); Reichstag building in Berlin destroyed by fire (February); commercial boycott of Jews begins and violence against Jews and their property escalates (April); Germany becomes a one-party state as Hitler bans all political opposition (June); use of concentration camps for Jews and opponents of the regime confirmed (August); Germany withdraws from the League of Nations (October) and walks out of the Geneva Disarmament conference (November).
- Communist uprising in Spain.
- Japan withdraws from the League of Nations.
- Economic legislation in US to combat the Great Depression (Roosevelt's 'New Deal').
- End of Prohibition in US.
  DEATHS
  Adolf Loos, Austrian architect.

1934
- Leopold III becomes King of the Belgians after death of Albert I.
- Hitler eliminates rivals in the Storm Troopers' Association (SA) in the 'Night of the Long Knives'.
- Austrian Chancellor, Englebert Dollfuss, is assassinated by Nazis.
- Death of President Hindenburg: Hitler announces the end of the Republic and the beginning of the Third Reich with himself as Führer and Reich Chancellor.
- King Alexander of Yugoslavia and Louis Barthou, French Foreign Minister, assassinated in Marseilles.
- Assassination of Sergei Kirov and purge of the Communist Party in USSR.
- Robert Graves' *I Claudius*.

DEATHS
Marie Curie, Polish-born French physicist.
Frederick Delius, British composer.
Sir Edward Elgar, British composer.
Roger Fry, British painter and art critic.
Gustav Holst, British composer.

1935
- Saar plebiscite for return to Germany.
- Bruno Hauptmann sentenced to death for kidnapping and murder of US aviator Charles Lindbergh's baby son.
- Germany repudiates Versailles Treaty and accelerates rearmament programme.
- Jews banned from public office in Germany.
- Stanley Baldwin becomes Prime Minister; forms new National Government.
- Mussolini invades Abyssinia: League of Nations imposes ineffectual economic sanctions against Italy.
- US Senator, Huey Long, assassinated.
- Long March of Communists from Nationalist-held areas in southern China ends: Mao Zedong (Mao Tse-tung) establishes Communist state in northern China.

DEATHS
Colonel T. E. Lawrence, 'Lawrence of Arabia', British soldier and author.

1936
- Death of George V and accession of Edward VIII (January); Edward VIII abdicates to marry US divorcee, Wallace Simpson, and is succeeded by his brother the Duke of York as George VI (December).
- German remilitarization of the Rhineland.
- Italy annexes Abyssinia.
- Spanish army led by General Franco revolts against the Republican government: Spanish Civil War begins.
- Mussolini and Hitler announce the Rome-Berlin Axis.
- Stalin initiates the great purges that are to last for two years and cost up to ten million lives.
- F. D. Roosevelt re-elected US President by landslide.
- March of unemployed workers from Jarrow to London begins.
- The first suntan lotion is launched by L'Oreal.

DEATHS
Alexander Glazunov, Russian composer.
Rudyard Kipling, British poet and author.
Ivan Pavlov, Russian physiologist.

1937
- Guernica bombed by German air force in Spanish Civil War.
- Neville Chamberlain becomes Prime Minister after the resignation of Stanley Baldwin.
- German airship *Hindenburg* explodes on landing in New Jersey.
- Second Sino-Japanese War: Japanese begin attempted conquest of China; Shanghai bombed (August); forces of Chiang Kai-shek unite with Mao's Communists to combat Japanese threat (September).
- Stalin stages show trials of ex-colleagues in Moscow and purges army generals.
- The shopping trolley is introduced by Sylvan Goldman, manager of a supermarket in Oklahoma.

DEATHS
Sir James Barrie, British author.
George Gershwin, US composer.
Jean Harlow, US actress.

Guglielmo Marconi, Italian engineer.
Maurice Ravel, French composer.
John D. Rockefeller, US oil tycoon.
Lord Ernest Rutherford, British scientist.
Bessie Smith, US blues singer.

1938

- Austria annexed by Germany.
- Singapore naval base opened.
- Japanese bomb Canton.
- Munich Agreement between Chamberlain, French Premier Daladier, Hitler and Mussolini appeases Hitler over Czechoslovakia.
- Germans march into Czechoslovakia.
- Kristallnacht: Jewish homes and businesses are attacked and looted throughout Germany (November); all Jewish property is confiscated (December).
- John Logie Baird demonstrates the colour television.

  DEATHS
  Gabriele d'Annunzio, Italian soldier and poet.
  Karel Capek, Czech writer.
  Constantin Stanislavsky, Russian stage director.

SECOND WORLD WAR

1939

- Madrid falls to Nationalist forces led by General Franco (March): end of the Spanish Civil War.
- Bohemia and Moravia annexed by Hitler.
- Britain signs treaty of mutual assistance with Poland.
- Conscription introduced in Britain.
- Mussolini invades Albania.
- Italy and Germany sign alliance.
- Germany and USSR sign a Non-Aggression Pact.
- September: Hitler invades Poland (1); war declared between Britain and Germany (3); first enemy air raid on Britain (6); British Expeditionary Force lands in France (11); Warsaw capitulates and Nazi-Soviet Pact signed in Moscow for partitioning of Poland (29).
- October: *Royal Oak* sunk in Scapa Flow with the loss of 810 lives (14).
- November: Finland attacked by Russia.
- December: Battle of the River Plate, *Graf Spee* scuttled by Germans after being trapped in Montevideo harbour by British warships.
- John Steinbeck's *The Grapes of Wrath*.
- James Joyce's *Finnegan's Wake*.
- Henry Miller's *Tropic of Cancer*.

  DEATHS
  Douglas Fairbanks, US actor.
  Sigmund Freud, Austrian psychoanalyst.
  W. B. Yeats, Irish poet and playwright.

1940

- January: Food rationing begins in Britain; Finnish Winter War.
- March: Finns defeated by Red Army.
- April: Hitler invades Denmark and Norway; British troops join fighting in Norway.
- May: Holland, Belgium and Luxembourg suffer German blitzkrieg: National Government formed under Winston Churchill; British troops encircled on French coast around Dunkirk (31).

- June: evacuation of British army from Dunkirk completed (4); Italy declares war on Britain and France (10); Paris captured by the Germans (14); France accepts terms for an Armistice (22).
- July: Channel Islands occupied by Germany (1); Battle of Britain begins (10).
- August: British Somaliland attacked by Italy (7); Britain begins night bombing of Germany.
- September: Blitz on London begins; Battle of Britain ends in victory for the Allies (15); Japanese invade Indochina.
- October: Bucharest occupied by Axis troops.
- November: Greek troops repel Italian attacks; Coventry bombed in worst air raid of the war, 1000 killed.
- December: Sidi Barani captured by British troops in North Africa; General Archibald Wavell begins destruction of Italian forces in the Western Desert; Germans drop incendiary bombs on London.

DEATHS
John Buchan, British author.
F. Scott Fitzgerald, US novelist.
Harold Harmsworth, Lord Rothermere, British newspaper baron.
Paul Klee, German artist.
Leon Trotsky, revolutionary socialist.

1941
- January: Tobruk captured by Commonwealth troops.
- February: Benghazi captured (7); Mogadishu in Somaliland captured by Imperial troops (26); General Erwin Rommel's Afrika Korps lands in Tripoli.
- March: President Roosevelt signs Lease-Lend agreement with Britain (11); British raid on Lofoten Islands off Norway (4); Italian fleet virtually destroyed by British in Battle of Cape Matapan, off Crete (28); Rommel begins campaign in North Africa (30).
- April: Addis Ababa captured by Imperial troops (4); Germans occupy Yugoslavia (17); Athens captured by Germans (27).
- May: Rudolf Hess parachutes into Scotland (10); heavy German bombing raid on London (11); Germans invade Crete and British forces withdraw (20); German battleship *Bismark* sunk (27).
- June: Clothes rationing begins; Germany attacks Russia (20).
- July: US troops take over Iceland (7); Smolensk falls to German advance in Russia (16); Syrian capital Damascus surrenders to Allied forces (21); Japanese troops move into Thailand and Cambodia, and occupy Saigon (27).
- August: British and Russian troops attack Iran (25); the Dnepropetrovsk Dam blown up by the Russians to halt German advance (27).
- September: Intense fighting around Leningrad (12); Kiev falls to the Germans (19); in London, General de Gaulle announces the formation of a French provisional government in exile (25).
- October: Germans attack Moscow (6); Soviet government leaves Moscow (20); Germans take Kharkov in the Ukraine (25).
- November: *Ark Royal* sunk by Italian torpedo (13); Eighth Army begins first offensive in Libya (18); Russians retake Rostov (30).
- December: German attack on Moscow stalls (4); Japanese attack Pearl Harbor (7); Britain declares war on Finland, Romania and Hungary (8); Japanese forces land in Malaya (8); Philippines invaded by Japanese (10); Hong Kong surrenders to Japanese (25).

DEATHS
Lord Robert Baden-Powell, British founder of the Scouting movement.

Henri Bergson, French philosopher.
Amy Johnson, British airwoman.
James Joyce, Irish author.
Rabindranath Tagore, Indian author.
Virginia Woolf, British author.

1942

- January: Manila captured by Japanese (2); Japanese forces land in New Guinea and Solomon Islands (23); German and Italian troops take Benghazi (29).
- February: Singapore falls to the Japanese (15); Battle of Java Seas (28).
- March: Java surrenders to Japan (9); German U-boat base at St Nazaire attacked by British commandoes (27); RAF begins intensive bombing campaign against Germany (28).
- April: George Cross awarded to the people of Malta (16); US B-52s bomb Tokyo (18).
- May: Battle of the Coral Sea (4–8); Britain allied with Russia (26); Rommel launches offensive in Libya (27); 1000 RAF bombers raid Cologne (31).
- June: US routs Japanese navy in Battle of Midway Island (3–7); Czech village of Lidice destroyed by Germans in reprisal for assassination of Reinhard Heydrich (10); Tobruk captured by Germans (20).
- July: Sevastopol falls to the Germans (1); RAF makes first daylight raid on the Ruhr (16).
- August: General Bernard Montgomery assumes command of the Eighth Army (6); Germans advance on Stalingrad (6); US forces attack Solomon Islands (7); Allied raid on Dieppe (19).
- September: Germans clear Warsaw Jewish ghetto (2); Germans halted at Stalingrad (8); Madagascar falls to Britain (18); Eighth Army seizes key German positions at El Alamein (30).
- October: Battle of El Alamein, Rommel in full retreat (30).
- November: Allies invade North Africa (7); Germans defeated near Stalingrad (26); French fleet scuttled in Toulon harbour (27).
- December: Physicists led by Enrico Fermi at Chicago University achieve first controlled nuclear chain reaction (2); Admiral Darlan, Vichy leader in North Africa, assassinated (24).

DEATHS

John Barrymore, US actor.
Carole Lombard, US actress.
Stefan Zweig, Austrian author.

1943

- January: Tripoli taken by the Eighth Army (23); conference of Allied powers at Casablanca (24); US bombers make their first attack on Germany (27); Germans surrender at Stalingrad (31).
- February: Japanese cleared from Guadalcanal in the Solomon Islands (9); Kharkow retaken by the Russians (16).
- March: Battle of Bismarck Sea (1–3); Rommel almost surrounded by US and British forces in North Africa (26).
- April: Mass grave of Polish officers discovered by Germans in Katyn forest near Smolensk.
- May: Remaining German and Italian forces surrender to Allies in North Africa (12); RAF Dambuster raid on the Ruhr dams (17).
- June: French Committee for National Liberation formed in Algiers.
- July: Allied invasion of Sicily (10); Germans routed in Battle of Kursk (13); Mussolini overthrown (25).

- August: Sicily falls to the Allies (17).
- September: Allies invade Italian mainland (3); Italy surrenders (8); US forces land at Salerno, near Naples (10); Germans occupy Rome (10); Smolensk taken by the Russians (25).
- October: Naples falls to Allies (1); Russians cross the River Dneiper and capture Zaporozhie and Dnepropetrovsk (29).
- November: Kiev taken by the Russians (6): Churchill, Roosevelt and Stalin meet at Allied conference in Tehran (28).
- December: General Dwight D. Eisenhower chosen as Supreme Commander of the Allied invasion of Europe (24); German battleship *Scharnhorst* sunk (26).

DEATHS

Leslie Howard, British actor and director.

Sergei Rachmaninov, Russian composer.

Thomas 'Fats' Waller, US jazz pianist.

Beatrix Potter, British writer.

Beatrice Webb, British socialist and writer.

1944

- January: Allied landings at Anzio (22); Russians raise German siege of Leningrad (19);.
- February: US forces land on the Marshall Islands (1); Russians destroy ten German divisions on the Ukrainian front (17).
- March: Monte Cassino destroyed by Allied bombing (15); Allied force lands in Burma (19); General Orde Wingate killed in air crash.
- April: General de Gaulle appointed head of the Free French Forces (9); Russians drive Germans from the Crimea (16).
- May: Sevastopol captured by the Russians (9); Monte Cassino falls to the Allies (18); 47 Allied airmen shot after mass escape from Stalag Luft III, prison camp in Silesia.
- June: Rome liberated by Allies (4); D-Day invasion of Europe (6); first V-1 rocket falls on England (18).
- July: Minsk captured by Russians (3); Caen falls to Allies (9); Bomb Plot fails to kill Hitler (20); Guam captured by Americans (21).
- August: Warsaw uprising (1); Allies land in southern France (15); Paris liberated (23); Romania declares war on Germany (25).
- September: Antwerp and Brussels taken by Allies (4); Boulogne taken by Allies (7); Bulgaria declares war on Germany (7); V-2 rockets begin to fall on England (8); Allies enter German soil (11); Allied landings near Arnhem (17); US forces attack Japanese near Manila (21).
- October: Warsaw rising crushed by Germans (3); British troops land on mainland Greece (5); Rommel commits suicide (14); Athens occupied by Allies (14); Aachen taken by Allies (20); Red Army liberates Belgrade (20); Battle of Leyte Gulf, Japanese sea power destroyed (25).
- November: British troops capture Salonika (1); German battleship *Tirpitz* is sunk by RAF bombs (12).
- December: Civil war begins in Athens (6); German counter-offensive in the Ardennes (16); Budapest surrounded by Red Army (26).

DEATHS

Sir Edwin Lutyens, British architect.

Glen Miller, US band leader.

Piet Mondrian, Dutch artist.

Edvard Munch, Norwegian artist.

Heath Robinson, British humorist.

Sir Henry Wood, British conductor.

1945

- January: US troops land on Luzon in Philippines (11); Warsaw captured by Russians (17); Hungary declares war on Germany (21); Red Army liberates Auschwitz (27); Ledo Road from Burma to China reopened (28).
- February: Allied Conference at Yalta (4); bombing of Dresden (14); US forces land on Iwo Jima (19).
- March: Cologne captured by Allies (6); Marshall Tito takes power in Yugoslavia (6); Allies cross the Rhine (25).
- April: US invades Okinawa (1); Red Army enters Vienna (11); death of President Roosevelt (12); US troops and Red Army link up in Germany (27); Mussolini and his mistress shot by Italian partisans (28); Allies penetrate Berlin (30); Hitler and his mistress commit suicide (30).
- May: Germans surrender in Italy (2); Berlin captured by Red Army (2); Rangoon falls to the British (3); war against Germany ends officially (8); naval air attacks on Japan (28).
- June: United Nations Charter signed in San Francisco (26).
- July: Polish government in Warsaw recognized by Allies (5); Labour Party wins landslide in general election; Clement Attlee becomes Prime Minister (26).
- August: Atomic bombs dropped on Hiroshima (6) and Nagasaki (9); Russia declares war against Japan and advances into Manchuria (8); unconditional surrender of Japan (14).
- September: Second World War ends (2).
- November: de Gaulle elected President of France (13); Nuremberg Trials begin (20).
  ### DEATHS
  Bela Bartok, Hungarian composer.
  David Lloyd George, British Liberal statesman.
  General George S. Patton, US commander.
  Anton von Webern, Austrian composer.

COLD WAR AND AFRO-ASIAN NATIONALISM

1946

- General Assembly of the United Nations meets in New York for the first time.
- Winston Churchill warns of 'Iron Curtain' descending across Europe in speech at Fulton, Missouri.
- Leon Blum forms Socialist government in France.
- Juan Péron elected President of Argentina.
- Abdication of Victor Emmanuel III as King of Italy; his son, Umberto II, reigns briefly then leaves the country after referendum in favour of a republic under Premier de Gasperi.
- King David Hotel, British military HQ in Jerusalem, bombed by Jewish terrorists.
- Leading Nazis executed at Nuremburg.
- Civil war between Nationalists and Communists resumes in China.
- Biro pen, invented by Hungarian journalist Ladislao Biro, goes on sale.
  ### DEATHS
  John Maynard Keynes, British economist.
  John Logie Baird, British scientist and pioneer of television.
1947
- Coal mines nationalized in Britain.
- Burma proclaimed independent republic.
- India becomes independent and partitioned into India and Pakistan.
- US Secretary of State, George Marshall, inaugurates US funding for European reconstruction (Marshall Plan).

- Cominform, a new international Communist organization, established in Belgrade.
- Edinburgh International Festival of Music and Drama launched.
- UN determines the partition of Palestine.
- Tennessee Williams's *A Streetcar Named Desire*.
  DEATHS
  Pierre Bonnard, French artist.
  Henry Ford, US car manufacturer.
  Max Planck, German physicist.
  Sidney Webb, British Socialist and author.

1948
- Railways and the electricity industry nationalized in Britain.
- Burma becomes independent.
- Mahatma Gandhi assassinated.
- Communists seize power in Czechoslovakia.
- Marshall Plan for $17 billion in economic aid to Europe passed by US Senate.
- First Arab-Israeli War: state of Israel established with Chaim Weizmann as president.
- Russian blockade of Berlin: Western airlift of supplies begins.
- National Health Service begins in Britain.
- North Korea becomes a republic: Korea now divided between Communist North led by Kim Il Sung and Republic of Korea in the south led by Syngman Rhee.
- Apartheid established in South Africa.
- Harry S. Truman elected US President.
  DEATHS
  Sergei Eisenstein, Soviet film director.
  Muhammad Ali Jinnah, Pakistani statesman.
  Franz Lehar, Austrian composer.

1949
- People's Republic of China founded with Mao Zedong as leader (October); Chinese Nationalist government establishes headquarters on Formosa (December).
- North Atlantic Treaty signed in Washington by 12 Western nations, establishing NATO.
- Republic of Eire proclaimed in Dublin.
- Berlin blockade lifted (12 May); German Federal Republic created with Bonn as capital (23 May); Konrad Adenauer elected first Chancellor of the FDR (August); Soviet sector becomes German Democratic Republic (October).
- Pandit Nehru elected Prime Minister of India.
- George Orwell's *1984*.
- Simone de Beauvoir's *The Second Sex*.
- Arthur Miller's *Death of a Salesman*.
  DEATHS
  Tommy Handley, British comedian.
  Margaret Mitchell, US author.
  Richard Strauss, German composer.

1950
- Britain recognizes Communist China.
- Sino-Soviet Alliance signed.
- Labour wins general election.
- Senator Joseph McCarthy begins communist witchhunt in US.
- US starts building hydrogen bomb.
- Klaus Fuchs found guilty of betraying secrets of atomic bomb construction to Russia.
- North Korea invades South Korea (25 June): US military forces dominate UN forces, led by General MacArthur, sent to repel Communist advance (June–July); Britain sends troops (August); UN landings at Inchon (September); UN forces

capture Communist capital, Pyongyang (October); massive Chinese offensive in North Korea (November); Chinese take Pyongyang (December).
- Vietnam partitioned between Communist North and regime in the south under Emperor Bao Dai.
- China invades Tibet.

DEATHS

Edgar Rice Burroughs, US author.
Al Jolson, US entertainer.
Sir Harry Lauder, British comedian.
Heinrich Mann, German author.
Vaslav Nijinsky, Russian ballet dancer.
George Orwell (Eric Blair), British author.
Cesare Pavese, Italian author.
George Bernard Shaw, Irish author and playwright.
Kurt Weill, German composer.

1951
- Korean War: Seoul captured by Communist forces (4 January); General MacArthur sacked by Truman after threatening invasion of China (April); cease-fire talks begin (July); truce-line established along the 38th parallel (November).
- Vietminh guerillas suffer heavy losses in offensive against the French in Tonkin.
- Treaty of Paris creates European Coal and Steel Community, soon to evolve into the European Economic Community (EEC) .
- British spies, Guy Burgess and Donald Maclean, escape to Russia.
- British troops seize Suez Canal Zone.
- Winston Churchill, Prime Minister after Conservative victory in general election.
- 22nd Amendment to the US Constitution limits presidents to two terms, a maximum of eight years in office.
- Julius and Ethel Rosenberg sentenced to death for passing wartime atomic secrets to Russia.
- Libya gains independence.
- Festival of Britain opens.

DEATHS

Ernest Bevin, British statesman.
André Gide, French author.
William Randolph Hearst, American newspaper magnate.
Sinclair Lewis, US author.
Ivor Novello, British actor and composer.
Arnold Schoenberg, Austrian-born US composer.
Ludwig Wittgenstein, Austrian philosopher.

1952
- Death of George VI (6 February) and succession of Queen Elizabeth II.
- Japan regains sovereign status.
- US launches air strikes against North Korea as peace talks stall.
- State of Emergency declared in Kenya after series of Mau Mau terrorist killings.
- General Neguib leads coup and seizes power in Egypt; King Farouk abdicates in favour of his infant son.
- Riots in South Africa against apartheid laws.
- US tests first hydrogen bomb on Eniwetok Atoll in the Pacific.
- Britain tests its first atomic bomb.
- Dwight D. Eisenhower elected US President.
- Anne Frank's *Diary*.
- Ernest Hemingway's *The Old Man and the Sea*.

DEATHS

Paul Eluard, French poet.

Eva ('Evita') Peron, Argentine political activist.

George Santayana, Spanish philosopher.

1953

• Marshall Tito elected President of Yugoslavia.
• General Naguib declares a republic in Egypt.
• Stalin dies: Nikita Krushchev emerges as Soviet leader after power struggle.
• Coronation of Queen Elizabeth II in Britain.
• US spies, Julius and Ethel Rosenberg, executed.
• Korean War ends: armistice signed at Panmunjom.
• Russia tests hydrogen bomb.
• Mau Mau leader Jomo Kenyatta jailed in Kenya.
• French Legionnaires capture Dien Bien Phu.
• Cambodia gains independence.
• Agreement signed for laying of the first transatlantic telephone cable.
• E. P. Hillary and Sherpa Tensing reach summit of Everest.

DEATHS

Hilaire Belloc, British author.

Eugene O'Neill, US playwright.

Sergei Prokofiev, Soviet composer.

Django Reinhardt, jazz guitarist.

Dylan Thomas, Welsh poet.

Hank Williams, US country singer.

1954

• Colonel Gamel Abdul Nasser seizes power in Egypt.
• St Lawrence Seaway approved by Eisenhower.
• French defeated by Vietminh forces at Dien Bien Phu (May); Geneva Agreement divides Vietnam into North and South along 17th Parallel.
• US Supreme Court rules against racial segregation in state schools.
• South East Asia Treaty Organization (SEATO) established.
• Senator McCarthy's anti-communist Senate hearings televised in US: McCarthy eventually censured and condemned by Congress (December).
• Food rationing ends in Britain.
• Anti-British rioting in Cyprus by EOKA supporters demanding union with Greece.
• Anti-polio vaccine, developed by Dr Jonas E. Salk, begins intensive trials.
• Roger Bannister is the first person to run a mile in under four minutes.
• Bill Haley and the Comets' 'We're Gonna Rock Around the Clock'.
• Kingsley Amis' *Lucky Jim*.
• William Golding's *Lord of the Flies*.

DEATHS

Lionel Barrymore, British actor.

Enrico Fermi, Italian physicist.

Wilhelm Furtwangler, German conductor.

Auguste Lumiere, French cinema pioneer.

Henri Mattisse, French artist.

1955

• Anthony Eden becomes Prime Minister after resignation of Churchill.
• Civil war between rival factions in Saigon, South Vietnam.
• East-West Geneva Conference.
• Warsaw Pact signed by USSR and Eastern Bloc nations.
• Germany becomes member of NATO.

- State of emergency declared in Cyprus after violent demonstrations against British rule.
- Eighty spectators die in crash disaster at Le Mans.
- Commercial TV begins broadcasting in Britain.
- Civil Rights Campaign emerges in US South: black campaigners begin a boycott of public transport in Alabama, under the leadership of the young Martin Luther King.
- Clement Atlee resigns as Labour Party leader; replaced by Hugh Gaitskill.
- Vladimir Nabokov's *Lolita*.
  DEATHS
  James Dean, US actor.
  Albert Einstein, German-born US physicist.
  Arthur Honegger, Swiss composer.
  Fernand Leger, French artist.
  Thomas Mann, German novelist.
  Charlie Parker, US jazz musician.
  Maurice Utrillo, French painter.

1956
- Sudan becomes independent republic.
- Nikita Khruschev denounces Stalin at 20th Communist Party Congress.
- Race riots in Alabama.
- British deport Archbishop Makarios, leader of the Greek-Cypriot community, to the Seychelles.
- Pakistan becomes Islamic republic.
- Suez Crisis (Suez-Sinai War): Colonel Nasser, President of Egypt seizes the Suez Canal Zone (July); Israel attacks Egypt (29 October); Anglo-French forces bomb Egyptian military targets (30 October); Allied forces retake Canal Zone (6 November); UN-imposed cease-fire (8 November); Canal blocked (16 November); British withdraw forces after financial pressure from the US (23 November).
- Uprising in Hungary against Soviet control crushed by Soviet tanks.
- Fidel Castro lands in Cuba to lead rebellion against President Batista.
- US film star, Grace Kelly, marries Prince Rainier III of Monaco.
- Premium bonds launched in Britain.
  DEATHS
  Sir Max Beerbohm, British author and cartoonist.
  Bertold Brecht, German playwright.
  Alfred Kinsey, US sociologist.
  Sir Alexander Korda, British film director.
  Alan Alexander Milne, British author.
  Jackson Pollock, US artist.

1957
- Harold Macmillan becomes Prime Minister after resignation of Sir Anthony Eden.
- Ghana gains independence.
- Treaty of Rome, signed by France, West Germany, Italy, Belgium, the Netherlands and Luxembourg, inaugurates the European Community (EC).
- The Federation of Malaya gains independence.
- Suez Canal reopened.
- Tunisia becomes a republic after Bey is deposed by Premier Bourguiba.
- President Eisenhower sends National Guard into Little Rock, Arkansas, to enforce school desegregation.
- Russia launches first man-made space satellites, Sputnik-I and Sputnik-II.
- Jack Kerouac's *On the Road*.

DEATHS

Humphrey Bogart, US actor.
Constantin Brancusi, Romanian sculptor.
Christian Dior, French fashion designer.
Jimmy Dorsey, US band leader.
Oliver Hardy, US comedian.
Diego Rivera, Mexican painter.
Jean Sibelius, Finnish composer.
Erich von Stroheim, Austrian actor and film director.
Arturo Toscanini, Italian conductor.

1958

- Anti-British riots in Cyprus.
- Seven members of Manchester United football team killed in plane crash at Munich Airport.
- Egypt and Syria proclaim union as United Arab Republic.
- Alaska becomes 49th US State.
- Dr Vivian Fuchs completes first overland crossing of Antarctica.
- Campaign for Nuclear Disarmament (CND) founded (February): organizes first march from London to Aldermaston (April).
- French Nationalist settlers rebel in Algeria.
- King Faisal of Iraq assassinated.
- Cardinal Giuseppe Roncalli becomes Pope John XXIII.
- EOKA terrorists step up campaign against British in Cyprus.
- First heart pacemaker inserted.
- Fifth Republic established in France with General Charles de Gaulle as first President.
- US nuclear submarine *Nautilus* sails under the icecap at the North Pole.
- Thalidomide drug implicated in birth defects.

DEATHS

Sir William Burrell, Scottish shipping magnate and art collector.
Ronald Coleman, British actor.
Robert Donat, British actor.
Tyrone Power, US actor.
Marie Stopes, British pioneer of family planning.
Ralph Vaughan Williams, British composer.

1959

- Fidel Castro overthrows Batista regime and takes power in Cuba.
- Indira Gandhi becomes President of Congress Party in India.
- Hawaii becomes 50th US State.
- China suppresses uprising in Lhasa: Dalai Lama flees.
- Conservatives re-elected under Harold Macmillan in general election.
- European Free Trade Association inaugurated as rival trading bloc to European Community.
- Archbishop Makarios elected as the first President of the new Republic of Cyprus.
- British Motor Corporation launches the Mini.

DEATHS

Raymond Chandler, US author.
Lou Costello, US comedian.
John Foster Dulles, US statesman.
Sir Jacob Epstein, British sculptor.
George Grosz, German-born US artist.
Errol Flynn, US actor.

Billie Holliday, US singer.
Buddy Holly, US singer.
Cecil B. de Mille, US film director.
Sir Stanley Spencer, British artist.
Frank Lloyd Wright, US architect.

1960

- Harold Macmillan delivers his 'Wind of Change' in speech to South African Parliament in Cape Town.
- Sharpeville Massacre in South Africa, 56 Africans killed by police.
- American U-2 spy plane shot down over Soviet territory.
- Adolf Eichmann captured by Israeli secret service, Mossad, in Argentina.
- Belgian Congo granted independence as Congo Republic under President Patrice Lumumba (1 June); Congolese army mutiny (6 June); Katanga Province declares itself independent from Congo and civil war begins (July); Congolese army takes power under Colonel Mobutu (September); Congolese army in conflict with UN troops (November); ex-premier Lumumba arrested (December).
- British rule ends and Cyprus becomes independent republic.
- Nigeria gains independence.
- US nuclear submarine *Triton* completes first underwater circumnavigation of the globe.
- Charles van Doren and 12 other contestants arrested for perjury in testifying that they were not given the answers in advance to questions on top US TV quiz '21'.
- 'Lady Chatterley' trial in London: Penguin Books found not guilty of publishing obscene material.
- John Fitzgerald Kennedy elected US President.
- Harper Lee's *To Kill a Mockingbird*.
    DEATHS
    Aneurin Bevan, British statesman.
    Albert Camus, French author.
    Clark Gable, US actor.
    Sylvia Pankhurst, British suffragette.
    Boris Pasternak, Soviet author.
    Mack Sennett, US film director.
    Nevil Shute, Australian author.

1961

- In referendum, French and Algerian voters support De Gaulle's policy of home rule for Algeria.
- British police arrest members of Portland spy ring.
- US severs diplomatic relations with Cuba.
- Contraceptive pill goes on sale in Britain.
- President Kennedy establishes US Peace Corps.
- Soviet cosmonaut, Major Yuri Alexeyevitch Gagarin, becomes first man in space.
- US-armed Cuban exiles stage unsuccessful invasion of Cuba at Bay of Pigs.
- Berlin Wall constructed.
- Dag Hammarskjöld, UN Secretary-General, killed in plane crash.
- Adolf Eichmann sentenced to death for war crimes at trial in Jerusalem.
- Britain begins negotiations to join the European Community.
- Joseph Heller's *Catch 22*.
    DEATHS
    Sir Thomas Beecham, British conductor.
    Gary Cooper, US actor.
    (Samuel) Dashiell Hammett, US author.

George Formby, British comedian.
Ernest Hemmingway, US author.
Augustus John, British painter.
Carl Jung, Swiss psychoanalyst.
James Thurber, US author.

1962

- US steps up military aid to South Vietnam.
- Adolf Eichmann hanged for Nazi war crimes.
- France recognizes independence of Algeria.
- Riots in Deep South of America as University of Mississippi enrols black student, James Meredith.
- Uganda and Tanganyika gain independence.
- Sino-Indian War: short border war results in a Chinese victory.
- Cuban Missile crisis.
- Trans-Canada Highway opened.
- Telstar communications satellite launched: brings first live trans-Atlantic television pictures.
- World's first passenger Hovercraft enters service.

  DEATHS

  Niels Bohr, Danish nuclear physicist.
  William Faulkner, US author.
  Herman Hesse, German-born Swiss author.
  Charles Laughton, British actor.
  Marilyn Monroe, US actress.
  Richard Tawney, British socialist historian.
  George Trevelyan, British historian.
  Victoria Sackville-West, British writer.

1963

- Harold Wilson elected leader of the Labour Party after the death of Hugh Gaitskill.
- Beeching Report recommends extensive cuts in British railway branch lines.
- Britain agrees to buy Polaris missiles from the US.
- President de Gaulle of France vetoes British entry into the European Community.
- Profumo Affair in Britain: Secretary of State for War John Profumo resigns after lying to Parliament about affair with prostitute.
- Civil Rights demonstrations in Birmingham, Alabama: Martin Luther King arrested.
- Cardinal Giovanni Battista Monitine elected Pope John XXIII.
- Great Train Robbery: £2.5 million stolen.
- 200,000 join civil rights 'Freedom March' on Washington DC.
- Buddhist riots in Saigon.
- Russia put first woman in space, Lieutenant Valentina Tereshkova.
- Sir Alec Douglas Home succeeds Harold Macmillan as Prime Minister.
- Test Ban Treaty signed by Britain, US and Russia.
- US President John F. Kennedy is assassinated by Lee Harvey Oswald in Dallas, Texas: succeeded by Vice President Lyndon Baines Johnson.
- Lee Harvey Oswald shot dead by Jack Ruby at Dallas police headquarters.
- Military coup overthrows regime of President Ngo Dinh Diem in South Vietnam.
- Kenya gains independence.

  DEATHS

  Georges Braque, French Cubist painter.
  Jean Cocteau, French artist and writer.
  Robert Frost, US poet.
  Paul Hindemith, German composer.

Aldous Huxley, British writer.
Max Miller, British comedian.
Edith Piaf, French singer.
Francis Poulenc, French composer.
Dinah Washington, US blues singer.
William Carlos Williams, US poet.

1964

- Zanzibar becomes a republic and unites with Tanganyika to form Tanzania.
- Northern Rhodesia becomes independent Republic of Zambia.
- Constantine II, King of Greece on death of King Paul I.
- Ian Smith, Premier of Southern Rhodesia.
- Violent clashes between Turkish and Greek Cypriots in Cyprus: UN peace forces intervene.
- Gulf of Tonkin incident: US destroyers are allegedly attacked by North Vietnamese torpedo boats; President Johnson orders air strikes against North Vietnam.
- Warren Commission finds Lee Harvey Oswald acted alone in assassination of President Kennedy.
- Harold Wilson leads Labour Party to victory in general election.
- Jawaharl Nehru, Indian Prime Minister since independence, dies after heart attack.
- Black leader, Nelson Mandela, sentenced to life imprisonment in South Africa.
- President Johnson signs Civil Rights Act.
- Soviet leader, Nikita Khrushchev, deposed; replaced by Leonid Brezhnev as Communist Party leader and Alexei Kosygin as Prime Minister.
- Martin Luther King awarded Nobel Peace Prize.
- Lyndon Johnson wins landslide victory in US presidential election.
- Kenya established as a republic with Jomo Kenyatta as President.

DEATHS

Lord Beaverbrook, Canadian-born British newspaper tycoon.
Brendan Behan, Irish playwright.
Ian Fleming, British novelist.
Alan Ladd, US actor.
Peter Lorre, US actor.
Harpo Marx, US comedian.
General Douglas MacArthur, US soldier.
Sean O'Casey, Irish writer.
Flannery O'Connor, US novelist.
Cole Porter, US composer.

1965

- Gambia becomes independent.
- Militant black leader, Malcolm X, assassinated in New York.
- President Johnson sends marines into Vietnam.
- Edward Heath elected leader of the Conservative Party.
- Race riots in Watts, Los Angeles.
- India and Pakistan at war over disputed territory of Kashmir.
- Singapore separates from Malaysia.
- Ian Smith announces Universal Declaration of Independence of Rhodesia; Britain imposes oil embargo.
- General de Gaulle wins French presidential election.
- Death penalty for murder abolished in Britain.

DEATHS

Sir Winston Leonard Churchill, British statesman.

Nat King Cole, US singer.
Thomas Stearns Eliot, US poet.
Stan Laurel, British-born US comedian.
Le Corbusier (Charles Edouard Jeanneret), Swiss-born French architect.
Albert Schweitzer, German-born French doctor and missionary.

1966

- Indira Gandhi becomes Prime Minister of India.
- British Guiana becomes independent as Guyana.
- Barbados becomes an independent state within the British Commonwealth.
- Moors murderers, Myra Hindley and Ian Brady, sentenced to life imprisonment.
- Mao Zedong proclaims 'Cultural Revolution' in China.
- Prime Minister Dr Hendrik Verwoerd assassinated in South Africa and is succeeded by B. J. Vorster.
- President de Gaulle announces that France is to withdraw her troops from NATO.
- Aberfan disaster in Wales: 116 children and 28 adults killed by collapsed slag heap.
- English football team win the World Cup.
- Truman Capote's *In Cold Blood*.
  DEATHS
  André Breton, French poet and author.
  Lenny Bruce, US comedian.
  Montgomery Clift, US actor.
  Walt Disney, US animator.
  Alberto Giacometti, Italian sculptor.
  Buster Keaton, US actor and director.
  Evelyn Waugh, British novelist.

1967

- Jeremy Thorpe elected leader of the Liberal Party.
- Six Day War between Israel and Arab nations (third Arab-Israeli War): Israel takes territory from Egypt, Jordan and Syria.
- 50,000 demonstrators against the Vietnam War gather at the Lincoln Memorial in Washington DC.
- Ernesto ('Che') Guevara shot dead in the Bolivian jungle.
- Britain reapplies to join the European Community.
- Oil tanker *Torrey Canyon* goes aground off Land's End causing major pollution of the coastline.
- Eastern region of Nigeria breaks away as independent state of Biafra.
- Brian Epstein, manager of the Beatles, commits suicide.
- US airforce intensifies bombing of North Vietnam.
- Christian N. Barnard performs first heart transplant in Groote Schuur Hospital, Cape Town.
- Cunard liner *Queen Elizabeth II* launched.
- Donald Campbell killed in jet-powered boat *Bluebird* while attempting to break the world water-speed record.
- Fire kills three US astronauts in Apollo spacecraft on launch pad.
- Expo 67 opens in Montreal.
  DEATHS
  Konrad Adenauer, German statesman.
  John Coltrane, US jazz musician.
  Sir Victor Gollancz, British publisher.
  J. Vivian Leigh, British actress.
  René Magritte, Belgian artist.
  John Masefield, British poet.

J. Robert Oppenheimer, US nuclear physicist.
Joe Orton, British playwright.
Dorothy Parker, US author and critic.
Claude Rains, US actor.
Arthur Ransome, British author.
Carl Sandburg, US poet.
Siegfried Sassoon, British poet.
Spencer Tracy, US actor.

1968

- Tet (New Year) Offensive in Vietnam: the Vietcong launch widespread attacks against southern cities.
- Alexander Dubcek named First Secretary of Czechoslovak Communist Party; begins reform of socialist system.
- US President Johnson announces he will not seek re-election.
- Violent anti-Vietnam war demonstrations in London.
- Martin Luther King assassinated in Memphis hotel.
- Robert Fitzgerald Kennedy assassinated in Los Angeles hotel.
- Student riots and street-fighting in Paris.
- Soviet tanks move into Prague to suppress 'Prague Spring' reform programme.
- Violent anti-Vietnam war demonstrations disrupt Democratic Party Convention in Chicago.
- Richard M. Nixon elected US President.

  DEATHS
  Enid Blyton, British author of children's books.
  Jim Clark, British racing driver.
  Anthony John Hancock, British comedian.
  Mervyn Peake, British author and artist.
  Upton Sinclair, US author.

1969

- British troops sent to suppress conflict between Protestants and Roman Catholics in Northern Ireland.
- Jan Palach, Czech student, burns himself to death in protest against Soviet occupation of Prague.
- Golda Meir, President of Israel.
- General de Gaulle resigns as French President: George Pompidou elected to replace him.
- Yassar Arafat appointed leader of the Palestine Liberation Organization.
- Neil Armstrong, commander of US spacecraft Apollo 11, becomes the first man on the moon.
- Chappaquiddick Incident: Senator Edward Kennedy fails to report car accident in which his passenger, Mary Jo Kopechne, is killed.
- Sharon Tate, pregnant wife of film director Roman Polanski, is brutally murdered in Beverly Hills mansion by Charles Manson gang.
- Colonel Muammar Gaddafi seizes power in Libya.
- 'Vietnam Moratorium': largest ever anti-Vietnam war demonstrations in the US.
- Oil discovered in the British and Norwegian sectors of the North Sea.
- Nigeria bans Red Cross aid for starving Biafrans.
- Concorde, British-built supersonic airliner, makes maiden flight.
- Kurt Vonnegut's *Slaughterhouse Five*.
- Philip Roth's *Portnoy's Complaint*.

  DEATHS
  Richmal Crompton, British author.

Otto Dix, German artist.
Judy Garland, US actress and singer.
Walter Gropius, German architect.
Brian Jones, British rock musician.
Jack Kerouac, US author.
John Wyndham, British author.

1970

- Conservatives win general election and Edward Heath becomes Prime Minister.
- Britain makes third application to join the European Community.
- Biafran Civil War ends with Biafran capitulation to Nigerian Federal forces.
- President Nixon sends US troops into Cambodia.
- Four students killed by National Guard during anti-Vietnam war demonstration at Kent State University, Ohio.
- Salvador Allende elected President of Chile.
- Palestinian commandos hijack and blow up three airliners at Dawson's Field, Jordan.
- Anwar Sadat succeeds Gamel Abdul Nassser as President of Egypt.
- Civil war begins in Cambodia.
- Typhoon and tidal wave kill 150,000 in East Pakistan.
- Germaine Greer's *The Female Eunuch*.

  DEATHS
  Sir John Barbirolli, British conductor.
  General Charles de Gaulle, French statesman.
  Edward Morgan Foster, British novelist.
  John Dos Passos, US author.
  Eva Hesse, German-born US sculptor.
  Jimi Hendrix, US guitarist.
  Yukio Mishima, Japanese author.
  Erich Maria Remarque, German author.
  Mark Rothko, US artist.
  Bertrand Arthur William Russell, British philosopher.

1971

- Fighting in Vietnam spreads to Laos and Cambodia.
- General Idi Amin seizes power from President Milton Obote in Uganda.
- Sixty-six football fans crushed to death by collapsed barrier at Ibrox Park stadium, Glasgow.
- Lieutenant William L. Calley Jr found guilty of massacre in My Lai village, Vietnam in 1968.
- 'Pentagon Papers' exposing secret history of US involvement in Vietnam begin to appear in the *New York Times*.
- Britain introduces internment (imprisonment without trial) to combat IRA terrorism in Northern Ireland.
- East Pakistan declares its independce as the new state of Bangladesh: it is occupied by the Pakistani army, composed of troops from West Pakistan, and civil war ensues.
- Jean-Claude Duvalier succeeds his father, Francois 'Papa Doc' Duvalier, as President of Haiti.
- China is admitted to the United Nations.
- Agreement signed to prepare Rhodesia's legal independence from Britain and settle issue of transition to African majority rule.
- Attica Prison revolt: 10 warders and 32 prisoners die in five days of mayhem.
- India defeats Pakistan in two-week war over India's support for Bangladesh.
- Decimal currency introduced in Britain.
- Open University inaugurated.

- Earthquake in Los Angeles kills 51 people.
  DEATHS
  Louis Armstrong, US jazz trumpeter.
  Gabrielle 'Coco' Chanel, French fashion designer.
  Harold Lloyd, US film actor and comedian.
  Ogden Nash, US poet.
  Igor Stravinsky, Russian composer.

1972
- Bangladesh (former East Pakistan) established as independent state.
- President Nixon visits Russia and China.
- Five burglars arrested in Democratic National Headquarters in the Watergate Building in Washington DC: beginning of Watergate Affair.
- George Wallace, Governor of Alabama, paralysed after assassination attempt.
- Lon Nol takes power in Cambodia.
- Bloody Sunday in Ulster: British paratroopers fire on civil rights demonstrators killing thirteen.
- Heath government imposes direct rule on Northern Ireland.
- Eire, Britain and Denmark become full members of the European Community.
- Japanese terrorists massacre 25 people at Lod International airport, Tel Aviv.
- Last US combat troops withdraw from South Vietnam: US bombing of North Vietnam and Viet Cong supply routes in the south intensified.
- 'Black September' Arab terrorists kill eleven Israeli athletes at Munich Olympics.
- Idi Amin expels 50,000 Ugandan Asians with British passports.
- Earthquake in Managua, Nicaragua kills 10,000 people.
- Philippine President Marcos declares martial law to combat so-called 'Communist rebellion'.
  DEATHS
  Maurice Chevalier, French actor and singer.
  J. Edgar Hoover, FBI director since 1924
  Dr Louis Leakey, British anthropologist.
  Cecil Day Lewis, British poet and novelist.
  Ezra Pound, US poet.

1973
- Cease-fire in Vietnam agreed at Paris peace conference.
- Yom Kippur War (Fourth Arab-Israeli War): Egyptian and Syrian forces launch surprise attack on Sinai and the Golan Heights, captured by Israel in 1967; ends with a UN cease-fire, largely negotiated by the US and the Soviet Union.
- Top Nixon aids resign as Watergate scandal penetrates the Oval Office (April); Senate Watergate hearings begin (May).
- President Salvador Allende killed during military coup in Chile.
- Greek army seizes power in Athens overthrowing President George Papadopoulos.
- Arab oil countries increase prices and cut production in protest at US support of Israel in Yom Kippur War.
- Miners' strike brings government announcement of three-day week to conserve fuel stocks.
- Value Added Tax (VAT) introduced in Britain.
- Aleksandr Solzhenitsyn's *Gulag Archipelago*.
  DEATHS
  Wystan Hugh Auden, British poet.
  Elizabeth Bowen, Irish writer.
  Sir Noel Coward, British playwright.

John Ford, US film director.
Bruce Lee, Kung Fu film star.
Pablo Picasso, Spanish artist.
Edward G. Robinson, US actor.
John Ronald Reuel Tolkein, British author.

1974
- Edward Heath resigns and Harold Wilson leads minority government after snap election (March); Labour win second election with tiny majority (October).
- IRA bombs kill 21 and injure 120 in two Birmingham pubs.
- Bloodless coup in Portugal: dictatorship ended by military intervention and democratic reforms inaugurated.
- Syria and Israel agree to cease fire on the Golan Heights.
- Turkish invasion of Cyprus.
- President Nixon resigns as White House tape recordings implicate him in Watergate cover-up and Senate moves to impeach him; Gerald Ford sworn in as new President.
- Greek military junta collapses and ex-Premier, Constantine Karamanlis, returns from exile to head new government.
- President Haile Selassie overthrown by coup in Ethiopia.
- Civil war in Cambodia ends in victory for the communist Khmer Rouge under Pol Pot; the country is renamed Kampuchea.

DEATHS
Duke Ellington, US jazz musician.
Samuel Goldwyn, US film producer.
Virttorio de Sica, Italian film director.
Eric Linklater, British novelist.
Walter Lippman, US journalist.

1975
- Angola achieves independence from Portugal (January); civil war breaks out (November).
- Margaret Thatcher elected leader of the Conservative Party.
- Saigon surrenders to North Vietnamese troops.
- Communist Khmer Rouge seize control of Cambodia: Pol Pot regime inaugurates 'Year Zero'.
- Beirut erupts in civil war between Christians and Muslims (till 1990).
- Spain reverts to monarchy after the death of General Franco: Prince Juan Carlos crowned as King Juan Carlos I.
- Suez Canal reopened for first time since 1967 Arab-Israeli War.
- First live broadcast of House of Commons debate.
- Internment (detention without trial) ends in Northern Ireland.
- Terrorists led by Carlos the Jackal raid Vienna headquarters of the Organization of Petroleum Exporting Countries (OPEC).

DEATHS
Sir Pelham Grenville Woodhouse, British-born US author.
Sir John Frederick Neville Cardus, British music critic and cricket writer.
Sam Giancana, Chicago Mafia boss.
Susan Hayward, US actress.
Graham Hill, British racing driver.
Sir Julian Huxley, British scientist and philosopher.
Aristotle Onassis, Greek shipping magnate.
Dimitri Shostakovich, Russian composer.
Thornton Wilder, US writer.

1976

- Harold Wilson resigns: James Callaghan becomes Prime Minister.
- Jeremy Thorpe resigns as leader of the Liberal Party: David Steel elected to replace him.
- Ian Smith accepts British proposals for majority rule in Rhodesia, ending 11 years of illegal independence.
- President Isabel Peron overthrown by Argentine military in bloodless coup.
- US celebrates its bicentennial.
- Dr Mario Soares elected Prime Minister of Portugal.
- North and South Vietnam reunified as Socialist Republic of Vietnam with Hanoi as capital: Saigon renamed Ho Chi Minh City.
- Death of Chairman Mao Zedong.
- Jimmy Carter elected US President.
- World's first scheduled supersonic passenger service inaugurated: two Concorde airliners take off simultaneously from London and Paris.
- Israeli commandos rescue 103 hostages held at Entebbe Airport in Uganda by pro-Palestinian hijackers.
- Widespread anti-apartheid riots in black townships of South Africa.
  DEATHS
  Dame Agatha Christie, British crime writer.
  Benjamin Britten, British composer.
  Max Ernst, German-born French artist.
  John Paul Getty, US oil tycoon.
  Howard Hughes, US tycoon.
  Chou En-lai, Chinese Premier.
  Fritz Lang, German film director.
  Man Ray, US artist and photographer.
  André Malraux, French writer and politician.
  Field Marshal Bernard Law Montgomery, First Viscount Montgomery of El Alamein, British commander.
  Paul Robeson, US singer and black activist.
  Laurence Stephen Lowry, British artist.

1977

- Liberal and Labour parties form Lib-Lab Pact.
- Moraji R. Desai, Prime Minister of India after resignation of Indira Gandhi.
- Menaham Begin, Prime Minister of Israel after resignation of Yitzhak Rabin.
- Convicted murderer, Gary Gilmore, executed by firing squad in Utah State Prison: first convict to be executed in the US in ten years.
- Egyptian President, Anwar Sadat, visits Israel: the first visit by an Arab leader since the Jewish state was founded in 1948.
- Two Jumbo jets collide at Tenerife Airport: 574 passengers killed in world's worst aviation disaster.
- Prime Minister of Pakistan, Zulfikar Ali Bhutto, overthrown by General Zia ul-Huq.
- Rock singer, Elvis Presley, dies of drug overdose at age of 42.
- South African black leader, Steve Biko, beaten to death in prison cell at Port Elizabeth in South Africa.
- US Space Shuttle makes maiden flight on top of a Boeing 747.
  DEATHS
  Maria Callas, Greek soprano.
  Sir Charles Chaplin, British actor and director.
  Joan Crawford, US actress.
  Bing Crosby, US singer and actor.

Peter Finch, Australian actor.
Julius 'Groucho' Marx, US actor and comedian.
Vladimir Nabokov, Russian-born US author.
Anais Nin, US author.

1978

- Former Italian Prime Minister, Aldo Moro, is kidnapped and murdered by Red Brigade terrorists.
- Military junta seizes power in Afghanistan.
- US establishes full diplomatic relations with People's Republic of China.
- Pieter Willem Botha, Prime Minister of South Africa after resignation of John Vorster.
- Military coup in Bolivia.
- Prime Minister of Israel, Menaham Begin, and Egyptian President, Anwar Sadat, agree on framework for Middle East peace in the Camp David Accords at a summit organized by President Carter.
- Shah of Iran imposes martial law to suppress anti-government demonstrations.
- Cardinal Luciani elected Pope John Paul I; he dies after 33 days in office and is succeeded by Polish Cardinal, Karol Wojtyla, as Pope John Paul II.
- Members of the People's Temple, a US religious cult led by Rev. Jim Jones, commit mass suicide in Guyana.
- Louise Brown, the world's first test-tube baby, born in Britain.

DEATHS

Charles Boyer, French actor.
Jacques Brel, Belgian singer.
Jomo Kenyatta, Kenyan statesman.
Margaret Mead, US anthropologist.

1979

- Shah of Iran is driven into exile by supporters of Muslim leader, Ayatollah Khomeini, who returns to Tehran after 14 years in exile.
- Vietnam invades Cambodia and crushes Khmer Rouge regime: evidence of mass killings under leader, Pol Pot, emerge.
- Regime of Idi Amin collapses in Uganda.
- Egypt and Israel sign Camp David Accords.
- Nationalist hopes for devolution in Wales and Scotland are killed by referendum results: a majority vote against a Welsh Assembly, and only 33% for a Scottish Assembly, short of the 40% required.
- Conservatives win general election: Margaret Thatcher becomes first woman Prime Minister.
- Leonid Brezhnev and President Carter sign SALT-2 arms limitation treaty.
- Accident at Three Mile Island nuclear plant in Pennsylvania.
- Sandinista rebels overthrow dictator, General Anastasio Samosa, in Nicaragua.
- Earl Mountbatten of Burma murdered by IRA bomb.
- Supporters of Ayatollah Khomenei attack US embassy in Tehran and seize Marines and staff as hostages.
- Sir Anthony Blunt, the Queen's art adviser, revealed as a Russian spy, the 'Fourth Man' in the Burgess, MacLean and Philby affair.
- Soviet troops invade Afghanistan.
- Lancaster House Agreement arranges cease-fire in the guerilla war in Rhodesia and elections to effect transfer to black majority rule in a new state to be called Zimbabwe.

DEATHS

Dame Gracie Fields, British actress and singer.

Herbert Marcuse, German-born US philosopher.
Mary Pickford, US actress.
Jean Renoir, French film director.
Nelson Rockefeller, US politician.
Jean Seberg, US actress.
John Wayne, US actor.

1980

- Robert Mugabe elected Prime Minister of Zimbabwe.
- In Tehran, US military bids to rescue hostages held by Iranians in the American Embassy aborted due to mechanical failures.
- SAS storm Iranian Embassy in London to release hostages held by terrorists.
- Archbishop Romero shot in San Salvador, El Salvador.
- Sanjay Gandhi, the 33-year-old youngest son of Indira Gandhi, killed in plane crash.
- Polish strikers led by Lech Walesa win concessions from Communist government on trade union rights; Solidarity, central workers' organization, formed with Lech Walesa as leader.
- Iraq attacks Iranian oil installations at Abadan: Iraq-Iran War begins.
- Ronald Reagan elected US President.
- Michael Foot succeeds James Callaghan as Labour Party leader.
- Jeremy Thorpe, former leader of the Liberal Party, acquitted in conspiracy trial.
- John Lennon murdered in New York by Mark David Chapman.
- William Golding's *Rites of Passage*.

DEATHS
Joy Adamson, naturalist.
Sir Cecil Beaton, British photographer and designer.
Jimmy Durante, US comedian.
Sir Alfred Hitchcock, British film director.
Oscar Kokoschka, Austrian artist.
Steve McQueen, US actor.
Henry Miller, US writer.
Jean-Paul Sartre, French philosopher.
Peter Sellers, British actor and comedian.
Mae West, US actress.

1981

- Iran releases US Embassy hostages after 444 days in captivity.
- General Jarulzelski appointed Prime Minister in Poland: strikes and demonstrations led by Solidarity intensify (February); martial law declared (December).
- President Reagan wounded in assassination attempt outside Hilton Hotel, Washington.
- Gang of Four (Roy Jenkins, David Owen, Bill Rodgers and Shirley Williams) break with Labour and announce the formation of a new party—the Social Democrats.
- Rioting in Brixton, Liverpool and Manchester in response to allegedly heavy policing.
- Hunger strike by IRA prisoners at the Maze Prison in Northern Ireland: 10 die.
- Peter Sutcliffe convicted of Yorkshire Ripper murders.
- Pope John Paul II survives assassination attempt by Turkish gunman in St Peter's Square, Rome.
- French elect François Mitterrand as new President.
- Prince Charles marries Lady Diana Spencer in St Paul's Cathedral: 700 million watch on television worldwide.
- Egyptian President Anwar Sadat assassinated at military parade in Cairo.

- Kampuchea is renamed Cambodia.
  DEATHS
  Samuel Barber, US composer.
  Karl Bohm, Austrian conductor.
  Bill Haley, US rock singer.
  William Holden, US actor.
  Bob Marley, Jamaican reggae star.
  Jessie Matthews, British actress and singer.
  Albert Speer, German architect.
  Natalie Wood, US actress.

1982

- Unemployment in Britain reaches over three million.
- Barbican Centre arts complex opens in London.
- Argentina invades the Falkland Islands in the South Atlantic (2 April); Thatcher sends Task Force (5 April); Argentine cruiser *General Belgrano* sunk by torpedoes (2 May); HMS *Sheffield* hit by Exocet missile (4 May); first land battles between Argentinian and British troops (21 May); Argentine attack on two British supply ships off Bluff Cove (7 June); Argentinians surrender (14 June).
- Israel invades Lebanon in reprisal for Palestinian guerilla activities (June); Israeli forces drives the PLO out of Beirut (August); Lebanese Christian militia massacre hundreds in Palestinian refugee camps of Sabra and Chatila in West Beirut.
- Leonid Brezhnev dies; Yuri Andropov becomes Soviet leader.
- Women's Peace Camp established at Greenham Common in Berkshire to protest against planned siting of US Cruise missiles at nearby US military base.
- Britain's fourth TV channel, Channel Four, goes on the air.
- Princess Grace of Monaco (Grace Kelly) killed in car crash.
- Thames flood barrier raised for the first time.
  DEATHS
  Ingrid Bergman, Swedish actress.
  Rainer Werner Fassbinder, German film director.
  Henry Fonda, US actor.
  Glenn Gould, Canadian pianist.
  Theolonis Monk, US jazz pianist.
  Carl Orff, German composer.
  Romy Scheider, Austrian actress.
  Jacques Tati, French film director and actor.

1983

- 'Star Wars' defence system proposed by President Reagan.
- 'Hitler Diaries' exposed as fake after extracts are published in the German news magazine *Stern* and the *Sunday Times*.
- Margaret Thatcher re-elected in landslide general election.
- Benigno Aquino, leading opponent of President Marcos, assassinated at Manila Airport.
- Soviet Union shoots down Korean Airlines' Boeing 747 flight 007 with the loss of 269 lives over Sakhalin Island off Siberia: Soviets claim the aircraft was on spying mission.
- Shia Muslim suicide bombers kill 241 Marines and 58 French paratroopers in Beirut by driving trucks filled with explosives into their compounds.
- Neil Kinnock elected leader of the Labour Party.
- US troops invade Grenada to remove Cuban presence from the island.
- Civilian rule restored in Argentina with the inauguration of Raul Alfonsin as President.

DEATHS

Luis Buñuel, Spanish film director.
George Cukor, US film director.
Arthur Koestler, Hungarian-born British writer.
Joán Miró, Spanish artist.
David Niven, British actor.
Ralph Richardson, British actor.
Gloria Swanson, US actress.
Sir William Walton, British composer.
Dame Rebecca West, British author.

1984

- Konstantin Chernenko succeeds Andropov as Soviet Communist Party leader.
- Pierre Trudeau resigns as Canadian Prime Minister.
- Diplomatic ties with Libya are severed after the shooting of WPC Yvonne Fletcher outside the Libyan Embassy in London.
- Discovery of the human immunodeficiency virus (HIV), the so-called AIDS virus, announced in Washington.
- Miners' national strike against pit closures begins.
- IRA bomb at Conservative Party Conference in Brighton kills five.
- Prime Minister of India, Indira Gandhi, assassinated by Sikh bodyguards: she is succeeded by her son, Rajiv.
- BBC television report on Ethiopian famine prompts massive aid effort.
- Gas leak from a chemical processing plant in Bhopal, India, kills over 2,000 people.

DEATHS

William 'Count' Basie, US jazz band leader.
Sir John Betjeman, British poet.
Richard Burton, British actor.
Truman Capote, US author.
Diana Dors, British actress.
Marvin Gaye, US singer.
Lillian Hellman, US author and playwright.
Joseph Losey, US film director.
James Mason, British actor.
Eric Morecambe, British comedian.
Sam Peckinpah, US film director.
J. B. Priestley, British author and playwright.
Sir Arthur 'Bomber' Harris, British Commander of RAF during Second World War.
Francois Truffaut, French film director.
Johnny Weismuller, US actor and athlete.

THE EMERGENCE OF A NEW WORLD ORDER

1985

- Miners vote to end year-long national strike.
- Mikhail Gorbachev appointed new leader of the Soviet Union: begins to initiate wide-ranging liberal reforms (Glasnost) and economic restructuring (Perestroika).
- House of Lords proceedings televised for the first time.
- British football teams banned indefinitely from European competition after 38 people die when Liverpool fans riot at Heysel Stadium, Brussels.
- Live Aid Concert raises £40 million for famine victims in Ethiopia.
- President Reagan and Soviet leader Mikhail Gorbachev meet at Geneva summit.

DEATHS

Laura Ashley, British fashion designer.
Yul Brynner, US actor.
James Cameron, British journalist and author.
Marc Chagall, Russian-born French painter.
Robert Graves, British poet.
Rock Hudson, US actor.
Philip Larkin, British poet.
Sir Michael Redgrave, British actor.
Orson Welles, US actor and director.

1986

- US space shuttle *Challenger* explodes on takeoff killing crew of seven.
- Construction of the Channel Tunnel begins.
- Cabinet Ministers, Michael Heseltine and Leon Brittain, resign over the Westland Affair.
- Swedish Prime Minister, Olof Palme, assassinated in Stockholm.
- Ferdinand Marcos overthrown and replaced by Mrs Corazon Aquino as President of the Philippines.
- Spain and Portugal join the EC: there are now 12 member countries.
- Jeffrey Archer resigns as Chairman of the Conservative Party after allegations of payments to a prostitute.
- US launches air strikes against terrorist targets in Libya.
- Russian nuclear reactor at Chernobyl is seriously damaged by fire and contaminates a wide area.
- President Reagan denies any knowledge of the 'Irangate' scandal whereby profits from US weapons sales to Iran were used covertly to fund the Contra rebels fighting the left-wing Sandinista government in Nicaragua.

DEATHS

Simone de Beauvoir, French author.
Jorge Luis Borges, Argentine author.
James Cagney, US actor.
Benny Goodman, US jazz clarinettist.
Cary Grant, British-born US actor.
Henry Moore, British sculptor.
Otto Preminger, US film director.

1987

- Terry Waite, special envoy of the Archbishop of Canterbury, is kidnapped in Beirut by members of the militant Islamic group, Hezbollah.
- The car ferry *Herald of Free Enterprise* capsizes off Zeebrugge with the loss of 188 lives.
- Margaret Thatcher re-elected for third term as Prime Minister.
- Government announces plans to introduce a Poll Tax to replace the rates system for funding local services.
- Former SS officer, Klaus Barbie (the 'Butcher of Lyons'), is sentenced in a court in Lyons to life imprisonment for war crimes.
- Rudolph Hess found dead in Spandau Prison after apparently hanging himself.
- David Owen resigns as leader of the SDP in opposition to talks about merging with the Liberals.
- 'Black Monday' in the City of London: over £100 billion wiped off the value of shares on the stock market.

- IRA bomb kills eleven people at a Remembrance Day service in Enniskillen, Northern Ireland.
- President Reagan and Mikhail Gorbachev sign treaty to arrange for the dismantling of Soviet and US medium-and shorter-range missiles.

  DEATHS

  Fred Astaire, US dancer and actor.

  Rita Hayworth, US actress.

  John Huston, US film director.

  Danny Kaye, US actor and comedian.

  Lee Marvin, US actor.

  Jacqueline Du Pré, British cellist.

  Andy Warhol, US artist.

1988

- Intifada uprising by West Bank and Gaza Arabs against Israeli occupation begins.
- *Piper Alpha* disaster: 167 workers killed in North Sea oil rig explosion.
- Iran and Iraq agree a cease-fire to end eight years of conflict.
- Floods in Bangladesh kill 300 and leave over 20 million people homeless.
- Social and Liberal Democratic Party formed by the merger of the Liberals and SDP.
- Canadian sprinter, Ben Johnson, is found guilty of using drugs and is stripped of his gold medal for the 100 metres at the Seoul Olympics.
- George Bush elected US President.
- President Gorbachev announces dramatic reduction in Red Army strength.
- Earthquake in Armenia kills over 100,000 people.
- Pan American jumbo jet blown up by terrorist bomb over Lockerbie in Scotland, killing all 259 passengers on board and 11 people from the town (December).

  DEATHS

  Sir Frederick Ashton, British ballet choreographer.

  Enzio Ferrari, Italian racing car magnate.

  Richard Feynman, US physicist.

  Trevor Howard, British actor.

  Roy Orbison, US singer.

  Kenneth Williams, British comedy actor.

1989

- Emperor Hirohito dies and is succeeded by his son, Crown Prince Akihito.
- Author Salman Rushdie goes into hiding after the Ayatollah Khomeini orders his execution for blaspheming Islam in his book *The Satanic Verses*; diplomatic relations between Britain and Iran are broken off.
- Soviet troops leave Afghanistan after ten-year occupation.
- Supertanker *Exxon Valdez* spills its cargo of oil in Price William Sound, Alaska: the worst oil spillage in US history.
- Ninety-four football fans crushed to death at Hillsborough Stadium in Sheffield.
- People's Liberation Army crush a student pro-democracy demonstration in Tiananmen Square in Peking.
- Poland elects Tadeusz Mazowiecki as its first non-Communist Prime Minister.
- Vietnamese troops leave Cambodia after eleven years of occupation.
- Hungary announces changes to its constitution to allow free elections.
- Guildford Four (Gerard Conlon, Carole Richardson, Patrick Armstrong and Paul Hill), convicted of IRA pub bombings in 1974, based on confessions fabricated by the police, are released.
- The Berlin Wall is dismantled as political reform in East Germany allows free movement of East German citizens to the West.
- House of Commons proceedings begin to be televised.

- Communist leadership in Czechoslovakia resigns; playwright, Vaclav Havel, is elected as President to prepare for free elections.
- Romanian dictator Nicolae Ceausescu and his wife Elena are executed by firing squad as Communist rule collapses.
- National Assembly in Bulgaria approves liberal political reforms in response to mass demonstrations.
- US troops invade Panama to oust dictator Manuel Noriega.

  DEATHS

  A. J. Ayer, British philosopher.
  Lucille Ball, US comedienne.
  Samuel Beckett, Irish writer.
  Irving Berlin, US songwriter.
  Salvador Dali, Spanish artist.
  Bette Davis, US actress.
  R. D. Laing, British psychiatrist.
  Herbert von Karajan, Austrian conductor.
  Daphne du Maurier, British novelist.
  Lord Olivier, British actor.
  Georges Simenon, Belgian novelist.

1990

- Ban on African National Congress (ANC) lifted in South Africa; black nationalist leader Nelson Mandela freed from prison in Cape Town after 27 years; Mandela and ANC enter talks with President F. W. de Klerk about political future of the country.
- Sandinista government in Nicaragua defeated in democratic elections by National Opposition Union led by Senora Violeta Chamorro.
- Anti-poll tax march in London turns into a riot.
- Boris Yeltsin elected Chairman of the Russian Soviet Federated Socialist Republic.
- David Owen disbands Social Democratic Party because of lack of support.
- Brian Keenan, one of several Western hostages held by militant Islamic groups in Beirut, is freed after 1597 days in captivity.
- Iraq invades Kuwait (August).
- West and East Germany are united (October); Helmut Kohl elected Chancellor of a united Germany (December).
- Britain rejects timetable for a single European currency by the year 2000 at EC summit in Rome.
- Margaret Thatcher withdraws from Conservative Party leadership contest and is replaced by John Major.

  DEATHS

  Leonard Bernstein, US composer and conductor.
  Aaron Copland, US composer.
  Sammy Davis Jr, US entertainer.
  Greta Garbo, Swedish-born actress.
  Ava Gardner, US actress.
  Rex Harrison, British actor.
  Barbara Stanwyck, US actress.
  A. J. P. Taylor, British historian.
  Paul Tortellier, French cellist.
  Irvine Wallace, US writer.

1991

- The British government replaces the poll tax with a new 'council tax' based on property values.

- Gulf War begins with operation 'Desert Storm', a massive air assault on Iraq by British, US and Saudi forces (17 January); land war begins (24 February) and Iraq capitulates after 100-hour conflict.
- Soviet troops crack down on Baltic states as demands for independence intensify.
- Last of the apartheid laws in South Africa are abolished.
- Saddam Hussein suppresses Kurd revolt in northern Iraq.
- Prime Minister of India, Rajiv Gandhi, is assassinated.
- Boris Yeltsin elected President of the Russian Soviet Federated Socialist Republic.
- Violence escalates in Yugoslavia as the Serbian-dominated federal army attempts to suppress demands for independence by Slovenia and Croatia (June).
- The Soviet Union comes to an end: President Gorbachev is temporarily ousted by hardline Communists opposed to his reform programme and then reinstated after Boris Yeltsin leads popular resistance to coup leaders (August); Russia, Byelorussia, Ukraine and eight other former Soviet republics form the Commonwealth of Independent States (8 December); Gorbachev resigns (25 December).
- British hostages in Beirut released by Islamic fundamentalist group, Hezbollah: John McCarthy (August), Jackie Mann (September) and Terry Waite (November).
  DEATHS
  Dame Peggy Ashcroft, British actress.
  Miles Davis, US jazz musician.
  Dame Margot Fonteyn, British ballet dancer.
  Graham Greene, British novelist.
  Sir David Lean, British film director.
  Robert Maxwell, publisher and fraudulent tycoon.
  Freddie Mercury, British rock star.

1992

- European Commission recognizes independence of breakaway republics, Croatia and Slovenia, legitimizing the disintegration of the former Yugoslavia (January); Bosnia-Herzegovina votes for independence (March); fighting between the Serb-dominated Yugoslav army and the secessionist republics intensifies; Macedonia declares independence; Yugoslavia now consists of Serbia and Montenegro.
- Judge Giovanni Falcone, Italy's chief anti-Mafia investigator, is murdered by the Mafia in Palermo.
- John Smith is elected leader of the Labour Party.
- US Marines land in Somalia to curb Somali warlords.
- Prince Charles and Diana, Princess of Wales, announce their separation.
- Bill Clinton is elected US President.
  DEATHS
  Isaac Asimov, US science-fiction writer.
  Richard Brooks, US film director.
  Marlene Dietrich, German-born US actress.
  Denholm Elliot, British actor.
  Alex Haley, US author.
  Benny Hill, British comedian.
  Frankie Howerd, British comedian.
  Robert Morley, British actor.
  Anthony Perkins, US actor.
  Sanjit Ray, Indian film director.

1993

- Oil tanker *Braer* runs aground off the Shetland Isles; environmental damage caused by oil spillage.
- Czechoslovakia is split into Slovakia and the Czech Republic.

- Inauguration of the Single European Market.
- President Bush and President Yeltsin sign START-II treaty cutting nuclear arsenals by two thirds.
- Bill Clinton takes office as US President.
- Queen Elizabeth II agrees to pay tax on private income.
- FBI siege of Branch Davidian cult headquarters at Waco, Texas, ends in mass suicide as building is deliberately set on fire.
- In South Africa, President de Klerk and ANC leader Nelson Mandela ratify a new democratic constitution (November).
- PLO-Israeli peace deal agreed after secret negotiations.
- State of Emergency is declared in Moscow: President Boris Yeltsin uses military force to oust opponents from the Russian Parliament building.
- There are elections in Cambodia and a democratic monarchist constitution is adopted, restoring Sihanouk to the throne.
- Two 10-year-old boys are found guilty of the murder of the 2-year-old James Bulger.
- European Union is inaugurated as the Maastricht Treaty comes into force.
- Downing Street Declaration on Northern Ireland by John Major and Taoiseach Albert Reynolds opens the way to all-party talks (December).

    ### DEATHS
    John Birks (Dizzy) Gillespie, US jazz musician.
    Anthony Burgess, British author, composer and critic.
    Sir William Golding, British author.
    William Randolph Hearst, US newspaper magnate.
    Audrey Hepburn, US actress.
    Rudolf Nureyev, Russian-born ballet dancer.
    Albert Sabin, US virologist.

1994

- Serb forces withdraw from around Sarajevo as NATOo threatens air strikes.
- Italian media tycoon, Silvio Berlusconi, becomes Prime Minster of Italy (March); resigns (December).
- Massacres of Tutsis by Hutus in Rwanda leave an estimated 800,000 dead and 1.5 million homeless.
- Nelson Mandela leads African National Congress to victory in South African elections (April); Mandela inaugurated as first black President (May).
- Israel and PLO sign a pact ending Israeli occupation of the Gaza Strip and Jericho.
- Labour Party leader John Smith dies; Tony Blair is elected new leader.
- President Kim Il-sung dies and is succeeded by his son, Kim Jong-il, as North Korean leader.
- Jordan and Israel sign peace treaty.
- US forces invade Haiti to oust military government.
- IRA announces cease-fire in Northern Ireland, opening way for political settlement (August); Loyalists announce cease-fire (October); peace talks begin between government and Sinn Fein (December).
- Roll-on roll-off car ferry *Estonia* sinks in Baltic with loss of 850 lives.
- Russia invades breakaway Caucasian state of Chechnya.
- Channel Tunnel opens.

    ### DEATHS
    Joseph Cotten, US actor.
    Peter Cushing, British actor.
    Burt Lancaster, US actor.
    Richard M. Nixon, US statesman.
    Henri Mancini, US composer.

Jacqueline Kennedy Onassis, former US First Lady.
John Osborne, British actor and playwright.
Dennis Potter, British TV dramatist.
Cesar Romero, US actor.
Telly Savalas, Greek-born US actor.
Mai Zetterling, Swedish actress.

1995

- Bosnian conflict: cease-fire begins (9 January); violated (11 February); Srebrenica, a Muslim 'safe area', falls to Serbs (July); Slobodan Milosevich, President of Serbia, Croatian leader, Franjo Tudjman, and Bosnian President, Alija Izetbegivic, agree to plan for unified Bosnia-Herzegovina at Dayton, Ohio (21 November); Accord is signed in Paris (14 December).
- Republic of Ireland votes for legalization of divorce.
- President Clinton visits Northern Ireland (November): the first US president to do so.
- Trial of actor and former football star, O. J. Simpson, starts in Los Angeles (24 January) for the murder of his estranged wife and her friend (in 1994); verdict is not guilty (October).
- Japanese city of Kobe hit by earthquake with loss of over 5000 lives (17 January).
- Oklahoma: Alfred P. Murrah building bombed with the loss of 158 lives.
- Merchant bank, Barings, collapses after rogue trader, Nick Leeson, loses an estimated £17 billion on the Japanese futures market.
- Israeli Prime Minister, Yitzakh Rabin, assassinated by right wing extremist, Yigal Amir (November 4); succeeded by Shimon Peres (November 15).
- Space stations *Mir* (Russian) and *Discovery* (American) rendezvous in space.
- Water is found on Mars.
- Ebola outbreak in Zaire kills 108.
- Nerve gas released in Tokyo subway kills 10 people and injures over 5000 (March); second attack in April in Yokahama; leader of AUM religious cult arrested and admits to attacks (May).
- Nigerian writer and political activist, Ken Saro-Wiwa, and eight other environmental campaigners hanged in Nigeria.
- South Africa wins Rugby Union World Cup.

DEATHS

Kingsley Amis, British novelist.
Mohamed Siad Barre, President of Somalia from 1969.
Robert Bolt, British playwright.
Peter Cook, British comedian.
Gerald Durrell, British author and conservationist.
Ronnie Kray, British gangster.
Dean Martin, US actor and singer.
Fred Perry, British tennis player.
Donald Pleasance, British actor.
Ginger Rogers, US actress.
Joe Slovo, South African Communist leader.
Harold Wilson, British Prime Minister 1964–76.

1996

- IRA bomb explodes at South Quay in London's Docklands killing 2 people, injuring 200 and causing extensive damage (9 February).
- More European countries ban import of British beef (March) because of BSE.
- At a Dunblane primary school, 16 children and a teacher are shot dead by gunman Thomas Hamilton, who then shoots himself (13 March).
- Robert Mugabe is re-elected President of Zimbabwe (17 March).

- Benyamin Netanyahu, Likud leader, elected as Prime Minister of Israel.
- Mary Robinson is the first President of the Republic of Ireland to make an official visit to Britain since foundation of Republic of Ireland (June).
- The Prince and Princess of Wales are divorced (28 August).
- Colonel Yayah Jammeh wins the presidential election in Gambia.
- France carries out a sixth nuclear test at Fangataufa.
- In Australia, Labor Party defeated by Liberal-National coalition.
- Bill Clinton re-elected as President of USA (5 November).
- Seven hundred people are killed when a cyclone hits southern India (6 November).
- Two aircraft collide in mid-air near New Delhi, India: all 351 passengers are killed (12 November).
- Fossils of bacteria discovered in a meteorite provide first evidence of life on Mars.
- Hutu-Tutsi crisis: fighting and massacres continue; 200,000 Rwandan Hutu refugees flee from camps in eastern Zaire (2 November); thousands of others are forcibly repatriated to Rwanda from Tanzania.
- Bosnian crisis: Serb soldiers and officers brought before International War Crimes Tribunal; exhumation of bodies of Muslims, massacred following capture of Srebrenica by Bosnian Serbs in July 1995.

DEATHS

Dorothy Lamour, American actress.

George Burns, American comedian.

Simon Cadell, British actor.

Ossie Clark, fashion designer.

Max Factor Jr., make-up artist.

Greer Garson, Irish-born actress.

Norman McCaig, British poet.

Timothy Leary, American psychologist.

Francois Mitterand, PM of France 1981–95.

Muhammad Najibullah, President of Afghanistan 1986–92.

Andreas Papandreou, Prime Minister of Greece 1981–89.

Willie Rushton, British satirist and comedian.

1997

- Ordination of first women priests in the Anglican Church in Wales (11 January).
- Inquest into the death of south London black teenager, Stephen Lawrence, finds that he was murdered by five youths in an unprovoked racist attack (13 February).
- Thirty-nine members of the Heaven's Gate sect in California, USA, commit suicide (27 March).
- Labour Party, with Tony Blair as leader, wins British general election with majority of 179 seats in House of Commons (1 May).
- IRA cease-fire announced to be in effect from 12 noon on 20 July; Sinn Fein invited to join the peace talks process (29 August).
- President Clinton is alleged to have sexually harassed Paula Jones when he was Governor of Arkansas; Supreme Court rules that he cannot claim constitutional immunity to escape a lawsuit (27 May).
- Liberal Party is returned to power in Canada (2 June).
- Hong Kong no longer a British colony: China assumes sovereignty (1 July).
- Mary McAleese becomes President of Ireland (31 October).
- Diana, Princess of Wales, her companion Dodi Fayed and their driver killed in a car crash in Paris.
- Referenda held in Scotland and Wales; a Scottish Parliament with tax-raising powers is approved by 63.5% of voters; a Welsh Assembly with fewer powers is approved by 50.3% of voters (17 September).

- Janet Jagan becomes President of Guyana (15 December).
- Socialist Party leader, Milan Milutinovic, elected President of Serbia (22 December).
  DEATHS
  Deng Xiaoping, leader of China since 1978.
  Jeanne Calment, the world's oldest person, aged 122.
  Denis Compton, British cricketer.
  Jacques Cousteau, French underwater explorer.
  Allan Ginsberg, American poet.
  Chaim Herzog, President of Israel, 1983–93.
  Ben Hogan, American golfer.
  Cheddi Jagan, President of Guyana since 1992.
  Laurie Lee, British poet and author.
  Sir George Solti, conductor.
  James Stewart, American actor.
  Gianni Versace, fashion designer.

1998

- Northern Ireland: Tony Blair addresses Irish Parliament, first British politician to do so since 1922 (26 November); Northern Ireland Accord, 'Good Friday Agreement', reached (10 April); Irish Parliament backs peace agreement (22 April); in two referenda Irish voters approve peace accord, 71% in favour in Northern Ireland and 94% in favour in the Republic of Ireland (22 May); new Assembly elected in Northern Ireland (26 June); Unionist leader David Trimble is elected First Minister (July); John Hume of the SDLP and David Trimble are awarded the Nobel Peace Prize (October).
- Sexual harassment case brought by Paula Jones against President Clinton dismissed (April).
- Investigation begins into alleged affair between President Clinton and White House intern, Monica S Lewinsky; the House of Representatives votes to impeach President Clinton on four articles (19 December).
- Iranian government withdraws its support of fatwa on Salman Rushdie, author of the *Satanic Verses* (24 September); Britain resumes diplomatic relations with Iran.
- Italian Prime Minister, Romano Prodi, is sacked in a vote of no confidence (9 October).
- Former Chilean dictator, General Augusto Pinochet, arrested in London (16 October).
- China signs agreement to improve human rights (5 October).
- German Chancellor of 16 years, Helmut Kohl, is defeated by Gerhard Schröder of the Social Democrats.
- Pope John Paul II makes his first visit to Cuba (21 January).
- Two boys, aged 13 and 11, kill 4 girls and a teacher and wound 11 others at Jonesboro Middle School, Arkansas, USA.
- Male impotence pill Viagra approved in USA.
- Canada's Supreme Court rules that Quebec does not have the right to separate from the rest of country.
- Daniel arap Moi is re-elected President of Kenya for a fifth term.
- Ezer Weizman is re-elected President of Israel (4 March).
- Islamic fundamentalist suicide bombers kill 43 people in Coimbatore, India.
- Football World Cup held in France (10 June); France wins (12 July).
- Burundi peace talks resume in Tanzania (20 July).
- The Council of the European Union in Brussels decide that eleven EU member states have fulfilled the conditions necessary for the adoption of a single currency on 1 January 1999 (3 May).

- Indonesian President Suharto resigns after 32 years in power; succeeded by his Vice President, B. J. Habibie (21 May).
- India stages underground nuclear testing (11, 13 May); Pakistan stages nuclear tests in response (29 May).
- Astronaut, John Glenn, aged 77, returns to space in *Discovery* to perform experiments on ageing (29 October).
- Operation Desert Fox: USA fires air missiles at Iraqi military sites (December).
- Conflict in Kosovo continues.

  DEATHS
  Frank Sinatra, American singer.
  Alan J. Pakula, film director and producer.
  John Derek, American film director.
  Joe Di Maggio, US baseball player.
  Lew Grade, British impresario.
  Florence Griffith Joyner, American athlete.
  Pol Pot, Khmer Rouge leader.
  Sir Alan Hodgkin, Nobel prize-winning scientist.

1999

- The euro, a single European currency, launched (1 January).
- UN troops pull out of Angola after ten years of peacekeeping in the Angolan Civil War (January).
- Earthquake in Colombia kills more than 2000 people (January).
- Barbados Labour Party wins power, leading the way for former British colony to become a republic (January).
- King Hussein of Jordan dies from cancer (8 February); Prince Abdullah becomes King.
- Kurdish leader, Abdullah Ocalan, arrested in Greece and returned to Turkey: Greek ambassadors in Zurich, Vienna and the Hague are kidnapped (February).
- A series of avalanches in the French, Italian, Austrian and Swiss Alps claim the lives of nearly 30 people (February).
- NATO countries now number 19: admission of Poland, Hungary and Czech Republic (March).
- Fire in the Mont Blanc Tunnel under Alps kills at least 40 people (March).
- Following a report on corruption, the entire European Commission, administrative arm of the European Union, resign (March).
- Libya agrees that the men suspected of placing a bomb in Pan Am Flight 103 which crashed at Lockerbie can stand trial under Scots law in Holland in front of a panel of three judges (March).
- The self-governing region of Nunavut in the Northwest Territories province of Canada comes into existence with a population of 85% Inuit (April).
- Ukrainian serial killer, Anatoly Onoprienko, is sentenced to death for the murder of at least 52 people (April).
- Two expelled pupils of a Colorado high school kill 12 pupils, a teacher and then themselves in the worst school massacre in US history (20 April).
- Elections for the devolved Scottish Parliament (6 May); Labour and the Liberal Democrats form a coalition; Labour comes top in Welsh Assembly elections but with no overall majority; official opening of the Scottish Parliament on 1 July.
- Worst tornadoes in living memory devastate Oklahoma City: 45 killed and 2000 homes destroyed (May).
- Allied jets attack missile site in Northern Iraq, bringing Allied aircraft responses to Iraqi 'provocation' to 150 since December 1998 (May).
- Johannes Rau of the Social Democrat Party is elected President of Germany (May).
- Lost Mayan city is found at border of Mexico and Guatemala (June).

- Indonesia holds its first democratic elections for 44 years; the Indonesian Democratic Party for Struggle, led by Megawati Sukarnoputri, win the most votes (7 June).
- President Nelson Mandela of South Africa stands down from politics (2 June); ANC led by Thabo Mbeki win 66% of vote in second democratic election since abolition of apartheid.
- Japan agrees to allow sale of birth control pill, ending a 40-year ban.
- 10,000 mummies found in a tomb in Bawiti in Egypt's Western Desert (June).
- Ehud Barak becomes new Prime Minister of Israel (May).
- German Parliament returns to Berlin.
- Kosovo peace conference begins at Rambouillet, France; thousands of ethnic Albanians flee the province (February); NATO launch air strikes against Serbia (24 March–10 June); Serbs agree to military withdrawal (9 June) leaving evidence of atrocities and 10,000 deaths; 40,000 Serbs flee from Kosovo into Serbia.
- China bans the popular Falun Gong religious sect (July).
- A new set of EU Commissioners is appointed, including some from the previous board (July).
- Vladimir Putin becomes Russian Prime Minister (August).
- Incursion from Chechnya into Dagestan is forcibly crushed by Russia.
- Western Turkey is ravaged by earthquake, with the death toll exceeding 13,000 (August).
- The inhabitants of East Timor vote for independence from Indonesia; Indonesian militias go on rampage and UN sends in Australian peace-keeping force (September).
- Yasser Arafat and Ehud Barak sign the Sharm el-Sheikh Agreement, hailed as charting the course to final peace (4 September).
- President Hosni Muhammad Mubarak of Egypt wins a fourth term in office.
- Accident at Tokaimura plant causes anxiety about nuclear safety in Japan (30 September).
- Train crash near Paddington Station, London, kills 31 people (5 October).
- Military coup ends civilian government of Nawaz Sharif in Pakistan (12 October).
- Armenian Prime Minister, Yazgen Sarkissian, and seven others are shot dead in the parliament building.
- Australians reject a Republican constitution in a national referendum held on 6 November.
- Boris Yeltsin resigns as Russian President (31 December).

DEATHS

Sir Dirk Bogarde, British actor.
Lionel Bart, British songwriter.
Boxcar Willie, American singer and songwriter.
Ann Haddy, Australian actress.
Stanley Kubrick, US film director.
Cardinal Basil Hume, British Roman Catholic Archbishop of Westminster 1976–99.
Joshua Nkomo, Zimbabwean politician.
Yehudi Menuhin, US-born British musician.
Naomi Mitchison, British author.
Brian Moore, Irish author.
Dame Iris Murdoch, British novelist.
Dusty Springfield, British singer.
Ernie Wise, British comedian.
Sir Alf Ramsay, British footballer and manager.
Julius Nyerere, First President of Tanzania.
Franjo Tudjman, President of Croatia.

2000

- Fears of a worldwide 'Y2k' computer systems crash fail to materialize (1 January).
- Chechen War: Federal Russian troops recapture Grozny (6 February).
- Mozambique floods: 800,000 to 1,000,000 people lose their homes (February).
- General Augusto Pinochet is allowed to return from the UK to Chile (2 March).
- Pope John Paul II apologizes for sins committed in the name of the Church over past 2000 years (12 March).
- Javed Iqbal, killer of 100 children, sentenced to public strangulation in Lahore (16 March).
- Acting President Putin is confirmed in office in Russian presidential election, with almost 54% of the vote (26 March).
- Zimbabwe Parliament approves legislation for white-owned farms to be confiscated without compensation.
- Israeli army withdraws from South Lebanon (24 May).
- A US district court orders the break-up of Microsoft into two businesses, because of monopoly abuse (7 June).
- Concorde crashes near Paris; 113 are killed (25 July).
- Russian nuclear submarine *Kursk* founders with 118 on board: none survive (12 August).
- Slobodan Milosevic loses presidential election but holds on to power in Belgrade; popular protest ends his regime (6 October).
- George W. Bush elected US President by a slender majority over Al Gore.
- President Fujimori of Peru decamps to Japan with vast amounts of loot.
- Dr Harold Shipman given life imprisonment in Britain for killing 15 patients (January); many more are believed to have been victims.
- Fifty-eight illegal Chinese immigrants to Britain found dead in container truck (June).
- The ozone layer over the Arctic is reported as being depleted by up to 60% in the winter of 1999–2000 (April).
- The Human Genome 'working draft' of three billion plus chemical letters denoting the human genetic blueprint is said to be complete (26 June).
- The Naua, a tribe unheard of since 1903, emerges from deep within the jungle in Amazonas, Brazil (August).
- First Olympic Games of the millennium, the XXVII Olympiad, held in Sydney, Australia (1 September–1 October).
- Oldest living microbe, a bacterium aged 250,000,000 years, found in a salt crystal 550 metres underground in New Mexico (October).

DEATHS

Hafez al-Assad, President of Syria.
Sirimavo Bandarinaike, three times Prime Minister of Sri Lanka.
Donald Dewar, First Minister of Scotland.
Pham van Dong, ex-PM of North Vietnam and Socialist Republic of Vietnam.
Douglas Fairbanks Jr., American actor.
Sir John Gielgud, British actor.
Hedy Lamarr, American film actress.
Pierre Pflimlin, ex-PM of France.
Ndabaningi Sithole, Zimbabwean freedom campaigner.
Pierre Trudeau, ex-PM of Canada.
Noboru Takeshita, ex-PM and 'patriarch of Japanese politics'.

2001

- Major earthquake in Gujurat causes up to 100,000 deaths and much devastation (26 January).

- Belgium decriminalizes cannabis, following example of Netherlands and Portugal (January).
- One of the two defendants at the Lockerbie trial, Abdel Baset al-Megrahi, is found guilty and receives a life sentence; the other is acquitted.
- The first genetically modified primate, a rhesus macaque monkey, is born in an American laboratory (January).
- Floods cause devastation and mass homelessness in Mozambique (February).
- Outbreak of foot and mouth disease rocks the British agricultural industry (February).
- The oldest-yet hominid remains are found in Kenya: 'Millennium Ancestor' goes back 6 million years (February).
- Russia's *Mir* space station undergoes planned destruction after 86,331 orbits of the Earth (23 March).
- First space 'tourist' goes into orbit; ticket cost is around $7,000,000 (April).
- Slobodan Milosevic is arrested and charged with corruption and war crimes (April).
- US President Bush announces his intention to ignore the Kyoto Agreement on reduction of 'greenhouse gas' emissions (April).
- Violence escalates in Palestine as Israel launches military operations inside the Gaza Strip (May): continues throughout the year.
- Philip Morris tobacco company is ordered by a Los Angeles jury to pay $3 billion damages to Richard Broeken, lung cancer patient and a smoker for 40 years.
- King Birendra of Nepal and seven family members shot dead by Crown Prince Dipendra; King Gyanandra succeeds to the throne (June).
- Labour win the UK general election with 418 seats out of 659, in a 59.4% poll, the lowest since 1918 (June).
- Final section of the Paris–Marseilles high speed rail link completed; the 700-km journey takes 3 hours (June).
- Slobodan Milosevic appears before the Hague War Crimes Court; he refuses to recognize it and claims he has been kidnapped (July).
- IMF lends $8 billion to Argentina to stave off financial collapse (August).
- Australia refuses to allow the MV *Tampa* to disembark 433 refugeees, mostly from Afghanistan, at Christmas Island (August); three further refugee vessels are turned away in October.
- Israeli cease-fire with Palestine collapses (August); suicide bombings become regular occurrences.
- America goes into shock as co-ordinated terrorist attacks use hijacked passenger planes to destroy the twin towers of the World Trade Center, New York and cause severe damage to the Pentagon, Washington (September 11); 2986 people are killed; the al-Qaeda terrorist organization, headed by Osama bin Laden, is held responsible.
- With the active co-operation of Tony Blair, UK Prime Minister, the US forms an 'international coalition against terrorism'.
- NASA reports discovery of a 'supermassive' black hole at the heart of the Milky Way galaxy (September).
- Further alarm is caused in the US by anthrax attacks: traces of spores are found in Washington DC government buildings, in the Supreme Court and at postal facilities; the source remains undetected; the US Senate enacts the 'Patriot Act', giving wide surveillance powers to the government (October).
- Military attacks by US forces, aided by the UK, are launched against Afghanistan (Operation Enduring Freedom) from October 7.
- The centenary Nobel Peace Prize is awarded to Kofi Annan and the United Nations.
- Swissair files for bankruptcy protection; Belgian airline, Sabena, also goes bankrupt (November).

- The United Islamic Front for the Salvation of Afghanistan, with US and British air support, defeats the Taliban government; many flee to the mountains or to Pakistan; the hunt for Osama bin Laden centres on the Tora Bora cave complex.
- Enron Corporation files largest corporate bankruptcy in US history: debts of $15 billion are revealed (December).

DEATHS

Sir Donald Bradman, Australian cricketer.
President Kabila of Congo Republic, assassinated.
Stanley Kramer, American film maker.
Sir Robert Mahuta, New Zealand Maori leader.
Dame Ninette de Valois, British ballet founder.
Douglas Adams, author of *Hitch-Hiker's Guide to the Galaxy*.
Gilbert Bécaud, French singer.
Mainza Chona, 'father of Zambian independence'.
Perry Como, US crooner.
George Harrison, former Beatle.
Sir Fred Hoyle, British astrophysicist and writer.
Spike Milligan, Anglo-Irish humorist.
Leopold Sedar Senghor, first President of Senegal (1960–80).
Isaac Stern, violinist.
Eudora Welty, US author.

2002

- Mt Nyiragongo erupts in Congo: 400,000 people have to flee (January).
- US troops are involved in a military campaign in Philippines against Muslim rebel group, Abu Sayyaf (January).
- In Australia, some 100 huge bush fires burn around Sydney (January) until the arrival of heavy rains; 28 suspected arsonists arrested.
- The euro, a single currency shared by 12 members of the EU, is launched successfully (January 1); former currencies of participating countries are abolished.
- Britain's foot-and-mouth disease outbreak is officially declared over, after 2030 cases; a public enquiry is refused (January 14).
- Robert Mugabe wins presidential election in Zimbabwe despite claims of irregularities (March 14).
- Protests are made to the World Trade Organization as the US slaps a heavy tariff on steel imports to protect its steel industry (March 20).
- An expelled pupil kills 16 staff and pupils at a secondary school in Erfurt, Germany (April 26).
- A referendum in Pakistan confirms General Pervez Musharraf's role as the country's President (April 30).
- Jacques Chirac wins a second term as French President in the landslide defeat of his far-right opponent, Jean-Marie Le Pen (May 5).
- Myanmar democratic leader Aung San Suu Kyi is freed from house arrest after 19 months (May 5).

DEATHS

Elizabeth, British Queen Mother, at the age of 102.
Ruth Handler, US creator of the Barbie doll.
Thor Heyerdahl, Norwegian explorer.
Peggy Lee, US singer.
Dudley Moore, British pianist and actor.
Jonas Savimbi, Angolan guerrilla leader.
Cyrus Vance, former US Secretary of State.
Billy Wilder, US film director.

2003

- China's unmanned space capsule, *Shenzhou IV* ('Heavenly Voyager'), lands safely (5 January).
- The NASA spacecraft *Columbia* breaks up on re-entering the Earth's atmosphere: 7 astronauts are killed (1 February).
- Worldwide demonstrations are held in protest against the impending US-British War on Iraq, including London's biggest-ever political demonstration (15 February); efforts by Britain and the US to obtain a second UN Security Council resolution authorizing or allowing an attack on Iraq fail when French President Chirac threatens to veto it; relations between Britain and the US, and the anti-war powers, France and Germany, reach a low ebb.
- During March, a new form of viral respiratory disease, Severe Acute Respiratory Syndrome (SARS), spreads westwards from China; with a 20% fatality rate, it is described as 'the first global epidemic of the 21st century'.
- Japan launches its first surveillance satellite, to protests from North Korea.
- The British House of Commons votes in favour of military action against Iraq.
- The US and Britain launch an aerial bombardment of targets in Iraq and begin a ground invasion (21 March); the military action is widely condemned as precipitate or illegal; British troops occupy Basra and American troops occupy Baghdad and other major cities; the National Library is destroyed in widespread looting; Saddam Hussein disappears; a US-led transitional authority is set up to oversee the transference of rule to a civilian Iraqi government (March–April); guerrilla warfare continues through the year.
- North Korea announces that it has the capacity to make a nuclear bomb.
- Winnie Mandela, former wife of Nelson Mandela, is sentenced to 5 years in prison for fraud and theft (April).
- A Papal Encyclical forbids Protestants and Roman Catholics to participate together in the Catholic Eucharist (April).
- In Myanmar, democracy campaigner Aung San Suu Kyi is again placed under 'protective' house arrest by the military rulers.
- Australian Governor, General Peter Hollingworth, resigns after press allegations about his past (May); replaced by Major General Michael Jeffrey (June).
- Referendum in Czech Republic shows 77.3% in favour of joining the EU (June).
- Finnish premier Ameli Jaatteenmaki resigns in 'Iraqgate' scandal over use of secret documents in anti-war campaign (June).
- Language research finds that 90% of the world's 6809 'living' languages are spoken by less than 100,000 people: the early extinction of many is predicted.
- Italy passes an immunity law which guarantees Premier Berlusconi freedom from trial while in office; his fraud trial is indefinitely suspended (June).
- For the fifth year running, Japan prevents the International Whaling Conference from organizing a South Pacific whale sanctuary (June).
- British defence official, Dr David Kelly, is found dead shortly after being named as the source of allegations that the government had 'sexed-up' its evidence on Iraqi weapons of mass destruction.
- Uday and Qusay Hussein, sons of Saddam, shot dead in a gun-battle in Iraq (22 July).
- A Nigerian peacekeeping force enters Liberia to help stop civil war; President Taylor flies into exile (August).
- Heatwave in Europe causes around 11,000 deaths in France, mainly among elderly persons ; record low water levels stop shipping on the Danube (August).
- The USA lifts its much-criticized tariff on steel imports.
- Swedish referendum on adopting the euro shows 56.2% against, 41.8% in favour (September).

- Latvian referendum on joining the EU shows 66.9% in favour (September).
- The UN Security Council votes to end sanctions against Libya following its agreement to pay compensation for the Lockerbie bombing (September).
- China's first manned space flight, by Yang Liwei, is successfully accomplished (15–16 October).
- Israel constructs a wall around the Palestinian West Bank (October).
- The Concorde supersonic aircraft makes its last commercial flight (24 October).
- Two suicide truck bombs kill at least 27 and injure over 400 in Istanbul (20 November); al-Qaeda and the IBDA-C ('Great East Islamic Raiders' Front') organisation claim responsibility.
- Georgian President, Eduard Shevardnadze, is deposed in a bloodless coup (23 November).
- Fifteen members of the 'November 17' terrorist group are convicted in Greece: Alexandros Giotopoulos receives multiple life sentences for 19 murders (December).
- In Iraq, Saddam Hussein is found and arrested by the US military (14 December).
- Elections in Russia leave President Putin's United Russia Party dominant with 37.1% of the vote; widespread ballot-rigging is claimed.
- An earthquake, 6.6 on the Richter scale, destroys the Iranian city of Bam: around 20,000 believed dead (26 December).

DEATHS

Giovanni Agnelli, Chairman of Fiat and a leading figure in the reconstruction of post-war Italy.

Roy Jenkins, British Labour and Social Democrat politician.

Daniel Patrick Moynahan, leading US Democratic Senator.

Sir Hardy Amies, British fashion designer.

Nina Simone, US singer.

Robert C. Atkins, US dietician.

Walter Sisulu, long-time South African anti-apartheid campaigner.

Bob Hope, British-born US actor.

Idi Amin, former Ugandan dictator.

Gregory Peck, US actor.

Katharine Hepburn, US actress.

Vasyl Bykau, leading Belarusian writer.

Madame Chiang Kai-shek, widow of the Generalissimo.

Leni Riefenstahl, German film maker.

Edward Teller, US 'father of the H-bomb'.

Gertrude Ederle, first woman to swim the English Channel (in 1926).

2004

- A world-wide scientific report expects global warming to eliminate around 1,000,000 animal and plant species by 2050.
- American NASA agency lands a mobile robot on Mars (January).
- The US begins fingerprinting all foreign visitors.
- Haitian President Aristide resigns and goes into exile.
- Three hundred die in Iranian train explosion (18 February).
- Vladimir Putin is re-elected as Russian President by a large majority.
- Bombs on Madrid commuter trains kill 202 and wound 1400: al-Qaeda held responsible.
- European Union fines Microsoft $603 million for breach of trade laws.
- African National Congress wins South African general election with 70% of the vote.
- Ten new members bring the number of countries in the EU to 25.

- Photographic evidence of abuse of prisoners by US soldiers in the Abu Ghraib jail in Baghdad, sparks outrage (April).
- Sudanese government and People's Liberation Army agree an end to civil war; but warfare and displacement of people continue in the province of Darfur through the year.
- Picasso painting 'Boy with a Pipe' fetches an auction record of $104.1 million (May).
- Interim government led by Iyad Allawi assumes power in Iraq (June).
- A UN report states that in seven African countries, average life expectancy has fallen below 40.
- In the summer, insurgency in Iraq reaches new heights of violence, in a sustained suicide bombing campaign.
- Venezuela votes to keep President Hugo Chavez in office by 52% to 48%.
- The XXVIIIth Olympiad opens in Athens, with over 10,000 contestants (13 August).
- Terrorists take over a school in Beslan, Russia; 340 children and adults were killed when security forces storm it (17 September).
- Five thousand US and Iraqi troops capture Samarra from insurgents (3 October).
- Investigators' final report concludes that Iraq had no illicit weapons prior to the 2002 invasion.
- Skeletons of a 'tiny people' from 13,000 years ago are found on the Indonesian Island of Flores (October).
- American forces storm the insurgent-held Iraqi city of Falluja (8–14 November).
- George W. Bush defeats John Kerry to win a second term as US President.
- In Ukraine, a disputed presidential election is re-run, resulting in victory for Victor Yevtushchenko.
- A UN report states that there are 852 million chronically hungry people in the world and that 5 million children die each year through hunger and malnutrition (November).
- The Millau Viaduct, the world's highest bridge at 1000 feet, is opened in France.
- Following an undersea earthquake on 26 December, a huge tsunami sweeps across the Indian Ocean, devastating shoreline communities in Indonesia, India and Sri Lanka: the final death toll is estimated at 283,000.

DEATHS

Ahmed Yassin, Palestinian co-founder of Hamas.
Ronald Reagan, former US President.
Alistair Cooke, British-American broadcaster.
Peter Ustinov, British actor and humorist.
Juliana, former Queen of the Netherlands.
Dom Moraes, Indian poet.
Marlon Brando, US actor.
Frances Crick, British co-discoverer of the DNA 'double helix'.
Ray Charles, US musician and singer.
Henri Cartier-Bresson, French photographer.
Red Adair, US oilfield fire-fighter.
Maurice Wilkins, New Zealand-born biologist.
Jacques Derrida, French literary theorist.
John Peel, British musician and broadcaster.
Christopher Reeve, US 'Superman' actor.
Yasser Arafat, Palestinian leader.
Susan Sontag, US writer and activist.

2005

- Prototype of super-jumbo jet Airbus A380 has maiden flight in France (January).
- North Korea admits possession of nuclear weapons.
- Rafik Hariri, former Prime Minister of Lebanon, is assassinated in West Beirut (14 February).
- Ellen McArthur makes a record female solo circumnavigation of the globe, in 71 days 14 hours (7 February).
- Through the year, fears mount of a possible pandemic of avian influenza, as known cases spread from China to Turkey.
- Earthquake in Iran kills over 500 people (February).
- Syria announces military withdrawal from Lebanon, in the wake of the assassination of Rafik Hariri in February (5 March).
- The new Iraqi Assembly meets for the first time.
- Steve Fossett makes the first non-stop solo flight around the globe (3 March)
- German Cardinal, Joseph Ratzinger, is elected as Pope Benedict XVI (19 April).
- Insurgency in Iraq continues at a high level; at least 844 US soldiers and an unknown number of Iraqis and others are killed during this year.
- Tony Blair forms his third government following a Labour victory in the UK general election, though with only 36% of the popular vote (5 May),
- The government of Zimbabwe ignores international protests to force through a 'slum clearance' programme, driving fringe town dwellers back to the countryside.
- Mikhail Khodorkovsky, once the richest man in Russia, is jailed for 9 years for fraud and tax evasion (May).
- After referendums in Holland and France reject the draft EU constitution, EU leaders abandon plans to ratify it by 2006.
- Gay marriages, already allowed in Holland, are approved in Spain, Canada and the UK.
- Pop singer, Michael Jackson, is cleared of child molestation charges after a sensational trial in California (13 June).
- Suicide bombers on underground trains and a London bus kill 52 people and wound over 700; British-born al-Qaeda activists are identified as responsible (7 July).
- The IRA renounces violence and pledges to pursue its aims by political means (July).
- NASA spacecraft *Deep Impact* hits target comet, Tempel 1, after an 83 million-mile journey (June); a tenth planet in the solar system is identified beyond Pluto.
- The Israeli cabinet agrees to enforce withdrawal from illegal settlements in the Gaza Strip (August).
- Hurricane Katrina, a category 4 hurricane, devastates the US Gulf coast: most of New Orleans is flooded and the city is temporarily abandoned amid scenes of disorder (29–31 August).
- In Germany, inconclusive parliamentary elections result in a 'grand coalition' and the appointment of the country's first woman Chancellor, Angela Merkel.
- The International Atomic Energy Agency and its director, Mohamed el-Baradei, are awarded the Nobel Peace Prize (7 October); British playwright, Harold Pinter, wins the Nobel Literature Prize.
- A massive earthquake on the Pakistan-India border causes over 54,000 deaths and leaves two and a half million people homeless (27 October).
- The trial of Saddam Hussein and seven aides opens in Baghdad.
- Violence erupts in the suburbs of Paris and spreads to other French cities (25 October); a state of emergency is declared.
- I. Lewis Libby, Chief of Staff to US Vice President Dick Cheney, is indicted on counts of obstruction of justice and perjury (October).

- UN investigators find evidence of Syrian involvement in the assassination of Rafik Hariri in Lebanon and ask to interview President Assad (October).
- Ellen Johnson Sirleaf is elected President of Liberia: the first woman head of state in Africa (11 November).
- Israeli Prime Minister, Ariel Sharon, quits Likud Party to form his own political party (November).
- Parliamentary elections held in Iraq: the Shiites are the largest party but they do not have a majority vote; coalition talks to begin in January 2006.
- US President Bush defends his government's policy of spying on suspected persons without an official warrant.
- In the US, controversy between creationist and Darwinian views of evolution result in a Pennsylvania court judgement ruling it unconstitutional for schools to teach 'intelligent design' as if it were a serious scientific theory (December).
- Hwang Woo-suk, Korean cloning pioneer, is discredited after an inquiry finds his research has been tampered with (December).
- By December, world crude oil prices are 40% higher than at the beginning of the year.

DEATHS

Hunter S. Thompson, US writer.
Rafik Hariri, former PM of Lebanon.
Arthur Miller, US playwright.
Saul Bellow, US writer.
Eduardo Paolozzi, Scottish sculptor.
Pope John II.
Ismail Merchant, Indian film producer.
Bob Hunter, Canadian Greenpeace co-founder.
King Fahd of Saudi Arabia.
Carlo Mario Giulini, Italian conductor.
Zao Ziyang, Chines reformist politician.
Robert A. Moog, US inventor of the synthesizer.
Edward Heath, former British Prime Minister.
James Callaghan, former British Prime Minister.
Simon Wiesenthal, German Jewish Nazi-hunter.
George Best, British football player.
John Fowles, British writer.
Birgit Nilsson, Swedish opera star.
Eugene McCarthy, US Democratic politician.

2006

- Canadian general election: Conservatives returned to power after ten years.
- Chile elects a woman President, Michelle Bachelet.
- Ariel Sharon suffers a stroke, causing political uncertainty in Israel and the Middle East; intensified when Hamas win a majority of seats in the most inclusive general election in Palestinian history (25 January).
- Coldest January in Central Europe for many years; the temperature in Bavaria reaches −33.8⁰ Celsius; severe flooding in Europe (April).
- Slobodan Milosevic is found dead in his cell in the Hague (March).
- UK government's chief scientist warns that the Earth is likely to experience a rise in temperature of at least 3°C over the next 100 years.
- The Commonwealth Games are held in Melbourne, Australia (March): Australia win the most medals (221) with England in second position (110).
- Tension mounts between Iran and the US over Iran's refusal to back down from developing what it claims is a civilian nuclear-power programme (April).

- Seventy commuters stranded in cable cars high above Manhattan are rescued by New York police (April).
- British hostage Norman Kember and two Canadian fellow peace activists are released by multinational forces in Iraq after being held for nearly five months by a group calling themselves the Swords of Truth Brigade (April).